THE UFO ENCYCLOPEDIA

John Spencer is Chairman of the world-renowned British UFO Research Association (BUFORA), an officer of the International Committee for UFO Research (ICUR), and a research specialist for MUFON, the Mutual UFO Network, the world's largest UFO research network. His previous books include *UFOs 1947–1987*, *Phenomenon* and *Perspectives*.

John Spencer is married with two daughters and lives in Harpenden, Hertfordshire.

Also by John Spencer

UFOs 1947–1987
Phenomenon
Perspectives
UFOs – The Definitive Casebook
The Paranormal – A Modern Perspective
Gifts of the Gods?
Ghostwatching

Also by John and Anne Spencer

The Poltergeist Phenomenon
The Encyclopedia of the World's Greatest Unsolved Mysteries
The Encyclopedia of Ghosts and Spirits
Spirit Within Her

The
UFO
Encyclopedia

Compiled and Edited by
John Spencer
for BUFORA –
The British UFO Research Association

HEADLINE

First published in 1991
by HEADLINE BOOK PUBLISHING

First published in paperback in 1991
by HEADLINE BOOK PUBLISHING

This edition published in 1997
by HEADLINE BOOK PUBLISHING

10 9 8 7 6 5 4 3 2 1

ISBN 0 7472 5797 3

Typeset by
Letterpart Limited, Reigate, Surrey

Printed and bound in Great Britain by
Cox & Wyman Ltd, Reading, Berks

HEADLINE BOOK PUBLISHING
A division of Hodder Headline PLC
338 Euston Road
London NW1 3BH

FOREWORD

by Major Sir Patrick Wall, M.C., V.R.D., R.M.(Retd), F.I.J.

It is commonly found that some people regard Ufology as a branch of science fiction; it never has been. However, due to the attitude of many devotees in its early years, it certainly suffered from an image problem. Researchers and research groups across the world have done much to move Ufology from the status of a hobby subject, akin to train spotting, towards that of serious study. Ufology is not a science, although it embraces many sciences, but in the modern day a great deal of research is conducted on scientific principles.

One of the leading figures in this subject in Britain, and indeed the world, is John Spencer, who has compiled this A to Z encyclopedia of the main facets of Ufology; including the personalities involved, the sightings and encounters reported, the abductions experienced, and much more. It is a stupendous work of world-wide research.

This collation of facts illustrates only too well how this relatively new discipline has advanced in the last few years. All serious-minded people will treat this encyclopedia with respect; even those who regard UFOs as fabrications of the simple-minded must consider this collection of facts as a proof that *something* extraordinary is taking place in and around our planet.

There are innumerable examples of such phenomena as crop-circles, sightings by aircraft pilots, radar traces, and the personal experience of witnesses, many of whom are clearly sincere people seeking to understand a true mystery that has sought out and affected them.

The subject is controversial, even amongst its advocates; many people believe that too much is taken for granted without examination of all the alternative possibilities – a criticism particularly levelled at the United States. For example, one

American expert told me that there had been thousands of abductions in his country each year, the point of these abductions being not to provide a joyride in a UFO but a chance for a medical examination of the human species. Perhaps so, but such a conclusion does not take account of the astonishing range of alternative studies which suggest an altogether more complex phenomenon. These alternatives are explained very clearly in this encyclopedia.

The particular value of John Spencer's work is that he keeps his feet firmly on the ground and does not allow himself to be swept away by simplistic interpretations; by the same token he is not dismissive of any reasonable theory. The encyclopedia sets out the findings of over forty years of observation and research and allows the reader to judge the phenomena without imposed bias. It is written with authority, but also humour, making it both informative and readable.

More and more people are taking an interest in Ufology and they will find this volume of particular interest, giving as it does a background of facts which will be of great value to those who seriously immerse themselves in this subject, as well as being of interest to the general reader.

It is published in association with BUFORA, the leading British UFO research organisation, of which John Spencer is Chairman.

Whether you believe in UFOs or not, and whatever you believe them to be, this book will give you an essential grounding in and work of reference to all that has happened in the world of Ufology. It is to be highly recommended.

INTRODUCTION

When I first discussed the idea of compiling an encyclopedia with BUFORA, the British UFO Research Association, principally its then-Chairman, Steve Gamble, and President, Major Sir Patrick Wall, I had little idea of the difficult task that would be facing me. I knew that for reasons of space I would be forced to select from the available material; not everything could be included.

That turned out to be probably the hardest part of the job. After twenty years of personal research in this subject – more than ten as a director of BUFORA – I thought I knew the scope of the material fairly well, but when I started compiling and classifying it the sheer weight of it surprised even me.

Nearly forty-five years have passed since the start of the modern era of UFOs, when in 1947 Kenneth Arnold sighted a formation of objects over Mount Rainier in Washington State, USA. In that time tens – perhaps hundreds – of thousands of people have reported seeing UFOs in just about every shape and size; thousands have reported entity sightings of humanoids and creatures; hundreds, probably going into thousands, have reported abductions – frightening stories of kidnap and manipulation by non-humans. Even to have tried to include all of the cases on all of the files in the world (actually an impossible task) would have left no room for adequate description.

The story does not stop there, however; it is the belief of most people working in this field that there is *more* unreported than reported. Everyone I know in this 'business' tells of experiencing what has happened to me time and time again; wherever I go to talk about the subject, a radio show, a local UFO group meeting, to address an astronomical society in a university, to lecture to businessmen in the local Rotary Club, or wherever else, one or two people will, usually with some embarrassment, take me aside and tell me: 'I saw something very strange once . . .' When you ask if they reported it to anyone the answer is almost always the same: 'No, I didn't know *how* to.'

Usually the report is of a distant light or disc sighting, of which so many are received that, frankly, there is little that can be done once time has passed other than to throw it into the database in case it should help correlate another known sighting. Occasionally, however, there are surprises. At a local meeting of the Round Table where I was a guest speaker, I was taken aside by one man early in the evening, before I had lectured. He was plainly embarrassed. He told me that he had seen something once, but that he hadn't reported it because he didn't know who to report it to, and he felt people might laugh at him, and so on. He was a well-dressed, well-educated man, obviously a successful career person, and clearly genuinely embarrassed by having to discuss this with me. I had seen this reaction in many sober and strait-laced people before; often they do not know just how common these experiences are. However, in this case I was astonished. The man went on to describe, with full memory recall, an extraordinary entity encounter and 'abduction' that had happened some twenty years earlier, and which he never reported, or even apparently discussed with his family.

In a case where the witness has asked me not to use any of the material in my talks or books, and certainly never to mention his name – I always comply with such requests and can say nothing here of the details, but it was very evident that just talking to me about it had relieved an enormous pressure that he had allowed to build up over the years – all because this subject is taboo in so many conventional circles. To reiterate the point I was making: we firmly believe that more goes unreported than reported; the subject is now so vast that it can never be fully catalogued, even if all the evidence was fully known.

This gives me the opportunity to make another very important point: it is a common supposition that those reporting UFOs and abductions are attention-seekers, or 'in it for the money'. Nothing could be farther from the truth. There will of course be cases of both, just as there will be hoaxes for a variety of reasons, but what is not often appreciated by the public is that the vast majority – we believe anything up to 70 per cent – of all reports are never placed on public record in books or magazines. They remain pure tools of research; held in secret by researchers for comparative and analytical purposes. The people reporting them make very clear that they do not want any publicity at all, they never seek to make money from their claims, they often won't discuss their sightings with even close family members. These are sincere, trustworthy people, often agitated and genuinely embarrassed by their experiences. They would not be doubted if they gave evidence in a court of law as witness to a road accident, why should they automatically be doubted when they testify to the existence of UFOs?

All of this proves beyond a doubt that the UFO phenomenon is *real*. I am not making any claims here as to what it really is; certainly I am not suggesting that it has to do with the visiting of our planet by alien creatures – by far the most popular interpretation. The UFO phenomenon, it seems to me, is about *people*: the things they see, and think they see, the things they experience, the things they fear. Not only do hundreds of thousands of people see strange things they cannot identify, they also feel so moved by them that they seek out – albeit sometimes decades later – someone to tell their story to.

I find it senseless and blinkered that conventional scientists refuse to examine this data. Even if every UFO report ever filed was a deliberate hoax (an absurd assumption), then surely that in itself would be enormously valuable material for study by sociologists or psychologists. Even if every report was accepted as 'real' and then explained as resulting from a natural weather or atmospheric phenomenon, then surely that would be an impressive body of evidence for meteorologists to study. And if only a handful remain unexplained and *may* represent some experience alien to humanity (whether originating from the Earth itself or elsewhere), isn't there an enquiring mind in the science establishment somewhere who wants to examine that?

I chose as my overall criterion for compiling this encyclopedia the aim that the reader should receive a complete and representative overview of the subject. I have taken cases from the forty-five years since the first UFO sighting; I have gone back farther even across the centuries, prior to 1947 to get the historical perspective; I have listed all of the major cases, and a cross-section of the rest, from the mundane 'I saw a light and it went away again' to the exotic 'I saw a light and ended up inside it'. I have tried to seek out a representative sample of the personalities involved over the years; military personnel by the plane- and boatload, police in their droves, politicians and a cast of thousands of others. Sometimes the selection has had to be random. Three similar reports from three police officers may be represented here by one typical report; the others were left out.

The cross-referencing is designed for a particular purpose. There may be a case with three witnesses, generally known by the location of the event, and the reader may find that I have cross-referenced only one or two of the witnesses' names to the main entry. The criterion chosen was to take the names by which the case is often found in UFO literature to allow for follow-up reading; if the second or third witnesses' names were not used in this way then there seemed no point in 'over-referencing' the entries. The same is true of the many official committees that have been set up by government agencies across the world. I have cross-referenced or briefly referred to those names by which the committees are sometimes known; other names will have been omitted.

The criterion was *balance* and if I have succeeded readers of this book should appreciate the sheer range of this subject over the years, the routine cases and the bizarre, the humour and the terror.

Most importantly, they will appreciate its mystery.

Anyone inspired by this book to follow up their reading will not be short of material. It is worth remembering that many of the entries herein, often just a paragraph or two in length, have been the subject of whole books – it is a complex subject.

I have tried not to impose any personal opinions on the data, but the nature of the subject sometimes makes that difficult. There were also times when I could not resist a comment or two; some of the 'explanations' offered for early sightings by the United States Air Force are simply asking for it! One pilot weaved around the skies 'dog-fighting' a UFO in full view of the personnel of the control tower only to be told he had seen a weather balloon. Another case that turned up on a radar screen was explained as the planet Jupiter (generally a bit outside the range of the average common-or-garden radar).

BUFORA has been invaluable in providing all sorts of help in putting this data together, whether in the form of library material, leads to follow up, or people to help with particular research tasks; my thanks are extended to the very many people who have helped, and particularly Arnold West, Steve Gamble, Lionel Beer, Jenny Randles and Bob Digby.

None of the above, or anyone else, is responsible for the selection of data included, and certainly not for my comments or opinions where they have crept in; I alone must take responsibility for both. Although I work for BUFORA, that organisation is similarly not responsible for any views expressed. Indeed, BUFORA has no corporate view to express as a matter of Association policy; it remains open to all theories and welcomes all serious research without bias.

The pages of this encyclopedia should prove one thing, if nothing else – the subject deserves to be taken seriously, whatever it turns out to represent. Just take a look at the number of policemen listed who have witnessed UFOs, often at alarmingly close proximity (and on occasion from inside!), and remember they are only a representative sample. Look at the number of military personnel, of civilian pilots, of respected public figures, of astronomers and so on who are listed. Remember that they, too, are only a sample. Consider the people who have lost their jobs, been vilified by the community, even suffered physical violence as a result of their reporting of UFO-related sightings; consider that they could not deny the truth even to the extent of protecting themselves by 'holding back', and surely there is impressive evidence here for something.

It would be inconceivable personally to have verified all of the cases listed here. I have used material from my own files, of course, but the vast majority of the book is compiled from other sources. I have checked what information I can and I have tried to use only reputable sources – this is no collection of tabloid press stories! Even so, errors will no doubt have crept in – I apologise in advance for them. The reference list at the back gives a great many of the sources I have used, but certain authors have proved invaluable: Cynthia Hind, Jenny Randles, Hilary Evans, John Keel, Major Donald Keyhoe, Budd Hopkins, J. Allen Hynek, John Rimmer, Paris Flammonde, Ralph and Judy Blum, Charles Hickson, William Moore. I would especially mention Timothy Good, whose book *Above Top Secret* is a very well-researched and documented summary of the 'official' attitude to UFOs. Timothy Good has done Ufology a great service by putting this wealth of material on public record.

I thank also those psychiatrists, psychologists, scientists and others who have helped many researchers such as myself over the years but who wish to remain anonymous; we would not be able responsibly to do what we do without them. I hope that one day peer pressure will lift and allow them to take credit for their work by name.

I thank the investigators and the researchers of the past forty-five years – even to have included all their names would have taken most of this encyclopedia, so long is the list. One or two whose influence on the subject has been in some way special are included. No slight to those not mentioned is intended. One of the most uplifting aspects of this work is the fact that so many people give so much of their time for little or no reward. It is a subject that has brought people from across the world together in a very special way.

And most of all, I thank the witnesses who have come forward to give us the information that *is* this subject. There have been many who have shrugged and walked away from their sightings or experience; there have been some for whom it was the greatest and most beneficial experience of their lives; and there have been many, like one man who comes to mind, who poured gallons of tears on to my shoulder and cried: 'I just wish more than anything that this had never happened to me. Please make it go away.'

I can't make it go away, and I wouldn't if I could because it may represent something beneficial that we have yet to comprehend, but I hope that I can make it better understood and that this book is a successful part of that process.

ABOUT BUFORA

The British Unidentified Flying Object Research Association (BUFORA) is dedicated to the scientific investigation of UFO phenomena, and stresses the importance of an objective approach. It has two interlinked roles of research and investigation, as well as activities of an educational nature. Details of BUFORA's aims are given in its entry in this encyclopedia.

BUFORA publishes a bi-monthly journal, *UFO Times*, which covers current developments, research activities, noteworthy investigations and discussions of broader issues. In addition, BUFORA publishes case histories, science papers and pamphlets on specific subjects.

BUFORA holds lectures, normally on the first Saturday of the month (apart from a summer break), which provide an open forum for lively discussion and debate. In addition, BUFORA sponsors international conferences periodically.

Membership of BUFORA is open to any person with a genuine and non-cultist interest in UFO research and who supports the general aims of the Association. Application forms and details of publications are available from: BM BUFORA, London, WC1N 3XX.

Those wishing to report sightings and experiences should also use this address; reports will be sent to the appropriate investigator or researcher for follow-up.

BUFORA operates a 24-hour UFOCALL information line on: 0891 121886 (special charge rates apply).

A

ABBIATE BUAZZONE

On 24 April 1950, near his home in Abbiate Buazzone, in Italy, Bruno **Facchini** saw sparks he thought were generated by a storm. When he left the house he saw that there was a dark UFO hovering some two hundred yards away. Nearby, a figure seemed to be working on the object, perhaps making repairs. Other entities were seen. They were dressed in tight-fitting clothes and were wearing helmets but their faces were also concealed behind masks from which emerged flexible pipes. During the encounter Facchini offered help but the entities fired a beam of light at him, pushing him along the ground for several yards. Shortly afterwards, when the repairs had apparently been completed, the object took off, making a heavy buzzing sound. The following day Facchini returned to the site, recovered metal fragments and noted circular imprints and patches of scorched grass. There were other anonymous witnesses who testified to the event.

ABDUCTEES (GENERAL DEFINITION)

Abductees are those witnesses who claim to have been temporarily kidnapped against their will by entities presumed by many to be alien in origin. Due to the extraordinary and dramatic nature of their claims abductees are often shunned in society by friends and relatives alike. In some extreme cases such witnesses have suffered the loss of their jobs, and physical abuse and attacks. For this reason they – assisted by therapists who work in the UFO study field – have often formed loose 'self-help' groups to counterbalance the lack of official support. Abductees are able to share their experiences; quite often just knowing they are not alone is as much help as they need. In America this is known as the 'buddy-system', employed also for rape victims; special conferences are held for abductees.

ABDUCTIONS

The most modern twists of the UFO phenomenon are claims by many witnesses of abduction. The typical scenario is that while in a reasonably isolated position, often driving on lonely roads at night, witnesses are captured by UFOs, removed from their cars and taken aboard the flying saucers where they are subjected to medical examination and interrogation. Recent claims indicate that abductions may occur at any time; from bedrooms – with cases of people being passed *through* the walls of their homes, or even from high-rise blocks in the middle of the day. In one case it appears that a woman was abducted from the middle of a party with many people around her, all of whom were somehow 'switched off' or 'suspended' to prevent their interaction.

After a period of some hours the witnesses are replaced in their vehicles, homes, etc., and generally given amnesiac blocks to prevent them remembering what has happened to them. It may of course be that the trauma of the perceived event causes the block. These blocks are allegedly lifted by the use of regression hypnosis and the truth then revealed to the investigator.

The first claim of forcible abduction was made by Antonio Villas **Boas** in 1957, and the first claim using regression hypnosis was by Betty and Barney **Hill** who had an encounter in 1961. Since that time there have been many subsequent claims, with recall often reaching further back in time to the 1930s and 1940s.

However, modern research has indicated that some abduction claims, and particularly some of the details, may be the result of poor investigative technique (of regression hypnosis itself, for instance) which has unwittingly built the abduction around a framework of expectation models. It would not be fair to accuse all investigators of such shortcomings. Many of them are very professional.

Budd Hopkins is one prominent American investigator into these cases who has stressed that the 'broad picture', the final answer to the UFO phenomenon, cannot always be of concern. Witnesses need help immediately, whatever the source of their difficulties, and the investigator therefore becomes a sort of therapist. While researchers may question the validity of certain data revealed by hypnotic regression, no one can doubt the therapeutic care given by those like Hopkins. One witness he had dealt with over a long term – Kathie **Davis** – told me in an interview in 1990 that had it not been for Hopkins she would probably have committed suicide, so difficult was it to deal alone with her experiences. Kathie Davis' case is dealt with in Hopkins' book *Intruders: The Incredible Visitations at Copley Wood* (see References and Background Material).

All cases of abduction have their own peculiarities and these are covered in the individual cases listed in this encyclopedia.

ACUFF, JOHN
In December 1969 John Acuff became Director of **NICAP**. Acuff was held to have links with the **CIA** and indeed it has been stated that he obtained the position when his predecessor, Major Donald E. **Keyhoe**, was ousted by a **NICAP** faction led by Colonel Joseph **Bryan III**, who was a former chief of the CIA psychological warfare staff. Acuff was later to be succeeded by Alan **Hall**, a retired CIA employee.

The involvement of agencies like the CIA in UFO research is very apparent, despite official denials.

ADAMS, CAPTAIN JON H.
On 14 March 1965, a rancher living at Fort Myers, Florida, Mr James W. **Flynn**, observed a low-flying brightly lit object in descent. Flynn was knocked out by a beam of light from the UFO which, after it had departed, proved to have left charred patches in the trees around the area where Flynn had observed it. It is alleged that the Pentagon was going to put out the story that this was a hoax but plans for this were dropped in the face of medical and other evidence. **NICAP** wrote to the Air Force base concerned and it was Captain Jon H. Adams, the Chief of Information, who dismissed the incident, saying, 'We here at Homestead have researched our files and found nothing concerning this particular incident where Mr Flynn saw a brightly lit UFO and experienced a "sledge-hammer" blow as you described.'

ADAMS, KEN
In 1966, in Australia, a series of 'cornfield circles' (see **Circles, Cornfield**) appeared. Gooloogong resident Ken Adams suggested that these were being made by a bird called the bald-headed coot. This theory has not been widely supported. (Though it probably ranks more highly than one British suggestion that the circles are caused by rutting hedgehogs in a frenzy!)

ADAMS, MOUNT

During Kenneth **Arnold**'s historic sighting of June 1947 in which he inadvertently coined the phrase 'flying saucer', Arnold estimated the speed of his sighted formation of objects by measuring the time it took to traverse between **Mount Rainier** and Mount Adams in Washington State, USA. Although generally known as the Arnold case, or the Mount Rainier case, it is less often referred to as the Mount Adams case in some early literature.

ADAMS, COLONEL WILLIAM A.

During the early 1950s the **CIA** is believed to have arranged a meeting of scientists and Air Force representatives at the Pentagon to study the confidential data collected on UFO phenomena. Colonel William A. Adams of **Wright Patterson Air Force Base** was one of the Air Force representatives. Although the meetings were held between 14 and 17 January 1953 the report was not completely declassified until 1975 and there are those who maintain that some information has never been declassified to this date. These meetings have been known variously as the **Robertson Panel** Report and the Durant Report.

Major Donald E. **Keyhoe** also notes that Colonel Adams was one of several Air Force personnel invited to review classified UFO film material in 1952, and authorised considerable analysis of some film.

ADAMSKI, GEORGE

The first and still the most famous of the early **contactees**. Born in 1891, he was 62 when he published his story in 1953 of alleged contactee meetings with aliens from another world. In his book *Flying Saucers Have Landed* (see References and Background Material) he revealed that he had been having sightings since 1946 and that he had met his first alien at 12.30 in the afternoon on Thursday, 20 November 1952, in the California desert ten miles from **Desert Center**, towards Arizona.

He and the alien apparently communicated in a combination of sign language and telepathy. Adamski referred to himself as Professor George Adamski though where he acquired the title of 'Professor' is not clear. Adamski also made much of his connection with Mount Palomar, the world's largest telescope, though in fact his real connection to this was that he served hamburgers in a tourist café on the slopes, a detail which he later clarified in his books. Adamski's alien indicated that he came from Venus which he described as being Earth's sister planet, although subsequent years have revealed that Venus is far from compatible with Earth.

During his conversations Adamski was told that the **humanoid** form was universal and it was also indicated that aliens were abducting human beings. On this point it is unclear whether the alien meant 'abduction' in the sense of this encyclopedia: he may have meant permanently kidnapping them.

Adamski later went on to travel in flying saucers throughout the solar system meeting Martians, Saturnians and Jovians. Adamski has many supporters to the present day though modern UFO researchers have called many of his claims into question. The most obvious problem is that science has overtaken many of his claims, in the way that we know Venus will not support humanoid life; so we now know that Adamski could not have stepped on to the surface of the gas giant planets – if they have surfaces!

ADDONIZIO, HUGH J.
In 1961 Congressman Addonizio was one of many legislators who publicly condemned secrecy over UFOs after studying **NICAP** reports on the subject of the UFO phenomenon.

AD HOC COMMITTEE
In the opening months of 1966 an Ad Hoc Committee of the Scientific Advisory Board, instigated by Major General E. B. LeBailey, the United States Air Force Director of Information, and chaired by physicist Dr Brian O'Brien, a member of the **National Academy of Sciences (NAS)**, recommended the official investigation of certain sightings, partly based on a review of Project **Blue Book**. On 5 April 1966 the House Armed Services Committee agreed that these recommendations should be implemented.

ADICKES, CAPTAIN ROBERT
At approximately 8.25 p.m. on 27 April 1950, Captain Robert Adickes was piloting a TWA DC3 towards Goshen, Indiana. The DC3, designated Flight 117, was at approximately 2,000 feet when it encountered what appeared to be a solid glowing saucer-shaped object. Although the DC3 was moving at approximately 175 miles per hour the object overtook it rapidly, then appeared to pace the plane and then dived off at a speed Adickes estimated to be nearly 400 miles per hour. If this is the case then it doubled its speed in approximately three seconds, a

feat which suggests either an unmanned object or a craft designed to negate the effects of G-forces on any occupants. Adickes' sighting was confirmed by his co-pilot, Robert F. Manning; both men were described as quiet, conservative, serious and careful.

AERIAL PHENOMENA GROUP
Throughout the 1950s the United States government had several successive projects investigating unidentified flying objects. Project **Grudge** became Project **Blue Book** in March 1952 (see reference **Condon Committee/Condon Report**). For a short time between the cessation of Project Grudge and the commencement of Project Blue Book the project carried the designation 'Aerial Phenomena Group' though in fact its only existence appears to be one sole reference in the Condon Report.

AERIAL PHENOMENA RESEARCH ORGANIZATION (APRO)
The world's oldest surviving UFO group founded in 1952 by Jim and Coral **Lorenzen**. The **CIA**'s **Robertson Panel** Report singled out this organisation for monitoring and it is therefore assumed they were subject to CIA surveillance. APRO was founded in Tucson, Arizona.

AERONAUTICAL INFORMATION SERVICE (MILITARY)
Based at the London Air Traffic Control Centre at West Drayton in Middlesex and it is held that Air Traffic Controllers have instructions immediately to telephone UFO reports received to this unit.

AEROSPACE DEFENSE COMMAND (ADC)
The unit responsible for the aerospace defence of the United States. According to a letter which was dispatched by the Pentagon following the termination of Project **Blue Book**, ADC was 'responsible for unknown aerial phenomena reported in any manner'. This was made clear by the military after the closure of Project Blue Book.

AETHERIUS SOCIETY
A research organisation that absorbs many of the paranormal aspects of study, but is held by many to be a cult group, and

more of a religion than a research group. It started life in 1954 when London cab driver George **King** was informed by the Cosmic Intelligence to prepare himself to become the Voice of **Interplanetary Parliament**. As such he formed the Aetherius Society which communicates between the cosmic masters and the Earth. King adopted many titles including 'Archbishop' and 'Sir' (when asked where he got the title 'Sir' from during a presentation in Sheffield in 1990 one of his supporters indicated vaguely that 'there are other powers than the Queen who can confer the honour'); his achievements include being taken into space by the aliens to destroy an intelligent meteor that was heading towards the planet. The aliens' UFOs were unable to stop the meteor and King was now needed to 'save the world'.

When challenged to prove the existence of their cosmic masters the Aetherius Society apparently arranged for an enormous flying saucer to hover motionless over Los Angeles. To protect the masses from fear, however, it was kept invisible from all but devoted followers.

The Aetherius Society's most famous achievement is the charging and storing of prayer power in 'batteries' which are then beamed to the Earth's trouble spots to relieve suffering and tension. I was privately informed that such batteries had successfully prevented a major earthquake and the Russian invasion of Poland.

AGREST, MIKHAIL
In the Tunguska region of Siberia, in 1908, there was an enormous explosion held to have left considerable radioactivity (see **Tunguska Meteorite**). Soviet physicist Mikhail Agrest interpreted this explosion as that of an interplanetary vehicle. Dr Felix **Zigel** of the Moscow Institute of Aviation apparently supported this by suggesting that the object had made manoeuvres before crashing. Since the explosion appears to have been airborne, and the devastation similar to the airblast from the atomic bomb dropped on Hiroshima, this is a thought-provoking circumstance.

AIR FORCE LETTER 200-2 (REGULATION)
Within a few months of the **Robertson Panel** meeting of January 1953 Air Force Regulation 200-2 went into effect which stipulated that 'the percentage of unidentifieds must be reduced to a minimum'. 200-2 was allied with Regulation **JANAP-146**, which made the release of information about

unidentifieds by military personnel a crime punishable by a fine of $10,000 and 10 years' imprisonment.

It appears that the Air Force instigated procedures to ensure that the public Project **Blue Book** was not the only reporting channel for UFOs, keeping some a little further from public reach.

AIR FORCE OFFICE OF SCIENTIFIC RESEARCH (AFOSR)

Based at the Pentagon this department was responsible for a variety of research projects; as one Air Force colonel said, 'Their task is to explore the far-out stuff.' It was AFOSR which was to choose a suitable university to implement the investigations of sightings as recommended by the **Ad Hoc Committee**. They suggested the University of Colorado, which was to culminate in the **Condon Report**.

The AFOSR acted as intermediary between the Air Force and the University, the Air Force wishing to remove itself from obvious direct involvement.

AIR FORCE OFFICE OF SPECIAL INVESTIGATIONS (AFOSI)

AFOSI, based at Bowling Air Force Base, DC, is held to have a long history of clandestine UFO research on behalf of the United States government. At one time Jim and Coral **Lorenzen** of **APRO** established that AFOSI had monitored their activities.

AFOSI documents leaked over the years have indicated their knowledge of UFO investigation by other services, such as NASA.

AIR MATERIEL COMMAND (AMC)

On 23 September 1947 the Commanding General of AMC, General Nathan F. **Twining**, reported on the subject of UFOs that 'the phenomenon reported is something real and not visionary or fictitious . . . the reported operating characteristics such as extreme rate of climb, manoeuvrability (particularly in roll), and action which must be considered evasive when sighted or contacted by friendly aircraft and radar, lend belief to the possibility that some of the objects are controlled either manually, automatically or remotely'.

AMC made recommendations for the study of UFOs who suggested liaison with American military and scientific bodies.

AIRSHIPS OF 1896–7

From November 1896 to the middle of 1897 thousands of people across the United States reported seeing the lights of an airship in the sky. As this was some four years before the acknowledged first flight of an airship it has been speculated that the airship was of extraterrestrial origin. However, the likelihood of its being a prototype experimental Earth airship is very high and indeed one E. J. **Pennington** is credited with being its owner. When asked, he admitted he had an airship undergoing repairs in Brown County, Indiana, which in fact correlated with a report by two witnesses from that area.

Some of the reported cases were undoubtedly the pranks of the media of the time, but other cases were thought-provoking.

If some of the airships were of extraterrestrial origin then it would confirm the theory of **cultural tracking** which suggests that many of the devices of the aliens are very similar to the technology of Earth of the time. This of course has led to speculation about the true nature of so-called alien intervention.

AIRSHIPS REPORTS 1909

Just as a few years before in America airships had been reported so a wave of reports was received across Europe in 1909. The strange language of the occupants has subsequently given rise to speculation that these were of extraterrestrial origin but against the tension in Europe of the impending First World War and the use of airships within that war, the explanation for these events is more likely to be 'down to earth'.

AIR TECHNICAL INTELLIGENCE CENTER (ATIC)

A unit of the United States government and military which received official reports of UFO phenomena and the organisation which, it is alleged, delivered a report to General **Vandenberg** on 5 August 1948 concluding that UFOs were interplanetary in origin. It is held that Vandenberg dismissed the top secret 'estimate of the situation' and ordered that the report be destroyed as it could cause panic and because it was not substantiated by sufficient proof. The unit was based at **Wright Patterson Air Force Base**.

AKHURST, LESLIE

In 1967, one of the most famous UFO sightings was that of **Moigne Downs**. The sighting was by former RAF Intelligence Officer J. B. W. **Brooks**. Leslie Akhurst investigated the report by interviewing Brooks in February 1968. Akhurst was from the MOD's **S4 (Air)** Unit which dealt with reports of UFO sightings by members of the public. Along with his colleagues, Akhurst concluded that the probable explanation for the Moigne Downs case was a vitreous floater in the witness's eyeball.

AKINESIA
A state of total paralysis, an inability to move or initiate activity. It is speculated that UFO encounters deliberately induce this state in some witnesses as a means of either temporary capture or temporary control. However, since a UFO/entity encounter has potential for trauma it is equally possible that the state is self-induced in some way as a result of shock or to self-protect the witness from his/her worst fears. The medical profession, let alone UFO researchers, are divided on the point.

AKKURATOV, VALENTIN
A Soviet pilot who in 1956, while flying a Tupolev 4 aircraft over Greenland, observed a saucer-shaped craft apparently pacing him. During the flight observation of the craft was obscured for approximately forty minutes as the plane flew towards Bear Island, but when the cloud cover lifted the object could again be seen pacing the aircraft and was seen to change course as the Tupolev did. After a further quarter of an hour the object accelerated and climbed out of sight. The nature of the sighting, with no obvious signs of technology seen, typical of many thousands like it, makes it impossible to determine whether or not the object was a solid physical structure, a mirage or some form of atmospheric phenomenon. Most notable is the suggestion that at one time it seemed to respond to the movements of the aircraft, yet later was able to make apparently intelligent movements independent of the aircraft.

ALAMOGORDO, NEW MEXICO
In the 1940s the location of the White Sands proving grounds where research was being conducted into German V2 rockets and which can be classed as one of the cradles of the birth of the American space programme. In the latter half of the 1940s there were many UFO reports from this area.
    Speculation has it that either UFOs were attracted to the area to 'keep an eye on' what our military and scientists were doing or alternatively that UFO reports were from people seeing the

experimental hardware of our own scientists and not recognising the secret devices.

Crash retrieval stories (of recovering crashed flying saucers) may in part be governments using the UFO phenomenon as a 'cover' for retrieving failed experiments from sites such as this.

A-LAN

Contactee Daniel **Fry**, while working at the White Sands proving ground in New Mexico, saw a flying saucer land and was contacted by an alien known as A-Lan, who later shortened his name to Alan. A-Lan took Fry for a trip around the United States and asked him to write a book about his experiences to prevent the world from destroying itself in a nuclear war, *The White Sands Incident* (see References and Background Material).

Many contactees have referred to telepathic communication with their alien companions, or to hearing them speak in a strange, alien tongue, but A-Lan was better prepared; he had an advanced understanding of slang. When Fry reached out to touch the hull of the flying saucer he heard a voice say, 'Better not touch the hull, pal, it's still hot.'

ALBERTA 'LURE'

There were frequent UFO sightings by the Royal Canadian Air Force over Alberta, Canada, in the late 1940s and early 1950s.

In a novel approach to attempt to contact a UFO, the Defence Research Board of Canada established a 'lure'. To this date jet pursuits were the only method used to attempt to engage and capture UFOs. This alternative method at least showed imagination and flair on the part of its authors.

The Defence Research Board established a restricted landing area near its own station at Suffield, Alberta, Canada, and all Royal Canadian Air Force and commercial aircraft were banned from the area. The object was to encourage UFOs to land at that particular location so that they could be studied and contacted. It is thought that capture was also considered. Defence Research officials also suggested using radio and searchlight signals to attract the visitors.

The plan was abandoned when it was realised that anything startling enough to attract aliens would also probably attract the general public, and might well alarm them. There have been similar projects suggested since, in the United States and France, though none is known to have come to fruition.

ALENÇON, FRANCE
Police Inspector Liabeuf, in the presence of several local officials, witnessed and investigated an extraordinary event during
summer near Alençon, France.

A large red globe flew across some farmland, scorching grass
and burning trees. The globe landed and a man emerged and
spoke to the gathered crowd who did not understand him.
Shortly afterwards the globe exploded into pieces and the man
disappeared.

The report appears to be well documented and corroborated
and is all the more thought-provoking because it occurred in the
year 1790!

ALEXANDER OF TUNIS, EARL
In 1954 Earl Alexander of Tunis was the British Minister of
Defence and made the following statement with regard to
UFOs: 'There are of course many phenomena in this world
which are not explained and it is possible to say that the
orthodox scientist is the last person to accept that something
new (or old) may exist which cannot be explained in accordance
with his understanding of natural laws.'

He may not have had the answers to the UFO phenomenon,
but he certainly understood scientists.

ALIENS: CONCEPT OF
It is a tenet of the most popular theory to attempt to explain
UFOs that they are extraterrestrial spacecraft visiting us from
worlds beyond the Earth or the solar system. As such, therefore,
their pilots are alien to this Earth and generally speaking are
referred to as aliens.

There has been a tendency in recent years, however, to
recognise the possibility that the UFO phenomenon represents
an unknown aspect of our own Earth's environment and as such
the term alien can now often be found referring to entities
where the meaning is 'alien to the human race' (but not
necessarily alien to the Earth). To combat this the Americans
tend to use the term 'space alien' to represent extraterrestrial
visitors (though also because the term alien is used in that
country to refer to a non-national).

Aliens, of whatever origin, come literally in all shapes and sizes
with such an enormous span of technologies, achievements,
understanding, and so on, that the basic concept that aliens are
extraterrestrial visitors requires at least careful consideration, if

not modification. If all the different aliens represent different races visiting the Earth, and even worse different points of origin, then the Earth must be some kind of inter-galactic stopping point and probably the greatest tourist attraction in the Universe. On the other hand if the aliens do represent an extraterrestrial visitation, then another possible explanation for this wide variety is that they come from one or a small number of points of origin, that they are basically similar but that there is room for imaginative interpretation on the part of the witness to see the alien 'through his own eyes'.

One alien in the **Beit Bridge** encounter in Africa suggested that he could appear however the witness wanted; if he wanted the alien to look like a duck, he could look like a duck, or a monster, or whatever. This of course would reconcile the problem of their various appearances.

Having stressed the variety reported, it is also fair to say that one 'type' is very frequently reported in America and some European cases: that of a dwarf-sized creature with a huge, bald head and prominent, slanting eyes.

The wide variety of alien forms also leads some researchers to the speculation that their very existence is subjective and basically in the minds of witnesses alone. While this possibility has merit it would need to overcome a great deal of physical and corroborative evidence to make it the sole explanation for the UFO phenomenon.

ALLEN, FRANKLIN
(See **Light, Gerald.**)

ALLINGHAM, CEDRIC
Following George **Adamski**'s revelations of his meetings with aliens in 1953 a British version of a supposed meeting between Martians and one Cedric Allingham, said to have taken place in Scotland, was published in 1955.

The book, *Flying Saucer from Mars* (see References and Background Material), exposing the material contained some highly unlikely photographs of a Martian walking away and of his spacecraft – predictably Adamski-like.

It is strongly suspected that Cedric Allingham's claims were a hoax and if so probably perpetrated to show the gullible attitudes of some UFO researchers. Publishers are usually very keen that their authors publicise themselves but in this case Allingham was most elusive. As pressure mounted it was conveniently announced that shortly after the book came out he had died, and was therefore now beyond the reach of proper questioning.

According to **BUFORA**'s Director of Investigations Jenny Randles, working on information given by researchers Chris Allan and Steuart Campbell, Cedric Allingham may be none other than astronomer Patrick Moore.

As I understand it, however, Patrick Moore has never confirmed these allegations, though Jenny Randles reports that he has never denied them either.

ALTAMIRA, SPAIN: CAVE DRAWINGS

It is held by many researchers that cave paintings by our pre-historic ancestors represent in part early UFO reports. Many such illustrations include oval and disc shapes and images reminiscent of space men, etc.

The artwork at Altamira in the province of Santander in Spain contains particularly thought-provoking imagery. Modern 'translations' of those images have some merit and indeed the early artists may well be depicting the same types of scene as modern day UFO reporters are describing, whatever their source stimulus. It must also be said, however, that there is a tendency on the part of such researchers to interpret liberally, and to find what they are looking for, with the result that in many cases ambiguous or vague images often take on some very exotic, and probably unreasonable, interpretations.

Art historian students of 'primitive' styles point out that many of the images have perfectly reasonable, down to earth, alternative possibilities. In one case a drawing of a ring of men apparently floating weightless (and therefore in space) would have been a normal way to paint a ring of men dancing, in certain styles of art.

ALTERED STATES OF CONSCIOUSNESS

Occasions when the human mind is not reacting to external stimuli in what would loosely be called 'normal' behaviour. Altered states of consciousness range from common and beneficial conditions such as sleep to the most extreme of psychotic aberrations. ASC can therefore occur spontaneously but can also be brought about by physical or mental illness, by excessive alcohol abuse, by the use of drugs or by forms of sensory and dream deprivation.

It is speculated that some UFO events take place during

altered states of consciousness and this gives rise to the suggestion that the event is internally generated (from within the witness's mind) rather than externally generated (viewed by the witness observing a phenomenon occurring independently).

It has, however, also been speculated that where a witness exhibits reactions which suggest an altered state of consciousness, this has been induced by the external event, i.e. either the trauma of the sighting or a deliberate intervention by extraterrestrial or other alien interference with the mind.

Not all cases of even the most exotic UFO experiences occur in what seem to be altered states of consciousness though the most symbolic imagery seems to arise when this is a possibility. However, since scientists and the medical profession are not completely clear as to what does or does not constitute the mind working in a 'normal' way, there is at least room for speculation that all UFO events occur in some altered states of consciousness. This still does not rule out the possibility that the event is real and creating the ASC.

Perhaps most thought-provoking of all is the suggestion that the UFO phenomenon is a manifestation of the paranormal which is around us all the time but which can only be 'tuned into' by certain people at certain times, of which altered states provide access.

ALVAREZ, DR LUIS
In 1952 and 1953 the Office of Scientific Intelligence in the United States convened the **Robertson Panel**. The conclusions of this panel are of great significance to those who believe UFO reports represent the sightings of **structured**, possibly alien, craft. The panel concluded that UFOs were easily explainable and no threat to national security. Dr Luis Alvarez was one of many members of the panel representing the physical sciences, and therefore important in a conclusion regarding the physical nature of the UFOs.

ALVARO, JOSÉ
On 3 March 1978 a significant abduction case occurred in Fragata Pelotas, Brazil. The case is all the more remarkable because it has features which echo the earlier claims of Antonio Villas **Boas** and yet has claims which predate the events at **Gulf Breeze**, Florida, in the late 1980s.

On 3 March 1978 José Alvaro walked towards a house owned by his father to check that it was locked up. He claims he was then struck by a blue beam and knocked out. (The blue beam is a significant feature of the Gulf Breeze encounters.) When he awoke Alvaro believes that the words 'The task is accomplished' were in his mind, together with violent images running as if in a movie. (Again, in the Gulf Breeze case there were two examples of the witness receiving changing visual images.)

Hypnosis sessions were set up by UFO investigators and a psychologist. During these sessions Alvaro claimed he was led into a room where a tall female humanoid rubbed him down and forced him to have sex with her. (This almost exactly mirrors the claims of Antonio Villas **Boas** in Argentina in the late 1950s.) Although reproductive material, semen and ova, feature in many UFO abductions, sexual intercourse is more rare; for a reason researchers have never agreed upon, most sexual encounter reports come from South America. It is considered that this is possibly a factor of the self-image of men on that continent. The alternative would seem to be that the phenomenon can react to the expectation model of witnesses.

AMANO, HIDEICHI

Although no UFO appears to have been reported during the case, this report from Japan in October of 1978 has features which clearly make it an abduction experience identical to what are referred to as UFO abductions.

While parked in his car with his infant daughter, Hideichi Amano observed the interior of the car 'swallowed up' by a glowing light. His daughter appears to have been knocked out and was being probed by a beam of light directed on her body. At the same time Amano was assaulted by a short slim being with 'strange eyes' and diminished nose. The being pressed what may have been a probe to Amano's forehead and paralysed him.

Amano reported kaleidoscope visual imagery very similar to many other cases including the José **Alvaro** case of just six months previously in Brazil and the **Gulf Breeze** encounters of the 1980s in Florida. Amano believes that the aliens planted a probe into him which will enable them to call him when they need him, again similar to events at Gulf Breeze, Florida.

There may be some **missing time** element but this has not been examined.

AMBERLEY, RAAF BASE

When hundreds of people sighted an aluminium-coloured, airship-shaped UFO over Darling Downs in Australia in August

1969, an RAAF Canberra bomber was dispatched from RAAF Amberley to engage the UFO. It was unable to make close contact; witnesses stated that the UFO fled when the plane approached it. The nature of the sighting coupled with the numbers of witnesses suggest strongly that something physical was being observed. That said, there is no evidence within this event to suggest that the object need be of extraterrestrial origin, as is so often speculated.

AMERICAN ASSOCIATION FOR THE ADVANCEMENT OF SCIENCE (AAAS)
On 26 December 1969, at their annual meeting, the American Association for the Advancement of Science discussed UFOs in a specially convened sub-committee. There were many productive contributions from prominent scientists and the committee strongly criticised the work of the **Condon Commission**. The result was that thirteen scientists signed a resolution to the Air Force Secretary requesting that all **Blue Book** files be preserved and housed for posterity.

Dr J. Allen **Hynek** was one of the contributors to this session and he used this to give the first serious report on UFOs by a scientist. Hynek went on to become one of the world's most prominent UFO researchers. When he founded the civilian study group **CUFOS** (the **Center for UFO Studies**) he brought many scientists into the work with him. They had formerly been 'in the closet' on the subject, and known as the '**invisible college**'.

AMERICAN INSTITUTE OF ASTRONAUTICS AND AERONAUTICS (AIAA)
This prestigious scientific body publicly rejected the findings of the **Colorado (University) UFO Project**, better known as the **Condon Report**, which had suggested that UFOs were not 'real'. It would have recognised, as most others did, that the conclusions were hardly borne out by the data within the report, and probably reflected a bias in the approach to the investigation.

ANAMNESIS PROJECT
In the mid 1980s **BUFORA** investigator Ken Phillips instigated the Anamnesis Project with Austrian psychologist Dr Alex Keul. The Anamnesis Project studies the life profiles of UFO-experience reporters and is a major analysis of the personalities involved in the UFO experience.

The Anamnesis Project concludes that by and large UFO-experience reporters are a reasonable cross-section of the population and not, as a group, psychotic in tendency or particularly fantasy prone.

However, certain characteristics do appear to have shown themselves in this group which early work suggests may be significant, statistically, to this sub-set. In particular, that there is a high incidence of self-reported ESP by UFO-experience reporters, that they report many more cases of flying-type dream imagery and that they have a tendency towards **status inconsistency**, i.e. they hold positions in society which are generally not what would be expected from their level of education or standing. This usually means that they hold jobs which are of a lower calibre than would be expected. There was also some tendency for UFO reporters to be what might be regarded as 'loners' in society.

ANCHORS DROPPED BY UFOS

During the 1897 **airship** wave in America there were reports of the airships trailing anchors, some of which were ensnared as they trailed along the ground. One such example from Merkel, Texas, found the anchor caught on a rail. A person was reported descending down a rope and cutting free the anchor which became an exhibit at the local blacksmith's shop.

There is great similarity between this and a case in approximately the year 1211 in Cloera, Ireland. In that case a similar event resulted in the anchor being caught on the roof of a church and again a man descended the rope and cut free the anchor. The anchor is reported to have been preserved in the church. None of the entities involved in these cases were captured, although an attempt was made in Cloera which was forbidden by the bishop.

Certainly the 1897 case could well have been a terrestrial airship though this hardly seemed to apply to the 1211 case. In any event, if these cases are held to be examples of extraterrestrial visitation then it is also a clear example of **cultural tracking** where the hardware of the aliens appears to mirror very closely the hardware of our own time. By the time we approach the space age the aliens' hardware has also approached space age technology, but in these early years they were apparently satisfied with propeller-driven airships.

ANDERS

Anders is the pseudonym for a witness who experienced an extraordinary abduction in 1974 in Sweden. Late on the night of 23 March 1974 Anders was walking along a dark road in Gustavslund, north of Stockholm. He was surrounded by light and apparently 'sucked up' into an overhead UFO where he underwent a reasonably 'classical' abduction experience, i.e. he was confronted by entities and subjected to a form of medical examination which included the insertion of a probe into the temple. When he arrived at his home he was in an extremely agitated state, bleeding from a wound in his forehead and his cheek was burned. Anders underwent two hypnotic regression sessions on 1 April and 20 May 1974 under the supervision of hypnotherapist Dr Ture **Arvidsson** of Danderyds Hospital.

At this point the extraordinary nature of the case becomes apparent because Anders appears to have rejected the UFO research being conducted and turned instead to researcher Arne Groth who explored, at Anders' request, areas not usually examined. Discoveries made included the facts that Anders was able to manipulate a compass needle by placing his hands nearby and to produce patterns of energy in fine iron filings placed under petri dishes. He could also see the vibrant aura of people and objects. Arne Groth and Anders have also experimented with a form of telepathic communication using energy lines which they believe to be the way in which the abduction was originally staged by the aliens.

Of some considerable interest is the fact that the case was corroborated by a number of witnesses, at least to some extent. It took place during a wave of reports of which over one hundred significant cases came to light during a two-year period and over thirty significant cases were reported within a few hours of the Anders encounter. Indeed, within minutes of the encounter there were many independent reports of lights and objects being sighted in and around the area of the abduction site, many of which did not come to the researchers' attention until after the abduction had been reported. Furthermore, there is one report which is clearly a corroboration of Anders' encounter itself where a witness – at precisely the time Anders was being abducted by the conical light from overhead – looked across a field and into the abduction site and reported seeing a conical light from an overhead object. She did not, unfortunately, see Anders himself but given the nature of the terrain this would not have been possible as Anders would have been taken from behind some trees which would have obstructed her view.

It is, however, clearly a corroborated abduction case with

every good reason to suspect that at least something physical was happening at the time.

Of such concern was the wave of sightings which included the Anders abduction that a **skywatch** was organised by **Home Guard** Chief Hardy **Broström** some two months after the abduction and this itself was unique in that Home Guard personnel vastly outnumbered Ufologists (fifty Home Guard to fifteen Ufologists). Although this 'stake-out' produced no event similar to Anders' abduction there were a number of **LITS** (Lights in the Sky) sightings corroborated by the three stake-out locations. This gives further weight to the supposition of some real physical event occurring and shows the degree to which official interest was awakened by this case. Skywatches as a technique caught on late in Sweden; they had been popular in the 1960s in England but reached other parts of Europe in the 1970s and 1980s. However, by that time many of the amateurish mistakes had been avoided, and this skywatch was efficiently organised and well supported by technical back-up.

ANDERSSON, MRS H.

There have been many attempts throughout the world, and particularly in America, to set up self-help groups for UFO witnesses and **abduction** witnesses. Some have been successful, particularly when set up by those researchers whose caring attitudes override other considerations, but as a general rule they tend to fail because of the 'organised' nature of the group. The production of newsletters, regular meetings etc., serve to 'institutionalise' these groups, which then lose their effectiveness.

Mrs H. Andersson of Sweden has more or less accidentally provided the role model for an abduction support group. Without apparently intending to do so she has become a focal point for UFO witnesses; there is no organised structure, common newsletter, and so on, but it is generally recognised that anyone in her local area having a UFO experience can seek her out and talk to her and receive the sort of genuine comfort needed from any self-help group. Mrs Andersson is herself a multiple witness and indeed had several sightings during the **Vallentuna** wave of 1974 which included the extraordinary **Anders** abduction.

After a series of sightings on the very day of the Anders abduction Mrs Andersson and her family were chased by a UFO and apparently scanned and probed by it, resulting in kidney pains in the case of Mrs Andersson and headaches and stomach aches in the case of her children. Mrs Andersson summed up her feelings towards that particular event thus: 'It was so horrible I wish it had never happened. I got the impression that we were checked out by someone – like a big torch that swept the area.'

ANDREASSON, BETTY

In 1974 Betty Andreasson wrote to the *National Enquirer* about her UFO abduction experience. Following this she contacted the **Center for UFO Studies (CUFOS)** and **MUFON (The Mutual UFO Network)**. MUFON's investigator Raymond Fowler took up the case. It was in the early part of 1977, ten years after the original incident on 25 January 1967, that Betty Andreasson undertook regression hypnosis to discover further details of her experience.

Betty Andreasson had been at her home in Ashburnham, Massachusetts, with her parents and seven children. Early in the evening a light was seen outside the kitchen window. Betty's father reported creatures outside the house and she reported seeing a number of humanoids entering it *through the wall*. Betty had no other recollections until the hypnotic regression sessions.

Under regressive hypnosis an extraordinary tale emerged. Betty and the alien leader exchanged books: she gave him a copy of the Bible and he gave her a thin religious book which she subsequently lost! The alien leader identified himself as Quazgaa (making this one of the very rare occasions when an alien attributes a name to himself). Betty was abducted on to the UFO and underwent a medical examination including a probe in the nose (very similar to subsequent reports – see **Abductions**). She also reported a probe through the navel (almost identical to the claims of Betty **Hill** some years earlier).

At a later stage of the abduction she was taken to a room and covered in fluid, with tubes enabling her to breathe. She reported small reptile aliens around her and reported floating over a crystal city.

Betty reported that she heard the 'voice of God'.

The case is extremely complex and described excellently in Raymond Fowler's books *The Andreasson Affair* and *The Andreasson Affair Phase Two* (see References and Background Material). In particular there is a great deal in Betty's accounts which is symbolic both of birth and sexual imagery.

Many comparisons are made between this case and that of Kathryn **Howard**, where it appeared that a physical reality was closely intermeshed with a personal reality and a good deal of symbolic imagery unlikely to have been objectively real. To what extent this experience may have been a product of Betty Andreasson's mind rather than induced by an outside agency cannot be determined.

Because of the complexity of the case the Andreasson affair is one of the most important abduction events on record. The work on this case continues and only recently a third book, *The Watchers*, was published, looking further into the case.

ANDREWS AIR FORCE BASE
(See also **Washington 'Flap'**.) July 1952 was an extraordinary peak period for UFO sightings over Washington DC. Several UFOs are alleged to have been tracked by radar at Andrews Air Force Base. The correlation between radar and visual sightings is not high and there is some doubt as to the significance of the radar traces. Explanations for the sightings have varied between the UFOs being caused by temperature inversion to the inevitable suggestion of alien (extraterrestrial) intervention. One problem that always arises in periods of intense reporting is what is known as 'me too' syndrome; people seeing ordinary lights in the sky have UFOs on their mind and imagine more than there is. There is some evidence that this played a part in the sheer weight of number of reports at Washington. However, there is no doubt that there was a hard core of real sightings as well.

A Commander **Boyd** of the current intelligence branch is reported to have advised that 'the object sighted may possibly be from another planet . . . at the present time there is nothing to substantiate this theory but the possibility is not being overlooked.'

ANGEL HAIR
Following some UFO sightings thin, cotton-like fibres have been recovered from the scene of the event. It has been theorised that these are tiny particles held together by the outrushing electro-static field of the UFO. However, these deposits closely resemble a spider's web and there is another theory which states that this is exactly what they are. Unfortunately angel hair disintegrates rapidly and has never been available for full, scientific study. There was one claim that angel hair had fallen on a witness from an overhead UFO, effectively trapping him, but this turned out to be part of a hysterical reaction to a mass sighting, and not substantiated.

At the time of writing these deposits, relatively commonly

reported in the 1960s and early 1970s, tend to be less frequently mentioned.

ANGELUCCI, ORFEO

Following the highly popular book by George **Adamski** telling of his contact with extraterrestrials, a rush of similar stories were published. In 1955 one of these was *Secret of the Saucers* by Orfeo Angelucci (see References and Background Material) telling of his contact with extraterrestrials in California. Like many others, Angelucci had several spiritually enlightening meetings with extraterrestrials, was taken aboard their flying saucer for a trip around the solar system and underwent various revelations. Angelucci met with the aliens in several public places, including cafés and a Greyhound bus station. On one occasion he met Jesus, who revealed himself to be an extraterrestrial. On one excursion to the aliens' home planet Angelucci met an attractive woman called Lyra and her companion, Orion, who explained to him that he – Angelucci – had once been an extraterrestrial named Neptune.

One of the 1955 predictions was that if the Earth people did not shape up, there would be a major catastrophe befalling the planet in 1986.

(See also **Contactees.**)

ANGIE

'Angie' was a serving member of the Armed Forces, holding a high-security clearance. She reported to an investigator that many years earlier she had had a UFO sighting. The investigation into her claims revealed a classic abduction experience. She had become afraid to walk alone in the woods following the sighting near her home. Regressive hypnosis revealed that when she was in the woods she had met an apparently alien figure who had taken her aboard a landed flying saucer where she was subjected to medical examinations which left scars on her body, remaining to the present time.

Subsequent investigations have revealed a series of earlier abductions during Angie's life which suggests a 'pattern' of abductions, a careful programme carried out over an extensive period of time. It is the belief of many investigators, particularly in America, that aliens are following certain human 'bloodlines', abducting the same people many times, and also their children, in what appears to be a programme of genetic manipulation.

(See also **Abductions**.)

ANN ARBOR, MICHIGAN
(See **Swamp Gas Débâcle**.)

ANTARCTIC BASES
There was a rumour that Nazis had prepared secret bases in the Antarctic and were developing flying saucers and that today's UFOs are the descendants of that research. There is practically no sensible corroboration for this theory.

There is also a theory that alien UFOs use the polar regions as secret bases from which to operate on Earth and even that there are enormous 'holes in the poles' from which UFOs operate. There is no more sensible evidence for this theory than there is for the former.

There are obviously fewer reports from the polar regions than elsewhere, not least because there are fewer people there to see anything, but the air of mystery that the poles exude seem irresistible to the mythological side of UFOs.

ANTI-MASS FIELD THEORY
The anti-mass field theory (AMF) is one of several which seek to explain the physical characteristics of observed UFOs. This particular theory was presented by a New Jersey engineering consultant, Kenneth W. Behrendt, and is given some detailed exposure in two publications by **BUFORA**: *UFOs 1947–1987* and *Phenomenon*. (See References and Background Material.)

Behrendt believes that the AMF rationalises the bulk of anomalous behaviours displayed by UFOs. It was originally developed to account for the UFOs apparently inertia-free and gravity-free flight characteristics but he believes it also explains why UFOs produce visible light halos, the physical effects close encounters can have on witnesses such as burned eyes and skin, how UFOs affect compasses and interfere with vehicles, how they can operate under water, and indeed may explain their propulsion system between the stars. Behrendt believes that the AMF theory is mathematically sound and also reveals what the crew aboard a flying saucer would experience from their perspective.

According to AMF theory, UFOs eliminate gravitational and inertial effects by withholding the craft's emission of mass field radiation. This is believed to be achieved by combining a second field of energy over the normal mass field surrounding the object. The second field has a 'polarity' opposite to the original, cancelling each other out. It is the second field which gives the AMF theory its name.

By varying the amount of anti-mass energy produced, the crew of a UFO would be able to vary the remaining uncancelled mass and therefore selectively create certain inertia and gravitational effects, enabling the vehicle to make otherwise inexplicable manoeuvres.

Behrendt points out that with two perfectly matched fields the UFO and its crew would become massless and the crew would therefore float around the cabin of the UFO unless their clothing gave some physical grip to the UFO's floors and other surfaces. Behrendt points out that if the second field exceeded the first then the excess could reduce the mass of nearby objects and he believes this may explain why vehicles are occasionally felt to be lifted from the road by passing UFOs and also why people in cars that have been 'buzzed' by UFOs have experienced weightless sensations.

Since the anti-mass field has the effect of altering the electromagnetic spectrum, then certain effects may become apparent with regard to the UFO, i.e. it may have the capacity for invisibility and for the emission of certain radiations which appear as light.

Behrendt believes that only a minimal amount of experimental work is still needed before the human race produces its own first crude AMF generators.

APEN (UK)

One of the most paranoid aspects of Ufology is the belief of some researchers in a sinister government cover-up and conspiracy theory. This is not to say that there is no cover-up, indeed documentary evidence proves that there has been, but there is every reason to believe that it is a cover-up of ignorance rather than of knowledge. However, some researchers cling to the idea that governments have a full working knowledge of UFO activity which they conceal from the public. An extreme form of this is the belief that governments control ufologists and what they can and cannot say to the public. **BUFORA** researcher Jenny Randles refers to a body called APEN which from 1974 has promoted this latter idea. Indeed, Ms Randles claims to be frequently cited in APEN dispatches and states that people have even received letters allegedly written by her offering governmental UFO research posts.

A more serious interpretation of the promotion of such ideas is that UFO researchers are a very small part of a very large plan generally to undermine trust in governments, and that the motives for these rumours are political rather than ufological, government agents seeking to undermine a perceived threat to their stability, etc.

Governments may not be very good at covering up their secrets for long but they do have a natural propensity for seeing 'reds under the bed' so this suggestion has more credibility.

APPLETON, CYNTHIA

In November 1957, Cynthia Appleton, a housewife from Birmingham, England, reported a contactee-type experience. In fact no UFO was reported but during the afternoon a figure materialised in Mrs Appleton's living room similar in description to the **Adamski** Venusians of a few years earlier, suggesting a similar experience and one validly included in the UFO field. Light outside the house had been disturbed shortly before the materialisation, and returned to normal after the figure had appeared. The entity was quite tall with long blond hair, pale complexion and elongated features.

There appear to have been four contacts and during these the presumed extraterrestrial gave a great deal of information apparently predating known technology of the time; displaying what seemed to be a hologram describing atomic structure physics, the laser, and cancer cures based on frequency modulation.

There were physical traces left once by the entity when he burned his finger; some skin in a bowl of water. Apparently these were analysed and found to resemble animal skin rather than human skin.

APRAKSIN, ARKADII IVANOVICH

In June 1948 Soviet test pilot Arkadii Ivanovich Apraksin encountered a cigar-shaped UFO cutting across the flight path of the aircraft he was flying. The object appeared to be descending. There was confirmation of the sighting by ground radar and Apraksin was ordered to engage the UFO and if necessary to attack it. It appears that the UFO defended itself admirably by striking the aircraft with rays which completely immobilised it, forcing Apraksin to glide the plane to a, fortunately, safe landing.

Astonishingly, less than a year later Apraksin encountered an identical object which again attacked his aircraft, leaving it immobilised and forcing him into emergency landing.

In his book *Above Top Secret* (see References and Background

Material) Tim Good reports that records of Apraksin's existence are skeletal and speculates on the possibility either that the story is fabricated or that, having become an embarrassment to the Soviet Union, his records were erased, making him – in the words of George Orwell's *1984* – an 'unperson'.

APRO
(See **Aerial Phenomena Research Organization**.)

ARCHER, JAMES
James Archer is the pseudonym given to a security officer of **Woodbridge RAF/USAF Base** in the book *Skycrash* by Jenny Randles, Brenda Butler and Dot Street. (See References and Background Material.) Archer allegedly encountered a landed craft in **Rendlesham Forest**, near the RAF/USAF base, in a controversial UFO event which took place in December 1980. In the classic telling of the event several base personnel encountered the object, suspected of being of extraterrestrial origin. Archer described the object as triangular and on three landing legs, with a blue light on top and other lights on the underside. Archer reported seeing shapes inside the object that 'did not look human. Maybe they were like robots.' He and his colleague followed the moving object in the forest and witnessed its departure at great speed.

ARCHETYPES (JUNGIAN)
Jungian archetypes are described as a universal pattern of response to particular images shared by humans. In his book *Flying Saucers: A Modern Myth of Things Seen in the Sky* (see References and Background Material), Jung proposed that the UFO represented the archetype of 'the mandala', the circular symbol of unity.

ARÉVALO, WILFREDO
Rancher Wilfredo Arévalo witnessed the landing of a flying saucer on 18 March 1950 at Lego Argentino in Argentina, and noticed a second saucer overhead apparently guarding its companion. Arévalo walked to within some 400 feet of the object which he described as being made of something like aluminium and giving off a smell like burning benzine.

In a transparent dome Arévalo could see four tall men wearing something like cellophane. Shortly after, they shone a light at Arévalo and took off, leaving an area of burned grass.

AREZZO, ITALY

In November 1954 Mrs Rosa Lotti-Danielli reported an extraordinary encounter at a cemetery. While walking past an open space she saw a landed conical UFO. The craft was metallic and seats were visible. Two beings appeared, both no more than four feet tall. The beings spoke in an incomprehensible tongue and took the pot of flowers Mrs Lotti-Danielli was carrying. When she called the police to the scene the UFO was gone although other witnesses saw it leaving.

ARMSTRONG, CAPTAIN

Following the **Roswell Incident**, William 'Mac' **Brazel**'s son reported that a Captain Armstrong had taken away a collection of debris from the reported flying saucer crash which had been accumulated by Brazel's son in his early years. In taking it away Armstrong apparently claimed that the 'stuff was important to the country's security'. One way or another the witnesses were left with very little to show for the Roswell crash; the Air Force was very thorough in its rounding up of every piece of debris.

ARMSTRONG, LIEUTENANT

Just four days after the Kenneth **Arnold** encounter, i.e. 28 June 1947, United States Air Force pilot Lieutenant Armstrong – cruising at 6,000 feet over Lake Mead, Nevada – reported sighting six discs in formation. This was one of many sightings at this time and gives weight to the belief that physical objects were in the air and being observed and reported.

ARNOLD, GENERAL H. H.

From time to time the American Military has had a tendency to explain away UFOs on a basis that seems less than satisfactory. On 8 July 1947 (the same day as a series of sightings at the now Edwards Air Force Base in the Mojave desert, and indeed the same day that a crashed flying saucer was believed to have been recovered from the **Roswell** area), General H. H. ('Hap') Arnold of the Army Air Force was quoted as saying in a United Press release that the saucers 'could be a development of United States scientists not yet perfected . . . or just plain fighting planes'.

He further speculated that the UFOs might be foreign aircraft that had gone out of control or were straying off course.

ARNOLD, KENNETH
Introduction of Term 'Flying Saucer'

During Kenneth Arnold's sighting he described the formation of the objects as moving 'like a saucer would if you skipped it across the water'. A newspaper man translated this expression into the term 'flying saucer' giving birth to an enduring title for these objects.

Although Arnold is commonly credited with the introduction of the term 'saucer', in fact the first usage of the term was in 1878 when a Texas farmer described a large flying object he had seen as a 'large saucer'. The significance of the Arnold usage, however, is that it provided the media with a term that it found highly appealing and thus brought to public prominence.

Arnold's sighting and use of the term 'saucer' therefore did not start the UFO phenomenon but did start the pronounced media interest in it.

There is, however, one remarkable point about this expression which is often overlooked. Although often held to be a description of the *shape* of the objects Arnold saw, it was in fact intended to be a description of their *movement* (the skipping motion of a saucer being flipped across water). Arnold in fact described the objects as boomerang-shaped, although he later referred to them as discs, but even then they were shown as discs with large chunks cut out to give a stylised boomerang shape. This point was not picked up at the time and there was a general perception that Arnold had reported a saucer shape. The significance of this is that it shows the power of the media in influencing the public's perception of events and indeed it could be held that the media misinterpretation of Arnold's phrase has created part of the mythology around UFOs which is incorrect, and worse, masks the reality.

Sighting By

It was on 24 June 1947 that Kenneth Arnold sighted the nine objects in formation which were to lead to the modern UFO era. He was a lone pilot in a Callair aircraft informally engaged on a search for a crashed C-46 marine transport plane, which he did not find. During the flight near **Mount Rainier** in the Cascade Mountains of Washington State, USA, he witnessed objects in flight formation; he estimated their speed to be between 1,300 and 1,700 miles per hour, which would have been faster than any plane of the day could fly. He estimated the length of their formation to be some five miles, at around twenty-three miles' distance from him. He believed the individual size of the objects was approximately two-thirds that of a DC-4 (one of which happened to be sharing the sky with him and gave him some point of reference).

The sighting was of short duration, at far distance, not corroborated by radar or other sightings, and in fact adds very little to our knowledge of the UFO phenomenon. The significance of the sighting has always been the media attention it attracted and the enormous public interest which started at that time and has never seriously abated.

AS2
A department of the Ministry of Defence, the full title of which is Air Staff 2, which succeeded **Defence Secretariat 8 (DS8)**. These departments are alleged to deal with UFO reports made to the government; in fact a spokesman for that department described AS2 as 'the focal point within the United Kingdom for UFO reports'.

Interestingly, a former head of this department, Ralph **Noyes**, has – since retirement – become a very active and diligent researcher into the subject of UFOs and at the time of writing is a consultant to **BUFORA**.

ASHLAND, NEBRASKA SIGHTING
(See **Schirmer, Patrolman Herbert.**)

ASHLEY, THOMAS L.
In the late 1950s **NICAP** published a revealing statement on the subject of UFOs by the Ohio representative to Congress, Thomas L. Ashley: 'I share your concern over the secrecy that continues to shroud our intelligence activities on this subject.'

ASHTAR
An alien, a high-ranking member of the Inter-Galactic Federation and the United Council of the Universal Brotherhood, and one of several aliens contacted by **contactees**. He frequently offers advice on raising our consciousness, and generally making the world a better place.

ASTRONOMICAL EXPLANATIONS
When examining UFO reports it is important to recognise that between 90 and 95 per cent of all reports are solved and that the number of unexplained UFO cases is very low relative to the

numbers of reports received. By far the largest category of answers, followed reasonably closely by aircraft lights, are astronomical explanations, i.e. stars and planets, some of which can be exceptionally and unexpectedly bright. Other explanations in this category include the less common occurrences such as meteor showers and we can reasonably include sightings of man-made satellites orbiting the Earth. No exhaustive list of this category could easily be prepared but it is a useful category for a would-be researcher to be aware of because of the predictable nature of most of the objects involved. For example, if there is a UFO report of a particularly bright light and it can be determined that a particularly bright Venus was in the sky at that approximate time, then it is reasonable to assume that it is Venus which has been seen unless the witness confirms that there were two sources of bright light.

The UFO phenomenon is, however, not as simple as this in all its manifestations and there is at least one case on record where a woman sighted a UFO and became greatly emotionally disturbed, reporting all kinds of associated phenomena including telepathy, etc., yet despite the obvious sincerity of the witness the UFO was unquestionably identified as the moon seen through clouds. Cases such as this strengthen the need for UFO researchers to be as aware of the characteristics of the witness as of the events reported.

ATKINSON, COLONEL IVAN C.

It was Colonel Ivan C. Atkinson, then Deputy Executive Director of the Air Force Office of Scientific Research, who on 31 August 1966 approached the University of Colorado requesting that they conduct a comprehensive examination of UFOs. This was to culminate in the **Condon Report**. It is worth noting that several other comparable institutions had already declined his offer to participate or assume responsibility for such a project.

AURA RHANES

Contactee Truman **Bethurum** met with a flying saucer in the California desert. The saucer's captain was a female alien, Aura Rhanes, whom Bethurum described as 'tops in shapeliness and beauty'. Aura Rhanes apparently came from the planet **Clarion** which is permanently hidden behind our moon, and is free from disease and danger. Mrs Rhanes apparently was a grandmother and human enough in appearance to avoid detection on Earth.

According to Dennis Stacy's analysis of the contactee era in *Phenomenon* (see References and Background Material), Bethurum met Aura Rhanes at a later time in a restaurant sipping orange juice, but she ignored him.

AUSTRALIAN SECURITY AND INTELLIGENCE ORGANIZATION (ASIO)

The intelligence and counter-espionage service of the Australian government. In 1959, Stan Seers, then president of the Queensland Flying Saucer Research Bureau, was approached by a person indicating he was from this intelligence organisation, allegedly requesting close co-operation in UFO research, and therefore suggesting a high-level governmental approach to the subject on that continent.

However, the Royal Australian Air Force stated in a letter to British researcher Timothy Good that there had been no participation by this organisation in UFO investigations.

AUTOKINESIS

UFO researchers have to be aware of the illusions which can be caused by bright lights against a darkened background. Autokinesis is one such illusion, where a bright light appears to move in relation to a dark background simply because of the lack of reference points. This can be most dramatically demonstrated if there is a reasonable cloud cover being moved by high winds when the relative movement of points of light can appear to be quite extreme, although a long-term detailed study could in fact show that the apparently moving light is a star which over even a reasonable period of time will show very little actual movement (based only, of course, on the Earth's own rotation).

AUTOMATIC WRITING

There are several instances where UFO experiences, and particularly **contactee** experiences, have subsequently led to the witness feeling compelled to write messages being received from, presumably, the alien contact. The messages come in the form of automatic writing where the witness's hand is guided by 'other forces'.

Generally these messages confirm the statements of the alien entity previously made to the contactee. Often the contactee claims to be in a trance while this is happening and reads the writing for the first time when they come out of the trance, not remembering actually recording it.

AVELEY, ESSEX, CE4 CASE
In October 1974 Elaine and John Avis were abducted on the outskirts of their village which is just outside the Greater London boundary in Essex. (I have used the generally accepted pseudonym for these witnesses although their real names are now very much in the public domain. Since I have not been able to ascertain whether this was with their permission, I have stuck to the pseudonym.)

The couple were returning to their home by car with their three children. Early on in the drive they saw a light in the sky which they discussed but by which they seemed not to have been greatly perturbed. Shortly after this they drove through a green mist covering the road.

When they arrived home John switched on the television to watch a programme he was waiting for but was amazed to find that broadcasting had ceased for the night and it was now one o'clock in the morning. They identified a two and a half hour **missing time** period.

Many of the incidents in this case mirror the Betty and Barney **Hill** abduction in America of the early 1960s. Afterwards there were recurrent nightmare dreams of being in a room with small alien-type creatures, and these led them to UFO researchers to investigate their case.

Under **hypnotic regression** the family revealed that they were taken out of their car with a floating sort of sensation. They were led into the UFO, there was a medical examination, and later they were led back to the car to go on their way again.

There appear to have been some subsequent changes of a spiritual nature to the family and it has been suggested that John has increased his skills in the artistic areas. It is understood that the family have also reported psychic experiences and apparitions.

The Aveley encounter is acknowledged to be the first British abduction to be explored with the use of hypnotic regression.

AVERY ESTATES, LOUISIANA
On 10 October 1973 several witnesses reported a UFO over Avery Estates which is a housing estate in St Tammany parish, New Orleans. There were reports of affected radio and TV and bad Citizen Band Radio static.

Jimmy Fisher saw a 'big silvery hamburger'-shaped UFO suspended some four or five hundred feet above his house. There were apparently some fifteen people or more watching the UFO when a police unit arrived including Lieutenant Robert Lonardo and Captain Huey Farrell. Lonardo had a tape recorder in the car and switched it on as the UFO departed, providing one of the very rare aural recordings of a UFO experience.

The noise was described as a generator hum, rising in pitch, displaying intense energy. It was apparently something like a cross between tyres at high speed and the noise a large train would make. It was also described as the sort of sound you would hear inside a tornado.

The incident led to UFO 'stake-outs' with many lights spotted on subsequent evenings. There was also one report of an entity with green reflective eyes.

AVEYRON, FRANCE

There were reports of sightings by people at an isolated farm in Aveyron, France, in the summer of 1966. The reports were of spherical fiery objects which appeared to be exhibiting a 'haunting' nature.

These sightings became all the more extraordinary in January 1967 when there was a report of one farmer getting close to the spheres and seeing what appeared to be a UFO inside the fiery light; he was also able to identify humanoids.

The events then almost turned into contactee experience, with the witness suffering changes to his sleep and behaviour patterns. The witness appears to have received messages from the aliens which he is later to impart to the world.

AVIANO (NATO BASE)

Aviano is a small town in Northern Italy, housing a NATO base. On the night of 30 June/1 July 1977 a bright light was seen hovering over the base by several personnel. During the time the light was visible in the area, the base was subjected to a power blackout which ended when the light left. The light was described as fifty metres in diameter and spinning. There were also independent witnesses from over a mile away. The official explanation was that the light was a reflection of the moon on the clouds.

AVIS, ELAINE AND JOHN
(See **Aveley, Essex, CE4 Case**.)

AVRO DEVICES

During the early 1950s there were rumours of collaboration between the Royal Canadian Air Force and A. V. Roe Ltd, an aeronautics firm in Toronto, Canada. They were apparently perfecting AVRO devices, i.e. terrestrially made 'flying saucers', and in particular the AV-9 and VZ-9.

It is alleged that at one time the Air Force was using the presence of AVRO devices as an excuse to explain away reports of UFO sightings but it appears that in fact the AVRO development was a monumental flop. These vehicles were reportedly highly unstable and were never able to fly very far or for very long.

However, there was a new twist to the story when it was believed that the Army was using the AVRO excuse as cover for the fact that it was actually test flying a captured alien flying saucer. This later claim was made by Lieutenant-Colonel George **Edwards**, a scientist and former USAF personnel member, who claims to have been involved in the AVRO VZ-9 project and stated, 'We know that the AF was secretly test flying a real alien space craft.'

AYRES, WILLIAM H.

NICAP in the late 1950s published a statement by the Ohio representative to Congress, William H. Ayres: 'Congressional investigations have been held and are still being held on the problem of unidentified flying objects. Since most of the material presented is classified the hearings are never printed.'

AZHAZHA, VLADIMIR

Vladimir Azhazha was Deputy Director of the Underwater Research Section of the USSR Academy of Sciences and in 1978 set up an official civilian UFO research organisation called **BPVTS**, the translation of which means 'Search for Extraterrestrial Civilisations in the Neighbourhood of Earth by Means of Radio Electronics'. The group included a chief of communications in the Navy, a deputy head of space flight control and a cosmonaut. One of its prominent members is quoted as stating, 'The UFO problem exists, and it is extremely serious. Thousands of people have seen UFOs, and up till now it is still not clear what they are.'

AZTEC, NEW MEXICO

There are many stories of recovery of crashed flying saucers, generally from the late 1940s and in the United States.

Although the principal and most famous of all stories – and the one likely to have some basis of truth behind it – is the

Roswell crash of 1947, there were others that became famous in publications of the time, shortly after the surge of media interest following the **Arnold** sighting of June 1947. One of these other cases is the Aztec, New Mexico, recovery of 1948.

According to legend a flying saucer approximately 100 feet wide crashed into the desert near Aztec in New Mexico and was recovered by the United States government and taken to **Wright Patterson Air Force Base** (as it is currently known). Details of the incident contain all the usual flying saucer crash retrieval mythology: the craft was of a superlight metal that resisted all attempts to cut or burn it; there were no seams or welding on the structure; writings in hieroglyphics were recovered, and inevitably a number of dead alien bodies. This story is almost certainly one of the more ludicrous hoaxes perpetrated within the field of UFO research, though by whom is not certain.

Readers requiring more information should turn to **Crash Retrievals** and **Majestic 12**.

Crash retrievals in general terms are almost certainly a mythology, though it must be admitted that their advocates include some of the most diligent researchers in the world. One of the classic characteristics of a mythology is that it 'improves with the telling'. This is certainly true of crash retrievals generally, and the Aztec recovery in particular.

Just when interest in crash retrieval research was at its lowest ebb, due to the lack of hard evidence being produced by researchers, a series of documents known collectively as MJ-12 (Majestic 12) came to light, seeming to give corroborative evidence in support of these events. In recent years the Aztec recovery has been linked with members of the Majestic 12 government group, apparently giving new life to this story.

B

BAHIA BLANCA
(see **Diaz, Carlos Alberto**.)

BAIKONUR COSMODROME
Just as in the United States there are many claims of UFOs hovering around military centres and centres of space exploration, so there are similar reports from the Soviet Union. One such report is that in June 1982 two UFOs hovered over the Baikonur cosmodrome for a short period.

On inspection the following day there was some structural damage to the launch towers including ripping apart of welded sections. There was also damage to nearby houses.

According to the report the cosmodrome was shut down for repairs for a period of some two weeks.

BAILEY, AL AND BETTY
The first reported contact with extraterrestrials by George **Adamski** was to some extent witnessed by four others, two of whom were Al and Betty Bailey. They had contacted Adamski because of their common interest in flying saucers and had asked to be with him at his next attempt to establish contact.

They apparently observed his meeting with the aliens from a distance of approximately one mile. Together with the Williamson family they had been placed at a distant location by Adamski when he went alone towards the saucer sighting, where he was to have his first face to face meeting.

BALL LIGHTNING
Ball lightning is regarded as a rare natural atmospheric phenomenon, thought by some never to have been photographed, and doubted, even until recently, to exist by scientists working in meteorology. There are still some who deny that there is proof of the existence of ball lightning. If it does exist, then

based on the reports of those who claim to have seen it ball lightning would appear to be glowing spherical energy, generally moving slowly, and igniting on impact or occasionally passing through solid matter.

Since the beginning of UFO reporting there has been a tendency to try to pass off all reports as ball lightning and the counter arguments have always produced those cases of extraordinary detail where ball lightning simply would not fit the explanation.

In reality it is highly likely that ball lightning, if it does exist, explains a great many UFO reports but would none the less leave open a great many others. It is generally well accepted that the questions raised by the UFO phenomenon will not be answered by any one simplistic answer.

The Peter **Day** film is considered by some to be the first capture of ball lightning on film, though that remains speculation.

More recently it has been suggested that an even more extraordinary possibility may exist, with a form of ball lightning actually harbouring intelligence capable of reacting with the human observer's. Many of the lights observed in the valleys of Norway (see **Hessdalen, Project**) seem to exhibit some of these features.

A further interesting variation on the theory that has been offered is that ball lightning is 'charged' in such a way that it can interfere with the electrical impulses in the brain and cause hallucination. This, it has been argued, could explain even the more exotic UFO sightings, though this still remains highly speculative.

BALLARD, MAJOR
In September 1951 a Lockheed T33 from Dover Air Force Base, Delaware, piloted by Major Ballard and Lieutenant Rogers of the 148 Fighter Interceptor Squadron, encountered a UFO over New Jersey. It was a silver disc flying at around 1,000 miles per hour. A radar trace of the object at Fort Monmouth confirmed the sighting.

BANANEIRAS, BRAZIL
(See **Gaetano, Paulo**.)

BARCLAY, JOHN M.
On 21 April 1897, during the American **airship** sightings, John M. Barclay at Rockland in Texas reported an airship UFO. He had been attracted towards it by a whining noise and the

agitated barking of his dog. It was oblong with detailed structure along its sides, including what appeared to be wings, and was noticeable mainly for its extremely brilliant lighting. Barclay watched the craft circle round, close to the ground, and then land. He stepped within 100 feet of the object where he was prevented from getting closer by a man presumed to be from the craft.

The man called himself Smith and requested some tools and equipment, lubricating oil and chisels, offering American money to pay for the articles. Barclay obtained these at the local store, and handed them over to 'Smith'.

When Barclay asked the man where he was from he said, 'From anywhere.' Asked where he was going, Smith said they would be in Greece the day after tomorrow – no mean feat for 1897. When the object left it was at remarkable speed, described as being 'like a shot out of a gun'.

There was some possible corroborative report from a farmer living nearby, a Mr Frank Nichols. Some thirty minutes after Barclay's sighting he woke up to hear a strange whirring noise and saw a brilliantly lit object in his field.

LAS BARDENAS REALES

In January 1975 military personnel at the bombing range of Las Bardenas Reales near Zaragoza airbase reported two UFOs hovering and landing for a period of around half an hour in the late evening. There were reports of structures with white and orange lights; one of the UFOs was estimated to be approximately the size of a lorry. The witnesses observed the objects fly close to the ground, at low speed, before suddenly accelerating and climbing away.

There was an initial belief that the military personnel had seen an optical illusion but a subsequent Air Force investigation showed that 'no contradictions were found, all coincided exactly in their descriptions'. This seemed to suggest that there was some basis of fact to the reports.

BARKER, CAPTAIN JOHN
(See **Bougainville Reef**.)

BARNES, HARRY G.
A significant radar contact case occurred in 1952 near **Andrews Air Force Base**. Harry G. Barnes, a senior traffic controller, and six (or, according to some reports, seven) technicians were

manning the air route traffic control at Washington National Airport when seven blips registered in patterned flight. During the sighting, two of the blips moved off the radar screen at incredible velocity, far outstripping anything any aircraft of the day was capable of. A check of the equipment showed that there was no malfunction and it was determined that the blips were being registered on radar facilities at other locations. One report has one of the objects moving at 7,000 miles per hour.

The objects also crossed flight-restricted areas above the White House and Capitol Hill. This event occurred during the 1952 **Washington Flap** where there were a number of corroborated sightings by commercial pilots.

BARNETT, GRADY LANDON

During the July 1947 **crash retrieval** activities in New Mexico, witness Grady Barnett reported a crash site west of **Socorro** which involved a complete but damaged saucer and the dead cadavers of its alien crew.

Barnett described the aliens as, 'Like humans but they were not humans. The heads were round, the eyes were small, and they had no hair. The eyes were oddly spaced. They were quite small by our standards and their heads were larger in proportion to their bodies than ours. Their clothing seemed to be one piece and grey in colour.'

The object itself was described as 'some sort of metallic, disc-shaped object about twenty-five or thirty feet across'. Barnett's observation of the crash site was interrupted by military personnel who cordoned off the area and removed the witnesses, telling them that on grounds of national security they must not talk about their encounter.

Although Barnett died before he was interviewed by the people investigating the crash retrievals in the area, he was described by those who knew him as 'the very model of a respectable and honest citizen – hardly likely to invent such a fantastic tale'.

BARRERA, JUAN

In the summer of 1965 Juan Barrera was Commander of the Aquirre Cerda base. Together with several other observers, including a Chilean Air Force pilot, Barrera reported sightings of UFOs exhibiting extraordinary speed and manoeuvrability. They were apparently affecting scientific instruments on the base. The objects were observed for over an hour by six observers, by the naked eye, binoculars and a theodolite.

Barrera reported that he believed it 'rash to say that we all saw a flying saucer' but went on to say 'that it could be an aircraft constructed on this Earth, I do not believe possible'.

BARRY, BOB

Jacques Vallée in his book *Dimensions* (see References and Background Material) refers to the statements of Bob Barry, director of the 20th Century UFO Bureau at Colinswood, New Jersey. This bureau is described as part of a fundamentalist religious movement.

In June 1978 Barry apparently stated that he had three high level sources who confirmed that the government was concerned with the UFO problem and had recovered alien bodies in crash retrieval situations.

Mr Barry has also apparently stated he believes the movie *Close Encounters of the Third Kind* was part of a government plan to condition the public to accept the existence of UFOs and aliens.

This belief that exposure to UFO material is a government policy for the long term would seem to be very similar to comments made by Jenny Randles, a British researcher for **BUFORA,** that there is an (unsupported) belief that she, and indeed all UFO researchers, are in fact government 'plants' who are helping to condition the public into accepting UFOs.

I cannot speak for Steven Spielberg or the film industry, though I personally find the suggestion an unlikely one, but certainly I cannot support the notion that all or even many UFO researchers are likely to turn out to be government plants. If any at all are, then it is difficult to see what achievements they can point to.

If the government did have a policy of releasing information about UFOs they need only feed certain data to investigators and then allow normal 'mythology' to take over; there are many who believe that this disinformation technique explains many of the more exotic crash retrievals situations in America, and is far more likely than a massive fraud involving hundreds, if not thousands, of people.

BASES OF UFOS

Over the forty-odd years of UFO reports there has been no shortage of claims that UFOs operate from bases on the Earth or in near-Earth space. Many people have speculated that they operate from a base on the moon but other suggestions have placed the aliens closer to hand.

One theory is that the polar regions contain cavities and that the UFOs operate from within the planet.

Another theory suggests that Hitler's Nazis escaped to secret bases in Antarctica where they have been developing weapons since World War II, and sightings of these have led to today's tales of UFOs.

Other locations have been within the **Bermuda Triangle**, in various deserts, in various jungles, and thanks to a spate of reports in South Wales, a rocky island off the Welsh coast. One of the most recent and ludicrous suggestions is that they have a base inside the hills around the Yorkshire moors, the entire theory being based on a photograph which has actually been identified as light reflecting on wet mossy rocks!

BASS STRAIT

Bass Strait is that area of sea running between southern mainland Australia and the island of Tasmania. Some of the most extraordinary UFO cases in Australasia have occurred in and around the Bass Strait area. Paul Norman, of the Victorian UFO society, **VUFORS**, and one of that continent's most prominent UFO researchers, has uncovered UFO reports reaching back into the early 1900s, including the loss of the ship SS *Amelia J*. This particular vessel was lost during a period of unexplained UFO sightings. In circumstances frighteningly reminiscent of the Flight 19 loss of the **Bermuda Triangle** some years later the search aircraft sent to investigate the UFOs also disappeared without trace. One of the most extraordinary cases is that of Frederick **Valentich** in 1978.

Bill Chalker, another prominent Australian UFO investigator and a member of the Australian Centre for UFO Studies, reports that some seventeen aircraft went missing in the area during the World War II period although no enemy action took place over the Bass Strait.

Bass Strait would therefore seem to be what is known as a 'window area', or '**ufocal**' – a place of highly concentrated activity. Such areas have been identified in various places across the world at various times, but no reasonable explanation for them has ever been found.

BATTELLE INSTITUTE STUDY

The Battelle Memorial Institute in Ohio was commissioned by the United States Air Force to make the first scientific study of

UFOs in 1952. It concluded that it was statistically improbable, if not impossible, for the UFO 'unknowns' to be mere misidentifications of mundane objects. Possibly surprised by its own results the Institute, and certainly the United States Air Force, backed away from the significance of the conclusion. Subsequent US Air Force investigations concluded the opposite, to the satisfaction of very few people, including those pilots who had seen UFOs.

BAVIC LINE

French researcher Aimé Michel, studying the 1954 French UFO sightings, found that there were many sightings along a line he called the BAVIC line (so called from the initials of Bayonne and Vichy, being the two towns at each end of the line) which may be similar to the interface between UFO sightings and ley line patterns.

This was an example of Michel's 'straight line theory' where he demonstrated that many UFO sightings in France were taking place along various straight lines (*The Truth About Flying Saucers*, see References and Background Material).

BEAN, JOHN B.

A well-observed and reported sighting took place in January 1953 at Livermore, California. The observer had seventeen years' experience as a pilot. John B. Bean was driving away from the Atomic Energy Commission research facilities and pulled over on to the hard shoulder of the road to take some papers from his case. While parked he watched a DC-6 descending for a landing at a nearby airport. Bean reported seeing a UFO, perfectly round, with a metallic sheen similar to aluminium. Light reflecting from the UFO was whitish in colour and the object apparently manoeuvred in swift changes of direction. Bean was familiar with the capabilities of the F-86 fighters which could climb almost vertically but he commented that the UFO was apparently far more technologically advanced than that aircraft. Bean also reported that he felt the UFO accelerated upwards to avoid collision with an incoming jet.

Being familiar with aircraft, and having different models in his sight range simultaneously, Bean was able to determine that the UFO appeared to have more power and more manoeuvrability than either a DC-6 or the jet fighter. His experience as a pilot and the conditions of the sighting make this a highly credible report.

BEARDSLEY, JAMES V.

In June 1969 FAA Traffic Controller James V. Beardsley was aboard an American Airlines flight from Phoenix to Washington. He was an observer watching pilot procedures. The aircraft was one of three in flight, the second being United Airlines and the third a National Guard plane.

Four UFOs appeared ahead and the co-pilot called the air traffic control centre who informed him that they were tracking 'unknowns' near them, thereby confirming on radar what the pilots were seeing visually. One of the UFOs was described as being approximately 18–20 feet long, 12–14 feet across and some 8 feet thick and displaying the colour of burnished aluminium. The other three were dart-shaped and smaller.

The UFOs had been on a collision course but made a strikingly quick manoeuvre and passed safely by the aircraft.

The pilot of the United Airlines plane also witnessed the event and the National Guard plane pilot exclaimed, 'Damn, they almost got me!'

Beardsley filed an official FAA report which was kept from the public for approximately three years.

BEDROOM APPARITIONS

Studies have revealed that there is a high incidence of self-reported paranormal phenomena in **abduction** and **contactee** witnesses of UFO events. One particular incident commonly occurring is the so-called bedroom visitation; the apparition or manifestation of entities within the witness's bedroom, or at other times of sleep.

Whether these are due to **altered states of consciousness** which might also exist at the time of the UFO sighting, whether they represent a heightened suggestibility or awareness which the witness is able to pick up on, or whether they are actually a part of the UFO event or not, is all open to debate.

Several witnesses have made closer connections in bedroom visitations by claiming that the UFO entities actually abducted them out of their bedroom and into flying saucers parked outside. These last incidences of bedroom visitation follow the pattern of other UFO abductions very closely.

It has to be remembered that one of the characteristics of the states of near-sleep, either nearly awake or nearly asleep, is a period of hallucination, which could account for some of the imagery; on the other hand some witnesses have then shown physical evidence of possible attack – scars on their bodies corresponding to memories of medical examination, or nose-bleeds corresponding to memories of nasal probes, and so on.

BEIT BRIDGE, ZIMBABWE

In the last days of May 1974 a young couple identified as Peter and Frances were driving from Salisbury (now Harare) to Durban in South Africa, making a border crossing over the Limpopo river at Beit Bridge.

Approximately ten kilometres south of the farming town of Umvuma, Peter, who had been exceeding the speed limit, slowed down thinking he could see a policeman ahead, but as they passed the 'policeman' they noticed he seemed to be wearing a plastic or metal sort of suit; when they looked back after passing him, he was not there at all.

A bright blue light appeared in the air to the side of the car and the light inside the vehicle faded (although other electrical equipment remained operative). The light from outside was bright enough to cast shadows. One particular feature Peter and Frances remember was feeling very cold. They had to wrap up in coats and blankets to keep warm, although when they later pulled into a garage and commented on this to the attendant, he – in vest and shorts – could not believe that they thought it was cold.

As they began driving fast again, Peter took his foot off the accelerator and found that he was not in control of the car. For some eighteen kilometres it seemed to be driven without his assistance. All the time a bright light UFO had been station-keeping above them and only disappeared as they began to approach Fort Victoria.

Some ten kilometres out of Fort Victoria and back on the road towards Beit Bridge the UFO reappeared again; at one point the witnesses believed that they were passing through a strange landscape of marshes and swamps that did not belong to their known geographical location.

They seemed to be in a 'cone of silence', an unnatural stillness which often accompanies UFO encounters. Peter seemed, again, not to be in control of the car. Eventually they arrived at Beit Bridge and discovered they had a one hour missing time period.

Analysis of the lost time by regression hypnosis revealed that during the drive Frances had been induced to sleep, shortly before an alien entity had materialised in the back of the car and remained there for the rest of the journey. Peter had some communication with the entity and was also able – in some **out-of-body experience** – to examine the inside of the space-craft, and discuss the entities' lifestyle and their purpose on Earth. They seek, apparently, to guide mankind without direct interference. They apparently live amongst us and there was one interesting suggestion that on board the spacecraft was an abduction 'room' where Earth people could be taken but simulated scenarios would be used to make them think they were still in their normal Earth surroundings.

Analysis of the car indicated that although it had travelled 288 kilometres it had only used petrol corresponding to, and had clocked up mileage of, seventeen kilometres. Furthermore, tyres which had been cheap retreads used for this one journey, which should have worn out by the time they arrived, had not worn out and indeed went on to do 8,000 kilometres of driving without harm at all – apparently quite unknown for such products.

BELIEVER BILL

During the extensively photographed **Gulf Breeze** case there was one occasion when the principal witness, Ed **Walters**, heard the humming sound which usually indicated the presence of the UFOs, but had no sighting. On this occasion, however, there was some suggestion that the object was in the vicinity because a second photographer using the pseudonym 'Believer Bill' sent photographs to the *Gulf Breeze Sentinel* of objects similar to those Ed had photographed.

The identity of Believer Bill has never been established. The investigators have indicated that they believe this is because he is afraid of attendant publicity.

BELLINGERI, CARLA AND MAURO

Carla and Mauro Bellingeri were driving home near Piedmont in Italy on 16 April 1974 when they encountered a bright UFO diving to within 50 feet of their house. They stopped on their frontage and stood together watching the object, which hovered soundlessly above them.

There seemed to be a transparent cockpit to the object and inside they believed they could see three humanoid shapes, one of which, at one point, seemed to look at them before turning away; the UFO fired its jets and disappeared rapidly in a north-easterly direction.

Mauro's sister-in-law was in the house at the time and heard the noise, but did not see the object.

BELO HORIZONTE, BRAZIL

One of the most extraordinary Brazilian contact cases dates from May 1969 when the witness, José Antonio da Silva, was fishing near Belo Horizonte.

Da Silva noticed figures moving behind him and appears to have been struck by a beam of light, causing some paralysis and forcing him to his knees. Two humanoids of approximately four feet in height, wearing matt silver suits and with masks covering their faces, abducted da Silva on to a landed craft resembling an upright cylinder.

The craft then took off and da Silva appears to have undergone symptoms similar to the pressures of acceleration and G-force, i.e. pressure and physical weariness, numbness and increased relative weight. During this flight da Silva was wearing a helmet given to him by one of his abductors. After the craft landed, da Silva was blindfolded and taken into a large room some 30 feet by 40 feet where he encountered another entity.

This new entity was a dwarf covered in long red hair, with a long beard and a face very similar to gnome- and troll-like descriptions in Europe. He had thick eyebrows, pale skin and large greenish eyes. He was joined in the room by many other similar creatures.

The room in which da Silva described finding himself is virtually unique to UFO literature; it seems it was made of stone. Around the walls were paintings of animals and other Earth scenes. More common to UFO reports, da Silva stated that the lighting in the room was very bright but he could not discern the source.

One particularly unpleasant sight which greeted da Silva suggests a sinister motivation on the part of the entities: da Silva believed he saw on a shelf near him the corpses of four humans.

The entities took from him many of the articles he had with him, presumably as specimens. These included flies for fishing, and currency notes.

Da Silva engaged in conversation with the entities and it appears that they attempted to get him to spy on Earth on their behalf, or possibly to be their emissary on Earth. Da Silva refused.

He also reported undergoing some religious revelations but has never disclosed of exactly what nature. There was one time however when some brawling between the 'gnomes' and da Silva was brought to an end by the intervention of a Christ-like figure.

The event ended when the machine took off again and landed elsewhere, da Silva finding himself some 200 miles away from where he had been. Even more strangely, over four days had apparently passed since his abduction had begun.

BENAVIDEZ, LIEUTENANT
Lieutenant Benavidez was a Chilean Air Force pilot who, in the summer of 1965, reported extraordinary UFO activity over the Acquirre Cerda (see **Barrera**, Juan).

BENCAZON, SPAIN
(See **Carrasco, Miguel**.)

BENITEZ, JUAN JOSÉ
In 1976 the Air Ministry in Madrid, Spain, handed over a file of extraordinary UFO cases to a reporter, Juan Benitez. The file included photographic support for several cases. In an article in *Flying Saucer Review* Benitez states, 'When you read these files . . . it becomes definitely and categorically clear that the UFOs exist and, quite evidently, are a matter of the deepest concern to the governments of the whole planet.'

BENJAMIN, DR E. H.
During the 1896/7 **airship** wave in the southern United States of America there was much speculation that the airships were terrestrial and invented by men then ahead of their time. One such candidate was a dentist, Dr E. H. Benjamin, who newsmen identified from a description given by lawyer George D. **Collins,** who claimed to be representing him. Benjamin, however, denied having anything to do with any aerial experiments.

At the time, finding an inventor for the airships was a media pastime rather akin to the modern-day desire of finding Elvis alive and well, or the umpteenth gunman in the Kennedy assassination.

BENNEWITZ, PAUL
There appears to have been some considerable UFO activity in New Mexico in the early 1980s, particularly around the area of the Manzano weapons storage area. Much of this activity has been photographed and filmed by Paul Bennewitz who runs a scientific firm in Albuquerque.

In correspondence with researcher Tim Good, as reported in his book *Above Top Secret* (see References and Background

Material), Bennewitz has revealed that he also recorded magnetic activity believed to be caused by the UFOs.

BENTWATERS/LAKENHEATH
On 13 August 1956 there was one of the most celebrated radar visual contacts with a UFO at RAF/USAF Bentwaters/Lakenheath in Suffolk.

The objects were traced by three ground-based radars, were confirmed on aerial radar by a Venom night fighter and were seen – visually – from the ground and from the plane. Gun camera film was made of the UFOs though the images were too obscure to make any positive identification possible.

Radar contacts indicated that the objects were moving up to 4,000 miles per hour, considerably faster than aircraft of the day were capable of.

Even the **Condon Report** concluded, 'The apparently rational, intelligent behaviour of the UFO suggests a mechanical device of unknown origin.'

BERKNER, LLOYD V.
Lloyd V. Berkner is reported to have been a member of the **Majestic 12** panel formed to investigate UFOs in the 1940s.

Berkner was Executive Secretary of the Joint Research and Development Board, directed a study into weapons systems evaluation and was a member of the **Robertson Panel**.

BERMUDA TRIANGLE AND UFOs
The Bermuda Triangle is the name popularly given to an area of sea off the Florida coast where hundreds of ships and planes have mysteriously disappeared over the years. Although not related to UFO reports, perhaps the most famous case of such a disappearance is that of Flight 19, five planes and a rescue plane that all disappeared without trace – there are similarities to UFO-related plane disappearances such as over the **Bass Strait** in Australia. Those who study the Bermuda Triangle often propose the intervention of UFOs as an explanation for the disappearances.

Although UFO activity has been reported in that area – as it has been in every area of America – there are, in fact, no reliable reports of UFOs in the Bermuda Triangle exhibiting any characteristics not found in those reported in any other area. It would seem therefore that if the Bermuda Triangle is a phenomenon in its own right, then UFOs are not necessarily a major part of that phenomenon. Furthermore, there are no specific reports of UFOs from ships or planes subsequently lost; most of the disappearances talk of 'strange seas' and bizarre magnetic effects.

It appears that the Bermuda Triangle and UFOs are linked mainly because they are both extraordinary mysteries, and that in the public's mind mysteries have an affinity for each other.

BERNSTEIN, PROFESSOR JEREMY

Professor Jeremy Bernstein of the Stephens Institute of Technology entered the argument about extraterrestrial life (a side issue of the UFO phenomenon) by pointing out that, 'The more technological our own civilisation becomes, in many ways the worse it becomes . . . one could imagine terrible civilisations with a very high degree of technology.' The message for those who believe UFOs might be the visitation of aliens is clearly that they might not be the nice guys we would like to hope they are.

BESSOR, JOHN PHILIP

Imaginative answers to the UFO phenomenon have never been in short supply. Even in the first year of the modern UFO phenomenon, 1947, John Philip Bessor was suggesting to the United States Air Force that flying saucers were 'various species of . . . life forms or craft propelled by telekinetic energy. Possibly originating in the ionosphere they have been forced to migrate to denser atmospheres periodically because of solar or cosmic disturbances. They are capable of changing shape in flight and possess the intelligence of the octopus, porpoise or chimpanzee.'

BETHUNE, LIEUTENANT GRAHAM

In 1951 US Navy pilot Lieutenant Graham Bethune reported what appeared to be an attack by a UFO on his aircraft.

Bethune described the object as circular and glowing orange. He believed it was at least 300 feet wide and travelling in excess of 1,000 miles per hour. His interpretation of the direction changes and manoeuvres of the UFO was that it was to some degree engaging the aircraft as if in hostilities.

BETHURUM, TRUMAN

In 1954, the year following the publication of George **Adamski**'s claims of meetings with extraterrestrials, Truman Bethurum published his own story of a similar meeting in the book *Aboard a*

Flying Saucer (see References and Background Material).

Bethurum had been laying asphalt in the California desert when, it was claimed, he was awakened by a number of aliens around five feet tall, olive-skinned and dressed in uniform. Unlike Adamski's aliens, Bethurum's spoke perfect English. The aliens arrived in a flying saucer approximately 300 feet wide and 18 feet high which was captained by a female, **Aura Rhanes**, described by Bethurum as 'tops in shapeliness and beauty'.

Bethurum's aliens came from the planet **Clarion** which is apparently hidden beyond the dark side of our moon. At the time of the claims no one on Earth had seen behind the moon but subsequent space shots have never located Clarion! The aliens were apparently capable of passing themselves off as human beings; Truman met Aura Rhanes at a later time in a restaurant sipping orange juice, but she ignored him.

BIOT, DR MAURICE
Dr Maurice A. Biot was one of the world's leading aerodynamicists and mathematical physicists. In April 1952 he joined many leading scientists in confirming his belief in UFOs. He stated, 'The least improbable explanation is that these things are artificial and controlled . . . my opinion for some time has been that they have an extraterrestrial origin.'

BIRCH, ALEX
One of the earliest, successful, self-confessed UFO hoaxers was Alex Birch who claimed to have photographed five UFOs over Sheffield in 1962. His photograph, actually images painted on to glass, was accepted as genuine for ten years. He even appeared at the inaugural meeting of **BUFORA**.

In defence of those who were fooled by the photographs, the analysis techniques available then were rudimentary; such photographs would be unlikely to be so easily accepted in the present time, where enhancement techniques often detect fakes.

BIRTH TRAUMA HYPOTHESIS
First suggested as a working, testable hypothesis by Professor Alvin Lawson of California, the birth trauma hypothesis seeks to explain why different people share an apparently common abduction experience, if that experience is not objectively real. The suggestion was that since we all share birth as a common experience then there might be parallels surfacing in abduction

claims. In particular, points were made regarding the foetus-like shape of the alien entities, the comparison between the birth canal and the corridors of UFOs, and other elements of the claims.

The work arose from Lawson's 'imaginary abductee' experiments where he showed that the claims of people deliberately prefabricating UFO abduction experiences (under his instruction, as part of the test) were not greatly different from those claiming the 'genuine article'. A 'common' experience shared by all was thought to be the source of this imagery and Lawson suggested birth as the one experience we all share.

The birth trauma hypothesis has not been widely accepted, and has been the subject of much criticism.

BISHOP, DENISE

In September 1981 Denise Bishop, twenty-three years old, sighted a large UFO hovering over her house. She described the object as dark grey with several beams of light emanating from beneath. The sighting apparently scared her and she hurried to get inside her house but was prevented from doing so by a green beam of light which appears to have paralysed her when it hit her hand. Later examination of her hand revealed that she had been burned, and it took some days for this to heal.

There have been many cases of UFOs using paralysing beams of light including the famous 'blue beam' in the **Gulf Breeze** case.

Denise Bishop described the UFO as huge although UFO investigators in the area were unable to find other witnesses to the sighting. However, researchers interviewing Denise believed her to be sensible and sincere and describing an event which she perceived as genuinely happening. Although reported to the RAF and the Ministry of Defence, neither body appears to have undertaken an official investigation into the case.

BITTENCOURT, JOSÉ VENANCIO
(See **Niteroi, Rio de Janeiro**.)

BLACKOUTS (ELECTRICITY GRID FAILURES)

It has been suggested that there is evidence that UFOs can cause power failures in the national electricity grid systems though it is fair to point out that this may only be a side effect rather than the UFOs' purpose.

Such events include one day in November 1965 when parts

of Minnesota lost electric power after residents had reported UFOs. The power company had no explanation for the blackout. December 1965 saw the failure of the grid system in the New Mexico and Texas areas following UFO sightings.

November 1965 was the date of the **Great North-East Blackout** in the United States when parts of eight states lost power: Connecticut, Massachusetts, Maine, New Hampshire, New Jersey, New York, Pennsylvania and Vermont.

Despite some twenty-five or more years to correlate these events, no specific evidence has been found to connect sighted UFOs to the blackout events.

BLAKE, JAMES
James Blake was the principal witness at the **Aviano** sighting.

BLAKESLEE, WING COMMANDER D. J.
Second World War fighter ace Wing Commander D. J. Blakeslee encountered a UFO over Japan. Guided by ground radar, following reports from other Air Force pilots, he sighted the object which he described as a machine with red, green and white lights. The UFO apparently manoeuvred rapidly to escape his attention. In debriefing, Blakeslee stated that the object was definitely an unidentified flying object. A lieutenant-colonel of intelligence commented on Blakeslee that he was stable and thoroughly reliable and had held responsible command assignments.

The Air Force explained the event as a sighting of the planet Jupiter. As Major Donald E. **Keyhoe** points out, the Air Force radar which tracked the UFO had a range of a few hundred miles – on the night in question Jupiter was 366 million miles away!

BLANCHARD, ROY
On 16 July 1963 farmer Roy Blanchard discovered a massive crater in one of his fields at Manor Farm, Charlton. This event, which attracted considerable media attention, became known as the Charlton Crater.

According to the description given, the ground appeared to have been scooped out as if by an enormous spoon. Mr Blanchard was in no doubt that the depression was formed by the landing of a spaceship. As he stated: 'I didn't actually see it but what else could it have been? Obviously some craft from outer space since it sucked out my barley and potatoes when it took off.'

The bomb disposal squad arrived on the scene and undertook some investigation which turned up what appeared to be an iron meteorite which may well have been the cause of the crater.

However, the investigation was somewhat diverted by the comments of an Australian 'expert'. He believed that on the basis of this damage to a potato and barley field, which had not been witnessed by anybody, he was able to conclude that it had been caused by a flying saucer 500 feet wide, weighing 600 tons and holding a fifty-man crew originating from somewhere around Uranus. He went on to add: 'We think their mission is peaceful and exploratory. They may well be worried or curious about our atomic explosions, for their stability may depend on ours. They are not more than 100 years ahead of us scientifically. The type of spacecraft to which we have evidence is a kind which we can comprehend and will quite likely be making ourselves inside a century.'

An impressive analysis for one hole in the ground!

BLANCHARD, COLONEL WILLIAM H.
Colonel William H. Blanchard was the Base Commander of **Roswell** Army Air Base in 1947.

During the now famous crash retrievals at Roswell in 1947 there was an apparently official press statement released by the Roswell Air Base, confirming that the United States Air Force had recovered the wreckage of a flying disc.

It was later stated that the release had not been authorised by Blanchard (though there is some debate about that), and a further statement to the press claimed that the wreckage recovered was that of a weather balloon.

It was Colonel Blanchard who ordered the removal of the wreckage to 'higher authority', **Wright Patterson Air Force Base**.

BLUE BOOK, PROJECT
The United States Air Force's official investigation of UFOs had many names, including Project **Twinkle** and the revealing name Project **Grudge** but it culminated in the most famous of all, Project Blue Book. This commenced in 1952 and was closed down in 1969.

The original head of the project was Captain Edward **Ruppelt**, an intelligence officer at **Wright Patterson Air Force Base** in **Dayton, Ohio**, where the operation was based.

One of the world's foremost Ufologists, Dr J. Allen **Hynek**, was scientific adviser to Project Blue Book for many years. Public dissatisfaction with the progress of official investigations – mainly Blue Book – led to the commencement of innumerable private UFO research groups, many of which exist in some mutated form to the present day. If the Air Force had hoped that a professional such as Hynek was going to assist them in 'wishing away' the UFO phenomenon, they were to be sadly disappointed; he concluded that there was a mystery which required proper investigation and eventually set up one of the world's most prestigious private UFO research groups, the **Center for UFO Studies (CUFOS)**, now, following his death, named the J. Allen Hynek Center for UFO Studies.

Scientists such as Dr James E. **McDonald**, a professor of meteorology at the University of Arizona, who have reviewed the work of Project Blue Book, have described its investigations as 'completely superficial' and carried out with 'a very low level of scientific competence'. McDonald also went on to add that he thought the work of independent organisations such as **NICAP** 'much more thorough'.

BLUE PAPER, PROJECT
According to Lieutenant-Colonel Lou **Corbin**, following the closure of Project **Blue Book** the Air Force continued to investigate UFO events under two project headings, one of which was Blue Paper. If so, it was much more clandestine than its predecessor.

BLUE ROOM
The Blue Room is supposed to be an area of **Wright Patterson Air Force Base** where UFO artefacts, photographs and exhibits are kept for exhibition to high-ranking visitors. Just how high the rank needs to be is suggested by the experience of Senator Barry **Goldwater**. It is reported that he once requested access to the Blue Room but was denied permission by General Curtis LeMay.

There have been rumours that people have accidentally seen inside the Blue Room and then reported what they have seen to UFO researchers. However, it is obvious that no one has yet managed to steal any unambiguous artefacts from the Blue Room as that would have ended forty years of debate and, incidentally, put the procurer of the artefact on the gravy train for life – a temptation to which it is remarkable no one has yet succumbed.

The Blue Room is held to have been the inspiration for the film *Hangar 18*, about the retrieval of a crashed flying saucer and its dead occupants.

BOAC FLIGHT 703/027

On 1 October 1973, BOAC flight 703/027 from Bangkok to Teheran, flying at a height of 45,000 feet, observed an object brightly lit and moving at irregular speed. There was a report from the crew that the object had a long line of portholes and was enveloped in a thin cloud. The observation lasted for approximately one minute before the object disappeared to stern as the aircraft overtook it. Subsequent investigation indicates that it was almost certainly the re-entry of the launching rocket of the Soviet satellite *Molnya*.

BOAS, ANTONIO VILLAS

On 14 October 1957, twenty-three-year-old farmer Antonio Villas Boas had an extraordinary abduction encounter, recognised as one of the first such claims.

At approximately 10 p.m. Villas Boas was ploughing with a tractor when he saw a light hovering over the northern side of his field. As Villas Boas approached the light it moved at high speed and he chased it. Despite several attempts to catch up with it, it evaded him.

On the following night the same event occurred but on this occasion the object landed in front of Villas Boas. It stood on metallic legs and was described as having a rotating dome on top and changing colour from red to green.

Villas Boas leapt from his tractor and tried to run away but was held by three small entities who dragged him into the machine. The abductors wore tight-fitting grey suits and helmets concealing all except their small eyes; they were humanoid in appearance.

Villas Boas was forcibly undressed and covered in a clear thick liquid, then taken into a second room aboard the UFO where he underwent a medical examination.

Shortly after this, Villas Boas underwent a reasonably unique aspect of UFO abductions when he was confronted by a naked woman of virtually human appearance. She was broad hipped, well proportioned, with slanted eyes.

The woman caressed Villas Boas and he responded with enthusiasm, engaging in sexual intercourse only slightly spoiled by her habit of growling like a dog.

Villas Boas was given his clothes back and shown around the craft during which time he attempted to steal one of its instruments but was prevented from doing so.

During the following weeks he noticed strange wounds on his hands, forearms and legs.

In 1980 Villas Boas made his first public comments on his experience after a twenty-one year gap and confirmed all of the detail in the account, adding only that the woman had also preserved a sperm sample in a container after their second act of intercourse.

Villas Boas died recently, never withdrawing his claims.

BOEDEC, JEAN-FRANÇOIS

French researcher Jean-François Boedec studied UFO cases in Brittany and introduced the concept of a 'build-up phase' to UFO abductions beginning long before the UFO event occurs. Boedec speculates that for a period of up to weeks before the abduction the witness is already beginning to break usual patterns of behaviour and have strange events happen to him. Part of Boedec's suggestion is that at the time of the event the witness is driven to isolate himself, making the abduction more easy for the abductors.

It is difficult to say whether or not this suggestion, if accurate, means that the witness is being affected by an alien force for a matter of weeks or whether the abduction is the culmination of **altered states of consciousness** in the witness.

BOGGS, MAJOR JEREMIAH

After the fatal plane crash in 1949 which took the life of Captain Thomas **Mantell** it was Major Jeremiah Boggs who issued the Air Force statement that it was believed Mantell had died while chasing the planet Venus. Major Boggs was a project intelligence officer serving as liaison between the Pentagon and Wright Field (now **Wright Patterson Air Force Base**).

As Major Donald E. **Keyhoe** points out, in contrast with his later denials Boggs admitted to him (Keyhoe) that 'the Air Force had put out a secret order for its pilots to capture UFOs'. Boggs is held to have stated, 'We were naturally anxious to get hold of one of the things. We told pilots to do practically anything in reason, even if they had to grab one by the tail.' Mantell could have been one of the pilots who tried, and died.

BOIANAI MISSION, PAPUA
(See **Gill, Reverend William**.)

BOLENDER, BRIGADIER GENERAL
It is generally held that the United States government's UFO investigations were conducted by Project **Blue Book** (the final of several project names for this work) and that since its closure in 1969 there has been no reason for the Air Force to continue investigating UFOs. An Air Force memo from Brigadier General Bolender indicates that this may well not be the case. It states: 'Reports of unidentified flying objects which could affect the national security are made in accordance with **JANAP 146** or Air Force Manual 55–11 and are not part of the Blue Book system.'

Few people seriously accept that the Air Force stopped investigating when it shut down Blue Book.

BONILLA, JOSÉ A.Y.
One of the earliest UFO sightings, and reportedly the first photographed, was by astronomer José A.Y. Bonilla of the Zacatecas observatory in Mexico. The sighting took place at 8 a.m. on 12 August 1883.

The sighting consisted of a series of flights of what looked like discs and ovoids crossing the sun. Several hundred such sightings were made and there were subsequent sightings the following day.

Although there has been much speculation about what Bonilla actually saw, including a flock of migrating geese, its unknown nature makes this report one of the birth places of the UFO phenomenon.

BOOTH, LARRY
The extraordinary abductee claims of Charles Hickson and Calvin Parker (see **Pascagoula, Mississippi**) appear to have been corroborated in part by Larry Booth who ran a service station nearby. From his home he saw an object in the air drifting slowly at around 30–40 miles per hour. The object had lights all around it and appeared to be spinning. Booth claimed the object was so close that had it been a helicopter 'it would have jarred everybody in the neighbourhood'. However, the object apparently made no sound at all.

Booth stated he was not scared by the sighting until he read about the abduction of Hickson and Parker the next morning, when he then connected his sighting with their experience.

BOREWA, ANNIE LAURIE
(See **Gill, Reverend William**.)

BORSKY, VALENTIN
Valentin Borsky was the forest ranger for the district of **Lake Onega** in the USSR where there was the alleged crash retrieval of an alien flying saucer.

BOTUCATU, BRAZIL
(see **da Silva, Joáo Valerio**.)

BOUAHMAMA
A French legionnaire at the Algerian camp of Bouahmama in March 1958 reported a midnight sighting of a UFO, an enormous object of some 1,000 feet in diameter landing only 150 feet from him. It appeared to land on a beam of emerald light which the witness described as beautiful and relaxing. No specific details of any abduction, contactee or other events are described by the witness but the event, in particular the emerald light, appears to have triggered an almost religious revelation in him; he regarded the presence of the object as inducing a remarkably peaceful state.

BOUGAINVILLE REEF
In May 1965 Captain John Barker was flying from Brisbane to New Guinea; he reported a UFO pacing his aircraft for some ten to fifteen minutes which was also witnessed by other members of the crew. The sighting took place off the Queensland coast at Bougainville Reef and Barker reported to ground control that he was photographing a UFO.

On returning to Australia, Captain Barker was flown directly to the federal capital at Canberra where both the film and the flight recorder of his aircraft were confiscated.

The official clampdown on this story appears to have been very thorough and makes it very difficult to verify the incident although it is believed that Captain Barker made an official report including the phrase 'it was under intelligent control and it was certainly no known aircraft'.

BOWERS, H. L.
H. L. Bowers is held to be the author of a **CIA** memorandum of 1949 which concludes that UFO investigation is important even if there is only a remote possibility that they may be interplanetary.

The CIA denied any involvement in UFO research, but according to American researchers that claim was untrue. Under the **Freedom of Information Act** they requested CIA documents, after a struggle were offered 400 pages, and eventually received 40,000 pages!

BOWLES, JOYCE

In November 1976 Joyce Bowles claimed to have seen a landed UFO and occupant near Winchester. It was held that she received telephone calls from someone in the government making threats to keep her quiet about her sighting. Mrs Bowles apparently replied to the threats, witnessed by UFO investigator Frank Wood, 'This is a free country and I shall talk to whom I please.'

This incident seems to have some echoes of the 1950s **Men in Black** stories from America though in fact, in this case, no government suppression ever materialised.

BOYD, COMMANDER

An extraordinary **FBI** memorandum of 1952, which refers to a briefing by Air Intelligence Officer Commander Boyd, is held to include the following statements, apparently made by Boyd: 'The objects sighted may possibly be from another planet . . . at the present time there is nothing to substantiate this . . . but the possibility is not being overlooked.' 'Intense research is being carried out by Air Intelligence.' 'The Air Force is attempting in each instance to send up jet interceptor planes.'

BOYD, LEE

Lee Boyd was co-pilot with Captain James **Howard** during the Goose Bay, Labrador, encounter of 1954.

BPVTS

There are few UFO research groups known in the Soviet Union. In 1978 one such group was set up by Vladimir **Azhazha**, the Deputy Director of the Underwater Research Section of the USSR Academy of Science.

BPVTS stands for *Blizhniy Poisk Vnezemnykh Tsivilizatsy S Pomoshch'yu Sredstva Radioelektronika*, which means the 'Search for Extraterrestrial Civilisations in the Neighbourhood of Earth by Means of Radio Electronics'. As such, it therefore seems to have been devised as a specific form of research organisation, rather than the general type more prevalent in the West.

There were several prominent members of this group including a cosmonaut. One of the members conceded that the problem of UFO sightings could include the possibility of communication with extraterrestrial civilisation.

BRACE, LEE FORE

An early report on UFOs comes from the Persian Gulf in May 1880 by Lee Fore Brace on board the British India Company's steamship *Patna*.

Towards midnight Brace saw two enormous luminous wheels, one on each side of the ship, the spokes of which were touching the vessel. The spinning wheels made a swishing noise and were some 500–600 yards in diameter.

The objects were apparently also seen by the commander of the ship, Captain Avern, and the third officer, Manning. The sighting took place over a twenty-minute period.

BRADLEY, V. L.

One of the committee members of Project **Second Storey**, Flight Lieutenant V. L. Bradley was also a member of the Defence Research Board.

BRAZEL, WILLIAM

William 'Mac' Brazel was the manager of the ranch on which the famous **Roswell** UFO crash occurred.

Brazel heard an explosion, which he thought might have been lightning from a storm, and connected this with debris he found the next day. It has been speculated that the saucer was damaged by being struck by lightning, exploded, and crashed.

Having located the debris Brazel reported it to Sheriff George **Wilcox** at the Chaves County Sheriff's Office who in turn contacted Roswell Army Air Base.

Brazel was held, apparently on grounds of national security, for several days while the debris was recovered and he was encouraged not to talk about the incident as a matter of patriotic duty.

BREEN, JOHN

October 1974 saw a rash of UFO reports by pilots in the area around Gander, Canada.

Canadian Armed Forces pilot John Breen reported such an encounter on a flight to Gander from Deer Lake. The object was a triangular green shape which pulsated regularly. Although not tracked on radar the object appeared to be reflected from water below, giving evidence that it was to some degree material in nature.

BREGUET, LOUIS
This French manufacturer and designer of aircraft joined the UFO controversy with the statement: 'The discs use a means of propulsion different from ours. There is no other possible explanation. Flying saucers come from another world.'

BRICKNER, SERGEANT STEPHEN J.
One of the most extraordinary groups of UFOs ever sighted was in August 1942 by Sergeant Stephen J. Brickner of the US Marine Corps. The sighting took place in the Solomon Islands and consisted of some 150 UFOs laid out in virtually an enormous square some fifteen objects long and ten objects deep. Although formations of UFOs have been seen many times, such a pattern is unique.

BRIGGS, FREDERICK
Frederick Briggs was the witness to the reported UFO landing and entity sighting which took place in February 1955 on Lord Mountbatten's estate at **Broadlands** in Hampshire.

BRIGHAM, LIEUTENANT DAVID C.
In March 1952 Lieutenant David C. Brigham was flying a T-6 in flight with two F-84s. Brigham noticed that a disc-shaped object was making a close pass to one of the F-84s and manoeuvring with extraordinary capabilities as it did so. What was particularly noteworthy about the sighting is that the disc was reported to be only eight inches in diameter.

BRITISH FLYING SAUCER BUREAU
In the early 1950s many private UFO study groups began, due mainly to dissatisfaction with the official investigations. In Britain the first of these began in Bristol, The British Flying Saucer Bureau, which was an off-shoot of an American group.

The British Flying Saucer Bureau is still in existence and is a member society and associate group of **BUFORA**.

BRITISH UFO RESEARCH ASSOCIATION (BUFORA)
(See **BUFORA**.)

BROADLANDS

In February 1955 bricklayer Frederick **Briggs** reported seeing a stationary UFO and attendant entity on the Broadlands estate owned by Lord Louis **Mountbatten** of Burma.

The object was described as being approximately 25 feet in diameter, dull silver and with portholes around its circumference. While the witness observed the saucer, what appears to have been some form of platform lift descended with a man standing on it dressed in dark close-fitting overalls.

The witness appears to have been struck by a bluish light emanating from the object which either paralysed him or at least held him motionless for a time. The blue light is a common feature of UFO reports and very frequently associated with paralysing effects on the witness.

Towards the end of the sighting the platform lift was retracted into the saucer, which then left rapidly. Although shaken by the incident Frederick Briggs appears not to have suffered from his encounter.

A subsequent statement by Lord Mountbatten of Burma appears to support the honesty and sincerity of Mr Briggs together with corroborating certain aspects of the sighting such as the tyre tracks of Mr Briggs' bicycle in the snow which Lord Mountbatten took the trouble to investigate personally.

BRONK, DETLEV W.

Detlev W. Bronk is reported to have been a member of the **Majestic 12** panel formed to investigate UFOs in the 1940s.

Bronk was Chairman of the National Research Council and an advisory member of the Atomic Energy Commission. He was also a member of the Scientific Advisory Committee of the Brook Haven National Laboratory.

BROOKE, ANGELA

In October 1977 Angela Brooke returned to her cottage in Keighley, West Yorkshire, in the early evening. She, together with her husband, reported that a bright white light had appeared to be following them home and that it remained above their cottage throughout the night. It has been suggested that the object may have been astronomical in origin, i.e. a planet.

Approximately one week later Angela was found by her husband staring at the sky late at night 'as if in a trance'. She has no clear recollection of the events of that night but believes that something happened during that time. There was no investigation which indicated an abduction but several abduction cases have started in this manner such as Shane **Kurz**'s in America.

BROOKS, J. B. W.
Known as Angus Brooks, this administration officer for British Airways and a former RAF intelligence officer was the witness to the famous **Moigne Downs** sighting of 1967.

BROWN, LIEUTENANT FRANK M.
Lieutenant Frank M. Brown was apparently a representative of military intelligence who interviewed Kenneth **Arnold** following what is known as the **Maury Island** mystery.

BROWN, DR HAROLD, SECRETARY OF THE AIR FORCE
In the 1960s congressional pressure forced the House Armed Services Committee to conduct an open hearing into the subject of UFOs. This is generally regarded as a farcical hearing as only three Air Force representatives were invited to testify, only one of whom had practical involvement with UFOs. One of the three was secretary of the Air Force, Dr Harold Brown.

Not surprisingly, no significant landmarks arose from this hearing.

(The two other representatives were Major Hector **Quintanilla** and Dr J. Allen **Hynek**.)

BROWN, THOMAS TOWNSEND
One of the most important early American UFO research groups was the National Investigations Committee on Aerial Phenomena known by its initials as **NICAP**.

The organisation was founded by Navy physicist Thomas Townsend Brown in 1956 although it is most famous for its years under the control of Major Donald E. **Keyhoe**.

BRUEN, CAPTAIN WILLIAM
Captain William Bruen may have discovered at least one appropriate reaction to close encounters by UFOs when piloting aircraft. When a UFO approached his plane as he was flying towards Washington he turned off all the lights in order to observe the object more clearly. On impulse he then switched all the lights on again, including the very powerful landing lights. The UFO pulled up and streaked away, not to be seen again.

BRUTON, DEMPSEY

In January 1965 it was reported that a huge disc flew over the NASA station at Wallops Island, Virginia. Dempsey Bruton, satellite tracking chief, calculated its speed at over 100 miles a minute. There were other reports of UFOs by the Navy on the same day.

The Air Force, apparently reacting to a deluge of inquiries, labelled Dempsey Bruton and his other space administration observers as incompetent, apparently without the slightest investigation.

The backlash of this event did much to discredit the Air Force's approach to the subject; they had issued their statement prematurely and without substance.

BRYAN, COLONEL JOSEPH J. III

Joseph J. Bryan III was the founder of the **CIA**'s psychological warfare staff. He was a special assistant to the Secretary of the Air Force and an adviser to NATO. Bryan became a member of the board of **NICAP**, the National Investigations Committee on Aerial Phenomena.

Bryan made the following extraordinary statements on the UFO phenomenon: 'These UFOs are interplanetary devices systematically observing the Earth, either manned or under remote control, or both.' 'Information on UFOs, including sighting reports, has been and is still being officially withheld.'

Since Bryan did not make clear his CIA connections until much later there has been some speculation that the statements he made were a form of government disinformation designed to lead UFO investigators into embarrassing claims which would make them appear foolish.

BUFORA (THE BRITISH UFO RESEARCH ASSOCIATION)

BUFORA is the British UFO Research Association, a company limited by guarantee and the only national coordinating network for UFO research in the United Kingdom, which is linked up through the International Committee for UFO Research to researchers across the world. The UK currently 'hosts' the administration of the International Committee (ICUR).

The association was founded in 1964 from the merger of the London UFO Research Association, which had been founded in 1959, and the British UFO Association, founded in 1962. Its aims are as follows:

1. To encourage, promote and conduct unbiased scientific research of unidentified flying object (UFO) phenomena throughout the United Kingdom.
2. To collect and disseminate evidence and data relating to unidentified flying objects (UFOs).
3. To coordinate UFO research throughout the United Kingdom and to cooperate with others engaged in such research throughout the world.

It is an article of faith for BUFORA that it does not hold corporate views in respect of any particular aspect of the UFO phenomenon which lets it work with researchers of all persuasions, and allows for an easier exchange of dialogue with all groups.

BULLARD, DR THOMAS 'EDDIE'
Dr Thomas Bullard holds a doctorate in folklore from Indiana University and has done some most detailed and important research into UFO abductions. His work with over 200 events analyses abductions on a global basis, studies the components and order of components of abduction events (i.e. capture, medical examination, discussions with aliens, etc.) and compares abductions to folklore stories around the world such as *Cinderella*.

His conclusions appear to indicate that while the UFO abduction phenomenon has many parallels to folklore stories there are sufficient differences to indicate that the phenomenon cannot be only the product of folklore.

BURGESS, JOHN
In May 1965 John Burgess, a World War II veteran, together with two other witnesses, was in an isolated hotel at Mackay in Australia. They reported an approaching UFO, solid and metallic-looking and at least thirty feet wide displaying a circular pattern of spotlights from below. Burgess attempted to shoot at the object but the witnesses kept their distance when it landed and the glowing lights dimmed. They observed the UFO on the ground for about thirty minutes and noticed tripod landing gear when it finally took off, moving rapidly. The landing site displayed a charred ring and damaged tree tops.

Top Australian researcher Paul Norman verified the case and the evidence.

BURNETT, COLONEL JOHN
Colonel John Burnett was Air Attaché in New Zealand in the 1960s during the time of the famous Bruce **Cathie** theories. Burnett appears to have been impressed by Cathie's beliefs and it is held to be Colonel Burnett who revealed UFO research being carried out at the **Wright Patterson Air Force Base** in America. UFO investigators have found little documentary evidence to support this last claim, though they point out that it is of a nature where documentary evidence will be unlikely to exist.

BURNS, HAYDON
Haydon Burns was Governor of Florida and in April 1966 he and a group of newsmen aboard his campaign aircraft were buzzed by a UFO. Burns instructed the pilot to close in but the UFO climbed away immediately.

Burns therefore became one of a number of prominent American politicians reporting UFO encounters.

BURNS, HORACE
In December 1964 an alarming **vehicle interference** case was reported by witness Horace Burns. He was driving near Staunton, Virginia, when a UFO approximately 125 feet in diameter closed in on his car, causing the engine to cut out. Engineers recorded a high incidence of radiation from their readings.

BURROUGHS, JOHN
During the **Rendlesham Forest** encounter an airman at the **Woodbridge** airbase in Suffolk, John Burroughs, was apparently one of the witnesses who saw the landed UFO in the forest. He was with another security officer, given the pseudonym James **Archer**, who made a report describing the object.

BURSON, HOLM
During the famous **Socorro** encounter of 1964 Holm Burson was the mayor of the locality. There has been the suggestion that since the event took place on his land, he faked it in order to drum up tourist activity in the area. Burson has dismissed this suggestion, stating that he did not plan it. Burson also supports the principal witness, Sergeant Lonnie **Zamora**, stating that he believes he is 'a very serious person and always has been'.

BURTOO, ALFRED

In August 1983 Alfred Burtoo, then in his late seventies, was fishing in the Basingstoke Canal in Aldershot.

During the small hours of the morning Burtoo saw a light approaching him to within a close distance. Shortly after that Burtoo saw two entities approaching him who indicated they wanted him to follow them, which he did, across the towpath to the canal and up to a landed object standing on the towpath. It was approximately 45 feet wide and resting on runners.

On board the object, Burtoo was subjected to some form of examination but rejected for whatever purpose he was being examined on account of his age. The aliens told him, 'You are too old and infirm for our purpose.'

Burtoo was allowed to leave the object; he returned to his fishing spot and his dog which he had left there. He witnessed the object take off at high speed, becoming a small light then disappearing out of sight.

The entities apparently wore one-piece suits in green, covering even their hands and feet, and their faces were masked by visors. Despite appearances, Burtoo was convinced that they originated from Earth.

What is perhaps particularly unusual about Burtoo's encounter is that he appeared to have suffered little physiological consequences from it. In fact, his predominant emotion was of irritation at being rejected by the entities. It appears that he took the view that at his age there was nothing to fear, although he also stated: 'It was the greatest experience of my life.'

Some three years later Burtoo died and researcher Timothy Good sensibly followed up the story by asking whether he had ever confessed that it was a hoax. His wife confirmed that he had not and supported his claims.

BUSH, DR VANNEVAR

Dr Vannevar Bush was apparently the head of a group of government-sponsored investigators responsible for the investigation of UFOs and allegedly the examination of crashed saucers and alien bodies. This group has been codenamed **Majestic 12**.

Dr Bush was head of the Joint Research and Development Board after the Second World War. Prior to that he had leading posts in the National Defense Research Council and the Office of Scientific Research and Development. This last organisation was responsible for the development of the Manhattan Project, developing the atomic bomb at a location near to many alleged crash retrieval sites.

BUSHROE, DEPUTY SHERIFF B.
In March 1966 Deputy Sheriff B. Bushroe, along with his companion Deputy Sheriff J. Foster, reported several disc-shaped UFOs over Dexter, Michigan. There appears to have been corroborative radar tracking at Selfridge Air Force Base.

Deputy Bushroe reported that, 'These objects could move at fantastic speed, and make very sharp turns, dive and climb, and hover, with great manoeuvrability.'

BUSTINZA, ADRIAN
Another important witness to the **Rendlesham Forest** encounter was Sergeant Adrian Bustinza of RAF/USAF **Woodbridge**. He was then the Acting Commander of Security Police.

He reported seeing the object hovering and making slow movements. He described it as having a red light on top, several blue lights below and many other hues of light emanating from it. He also described it as being of enormous size and stated that he was surprised it would fit into the clearing where he was seeing it.

Bustinza also witnessed the departure of the object and described it as being 'gone in a flash'. He said that the event was 'a really scary feeling'. Bustinza also reports that photographs were taken by personnel from the base.

C

CABELL, MAJOR GENERAL C. P.
In October 1951 Major General C. P. Cabell was the director of
Air Force Intelligence and was responsible for the reactivation
of Project **Grudge**, the Air Force project to investigate UFOs
which had apparently been closed down at the end of 1949.
The reactivation arose from the discovery that a radar operator
had miscalculated the speed of a UFO on a radar return, stating
it to be much too high a velocity; presumably the Air Force
hoped that here was an opening for debunking UFOs.

Project Grudge eventually terminated in Project **Blue Book**.
Major Cabell was replaced at the end of 1951 by Major General
John S. **Samford**.

CALIFORNIA: 'HOME' OF THE CONTACTEES
It may be coincidence but the vast majority of **contactee** claims
have arisen from the state of California in the United States and
even some of the contactees or cult groups that have developed
elsewhere have migrated to that state over the years.

One school of thought for this fact is that the 'new age' wave
in California leads the population there to be more gullible in
respect of fraudulent claims, but the counter-argument to this is
that the 'new age' wave reflects a willingness to accept phenomena and aspects of our world which less open minds deliberately
close off from.

Certainly California can be regarded as the natural home of
the contactee claims, for whatever reason.

That said, some of the modern contactee claims have a more
probable basis in truth than the early claims, and are originating
world-wide, and frequently in Europe.

CALL, CAPTAIN WILLIAM
In 1954 Captain William Call, of Eastern Airlines, was circling
the airport at Hartford, Connecticut, when he saw a massive

flash which made him think of an atomic explosion.

There has been speculation that this was an attack of a UFO by Air Force jets scrambled to intercept the object. This idea is based on information relayed to Major Donald E. **Keyhoe** by a source in the Pentagon.

There has never been a confirmation of this attack, which would surely have been spectacular if it manifested as Captain Call suggested.

CAMP DRUM
In September 1952 several soldiers at Camp Drum in Canada witnessed a round, red UFO circling the camp. They several times heard a humming sound similar to that of a generator and witnessed the machine operating at low altitude and making swift, accelerating climbs.

CAMPBELL, ROBERT
When Texas newscaster Robert Campbell photographed an oval-shaped UFO in 1965 the photographs were examined by *The Christian Science Monitor* who commented, 'It makes the clearest case yet for a thorough look at the saucer mystery.'

CARLOCK, PROFESSOR HENRY
In 1957 Henry Carlock, using × 100 magnification telescope, witnessed a UFO over Jackson, Missouri. He described it as 'a manoeuvring device with three portholes'. What made the sighting of significance was that Professor Carlock was the head of the Physics Department at the University of Mississippi and an Air Force reserve colonel.

It is held that the **CIA** instructed a debunking explanation to be put out though there is no trace that it was ever published. It was generally accepted that Air Force officers should bow to CIA pressure not to release details of their sightings.

CAROLINE, HMS
In February 1893 HMS *Caroline* was cruising in the North China Sea when the officer of the watch reported to Captain J. N. Norcross an unusual light, 'Sometimes as a mass; and others, spread out in an irregular line, and, being globular in form they resembled Chinese lanterns festooned between the masts of a lofty vessel.'

On the following night the objects reappeared; they were a

reddish colour and emitting some smoke.

The UFO phenomenon has been with us for a long time!

CARPENTER, CAPTAIN PAUL L.
In July 1952 Captain Paul L. Carpenter was flying an American Airlines DC-6 near Denver. He received a warning by radio, from an aircraft ahead of him, that a formation of flying saucers had just raced past their plane. Carpenter turned down the cockpit lights to see ahead. He saw four lights moving at incredible speed but they were too far from him to make out detail. Carpenter estimated their speed at 3,000 miles per hour, far faster than the capabilities of planes of the day.

CARPENTER, SCOTT
There have been many reports of UFOs apparently sighted by astronauts and perhaps the most often repeated of these is that astronaut Scott Carpenter saw and photographed UFOs during his Mercury flight of May 1962.

Carpenter has apparently been questioned on this point at length and has made a quite clear and categorical statement denying these reports.

CARR, ROBERT SPENCER
Retired university professor Dr Robert Spencer Carr has reportedly stated to UFO researcher Leonard Stringfield that he has received evidence from several sources proving participation in the recovery of crashed UFOs and occupants in the late 1940s.

Following Carr's wishes, Leonard Stringfield has revealed very little detail of the people involved but was apparently impressed by the names given by Carr.

It is presumed that the recovery is that of the **Aztec** crash in New Mexico, or the **Roswell** crash nearby.

CARRASCO, MIGUEL
In January 1976 Miguel Carrasco was walking home late at night in the town of Bencazon in Spain. Above him, a UFO was seen hovering. When Carrasco attempted to run from the sighting two tall non-human entities appeared, firing a beam at him which temporarily paralysed and blinded him. A local doctor discovered a burn mark on the witness's cheek and he was taken to the local hospital in Seville for treatment. The doctors were unable to say what the marks were caused by.

CARRIZOZO AIRFIELD
Some corroboration of the **Roswell** crash retrieval may come from the fact that five witnesses at Carrizozo airfield, thirty-five miles from the crash retrieval site, all claimed to have seen a UFO on the same day moving at approximately 200–600 miles per hour in the general direction of the crash site. There were, of course, many sightings from the area around that time suggesting some physical object in motion.

CARSWELL AIR FORCE BASE
There have been several radar-visual reports of UFOs. One well-supported sighting took place in February 1954 at Carswell Air Force Base in Texas. The object was first detected on radar some ten miles from the base, and was shortly afterwards seen by the control tower personnel as it passed over the base. The object was silent and appears to have been somewhat aircraft-like in shape although no aircraft activity is thought to have been responsible. The witnesses are described as being completely reliable.

CARTER, PRESIDENT JIMMY
One of the most celebrated sightings, because of the identity of the witness, was the UFO reported by Jimmy Carter in 1969, some years before his ascendency to the presidency of the United States. Carter reported the object as being approximately the size of the moon, very bright and changing colours.

The sighting led Carter to claim that he would 'make every piece of information this country has about UFO sightings available to the public and the scientists' if he became president. He apparently tried to fulfil this pledge but found that the stubborn bureaucracy of the various government agencies can be obstructive even to a president. Whether Carter saw this pledge as a vote-catcher or not is speculation, but we should remember that many witnesses to UFOs have found their 'world-view' changed by even distant sightings.

CARTER, DR LAUNOR F.
On 3 February 1966 the United States Air Force Scientific Advisory Board **Ad Hoc Committee** met to review Project **Blue Book**. Dr Launor F. Carter was a member of the assembly.

CARVALHO, BERNARD J.
It is held that during the formative years of the National Investigations Committee for Aerial Phenomena (**NICAP**), the

organisation was infiltrated by many **CIA** agents. The Agency was apparently concerned at the close approach of civilian groups to matters that could involve United States **national security**.

One such person is believed to have been Bernard Carvalho who was at one time Chairman of NICAP's membership sub-committee.

CASCADE MOUNTAINS
(See **Arnold, Kenneth**.)

CASE, CAPTAIN RICHARD
In July 1952, during a wave of many sightings, Captain Richard Case was flying an American Airlines Convair near Indianapolis. He was one of several who sighted a UFO that had startled the citizens of Indianapolis by making a low pass above the city. He commented that it seemed to be a controlled craft moving at some 1,000 miles per hour and he witnessed it dropping from approximately 15,000 to 5,000 feet before heading in over the city.

CASH, BETTY
One of the most unfortunate UFO encounters is that of Betty Cash and co-witnesses Vickie and Colby Landrum. The event took place on 29 December 1980 near **Huffman** in Texas.

At approximately nine in the evening the witnesses in their vehicle encountered a diamond-shaped object at treetop height, hovering in front of them. The object was bright and making a considerable noise. Flames were shooting from it and its proximity to the car made the vehicle so hot that Betty was unable to touch the door safely.

They and other independent witnesses also reported a considerable number of Chinook helicopters apparently escorting the object.

It is clearly apparent from what followed that the witnesses were subjected to intense radiation. Betty suffered pains in her head and neck, her eyes swelled and she suffered nausea, sickness and diarrhoea. She lost patches of hair and developed breast cancer leading to a mastectomy. Vickie Landrum also suffered hair loss and swelling in the eyes and Colby Landrum appeared to have burn marks on his face and also suffered difficulties with his eyes.

There appear to be some grounds to the rumours that the

object was of military origin and may have been an unshielded nuclear reactor, perhaps following an accident of some sort. Suggestions that the object was a recovered alien craft being moved by the government have no apparent foundation, though cannot be disregarded entirely as when two of the witnesses sued the United States government on the grounds that the craft was some form of American device, the case was dismissed on the basis that the American military and civilian agencies did not own or operate any such object.

The implication of this, if true, is important. There appears to have been no official investigation, and yet if the American government denies that the object belonged to them they should surely be concerned that somebody, terrestrial or extraterrestrial, is toting unshielded nuclear reactors around in their airspace.

To date, Betty and her companions have suffered great financial loss due to medical bills and are appealing for help while their case is being re-presented.

CASSELS, MR
Ministry of Defence involvement in UFO investigation was, in the 1960s, the province of the department **S4 (Air)**.

Mr Cassels was an official of this department and stated that the Ministry did not make field investigations on UFO reports due to lack of resources. He stated that UFO reports were regarded as serious but were only of interest to the Ministry where there appeared to be a defence aspect.

CASSIE, ALEC
Alec Cassie was a Ministry of Defence official who investigated the **Moigne Downs** sighting of 1967. The Ministry undertook a serious investigation of the case (more so than their efforts since, it would seem), though they concluded the UFO was a 'floater' in the witness's eyeball.

CATALINA ISLAND
In April 1966 professional cameraman Lee Hansen filmed a UFO over Catalina Island, California. The film clearly showed a silver disc-shaped object manoeuvring about the mountains. For twenty years the film had remained unchallenged but recent **computer enhancement** techniques showed that in fact the UFO was a small light aircraft filmed out of focus and seen from the same level as the photographer, which produced the apparent absence of wings.

After enhancement the cockpit and even the pilot could be clearly seen.

CATHIE, BRUCE

In the early 1970s New Zealand pilot Captain Bruce Cathie produced a remarkable theory to suggest that there was a global grid being used by UFOs in their surveillances. His theory contends that there is a long-term plan for the Earth being executed by the UFOs.

His theories are known to have been considered by the American Defense Intelligence Agency; the Air Attaché to the Foreign Technology Division (at **Wright Patterson Air Force Base**) – Colonel John **Burnett** – stated in a memo that he believed Cathie to be 'not only rational but intelligent and convinced that certain UFOs he and others have seen are from outer space'.

Cathie alleged that it was Colonel Burnett who told him that Wright Patterson was undertaking UFO research.

Eventually the officials seem to have lost interest in Cathie's ideas, which have not been pursued in recent years.

CATTLE MUTILATION

There have been many reports linking so-called cattle mutilation with UFO encounters. It has been held that the bodies of cattle have been found minus surgically removed eyes, ears, tongues, genitals and internal body organs, and it is believed that this forms part of a general programme of genetic and biological study of the Earth by visiting entities.

Like most facets of the UFO phenomenon the vast majority of the claims made in this regard are either unsupported or in any case unconnected to UFO sightings and therefore not even subject to correlation let alone cause and effect.

However, some very good analysis has been done by some researchers, such as Linda M. Howe, showing a connection in some cases. **MUFON** States Section Director Bob Oechsler has demonstrated a likely connection between cattle mutilation and the wave of sightings and events at Chesapeake Bay, USA, known collectively as the Chesapeake Wave. His very thorough analysis, published privately as *The Chesapeake Connection*, shows the mutilations may be linked to a long-term study being conducted since the **Roswell** crash retrieval, with animal tissue being used as nutrition for the aliens.

There are mutilation stories from other sources which refer to mutilation of Dartmoor ponies, wild cats and other animal life.

CAUS
(See **Citizens Against UFO Secrecy**.)

CAVE PAINTINGS
Many researchers have speculated that prehistoric cave paintings depict UFO encounters. One of the most dramatic such
collections is at **Altamira** in the Santander province of Spain.
There are many disc-like symbols to be seen there.

Other locations include the caves at La Pasiega, at Les Trois
Frères in the Pyrenees in France and the Tassili plateau in the
Sahara.

At **Niaux** there are what appear to be depictions of UFOs
in flight and of a landed craft on legs complete with
antennae. Though these paintings give food for thought about
a possible extraterrestrial visitation, they are clearly open to
interpretation. However, whatever it was that fascinated prehistoric man, something similar still continues to fascinate
modern man. As has been pointed out, if we faithfully trust
prehistoric man's ability to transmit pictures of mammoths,
etc., then we should trust the other pictures he has given us
alongside them.

CAVITT (CIC AGENT)
The recovery of debris from the **Roswell** crash site was carried
out primarily by Major Jesse A. **Marcel**. One of the task force
he took with him was a counter-intelligence corps agent from
West Texas whose name was only given as Cavitt. Cavitt
assisted in the collection and retrieval of the debris.

CELTIC LEGENDS
There are many thought-provoking stories in the fairy-faiths of
Europe and particularly the Celtic countries of Scotland, Ireland, Wales, parts of England, and Brittany in northern France.
In particular there are remarkable abduction stories which
parallel UFO abductions to a great degree. Many of these
stories tell of victims of fairy abductions suffering considerable
time lapses, of being abducted into fairy circles where they
undergo strange reality distortion, and include such aspects as
'changelings' where non-human entities substitute their child
for the child of a human, a facet beginning to appear in the
most advanced UFO abduction stories today.

One school of thought for explaining the comparison
between these is that the claims of earlier centuries are in fact

extraterrestrial abductions described using the terminology of the time, i.e. fairies.

A second school of thought suggests that the unexplained phenomena, whatever their nature, are always interpreted in the terminology of the time, so that what may today be explained as alien abductions would have been blamed on the fairies in the sixteenth century – neither of which is necessarily correct.

Other possibilities include the 'psychological theory'; i.e. that abductions in any form represent mankind's basic fears and that those fears are surfacing in the claims being made in whatever time they arise. Since abductions may contain elements of rape and kidnapping, there is reason to give consideration to this.

Whatever the truth, there can be no true full understanding of the UFO phenomenon until these earlier accounts are reconciled with the modern day accounts.

CENTER FOR UFO STUDIES (CUFOS)

Following the closure of Project **Blue Book** the American Association for the Advancement of Science debated the subject of UFOs in sub-committee at the end of 1969. Many prominent scientists expressed the positive need for proper UFO investigation and were heavily critical of the Air Force's own work.

Astronomer J. Allen **Hynek** brought his scientific colleagues with him into the creation of an independent UFO research network known as the Center for UFO Studies (CUFOS) in 1974 which was designed to continue the work of Project **Blue Book** with the emphasis on a scientific approach. CUFOS operates from its base in Illinois.

Since Hynek's death, CUFOS has been renamed the J. Allen Hynek Center for UFO Studies.

CENTRAL INTELLIGENCE AGENCY
(See **CIA**.)

CHABEUIL, FRANCE

During the French wave of entity sightings in 1954 a close encounter case with apparent physical traces was witnessed by a Mme Leboueuf during September of that year, at Chabeuil in France.

The witness was near a field in which she could see a small entity. The humanoid, some three to four feet tall, was wearing an all-over transparent suit. It began to walk towards her;

understandably the witness ran and hid amongst nearby trees. Shortly after this, a metallic disc took off from behind the trees, disappearing into the sky.

Further investigation revealed that in the area from which the UFO had risen there was a circle of crushed shrubs and bushes.

CHADWELL, H. MARSHALL

In December 1952 the Assistant Director of Scientific Intelligence, H. Marshall Chadwell, sent a memorandum to the Director of the **CIA** regarding the UFO phenomenon. Part of that memorandum includes the following statement: 'Sightings of unexplained objects at great altitude and travelling at high speeds in the vicinity of major US defense installations are of such nature that they are not attributable to natural phenomena of known types of aerial vehicles.'

CHAMBERS, E. W.

The reaction of some witnesses to events is sometimes apparently out of proportion to the event itself. When radio engineer E. W. Chambers saw five discs circling in formation which then climbed steeply into the sky, he commented, 'I am sorry I ever saw them. I keep worrying about what it means.'

Modern UFO researchers would take this as their key to begin in-depth analysis of whether or not Mr Chambers' reaction was to some memory-suppressed part of the event he could not consciously recall as his comments mirror more the statements of abductees than distant encounter witnesses. However, it is equally rational to believe that it is simply the difference in response of one man to another. We do not know how much people's predisposition to the UFO phenomenon affects their reactions; in-depth analysis of a case where a witness has obvious misapprehensions on such a low-definition sighting could produce unreasonable fears under hypnotic suggestibility.

CHARLTON CRATER, THE
(See **Blanchard, Roy**.)

CHÂTEAUNEUF-DU-PAPE, FRANCE

Occasionally, the reaction of people to UFOs can be extraordinary to say the least! On 17 October 1954 the mayor of Châteauneuf-du-Pape, France, issued a proclamation forbidding the landing of any spacecraft within his area of jurisdiction and ordered that any spacecraft disobeying his instructions was to be impounded.

CHATELAIN, MAURICE

Maurice Chatelain is a former Chief of NASA Communications. It has been reported that he believed all the manned Gemini and Apollo United States space missions were shadowed by extraterrestrial spacecraft.

Generally speaking, however, there is little public support for this from the astronauts themselves, though their names have often been linked to specific events.

CHAVEZ, SERGEANT SAM

During the **Socorro** encounter of 1964 (see **Zamora, Lonnie**) where Police Sergeant Zamora reported a close encounter, it was Police Sergeant Chavez who was first on the scene having picked up Zamora's radio communications and having been guided to the site by Zamora during the event. Zamora later informed researcher Ray Stanford that he had especially requested Chavez come to the site alone, because he might have sighted a top secret research device and because he wanted one reliable witness who could be trusted to keep the secret, if necessary. It shows both the seriousness and the professionalism of Zamora in this event. Chavez unfortunately arrived just moments too late to see the departing object.

CHERKASIN, IGOR

In January 1985 the official Soviet news agency, TASS, circulated a UFO report relating to an Aeroflot flight captained by one Igor Cherkasin.

The aircraft apparently encountered a yellow and green cloud; at times the cloud appeared to take on the shape of an aircraft and there was some speculation that it was in fact mimicking the shape of the Aeroflot aircraft itself. The UFO apparently scanned the ground below with a powerful searchlight which it eventually locked on the Aeroflot aircraft, a Tupolev TU-134A. The UFO was also seen by passengers of the flight.

There was some corroboration from another flight in the area at the time although the official Soviet newspaper *Red Star* dismissed the sighting as explainable. It suggested that it might be re-entering space debris and further suggested that all UFOs could be explained without the need for an extraterrestrial hypothesis.

CHIDLAW, GENERAL BENJAMIN
During the early 1950s it was reported that former Commanding General of Air Defense Command, General Benjamin Chidlaw, stated, 'We have stacks of reports of flying saucers. We take them seriously when you consider we have lost many men and planes trying to intercept them.'

CHILES, CAPTAIN C. S.
In July 1948 an Eastern Airlines DC-3 over Alabama reported a near collision with a UFO. The captain, Clarence S. Chiles, together with his co-pilot, John Whitted, sighted the object as it sharply manoeuvred to avoid collision, rocking the DC-3 in its 'wash' so near did it approach.

The object was described as a wingless aircraft with a pilot cabin compartment. It was glowing blue and orange, and approximately 100 feet long.

An Air Force investigation concluded that the only other aircraft in the vicinity would not have matched the description given, but offered no further explanation.

CHINA UFO RESEARCH ORGANISATION
The main Chinese body investigating UFO reports is the China UFO Research Organisation (once the Chinese UFO Studies Association) which is an official branch of the Chinese Academy of Social Sciences. It is reported that membership of the organisation is 20,000.

CHINESE UFO STUDIES ASSOCIATION
(See **China UFO Research Organisation**.)

CHURCH STOWE, NORTHANTS
(See **Oakensen, Elsie**.)

CHURCHILL, SIR WINSTON
In July 1952 the then Prime Minister Winston Churchill wrote the following memorandum to the Secretary of State for Air: 'What does all this stuff about flying saucers amount to? What can it mean? What is the truth? Let me have a report at your convenience.'

In August 1952 the Prime Minister received a reply stating

that flying saucers could all be explained as known astronomical or meteorological phenomena, mistaken identifications of mundane objects, optical illusions and hoaxes.

The memo indicated that the Americans believed the same. Subsequent analysis of the situation at the time shows, however, that neither the British nor the Americans were that confident in explaining away all UFO sightings and the Americans were at that time admitting that some UFO sightings were not capable of explanation.

CIA

The precise involvement of the CIA in UFO investigation over the years is vague, as it would logically be given the nature of that organisation. Many of the individual details relating to CIA activity are included where appropriate in this encyclopedia and it remains sufficient to say that documents released under the American **Freedom of Information Act** have revealed a considerable difference between the stated lack of interest by the CIA in the UFO phenomenon and their secret instructions to the Air Force over the years. When American researchers requested documents from them, under the Freedom of Information Act, they first stated that they had none, then they released 400 pages. Eventually they released 40,000 pages.

CICCIOLI, GILBERTO

In October 1974 Gilberto Ciccioli, in Buenos Aires, woke early in the morning to investigate noises near his house. He was hit by a beam of intense white light and subjected to 'classic' abduction events such as medical examination and sample extraction of blood and sperm.

What makes the event special in the context of abductions is that it is one of the few which have not required regression hypnosis to reveal the memory, apparently still within the witness's conscious recall, yet closely mirror the stories of those who are regressed.

CIRCLES, CORNFIELD

This is a curious aspect of the UFO phenomenon in which UFO researchers have become embroiled thanks to the attention of the media and to some reckless members of our own groups. The circles may have little to do with UFO research and certainly nothing to do with extraterrestrial activity, if there is any.

'Cornfield circles' is the description generally given to circular flattened areas of wheat and other crop fields which periodically occur during the spring and summer in many areas of southern England. They have also been reported in Europe, Australia and America. They are striking because of their symmetrical patterns, sometimes appearing as a large central flattened circle with four symmetrically positioned smaller circles at north, south, east and west, and indeed a whole variety of similarly extraordinary symmetrical layouts.

Although there have been few reliable reports of UFO sightings in conjunction with the appearance of these circles, the media continually refer to them as 'saucer nests' or 'UFO landing nests' and **BUFORA** was forced to clear the matter up by undertaking a survey and investigation alongside various appropriate bodies.

It is worth noting at this point that the one or two reliable sightings of UFOs seen in conjunction with flattened areas of fields, particularly from France in the 1950s and 1960s, describe circles quite *unlike* the so-called cornfield circles in that the grass is randomly crushed rather than flattened into a spiral.

BUFORA's investigators, principally Paul Fuller and Jenny Randles, worked with the National Farmers' Union and the Tornado and Storm Research Association, amongst others, and concluded there was a high probability that the cornfield circles were a natural phenomenon, the result of hurricane vortex action. The symmetrical patterns are apparently a natural aspect of such complex vortices and although they are strikingly symmetrical it was pointed out that most things in nature are (i.e. a bubble is a perfect globe because of the arrangement of perfect 'pressures').

Using the information collected over a study period of several years there was some degree of accuracy about predicting the appearance of the cornfield circles and eventually we were able to receive reports from people who had been able to witness their formation.

There are still some mysteries related to the cornfield circles and one in particular which still suggests a 'UFO' connection; during the formation of the circle there is a frequently reported glowing orange ball just above the site. It is theorised that this may be the product of ionized air caused by the friction of the fast movement of the hurricane vortex, but this remains to be investigated more fully and work is continuing in this regard.

Despite the scientific efforts of those involved there are still a number on the UFO fringe who insist on trying to ascribe to the circle all manner of extraterrestrial interpretation.

It is interesting to note that Ufology in the late 1980s was beginning to achieve the kind of serious credibility which would attract scientists to its folds once it had shed the more extreme lunacy, and particularly the blatantly fraudulent claims, which had been a feature of the early years. However, it appears that there has been a backlash and cornfield circles appear to be the means by which poor, imaginative and unscientific research will again denigrate the work of serious UFO researchers and provide the media with the kind of image of UFO research which it has always sought to promote.

During the 1990 summer season, the circles debate took on a new dimension when incredible pictograms appeared in several fields in southern England. They were multi-circles, joined together by bars and displaying detailed appendages. Although some researchers have suggested they could be entirely natural, that seems very unlikely. If artificial, then the likeliest cause must be hoaxes, coming as they did just when the media were being attracted to the phenomenon.

CIRVIS
In the United States there were various directives issued with regard to sightings of UFOs by military personnel covered by the Joint Army/Navy/Air Force Publication (**JANAP**).

JANAP 146 refers to CIRVIS, Communication Instructions for Reporting Vital Intelligence Sightings. The directive is as follows: 'CIRVIS reports contain information affecting the national defense of the United States within the meaning of the espionage laws, 18 US code 793 and 794. The unauthorised transmission or revelation of the contents of CIRVIS reports in any manner is prohibited.'

It is known that many CIRVIS reports referred to UFO encounters and in some cases contained clear descriptions of saucer-like shapes.

CISCO GROVE, CALIFORNIA
A witness, identified only as Mr S., on 5 September 1964 was besieged by a UFO after a day's hunting at Cisco Grove. Separated from his companions he took shelter in a tree, strapping himself to a branch to prevent himself falling out; at one point he saw three objects with rotating lights approaching

The Mysterious Flying Light That Hovered Over St. Mary's College, Oakland, and Then Started for San Francisco. It Is Exactly Like That Described by Sacramentans, and Similar to the Cut Published a Few Days Ago in "The Call" From a Description Furnished by One Who Saw It.

An early UFO? An artist's impression of a craft seen during the 1896/7 airship wave of reports across the United States. (*Mary Evans Picture Library*)

Abductee George Adamski arrives in England as part of his world tour, bringing a new gospel to a new audience. (*Mary Evans Picture Library*)

Adamski with a portrait of a male Venusian visitor. (*Mary Evans Picture Library*)

Close-up shot of one of the saucers photographed by George Adamski over Palomar Gardens, California in December 1952. (*Mary Evans Picture Library*)

'Tops in shapeliness and beauty', Aura Rhanes was the female captain of the flying saucer that contacted Truman Betherum in 1954. (*Mary Evans Picture Library*)

Overlaid drawing of the UFO and occupants encountered by French lavender farmer Maurice Masse on 1 July 1965. (*GEOS*)

One of the early contactees was Daniel Fry, who photographed a number of variously shaped objects, including this one, during a series of encounters. (*Daniel Fry*)

Kenneth Arnold, the man whose description of his sighting in 1947 led to the coinage of the term 'flying saucer'. (*Mary Evans Picture Library*)

The staff of the USAF's Project Blue Book, headed by Major Hector Quintanilla (seated). (*Mary Evans Picture Library*)

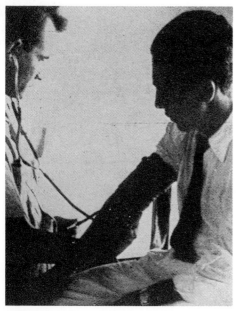

Following his extraordinary encounter in 1957, Argentinian farmer Antonio Villas Boas underwent physical and other examinations to verify his story. (*Mary Evans Picture Library*)

Scoutmaster Desverges encountered a UFO near West Palm Beach, Florida in August 1952. The encounter resulted in an attack, leaving Desverges and the area around him burned by a beam from a flying saucer. (*Mary Evans Picture Library*)

Pilot Frederick Valentich, whose plane was lost without trace during a flight over the Bass Strait in Australia in 1978. (*Paul Norman (VUFORS)*)

Clifford Muchena was the principal witness of a ball of light 'attack' and related entity sightings at La Rochelle in Africa in August 1981. (*Cynthia Hind*)

Originally known as 'Mr Ed', Ed Walters is the principal witness in the Gulf Breeze multi-photographic case. (*John Spencer*)

him. He believed them to be part of a search party and attracted their attention with signal fires.

The objects landed and dispatched two silver-suited **humanoids** with extraordinary, prominent eyes. The two humanoids and a third robot-like entity apparently tried to get Mr S. out of the tree. This resulted in Mr S. firing arrows at the robot, tearing off strips of his clothing and setting them alight to frighten the entities away. Eventually he succeeded and they left in their UFO, the backlash from which caused him to black out.

At daybreak the following day he awoke and discovered that the UFO and the entities were gone.

CISTERNAS, MARCELO

In 1965 the Captain of a Chilean National Airlines flight aboard a DC-6B, Marcelo Cisternas, reported a UFO event, describing the object as 'something mechanical'. The sighting lasted approximately a quarter of an hour and the pilot was certain it was not an optical illusion and confirmed that it was also seen by other members of the crew.

The object eventually left, characteristically of UFOs, at an amazing speed.

CITIZENS AGAINST UFO SECRECY (CAUS)

In 1978 Citizens Against UFO Secrecy was founded by Todd Zechel as a United States pressure group designed principally to force the government to release its secret files and documents regarding the UFO phenomenon. Since the **Freedom of Information Act** this organisation has been foremost in forcing the government to release hitherto secret documents, many of which have exposed contradictions in statements on the part of the American establishment.

The organisation has also been at the forefront of many legal battles to force the government to release even more data than they are obliged to do at present.

CLANCARTY, EARL OF

The Earl of Clancarty is also known to UFO enthusiasts as the author Brinsley Le Poer Trench.

In January 1979 Clancarty instigated a debate in the House of Lords to discuss UFOs. There was incredible public interest in the debate resulting in one of the few times when copies of *Hansard*, the official record of House proceedings, were sold out almost immediately.

As a result of the debate the Earl of Clancarty formed a UFO study group within the House of Lords though it is, regrettably, not presently active.

CLARION (PLANET)
Planet Clarion is the home world of Truman **Bethurum**'s aliens and their female captain **Aura Rhanes**. It is apparently hidden from Earth's view, being beyond the far side of Earth's moon. When this story was told to the contactee there had been no manned flights into space which could have disproved the claim, and indeed such flights may then have seemed quite unlikely, but subsequent flights have singularly failed to locate the planet. This is a pity since apparently Clarion is free of disease, politics and taxation.

The planet Clarion reappeared during Marian **Keech**'s report of contact, though it may have been a different planet Clarion.

CLARK, EVERETT
In the early morning of 6 November 1957 Everett Clark, a young boy living at Dante, Tennessee, was walking his dog. From his house he could see an object approximately one hundred yards away, in a nearby field. Next to the object were two men and two women who, the witness claimed, walked through the solid wall of the object which then took off silently.

CLARK, RALPH L.
Ralph L. Clark was Acting Assistant Director for the Office of Scientific Intelligence and issued a telling memorandum in July 1952 which indicated government interest in the UFO phenomenon. It stated: 'Although this office has maintained a continuing review of such reported sightings during the past three years, a special study group has been formed to review this subject to date.'

CLASSIFICATION OF UFO EVENTS
Generally speaking, UFO events are classified according to type. There are a number of possibilities available. The accepted present categories divide the phenomena into two broad groups, i.e. the distant encounters and the close encounters. One division of the distant encounters is simply that between daylight discs (i.e. phenomena observed during daylight hours) and night lights (i.e. phenomena observed during

night time hours). Another classification breaks the distant encounters into three sub-headings:

1. Low-definition cases with no definitive shape or effects.
2. Medium-definition cases where clear shapes are witnessed.
3. Instrumentally detected cases such as radar or photographic observations.

The close encounters are generally divided into four categories as follows:

1. Close encounters of the first kind (CE1 cases). This is the close approach of an object giving some time for pertinent observation and possibly giving some interactive experience between the event stimulus and the witness.
2. Close encounters of the second kind (CE2 cases). These are those encounters which leave permanent or semipermanent physical traces (which can be subject to subsequent investigation) such as ground markings, radiation traces, etc.
3. Close encounters of the third kind (CE3 cases). This is generally accepted to be simply those cases where non-human entities are seen in association with the event stimulus.
4. Close encounters of the fourth kind (CE4 cases). These are the events which are generally called abductions but which more specifically create severe reality distortion for the witness such as memory lapse, physiological effects, time and space disorientation and 'post abduction' trauma, such as inexpressible fear and anxiety.

The above classifications are suitable for certain types of analysis but have fallen short of providing analysis in respect of the psychological component of UFO events. At the July 1989 London UFO Congress delegates from many countries of the world speculated on a classification system which would divide events between those which are witnessed (i.e. with no interaction), and those events which are experienced (i.e. with interaction). The need for this classification system is most obviously seen where cases occur which affect witnesses quite differently from the main stream of cases in the earlier classifications. For example, abductions generally create a great deal of personal reality distortion, discomfort or fear in witnesses and yet in the case of Alfred **Burtoo** there was a classical abduction with no apparent ill effect on the witness. On the other hand there is at least one case on record where a witness suffered

severe emotional distress at sighting what was later proved
beyond doubt to be the moon behind cloud. Other investigations have shown that witnesses often react to IFOs (identified
flying objects) in the same way as they respond to UFOs. This
new proposed classification system would give some additional
weight to the witness's own response to the phenomenon.
Analysis under this division would have to take account of the
predisposition of the witness towards the UFO phenomenon –
modern research is beginning to build this into its studies.

CLEM, SHERIFF WEIR

In November 1957, during a localised but intensive spate of
UFO reports, Sheriff Weir Clem, together with his deputy, was
driving along the Oklahoma Flats road following up the many
reports of UFOs which had been received when they suddenly
saw an enormous ovoid-shaped light across the highway.

There were corroborative reports from other police officers
and reports of vehicle interference, although none actually
affecting Sheriff Clem.

CLOSE ENCOUNTERS
(See **Classification of UFO Events**.)

CLOSE ENCOUNTERS OF THE THIRD KIND

The film *Close Encounters of the Third Kind* was the movie
industry's major exposure of UFO material, albeit with a solely
extraterrestrial bias. Although fictional, and not documentary,
the events depicted are very similar to events reported by UFO
witnesses throughout the world, particularly in the portrayal of
the alien pilots at the end of the film. Dr J. Allen **Hynek**, the
late head of the Center for UFO Studios (now the J. Allen
Hynek Center for UFO Studies), was a consultant to the film
and indeed makes a cameo appearance during the landing of
the mothership craft.

The film did much to 'legitimise' material of UFO witnesses
but at the same time reinforced the belief that UFOs were
visiting alien spaceships, leaving this mark indelibly on millions
of people throughout the world.

There have been suggestions that the film's director, Steven
Spielberg, was part of an American government plan gradually
to increase public awareness of the UFO phenomenon but there
is no solid evidence to support this. More likely, if the government wanted to do this, it would know it could rely on 'normal'

public interest to demand such films, and that such films would draw from known data. If the government has an 'angle' to promote then it could do so by releasing certain information to certain individuals in order that it become part of that background data; there is more evidence to suggest this possibility than the outright conspiracy theory.

COLEMAN, LIEUTENANT SID

In December 1952 Lieutenant Sid Coleman was Radar Officer aboard a B-29 bomber near Galveston. When watching the radar scope Coleman observed two UFOs which he tracked at a speed in excess of 5,000 miles per hour, quite impossible for planes of the day. The captain of the plane, John Harta, suggested that Coleman recalibrate his set as the sighting was impossible but the sighting was immediately confirmed by the navigator on *his* radar scope. Eventually four UFOs were seen on the radar screens.

From the plane, they were also able to make visual contact with the object, watching it as a blue-white streak moving fast near the bomber. Shortly after this there was a repeat with several more objects whizzing past their plane. Crew members watched the UFOs perform incredible manoeuvres to avoid hitting the plane. There were reports of a mothercraft absorbing smaller craft and one report of one UFO moving at over 9,000 miles per hour.

COLLECTIVE UNCONSCIOUS

The 'collective unconscious' was a theory of Swiss psychologist Dr Carl Jung. In his book *Flying Saucers: A Modern Myth of Things Seen in the Sky* (see References and Background Material) he views UFOs within this framework.

He suggests that the human mind has developed a common pattern of response to the UFO image which he regards as an archetype; in the case of the UFO the archetype is the circular symbol of oneness (mandala).

Many people have held Jung's book to be an explanation of UFOs, and many have indeed twisted his words to suggest he was explaining them as extraterrestrial spacecraft, but it seems clear that his intention was to explain the interaction between people and UFOs, and their responses to them, and possibly the degree to which they can create them from their own minds. Jung's book made no attempt to explain the physical evidences, radar sightings, etc. in any investigative way.

COLLETT, W.

Driving a Ford Transit bus towards Reading, England, on 26 October 1967 during the early hours of the morning, Mr W. Collett was alarmed when the electrical system of the bus cut out, causing total power failure. He got out and checked the engine but could find no problem. He noticed as he did so a dark unlit shape hovering above the road ahead of him.

This sporadic interference with his vehicle happened twice more and again he could see the object nearby. Eventually he was able to complete his journey after the object had moved away across the treetops.

There were certain physiological effects on Mr Collett resulting from this; he felt a lack of co-ordination and almost had to relearn how to use the controls of his bus, and he began to remember his dreams more vividly than he had done before. London doctors examining him concluded that he may have been affected by a strong electromagnetic force field, though commented that a more powerful backlash could have had a serious effect on his nervous system.

COLLINS, GEORGE D.

George D. Collins was an attorney in the city of San Francisco during the **airship** waves of the 1896/7 period. He claimed to be the personal representative of the inventor of the airship and through various methods made clear that he attributed the machine to Dr E. H. **Benjamin**.

COLLINS, HAROLD B.

Harold B. Collins was Deputy Director of Intelligence at the British Air Ministry between 1950 and 1953. In a summary of results of UFO studies he indicated that there were '10% where the reporter was well qualified, i.e. Farnborough test pilot etc., where there was corroboration and where the report itself carried conviction; but where we could find no explanation'.

The main significance of this statement is that it contradicts the official stand being taken at that time, as presented to the public.

COLLINS, PAUL T.

In February 1942, shortly after the Japanese had invaded the Hawaiian base at Pearl Harbor, there were reports of unidentified aircraft over the United States mainland in California, and specifically near Los Angeles.

Paul T. Collins was one principal witness who described seeing lights moving in 'a strange manner'. There was also a report that there was an enormous UFO seen by many observers.

Collins was warned by an air raid warden to black out his car and stay parked until the 'all clear' sounded. During the ensuing shelling there were several deaths and some considerable damage to buildings. However, the target of the defensive barrages was never identified.

Mainland America had never been the target of bombing raids of external invasion and the hysterical reaction to the claims of the time are possibly partly due to this fact. In Europe bombing raids had become 'normal' and so did not cause such hysteria.

It has been suggested that the American reaction to the UFO phenomenon in general is due to the fact that America, unlike most other countries, does not have a history of invasion and conquest, and so is a result of the xenophobia born of this.

COLORADO (UNIVERSITY) UFO PROJECT
(See **Condon Committee/Condon Report**.)

COMET EXPLOSION
In May 1953 a British Comet jet took off from Dumdum Airport, Calcutta. Six minutes later the Comet, totally destroyed, was strewn over five square miles. There had been no distress call or any warning of difficulty.

After a Civil Air Ministry investigation a report was issued stating that the Comet had been hit by an unidentified flying body.

Although there is no evidence as to what exactly struck the Comet there has never, in the years since, been any documented suggestion that it was destroyed by the hostile action of a foreign terrestrial country.

COMMISSION FOR THE INVESTIGATION OF ANOMALOUS ATMOSPHERIC PHENOMENA
Established in Moscow in 1984 and comprised of distinguished scientists and others, including a cosmonaut, Pavel Popovitch.

There is close association with the very important USSR Academy of Sciences.

COMPUTER ENHANCEMENT
One of the principal new analysis techniques available to researchers is that of computer enhancement of photographs

purporting to support case reports.

One typical such technique is to use a television camera to scan the photograph, breaking it down into picture elements. Often this can be up to a quarter of a million picture elements per picture. The scanner then analyses the degree of brightness for each picture element and the computer can use this information to heighten and darken areas of the picture to emphasise images that are very unclear. This can enable, for example, strings and wires supporting models to be seen where they cannot easily be identified by the naked eye; they can effectively 'refocus' out-of-focus images such as the computer enhancement of a film of a disc-shaped object which proved to be a light aircraft; and they can perform edge enhancement which shows the break of continuity between objects and surroundings when the object is in fact two-dimensional, i.e. pasted on glass, and so on.

The Arizona-based group **Ground Saucer Watch** has been most prominent in pioneering such analysis.

CONDON COMMITTEE/CONDON REPORT

In 1966 Senator Gerald Ford (later President of the United States) opened the way for a scientific investigation of UFOs by the government which was to become the Condon Committee. Dr Edward Uhler **Condon** led a team of scientists at Colorado University in a two-year study of the UFO phenomenon.

In December 1968 the committee concluded its work and published the Condon Report which broadly concluded that UFOs were not of significance for scientific study. There is some doubt as to Dr Condon's impartiality in respect of this conclusion (see next entry) and in any case it appears clear that the conclusions of the report do not necessarily mirror the actual findings of the investigation. In short, the investigation seems to have revealed that there was something of significance to study, but the conclusion published was that which it appears the government insisted on.

The Air Force drew the following conclusions from the Condon Report: 'The report concluded that little if anything had come from the study of UFOs in the past twenty-one years that had added to scientific knowledge', and also, 'The panel concurred in the University of Colorado's recommendation that no high priority in UFO investigation is warranted by data of the past two decades.'

CONDON, DR EDWARD UHLER

One of the most important studies of the UFO phenomenon commissioned by the United States Air Force was that undertaken by the University of Colorado. Dr Edward Condon headed the investigative team and gave his name to the investigation generally known as the **Condon Committee** and its findings, the Condon Report. The committee was established in 1966 and the report published in 1969.

Dr Condon was a former director of the National Bureau of Standards, and a prominent nuclear physicist who had worked on such projects as the development of radar, the atomic bomb, and space capsule design. He was born near Alamogordo, New Mexico, on 2 March 1902, and during his early years he had been a journalist. He was no stranger to controversy and had several heated disagreements with the American establishment, who nonetheless were never able to deny his abilities.

CONGAREE AIR BASE, SIGHTING AT

In August 1952 there was a report from Congaree Air Base near Columbia, South Carolina, that radar officers at the Air Defense command post had sighted on radar a UFO travelling at some 4,000 mile per hour, considerably faster than aircraft of the day would have been capable of. No jets were scrambled to intercept the object as it was recognised from the outset that the UFO would outpace any jet and would indeed appear as little more than a blur to any jet pilot sent to investigate.

Investigation concluded that the radar had not been malfunctioning and Air Technical Intelligence Command admitted that it had no explanation for the sighting.

CONLEY, JAMES

(See **Ford Meade**.)

CONTACTEES

The expression 'contactee' refers to those people who claim an interaction with alien entities. Generally these entities are held to be extraterrestrial, but the overriding characteristic is only that they are non-human, i.e. alien to the human race. Some claims suggest they are non-human inhabitants of the Earth itself.

Contact is sometimes established in face to face meetings, but can be by means of telepathic messages, automatic writing and so on. Recent claims include those people who simply find themselves motivated to change their life-styles, or read particular literature which has a life-changing effect, etc.; it is held that they are being 'directed' in their endeavours.

Early claims of contactees contained much material that has not stood the test of time; claims of planets in our own solar system that have not been located, and so on. There were almost certainly some fraudulent claims amongst these contactees, as happens in all aspects of the subject.

However, recent contactee claims have been less obviously financially motivated, and even sometimes to the detriment of the claimant, suggesting at least a true belief in the claims being put forward.

The personality cults and personal power that these claims may give the contactees has been another reason for doubting some claims; again, recent claims have been less overt and contactees have not sought out this attention, giving further weight to their sincerity.

Some cases have indicated a close interface between the contactees and the abductees, suggesting that if a non-human power is seeking to direct the human race it may be a more complex design than was supposed by early researchers.

COOK, DUANE

During the incredible encounters at **Gulf Breeze**, Florida, which affected the witness, Ed **Walters**, there was an occasion on 24 January 1988 when he was able to get Duane Cook, the editor of the *Sentinel* local newspaper, to accompany him to an expected encounter.

It appeared for some time that the encounter was not going to happen but as the potential witnesses were getting back into their vehicle, a UFO appeared. Walters was able to take a photograph of the UFO. Duane Cook, who was videotaping at the time, could not get the camera up to sight the UFO but was able to film Walters at the time he was taking his picture.

This provided some skeletal corroboration of Walters' claim of that day.

COOK, JAMES

In September 1957 James Cook was apparently contacted by aliens and asked to meet them on the top of a hill near Runcorn in Cheshire. This he did, and was taken aboard their flying saucer which then flew him to the aliens' home planet of Zomdic (an alien planet never heard of before or since).

Mr Cook was warned about upsetting the balance of nature, presumably with the development of atomic weapons and ecological destruction, and then returned to Earth and sent on his way.

For many years following the event he apparently kept up a telepathic communication with the aliens. He eventually started up a church and later disappeared into obscurity.

COOKE, LIEUTENANT-COLONEL CHARLES
Lieutenant-Colonel Charles Cooke was one of the United States Air Force's top authorities on UFOs. During World War II and in the years following he analysed many hundreds of reports from Air Force officers.

When he published an article on 7 August 1966 strongly supporting the theory that UFOs were of an interplanetary nature, it created some considerable pressure for the Air Force to halt its cover-up activities.

COOPER, ASTRONAUT GORDON
Astronaut Gordon Cooper, one of the original Mercury astronauts and the last American to fly in space alone, announced that he has seen UFOs over Germany in 1951. They were metallic, saucer-shaped discs at considerable altitude and apparently able to outmanoeuvre the American fighter planes.

Timothy Good in his book *Above Top Secret* (see References and Background Material) reports that Cooper has stated to the United Nations: 'I believe that these extraterrestrial vehicles and their crews are visiting this planet from other planets.' Good also points out that Cooper states, 'Most astronauts were reluctant to discuss UFOs.'

COPELAND, MILES
Miles Copeland was a former **CIA** officer and has confirmed that the Agency has used the mythology that surrounds belief in UFOs to spread disinformation. In the case cited the UFO exercise was aimed at the Chinese and designed to disinform them about research activities.

Copeland made the point that some of the data 'got picked up by a lot of religious nuts in Iowa and Nebraska'.

Ufologists must wonder to what extent disinformation, of which there could be a considerable amount, has polluted the data held by many to be 'real'.

COQUIL, EUGENE
In the early hours of the morning of 16 January 1966 Eugene Coquil saw lights in a field where he was driving in Brittany, France. Believing there might have been an accident, he got out of the car and walked across the field towards the light.

When he got closer he realised that not only were the lights on an object moving towards him but they were moving some fifteen feet *above the ground*. At this point discretion became the better part of valour. He ran back to his car and got in but the object hovered above the car, possibly causing **vehicle interference**. Certainly he had difficulty in starting it. Eventually he drove off in a somewhat agitated state, leaving the object behind.

CORBIN, LIEUTENANT-COLONEL LOU
Lieutenant-Colonel Lou Corbin was a former Army intelligence officer who had for many years released evidence for the existence of UFOs and evidence of censorship surrounding them, obtained through connections in the Pentagon. He stated, 'The UFOs are no figment of imagination.'

Corbin also revealed that the Air Force was still investigating UFOs under two projects, the names of which have not been confirmed elsewhere; these were **Old New Moon** and **Blue Paper**. This occurred in 1972, after the closure of Project **Blue Book**, and was made public to a meeting of the Retired Military Officers' Association in Baltimore.

CORNING, NEW YORK: LECTURE BY E. U. CONDON
On 25 January 1967 Dr Edward **Condon** lectured to a scientific fraternity in Corning, New York. Part of his speech gives considerable doubt as to the objectivity of the Condon investigation and report and gives some weight to the claim that the conclusions were reached before the study was even under way.

Condon said: 'It is my inclination right now to recommend that the government get out of this business. My attitude right now is that there is nothing in it. But I am not supposed to reach a conclusion for another year.'

CORVALHO, BERNARD
Bernard Corvalho was one of the leading lights of **NICAP** (National Investigations Committee on Aerial Phenomena) which was one of the first private UFO research organisations to develop. It is held that he was a well-known intelligence

operative and therefore it is suggested that there may have been early government manipulation of this key organisation.

COVAS, ALBERTO GOMES
(See **Ferreira, José Lemos**.)

COYNE, CAPTAIN LAWRENCE J.
Captain Lawrence J. Coyne was the pilot of a Bell helicopter which in October 1973 had a close UFO sighting near Mansfield, Ohio.

The object apparently flew at approximately 600 knots on a collision course towards the helicopter. Coyne had to make a sudden descent to avoid the impact.

For a time the object appears to have paced the helicopter; the object was described as cigar-shaped and grey with a dome on top, and some sixty feet long. It was held probably to have been manned, and operated a light which scanned the helicopter.

There were several witnesses on the ground below the event, confirming the encounter.

Coyne and his companions filed a very detailed report of what was held to be one of the most important sightings of that year.

CRAIGIE, MAJOR-GENERAL L. C.
In December 1947 Major-General L. C. Craigie was Director of Research and Development for the United States Air Force, Office of the Deputy Chief of Staff. He wrote to the commanding general of **Wright Patterson Air Force Base** effectively forming a project to study UFOs. The project was assigned priority 2-A (second highest priority) and designated 'restricted'. This was the birth of Project **Sign**, often known as Project **Saucer**.

CRASH RETRIEVALS
This is the general name given to supposed retrievals of crashed flying saucers by government and military agents. There have been many such claims in the past, almost exclusively in the United States, and the stereotypical version of this is the **Roswell** crash of July 1947.

CREIGHTON, GORDON
Gordon Creighton has for many years been the editor of the well-known magazine *Flying Saucer Review*, often known

also by its initials *FSR*. He is a former intelligence officer. His obvious passion for the subject, and a working knowledge of many languages, makes him an important figure in the release of case data from non-English-speaking countries such as those of South America.

CRENSHAW, WILLIAM
At the time of Captain Thomas **Mantell**'s failed and fatal attempt to chase a UFO there were other National Guard planes attempting the same. William Crenshaw from Hopkinsville, Kentucky, reported pursuing a UFO although he appears to have identified it as a balloon.

CRISMAN, FRED L.
Fred L. Crisman was one of the two 'harbour patrol men' involved in the **Maury Island** incident.

CRONIGER, GEORGE
Together with his pilot Jerry Whittaker, George Croniger witnessed two UFOs over Tidioute, Pennsylvania. The event happened shortly before the **Great North-East Blackout** in 1965 and according to the witnesses the UFOs were chased by Air Force jets though they managed to outpace them.

CUERNAVACA BLACKOUT (MEXICO, 1965)
(See **Riva Palacie, Governor Emilie**.)

CUFOS
(See **Center for UFO Studies**.)

CULTS
Selected specific cults are mentioned under the appropriate heading in this encyclopedia. The existence of cults as part of the UFO phenomenon arose in the early 1950s and has remained a part of it since, although the early 1950s were probably the time of peak popularity for these groups. Generally speaking, cult members are distinguished from other UFO enthusiasts by a reliance on belief rather than proof and are generally categorised by the existence of a channel, i.e. a human contact with the aliens towards whom all the other members of the cult direct their worship. This of course gives the cult leader considerable kudos and, in many cases, considerable wealth.

The cults are forms of the 'new age' religion which has sprouted up in many areas in the past three decades.

CULTURAL TRACKING

Many UFO researchers in the forty-odd years since Kenneth **Arnold**'s sighting have noticed that there is a tendency for UFO sightings to mirror the capabilities of Earth technology of the time.

This extends as far back as the **airship** waves of 1896/7 and 1909 when the UFOs were reported as airship-shaped, even including propellers and passenger compartments beneath. In these times we find that UFOs appeared to be able to fly at speeds somewhat in excess of, but not greatly beyond, the scope of our own airships. As our own aircraft have increased their capabilities so too have UFOs. As we have come to accept the possibility of much greater speeds, so we find them being reported.

Witnesses aboard flying saucers have reported, for example, chunky number counters on the saucer control panels, but we did not have reports of liquid quartz readouts until we ourselves had invented them.

In the cases of many contactees, the messages given by the aliens related to the human fears of the time – such as the development of the atomic bomb. It might have been useful had those contactees been given messages back in the 1950s warning us of the impending problems we were going to create with, say, the ozone layer, but again these are conspicuous only by their absence.

The precise relationship between 'their' technology and ours is therefore a matter of study though no conclusions are easy to reach. To some extent it may be a case of our interpreting what we see through our own terminology and experience, which might account for the similarity of modern reports to those in the sixteenth century of abductions ascribed to fairies and elves. To some extent it may relate to an outside agency, i.e. the speculated extraterrestrial visitors, only needing to match our capabilities in order to do their work and having to step up their own abilities when we stepped up ours.

However, there must be some suspicion that witnesses are, possibly subconsciously, modifying the claims of their genuine experiences in order to make them credible within the context of the time. This is not to suggest that witnesses are lying but possibly only that they themselves are unable to believe what they are really seeing and thus reducing the extent of the extraordinary nature of the sightings. To this extent researchers must be aware that evidence could be unreliable.

There are cases where cultural tracking appears to have been 'overridden'; in the case of the Betty **Hill** abduction, and a similar report received in the case of Betty **Andreasson**, the witnesses reported the insertion of some kind of probe through their navel. It is held that this kind of medical examination was not made at the time of these claims but in fact such probes are now used.

CULVER CITY
One of the most spectacular 'mothership' reports came from Culver City, California, in July 1952.

Workers in an aircraft plant sighted a silver UFO over Culver City and one, watching it through binoculars, described it as egg-shaped and flying in a rocking motion.

It appears that the object dispatched two small UFOs which circled over the area and later re-entered the mothership which then climbed at enormous speed before disappearing.

CUNNINGHAM, NATHAN
In October 1973 Sheriff Nathan Cunningham of Tennessee reported witnessing three UFOs over his house, moving at approximately 100 miles an hour.

Sheriff Cunningham therefore became one of many 'officials' to have reported UFO events. The incident took place during a considerable wave of UFO reports.

D

DA SILVA, JOÁO VALERIO

In November 1982 Joáo Valerio da Silva was apparently abducted from his home in Botucatu, Brazil, by a beam of light and taken aboard a UFO.

On board the UFO he was approached by several entities, including a naked woman, and passed out. He was found by his family on the floor of his house, naked and unconscious, his clothes piled next to him. His skin was covered in red marks and his watch had stopped. His penis also had strange lesions on it.

There were reports of poltergeist activity around the home.

There are some obvious similarities here to the case of Antonio Villas **Boas** though no similar level of investigation is yet reported.

DA SILVA, JOSÉ ANTONIO

(See **Belo Horizonte, Brazil**.)

DAHL, HAROLD

Harold Dahl was one of the two 'harbour patrol men' involved in the **Maury Island** incident.

DANIEL, KEITH

On 12 July 1981 Keith Daniel, together with a friend, was camping with a group of children near the Dee estuary.

At approximately two o'clock in the morning they saw a bright yellow-white light some way off. The light apparently turned blue-white and streaked away rapidly. The sighting was corroborated by a report from a Dan Air crew flying over the area at the time.

Investigator Jenny Randles researched Keith Daniel's background and discovered that there was a family history of possible UFO encounters and dream imagery related to UFO events, reminiscent of many **repeater witnesses** and a factor emerging in many **abductees**, particularly where abductions are suspected but not confirmed.

There is much in the imagery of some of the impressions he has received that is similar to those of Kathryn **Howard**. In particular his convictions that the Earth may be approaching a holocaust, though Kathryn's convictions were that her messages reflected – hopefully – warning rather than certain fate, giving us a chance for compassionate change.

There are also many aspects of his history of encounters which suggest a parallel to the Kathie **Davis** case.

DANIKEN, ERICH VON

Erich von Daniken has published a series of books starting with *Chariots of the Gods?* (see References and Background Material) speculating that many of the artefacts of early man represent proof of visitation by extraterrestrials in ancient times. This 'ancient astronaut' theory has been used by many to suggest that the UFO phenomenon has been going on for many thousands of years.

One interesting facet is that the ancient astronaut theory includes the belief that the aliens used genetic manipulation and breeding experiments to create the human race as it is today, and there is now some suggestion coming through from modern UFO abductions that similar events are being undertaken. To what extent modern events are a copycat of this popular theme is unclear.

The ancient astronaut theory is popular at the present time, but largely ignored by researchers in view of the limited scope for 'on-site' conclusive investigation.

DAPPLE GREY LANE, CALIFORNIA

Two witnesses known as John Hodges and Peter Rodriguez were visiting a friend at an apartment in Dapple Grey Lane in South Los Angeles.

It was two o'clock in the morning when the two witnesses apparently saw two objects like human brains on the roadway. The objects seemed to be alive; each was approximately three feet high. Hodges drove Rodriguez to his home, having to pass the objects, and then returned to his own home but arrived back realising that he had lost two hours of time. Under regression hypnosis it appears that Hodges was telepathically contacted by the entities telling him that they would meet again.

There was also some imagery of being inside a large room where there were humanoid entities. This occurred in 1971 and John apparently met the creatures again in 1978 when he was somehow removed to the same room. The message from the entities appeared to be warning Hodges of the dangers of nuclear war.

Further revelation from the aliens suggested that they had been implanting small objects in abductees to heighten psychic abilities. There are stories of implantations in abductees – for various speculated reasons – in many more recent claims. It was suggested that present day humans are the result of biological experimentation over millions of years. This case very neatly ties up the modern abductions with aspects of the 'ancient astronaut theory' (see previous entry), both becoming dependent on aliens' genetic manipulation of the human race.

DARBISHIRE, STEPHEN
Along with his cousin Adrian Myers, Stephen Darbishire photographed a flying saucer near Coniston in the Lake District in February 1954. There was considerable similarity between the object in this photograph and those photographed by George **Adamski**.

The report attracted the attention of the Duke of Edinburgh who invited Stephen Darbishire to Buckingham Palace to relate his story to an aide.

There had been much speculation that these photographs were faked, and Darbishire then admitted they were, but apparently later maintained that he admitted they were faked only to reduce the pressure being directed at him because of the report.

DAUDPOTA, AIR MARSHAL AZIM
In July 1985 there was a radar and visual contact of a UFO in Zimbabwe. Air Marshal Azim Daudpota stated: 'This was no ordinary UFO. Scores of people saw it. It was no illusion, no deception, no imagination.'

Two jets were scrambled to intercept the UFO, which then accelerated away at considerable speed. No clear observation was made and no gun camera footage taken.

DAVIDSON, CAPTAIN WILLIAM
Captain William Davidson was apparently a representative of military intelligence who interviewed Kenneth **Arnold** following what is known as the **Maury Island** mystery.

DAVIS, EVAN

On 7 July 1947 patrolman Evan Davis was one of two witnesses at **Maury Island** in Washington State, USA, during the sighting known as the Maury Island incident. He witnessed three UFOs radiating sparks and making extraordinary manoeuvres.

DAVIS, KATHIE

The extraordinary multiple abduction of witness Kathie Davis (pseudonym) is the central theme of Budd Hopkins' book *Intruders – The Incredible Visitations at Copley Wood*. (See References and Background Material.)

According to Hopkins' analysis, Kathie Davis and other members of her family have been abducted on many occasions and appear to be part of a long-term genetic study and manipulation by alien entities.

There is the suggestion that Kathie Davis was abducted at approximately the age of six when skin, and possibly blood, was removed, leaving a scar on her leg to the present day. Then at the age of approximately eighteen she was abducted and apparently subjected to some form of penetration into her uterus and possibly artificially inseminated. Some months later there appears to have been another abduction where the unborn foetus was removed, and some eight years later a further abduction when she was shown nine babies and allowed to interact with them in a sort of bizarre 'mother bonding' arrangement.

Other incidents had occurred in the meantime where it appeared that Kathie's own human children were being subjected to abductions.

DAVIS, WILLIAM O.

Following the wave of sightings at Exeter, New Hampshire, in 1965 the Air Force Office of Scientific Research held a discussion on communication with extraterrestrials. Dr William O. Davis, a former Air Force physicist, suggested that the UFO occupants, out of concern for humans, would delay meeting directly and would use a period of time to acclimatise the human race to acceptance of their existence.

This suggestion is, of course, very significant in the debate as to why direct contact between extraterrestrials and aliens on an official basis appears to have been stalled over many years.

There have been many suggestions that the release of UFO-related material to UFO groups by governments has been part of an acclimatisation process. In that light, Davis' point could lead to speculation that the release is being authorised by governments and aliens working in collusion.

DAY, PETER

In January 1973 Peter Day was driving between Thame and Aylesbury when he saw an orange ball of light some three quarters of a mile away, at an estimated height of approximately 2,000 feet.

He was able to capture the sighting on film which remains today one of the most important pieces of film available to UFO researchers.

The object disappeared instantaneously and this can be seen from the frame by frame analysis of the film. Of particular interest is the fact that in the last frame of film, when the object disappears, all the nearby trees appear to be bending over sharply, suggesting some form of powerful, airborne explosion. However, recent photographic analysis has suggested that camera shake could have caused the image.

There were many independent witnesses from a nearby school, including children and staff. The fireball may have been the by-product of a crashing Air Force plane. The suggestion has been made that the aircraft may have dumped fuel during its last minutes of flight, which subsequently ignited. The Air Force may not have wanted to make this public given the potential damage that could have resulted. There was a plane crash that day but a detailed investigation suggests the plane crashed at least a quarter of an hour after the sighting, verifiable by the strict timetable at the school. There has also been a suggestion that Peter Day has captured **ball lightning** on film, for the first time.

DAY THE EARTH STOOD STILL, THE

Released in 1951 this was one of the first fictional films based on UFO experiences. Many of its basic images were drawn direct from UFO reports though it is important to note that there had been no reports of encounters with aliens by this time (**Adamski** was to make his claims in 1952). However, many of the images in the film have been mirrored in the accounts of subsequent abductees. In particular, the film's depiction of the inside of the flying saucer is identical to many reports received; including circular corridors around a central room which itself not only contains certain futuristic equipment but also a platform bed where, in the film, a medical operation is undertaken (in this case to resuscitate the 'dead' visitor from the stars).

The precise link between science fiction and UFO reports is a matter for some conjecture, although the link is without question a valid one and to this extent the film has significance.

DAYTON, OHIO (TWA SIGHTING)
In March 1950 a TWA pilot reported a UFO virtually directly over the Air Technical Intelligence Center at **Wright Patterson Air Force Base** and reported it to Dayton Municipal Airport. The Ohio Air National Guard scrambled F51 jet interceptors to pursue the object which was eventually lost in clouds at around 15,000 feet.

At Wright Patterson there was radar confirmation of the contact. The official explanation was that the sighting was of the planet Venus and that the radar return had been caused by an ice cloud.

DE BONISE, ALFRED
(See **Fort Meade**.)

DE NARDO, DENIS
Denis de Nardo and his wife were among the dozen or more residents of Belfast, Pennsylvania, who reported a flight of seven UFOs in V-formation on 23 March 1973, during a wave of sightings across the United States. The UFOs were apparently flying in formation throughout the sighting.

De Nardo was familiar with planes, having served in the Marine Corps. An official of Allentown-Bethlehem Airport stated that aircraft had been circling the field that evening (implying an explanation for the sighting) but de Nardo's wife commented that they saw the planes 'but these [the UFOs] weren't planes. Whenever the planes came close . . . they would zoom away.'

DE ROCHEFORT, COUNT NICOLAS
Count Nicolas de Rochefort became Vice Chairman of **NICAP** in 1956. It has been suggested that he represented an infiltration by the government as he had been a member of the **CIA**'s psychological warfare staff.

DEBUNKING
'Debunking' is the term applied to the absolute rejection of the UFO phenomenon, usually by government or official

bodies, but also by scientists as a body and by individuals. It is not a rejection based on critical analysis nor is it the result of healthy scepticism but seems to arise for a number of reasons.

Firstly, governments and official bodies seem to wish to debunk the subject of UFOs in order to cover up either their own ignorance or their own knowledge of the phenomenon. Documents released in America under the **Freedom of Information Act** show that while the **CIA** was debunking UFOs (i.e. stating that the subject was nonsense and not to be considered seriously), it was, in fact, undertaking intensive UFO research. It has further been suggested that debunking goes hand in hand with **disinformation** (i.e. feeding UFO investigators false data in order to make them seem increasingly foolish and thereby discredit them).

A second reason for debunking seems to be fear; some people insist that the UFO phenomenon is nonsense and non-existent because they do not wish to face up to the possibility.

Thirdly, science and scientists debunk UFOs out of a need to preserve the status quo. To be fair, most such debunking is a rejection of the extraterrestrial hypothesis, a standpoint which would be shared by many Ufologists, but equally many prominent scientists have rejected every aspect of the UFO phenomenon – usually without even a cursory examination of the evidence – thereby ignoring the claims and needs of many tens of thousands of people throughout the world and rejecting, en masse, a wealth of evidence deserving of proper scientific scrutiny.

It must fairly be said that many scientists who are also TV and media personalities appear to use debunking as their one way of becoming a media part of the subject – in effect, shouting from the highest hilltop that there is nothing to shout about!

DEFENCE SECRETARIAT 8 (DS8)
Known as Department DS8 of the Ministry of Defence this was one of two departments (along with **S4 (Air)**) to deal with UFO reports from the public.

DS8 was formed after the Ministry of Defence was created from the old Air Ministry and War Office.

A former head of DS8, Ralph **Noyes**, has become an active UFO researcher in recent years, a consultant to **BUFORA** and an important advocate of UFO research.

DEFENSE INTELLIGENCE AGENCY (DIA)
Set up in 1961, the Defense Intelligence Agency in America became something of a competitor to the **CIA**.

Although officially denying involvement in UFO research, the release of recent documents indicates that they have been involved in studies across the world. Their work would seem to be an analysis of the national defence implications only.

DELK, CONSTABLE CHARLIE
In October 1973 Constable Charlie Delk of Petal, Mississippi, reported chasing a UFO for some thirty miles in the hopes that it would land so that he could see if anyone got out.

The chase was interrupted when both his vehicle and police radio cut out, implying **vehicle interference** directed from the UFO, and a certain coyness on the part of its occupants.

DELPHOS RING, KANSAS
In November 1971, at Delphos, Kansas, a brightly coloured UFO was seen hovering over a farm field. Sheep in the field appeared very agitated. The witnesses saw the UFO disappear into the distance but noticed that there was a glowing grey-white circle under where the UFO had remained stationary. The farmer touched the soil and his fingers were numb for several days.

After-effects of the event were that the soil would not absorb water, and there seemed to be some other effect on plant growth. None appeared within the circle. The Delphos ring case was one of the best documented close encounters of the second kind on record, and won a *National Enquirer* award of $5,000 for that year's best report. There were some doubts about the case, based on the credibility of the witnesses, principally Durel and Ronald Johnson; researchers pointed to the fact that they seemed to enjoy the publicity they received, and stated they thought it strange that despite the implications of numb fingers after touching the ground traces, the witnesses went first not to a doctor but to a newspaper.

Subsequent cases have displayed similar features; one of the abductions of Kathie **Davis** left ground traces in the form of damaged plant growth and baked soil that were visible for many years afterwards.

DESERT CENTER, CALIFORNIA, USA
Desert Center, California, makes history in UFO lore as the first location of a widely reported contact between man and

extraterrestrial. On 20 November 1952 George **Adamski** apparently encountered his Venusian at this site.

DESVERGES, D. S.

In August 1952, near West Palm Beach, Scout Master D. S. Desverges and three scouts encountered a strange light in the woods when they were travelling towards home. The scouts remained in the car while Desverges investigated, carrying a machete and torch.

The scouts were alarmed when they saw a reddish light and a ball of fire shooting down from the height of the trees to where Desverges had been last seen. The scout master failed to return and one of the scouts telephoned the sheriff, from a nearby home.

As the sheriff arrived Desverges returned from the woods in a very shaken state. He recalled that he had reached a clearing and pointed his torch towards a metallic disc-shaped machine above him. The saucer had fired a shot at him, scorching his arms and burning his hat. When he recovered shortly afterwards, the saucer was gone. Desverges' arm was reddened and his hat was burned and the sheriff confirmed that he had located a scorched area in the clearing.

Some doubts were apparently raised when Desverges refused to give his story to reporters and held out for a sale to a magazine. However, while holding out for profit might count against a claimant, it cannot alone discount a claim, and there were other witnesses.

DETCHMENDY, CAPTAIN E. B.

In June 1947, just days before the **Roswell** crash, there were many sightings of UFOs in the general area, in New Mexico. On 27 June Captain E. B. Detchmendy witnessed a white glowing object passing over the White Sands missile range and reported it to his commanding officer.

DEWILDE, MARIUS

One of the most famous waves of UFO reports is the French sequence of 1954.

In September of that year Marius Dewilde at Quarouble was alerted by the howls of his dog outside during the late evening. Dewilde saw two entities close to the house, wearing what appeared to be diving gear. They were approximately three to four feet tall with large heads.

He attempted to grab the entities but was beaten away by a powerful light blasted from an object nearby. The beam paralysed him and by the time Dewilde could continue his assault the object had taken off and disappeared.

DI SALVATORE, ATTILO
In July 1978, near Mount Etna in Italy, Air Force Sergeant Attilo Di Salvatore, together with a colleague, Franco Padellero, navy officer Mauritzio Esposito and Antonino Di Pietro witnessed the landing of a red light near their group.

They drove to the scene and witnessed a saucer-shaped object approximately forty feet wide on the ground. It displayed an illuminated dome and a variety of blue and red lights.

The group reported six tall entities, described as human and beautiful. Two of the entities walked towards the group who found themselves paralysed although there was apparently no contact between them.

The witnesses did not see the UFO depart though they did witness it dim all its lights to disguise itself from a passing vehicle, a subterfuge not often reported.

DIAZ, CARLOS ALBERTO
In January 1975 Carlos Alberto Diaz was returning to his home at Bahia Blanca, Argentina, at four o'clock in the morning. He heard a strong humming noise, was paralysed by a ray of light and floated upwards, apparently into a UFO. (Note that the humming noise is very reminiscent of the claims of the **Gulf Breeze** witness, Ed **Walters**.) Inside the UFO he was approached by an entity wearing an overall suit who used a device to remove some hair from the witness.

Four hours later, he was found on the road by a motorist – 300 miles away from where he had been!

Diaz was able to show that he had indeed been in Bahia Blanca just a little earlier as he had a newspaper which had only just been published in that city. He admitted, 'I don't know if you will believe me. If someone were to tell me, I surely wouldn't.'

DICKERSON, POLICE OFFICER ROBERT
In September 1959 there were many reports of UFOs near Redmond, Oregon, the first of which was from Police Officer Robert Dickerson who was surveying the edge of the town at the time. He saw a glowing object drop from the sky which then

levelled out at approximately 200 feet, showing a clear disc shape. The object then passed Redmond Airport, and stopped again, hovering over the airfield.

Dickerson reported the UFO to the airfield and several federal aviation authority officials watched the disc for several minutes.

DICKISON, JOHN

Following the **Moigne Downs** incident in 1967 John Dickison was one of a team from the Royal Aircraft Establishment at Farnborough who interviewed the witness.

DISINFORMATION

Disinformation is the method used, particularly by security services and the military, to put false stories into either the public domain or the domain of enemy intelligence services, to take them off the correct track and on to a false one.

It is speculated that many government and military agencies over the past forty years, and perhaps particularly in America, have used disinformation techniques to discredit the subject of UFOs and flying saucers.

In particular, it has been suggested that the technique has been used with great subtlety, not starving UFO researchers of material but feeding ludicrous information to them to discredit the valid material. Unfortunately, there are many UFO researchers who accept every crackpot story without verification and to this extent make themselves a prime target for disinformation.

It must also be said that there is some evidence of very intricate disinformation being used, even to the point of allowing genuine, but nonetheless misleading, documents to be uncovered by researchers who have deliberately been given limited access to government files.

Whether this means that the governments are covering up their knowledge of UFOs or their ignorance of them is debatable, though the latter seems more probable.

DOBBS, W. C.

On 27 June 1947 W. C. Dobbs reported a white glowing UFO over Pope, New Mexico.

This would appear to be a corroboration of a sighting by Captain E. B. **Detchmendy** who reported a similar object just minutes later over the White Sands missile range.

DONAHOWER, MR AND MRS CLYDE O.
In March 1973 Mr and Mrs Clyde O. Donahower reported to the local authorities that they had watched an unidentified craft land on their farm at Robesonia, Pennsylvania. The vehicle remained stationary for some thirty minutes and the witnesses claimed that they could see entities moving within it.

The police were called but the craft had gone before they arrived.

DONATHAN, DEWAYNE
In October 1973 in Blackford County, Indiana, DeWayne Donathan had an extraordinary entity sighting.

Donathan and his wife were driving home in the early evening and encountered what appeared to be a tractor parked near the road. As they approached it they saw two silver-suited figures dancing as if to music. The Donathans drove past the pair, and looking back saw them standing beside the road. There was something unearthly about their movements and they appeared unable to leave the road where they were.

The Donathans turned around but found the silver-suited entities were gone. Up in the sky two separate bright lights were flickering in an 'up and down' motion.

What makes the sighting all the more extraordinary is that there was a virtually identical sighting some three hours apart approximately a mile away by witness Gary **Flatter**.

DONOVAN, MAJOR-GENERAL WILLIAM
Major-General William Donovan was the Head of the Office of Strategic Services shortly after World War II when it concluded that **'foo' fighters** were an unusual but natural phenomenon and probably not a secret German weapon.

DOUGLAS, EUGENIO
In October 1963, at Islaverda, Argentina, Eugenio Douglas encountered a bright light on the road ahead of him while driving through a heavy rainstorm. The light became so intense he had to slow down, but when he stopped the truck and got out the light was nowhere to be seen.

However, Douglas saw a disc-shaped craft approximately ten metres high from which three entities emerged. The entities were wearing helmets with antennae and were over twelve feet tall. From either the entities or the disc a red beam hit Douglas, burning him; he fired back at the entities with a gun and then ran away. However, the red beam followed him into the village of Montemaiz where it apparently affected street lighting.

Douglas ran to a nearby house. The people within reported that at the same time their own lighting was being interfered with and they smelt a strong odour which Douglas himself also noted.

Douglas had apparently been burned by some form of radiation; the marks on his face and hands were evident. Villagers went to the site of the encounter and found large footprints some twenty inches long.

DOWDING, AIR CHIEF MARSHAL LORD HUGH

Air Chief Marshal Lord Dowding was commanding officer of the Royal Air Force during the Second World War. In August 1954 he issued the statements: 'Of course the flying saucers are real – and they are interplanetary' and 'The cumulative evidence for the existence of UFOs is quite overwhelming and I accept the fact of their existence.'

DOWSING

Dowsing is a method of searching for hidden energies in the earth. It is commonly used to locate hidden water courses but can also be used to discover hidden lines of energy. Such lines include the famous ley lines (see **Leys**) humorously referred to as 'flying saucer runways'.

Recent projects correlating ancient sites of apparent mystical importance to sites of UFO encounters often use dowsing to show the connections.

In Sweden, investigator Arne **Groth** has used dowsing for many years and in one case has thoroughly dowsed the site of a corroborated abduction report, revealing considerable concentration of energy lines around the location of the event (also a site peppered with ancient runic symbols). His work shows that the abduction took place precisely on the junction of major energy lines.

DRAKENSBERG MOUNTAINS, SOUTH AFRICA

In the spring of 1951 a witness (name withheld) was driving up to the Drakensberg mountains in South Africa late one night when he was hailed by a man claiming he needed some water. The man was under five feet tall with a domed, bald head and spoke in a strange accent.

Water was obtained from a nearby stream and the witness

returned the man to the same spot where he now saw a disc-shaped craft hidden. The witness was invited inside and shown one of the 'alien's' colleagues who required the water because he had burned himself. When asked where they came from, the entity apparently pointed at the sky and said, 'From there!'

DREAM DEPRIVATION

Dream deprivation occurs when a subject, even though able to sleep, apparently does not dream. Research – including rapid eye movement observation – shows that some people appear to suffer from this at certain times and the effects are mental stress, exaggerated anxiety and waking hallucinations.

It is suggested that this condition could either be the cause of some UFO abduction reports or the condition which makes one particular person susceptible to a real external event where another would not be. The difficulty in deciding which is the case for any given report lies in the fact that some 'contact' reports are extraordinary in nature and not unlike hallucinations, particularly since they usually cannot be checked out for evidence.

DREAMS AND UFOS

There is much speculation regarding the connection between dream imagery and UFO reports. At one end of the speculation there are various people who believe that UFO abductions and close, more exotic, sightings are in fact no more than dreams themselves. To this end people turn to the so-called 'waking dream' where the person lapses momentarily during a waking period into a dream state.

There is also the importance of the heightened suggestibility of a person near the sleep state, i.e. hypnogogic state (the state between fully awake and fully asleep) and hypnopompic (the state between fully asleep and fully awake). In these states studies show that hallucination is a natural concomitant.

The 'middle range' viewpoint on the connection between dreams and UFO reports is that a genuine event can be overlaid by exotic imagery in the above states, heightening belief or creating unreal aspects to the event. Disproving these unreal aspects may discredit the report, whereas in fact there may still be some credibility to certain aspects if it can be determined which to reject as hallucinatory.

At the far end of the spectrum there is the belief that

UFO-related dreams are not dreams at all but are memories of actual events or the receiving of messages from extraterrestrials, creating the illusion of physical contact while at the same time being a contact by communication.

DRURY, TOM
In August 1953 Tom Drury, then Deputy Director of Civil Aviation in New Guinea, filmed a UFO over Port Moresby. Drury estimated the UFO to be travelling at five times the speed of sound.

DUBOSE, COLONEL THOMAS JEFFERSON
Colonel Thomas Jefferson DuBose was a former adjutant to Brigadier General Roger M. **Ramey** at the time of the **Roswell** incident.

   DuBose confirmed that there had been orders to 'ship the material from Roswell directly to Wright Field by special plane'. It appears that he was confirming that the weather balloon story used to cover recovery of Roswell debris was a fabrication designed to meet press interest. Ramey and DuBose posed together with the apparently substituted material in a widely publicised photograph.

DUGINOV, V. I.
V. I. Duginov was director of the Soviet Katrson Hydro-meteorological School and in 1966 witnessed a disc-shaped UFO, as did forty-five other witnesses.

DURANT, FREDERICK C.
Durant was one of the associate members of the **Robertson Panel**. He was a specialist in missiles and rockets.

E

EAGLE RIVER, WISCONSIN
(See **Simonton, Joe**.)

EARLY WARNING SYSTEM
The Early Warning System is the defence boundary which warns a country of any incoming attacks to its national borders. It has been held that one reason for wishing to understand the true nature of UFOs is that whatever they are they could trigger a response to the Early Warning System and – at the one extreme end of the hypothesis – cause an accidental commencement of the Third World War.

The obvious true concern over such a scenario may well be one reason why there are official documents issued by military and government sources to 'official' personnel on the subject of UFOs. This perhaps makes more sense than having to believe that governments and military bodies have secret knowledge of what UFOs really are.

EARTHLIGHTS
Several investigators, and predominantly Paul Devereux in the United Kingdom, have made the link between tectonic, geophysical activity and anomalous sightings, suggesting strongly that at least some UFOs are the by-product of natural energies released from inside the Earth. Such analysis charts the association of reported UFOs with earthquake activity and other periods of tectonic strain.

Experiments conducted in the 1980s have suggested that if certain types of rocks are brought under extreme pressure this can result in complex patterns of light emission, though the precise mechanism is not yet understood.

There are also suggestions that the energies may be capable of affecting the electrical patterns of the human brain, creating hallucinations which may account for the more exotic UFO sightings. Such effects may also be responsible for electrical interference in cars, etc. quite commonly reported in connection with UFO encounters.

It would, however, be naïve to believe that earthlights could account for all UFO activity, particularly since people would not have the same hallucinations, but clearly it might represent a significant factor.

EDWARDS, C. P.

In December 1950, Commander C. P. Edwards, Deputy Minister of Transport for Air Services, started Project **Magnet**, an official Canadian government investigation thought to be looking into the origins of UFOs. It has also been suggested that it is examining magnetic anomaly reports in the **Bermuda Triangle**.

EDWARDS, D. M.

In addition to Project **Magnet** the Canadian government also investigated UFOs under the title Project **Second Storey**. Group Captain D. M. Edwards was a prominent member of the project.

EDWARDS, LIEUTENANT-COLONEL GEORGE

Lieutenant-Colonel George Edwards USAF (Retd) is a scientist listed as having been involved in the production of man-made flying saucers such as the **AVRO** vehicles.

Edwards is quoted as having said, 'We know that the AF was secretly test-flying a real alien spacecraft. The VZ-9 was to be a cover so the Pentagon would have an explanation whenever people reported seeing a saucer in flight.'

EDWARDS, KEN

In March 1978, Ken Edwards, of Warrington in Cheshire, UK, had an entity encounter although no UFO was reported.

The entity crossed the road in front of his van, beamed rays at him making him dizzy, stopping his watch and burning out equipment on the vehicle, before dematerialising through the wall of a nearby atomic energy research centre.

The similarities between this and UFO entity reports is clear, but also demonstrates the interface between various entity reports.

EDWIN

Edwin is the name of a contactee who corresponds frequently with a space being, Valdar. Originally they met when Valdar was the foreman of a factory where Edwin worked – Valdar was then known as George – and they would go fishing together. Valdar apparently confessed his alien background to Edwin and shortly after that returned to his home planet, Edwin having watched him leave by flying saucer from Richards Bay, Natal, South Africa.

Valdar still sends messages to Edwin by radio telling us to improve our ways and warning us of the impending destruction of the Earth if we do not do so.

Top African researcher Cynthia Hind has listened in to one of the messages being received and appears to have been impressed; although remaining non-committal, she points out that we cannot just laugh off such claims – they deserve full study.

EEDLE, ARTHUR
Physicist and astronomer Arthur Eedle has been quoted as saying, 'The basic purpose behind all UFO phenomena today is to prepare for the coming of the Anti-Christ, and the setting up of world domination under the Devil.'

EICKHOFF, THOMAS
In 1954 Thomas Eickhoff attempted to prove or disprove the claims of contactee George **Adamski** by bringing him to court. Adamski had claimed he had made trips into space which had been witnessed by two scientists. Eickhoff believed he would be unable to produce them and he could therefore be prosecuted by the government for fraud.

The government seemed reluctant to press the point on the basis that they were not going to court on the contents of a book, though it is said that the **CIA** would, if necessary, have prevented testimony in court concerning Adamski's claims because 'maximum security exists concerning the subject of UFOs'.

EISENHOWER, PRESIDENT DWIGHT
During his early years as President, Dwight Eisenhower apparently showed interest in the recovery of crashed saucers. It is held that he was alarmed to discover that even though he was President, and indeed a former Army General, he did not have the necessary security clearances to be given access to such information.

There is, however, a suggestion that Eisenhower eventually

obtained such clearance. Having managed to leave his own entourage and press corps for a day, it is held that he visited the Edwards Air Force Base to examine crashed discs and recovered alien cadavers.

Needless to say conclusive verification of this is not available though witness testimony holds it to be true. There does seem to have been some official concern over where the President was for a twenty-four hour period though the official story was that Ike had gone to the dentist, having knocked the cap off a tooth.

ELECTRO-MAGNETIC EFFECT (EM)
Many close encounter reports of UFOs indicate considerable electro-magnetic effects on electrical apparatus. The most common of these is the effects on cars when 'buzzed' by UFOs, often stalling, and restarting only after the UFO has left the area.

Another very common effect is on television sets in areas where UFOs are reported. In the **Vallentuna** wave in Sweden, for example, there were many corroborative reports of television interference during a period of intense UFO activity.

It is a curious fact that although many cars are stalled by passing UFOs, it apparently rarely happens to aeroplanes, indeed the only significant cases in the very many UFO/aircraft encounters reported over the years occur in Asia. No explanation is offered as to why this should be.

It has been suggested that the electro-magnetic effect is not so much likely to be a directed deliberate attack by the UFO but rather some kind of manifestation of its energy sources. If the UFO is in fact natural then it may be some unknown natural high-intensity phenomenon which we have yet to understand. If the UFOs are in fact extraterrestrial spacecraft, then it may be some kind of backwash from their power system.

EMARD, FRED
In April 1959 an Air Force C-118 transport plane taking off from McCord Air Force Base in Washington hit an object in flight. The pilot radioed back, 'We have hit something – or something has hit us', and the pilot stated he would attempt to return to the Air Force Base. However, he failed, and the plane crashed, killing himself and his three-man crew.

Chief of Police Fred Emard at Orting, Washington, confirmed UFO reports of glowing objects following the plane shortly before the incident, suggesting a relationship between the sightings and the eventual fate of the aircraft.

ENGLUND, LIEUTENANT BRUCE

Along with Sergeant Adrian **Bustinza**, Lieutenant Bruce Englund was one of the witnesses to the events at **Rendlesham Forest**.

A tape-recording apparently made by Colonel **Halt** while investigating the UFO event includes the voice of Lieutenant Englund among others. It must be said that the authenticity of the tape has been called into question.

EPOSITO, MAURITZIO
(See **Di Salvatore, Attilo**.)

ESTIMATE OF THE SITUATION: 1948 'TOP SECRET' REPORT ON UFOS

It is held that in August 1948 the Air Technical Intelligence Center at **Wright Patterson Air Force Base** published a 'top secret' classified document stating that in their estimation UFOs were interplanetary. It is believed that it was suppressed by the Air Force as it did not want that particular viewpoint disseminated.

ET – THE EXTRATERRESTRIAL

While some films, such as *Close Encounters of the Third Kind*, can be shown to be directly drawn from UFO reports there have been a number of films such as *ET – The Extraterrestrial* which are inspired by the UFO phenomenon but not drawn directly from specific cases. It is interesting to note that in the wake of the publicity for films such as *Close Encounters of the Third Kind*, which purport to be 'real' or depicting real events, UFO researchers often receive a number of similar, even 'copycat', reports. However, there were no such reports following the release of *ET*, presumably because the material was not presented as 'real' and was in fact an emotional story of childhood friendship, albeit with an extraterrestrial.

This serves to show that at least a part of the UFO phenomenon is a reaction to social events at any given time.

ETH
(See **Extraterrestrial Hypothesis**.)

ETTENSON, COLONEL B. M.

When doubts were raised as to the impartiality of the **Condon Committee** investigation it was Colonel B. M. Ettenson who issued the reply from the Air Force Secretary's office stating, 'The Air Force awarded the UFO contract convinced that an impartial, open-minded, independent and objective scientific report would be forthcoming and we expect Dr **Condon** will fulfil the terms of the agreement.'

Subsequent analysis of the **Condon Report** suggests that it may have failed in some ways to live up to Colonel Ettenson's beliefs.

EUSTAGIO, FERNANDO

In August 1963 Fernando Eustagio, his brother and a neighbour were getting water from their well in the garden when they saw a globe hovering above the trees near them. They apparently could see rows of people inside the globe and light rays beaming downwards.

Apparently a very thin, very tall being glided down the light beams into the garden and sat down. The entity had one eye in his forehead and carried a flashing box on his body. Apparently the entity attempted to abduct one of the boys and paralysed Fernando Eustagio when he tried to intervene.

At the end of the encounter the boys felt that in fact the entity had not wished to harm them, and believed that he would return again to them.

EVANS-WENTZ, WALTER

Walter Evans-Wentz wrote *The Fairy Faith in Celtic Countries* (see References and Background Material). In his study he relates many tales of interaction between humans and fairy folk, and many UFO researchers have drawn close parallels between these stories and accounts of modern day UFO encounters – particularly abductions. Probably no one book on the subject is as thought-provoking in this comparison.

EXETER 'FLAP'

During the mid-1960s there was a considerable number of reports of UFOs from the area of Exeter, New Hampshire. The reports were generally of lights in the sky and distant sightings and were probably not as significant as earlier or later UFO flaps in America or other places.

The reason the Exeter 'flap' gained such prominence is that it received the attention of a prominent investigative reporter who published a detailed account of the sightings. This is yet another example of the media's power in directing public attention to this subject.

One American UFO investigator believes that all or most of the UFOs were balls of fire hovering on or near high-tension power lines.

EXTRATERRESTRIAL HYPOTHESIS (ETH)

The 'extraterrestrial hypothesis' is the very popular theory that UFOs are the product of an extraterrestrial visitation or intervention. In other words, aliens are visiting the planet Earth. There are of course many hypotheses devised to explain UFOs and abductions but the ETH is so popular that both the expression 'extraterrestrial hypothesis' and 'ETH' have become 'buzz words' in UFO literature.

EZEKIEL

One of the most often quoted biblical accounts held to be of a UFO is that of the prophet Ezekiel. The incident took place in the land of the Chaldeans by the river Chebar: 'Now it came to pass in the thirtieth year, in the fourth month, in the fifth day of the month, as I was among the captives by the river of Chebar, that the heavens were opened . . .

'And I looked and behold a whirlwind came out of the north, a great cloud and a fire unfolding itself, and a brightness were about it, and out of the midst thereof as the colour of amber, out of the midst of the fire. Also out of the midst thereof came the likeness of four living creatures. And this was their appearance; they had the likeness of a man. And everyone had four faces, and everyone had four wings. And their feet were straight feet; and the sole of their feet was like the sole of a calf's foot; and they sparkled like the colour of burnished brass.

'Now as I beheld the living creatures, behold one wheel upon the Earth by the living creatures, with his four faces. The appearance of the wheels and their work was like unto the colour of a beryl; and they four had one likeness; and their appearance and their work were as it were a wheel in the middle of a wheel. When they went they went upon their four sides; and they turned not as they went. As for their rings, they were so high that they were dreadful; and their rings were full of eyes round about them four. And when the living creatures went, the wheels went by them; and when the living creatures were lifted up from the Earth, the wheels were lifted up.'

It is held by many that Ezekiel was describing the arrival and departure of a flying saucer and entities within. In common with many contactees he also appears to have received a warning that Earth dwellers should mend their ways and create a more peace-loving, compassionate civilisation.

EZEIZA INTERNATIONAL AIRPORT
On 22 December 1962 a UFO landed on the runway at Ezeiza International Airport in Buenos Aires. A DC-8 jet was just approaching, and was forced to abort the landing and fly back up into a holding pattern. The UFO remained on the ground for a few minutes, but when it seemed that it was going to be ignored, it slowly lifted off. The pilots of the DC-8 were surprised at the lack of response from the airport staff.

Six months before a similar event had occurred at Camba Punta airport in Argentina, witnessed by the airport director Luis **Harvey**.

F

FACCHINI, BRUNO
(See **Abbiate Buazzone**.)

FAHRNEY, REAR-ADMIRAL DELMAR
Rear-Admiral Delmar Fahrney, a former US Navy missile chief, is quoted as saying, 'Reliable reports indicate there are objects coming into our atmosphere at very high speeds and controlled by thinking intelligences.'

FAIRIES AND FOLKLORE ENTITIES
There has been much speculation on the comparison between abduction reports and the reports of fairy and other entities in Celtic lore. Probably the most provocative book on this subject is *The Fairy Faith in Celtic Countries* by Walter **Evans-Wentz** (see References and Background Material).

In particular there are the reports of abduction into fairy circles, which contain elements of **missing time**, strange foods, etc., all of which have similarly appeared in UFO abduction reports.

One suggested reason for this similarity is that a single event is being described by the language of the time and that therefore the entities may be extraterrestrials described as fairies in the past or indeed may be fairies being described as extraterrestrials in the present. Alternatively, the experiences may be different forms of interpretation of a single stimulus, as yet not understood by science.

A further alternate suggestion is that the UFO phenomenon is a modern extension to an existing mythology.

Whatever the answer, there is evidence that UFO stories across the world mirror, to some extent, the legends of that location; Europe and Scandinavia have many folk-legends of 'little people' and aliens reported are often dwarf-like, whereas in the Soviet Union, for example, there are many legends of giants, and many giant aliens reported. This comparison should not be stretched too far, but must have some relevance.

FALCONBRIDGE
In November 1975 there was a radar-visual encounter with a UFO at the Canadian radar station at Falconbridge, Ontario. Studied through binoculars the object appeared to be approximately 100 feet in diameter, spherical and displaying rings (perhaps portholes?) around its rim.

F106 jets from the United States Air Force National Guard Squadron were scrambled but there was no contact reported with the UFO.

FALLING LEAF MOTION
There are many reports of UFOs swinging from side to side, particularly when descending, seeming almost without weight. It has been speculated that the objects may actually be weightless though critics at this point have suggested that weightlessness in reasonably dense air would produce a more erratic motion.

A further suggestion with regard to this widely reported observation is that the UFO is not weightless but that its shape is such that it constantly seeks a position of equilibrium between the point of maximum drag and the point of maximum weight. To achieve this the object would normally need thin trailing edges and a heavy centre section, certainly the case in many reports of UFO design.

A sinking ship exhibits 'falling leaf motion' as it seeks equilibrium in the water, vacillating between its streamlined bows pulling it forwards and its bulk of weight at the stern pulling it backwards.

UFOs have been photographed exhibiting 'falling leaf motion' when *ascending*.

FALLOWS, ALAN
In August 1975 Alan Fallows was driving towards the village of Mossley in West Yorkshire when he was surrounded by a thick hill mist. He noticed a bright light to the side of his van and saw that it was a huge egg-shaped glowing white object, drifting across his field of view. There was some evidence of **paralysis** and **missing time**, and when he fully came to himself, he found he was clutching a screw driver as if to defend himself though he does not recall picking it up.

The witness did not encourage further investigation, possibly due to a local press report suggesting the object was an illusion caused by the mist.

These various factors suggest an abduction, but clearly this cannot be explored further if the witness feels unwilling to cooperate, for whatever reason.

FARLOW, KARL
In November 1967, near Avon, Hampshire, Karl Farlow encountered a glowing egg-shaped UFO which cut out the lights of his diesel truck. The UFO moved across the road slowly, then picked up speed and disappeared. The witness reported both sounds and a smell like burning wood.

Although a comparatively mundane encounter in UFO terms, Farlow reported that it was 'like nothing on Earth . . . I sat in the cab petrified.'

The sighting was corroborated by the driver of a Jaguar car which was stalled nearby; together the witnesses called the police, who arrived quickly.

Investigation indicated the road surface might have melted in the area of the encounter and the following day it was reported that there was a group of investigators on site with instruments, and building workers repairing the road.

FARMINGDALE AGRICULTURAL COLLEGE
In August 1967 there were many reports of flying saucers and power failures in the area around Farmingdale Agricultural College, near New York City.

What made this particular set of reports notable was that several pigs had reportedly vanished from their pens at the college, although enclosed by high fences.

Researchers have many cases of what are generally referred to as **cattle mutilations** but which are not completely restricted to cattle – this may have been a related case. There is also the suggestion that these mutilations are a form of genetic study; one zoologist reminded me that the pig has many similarities to man, and is often used to test products to be used on humans.

FARNSWORTH, ROBERT L.
Robert L. Farnsworth was President of the US Rocket Society in the 1940s and protested against the Air Force order that if saucers refused commands to land and identify themselves, pilots were to open fire on them. Farnsworth's statement, given to United Press and copies to the White House, read: 'I

respectfully suggest that no offensive action be taken against the objects . . . should they be extraterrestrial such action might result in the gravest consequences.'

This Air Force order received considerable criticism at the time; one cartoon of the day depicted two Air Force generals hunched over a radar screen full of UFOs, and one saying: 'Why don't we shoot one down, and see if they're friendly?'

FATIMA, PORTUGAL
In May 1917, at Fatima in Portugal, there was a celebrated vision of the Virgin Mary.

In fact the apparitions were much more complex than the simple apparition of one vision and included many aspects common to UFO reports. In particular, the descriptions offered by witnesses include that of luminous spheres, the much reported **'falling leaf motion'** of descending lights, and the apparition of a disc-shaped object. Witnesses also reported heatwaves, falls of **angel hair**, and many sights and sounds often associated with UFO reports. There were also claims of prophecy by some of the witnesses.

FEDERAL BUREAU OF INVESTIGATION (FBI)
The FBI is one American official body which can be demonstrated to have lied about its involvement in the UFO phenomenon, an accusation that can be levelled at many agencies in that country. In 1973 the Director of the FBI stated that: 'The investigation of UFOs is not and never has been a matter which is within the investigative jurisdiction of the FBI.'

In 1966 investigator Dr Bruce Maccabee obtained approximately 1,100 pages of documentation on the subject from them, released under the **Freedom of Information Act**. A recent FBI document indicates that UFOs are 'considered top secret by intelligence officers of both the Army and the Air Force'.

FERREIRA, ANTONIO
In January 1975 Antonio Ferreira, of Sao Luis, Brazil, appears to have had a strange abduction encounter with extraterrestrial roughnecks.

First a UFO apparently hit the wall of his house and then came back and fired a beam of light, hitting Ferreira. He was dragged aboard the UFO by short, dark-haired, dark-skinned aliens and interrogated by one of them about Earth, cars and food. The interrogation seems to have been less than subtle with one alien punching Ferreira in the chest if he was not happy with the answers he got.

Ferreira made a deal, exchanging flying saucer trips to other planets for supplying the aliens with subjects for vivisection. The aliens accepted various animals for this purpose and rewarded Ferreira with objects including a gun that can destroy anything in its path, but which Ferreira appears to have misplaced.

On one trip an alien was apparently turned into a double of Ferreira, sent to Earth and successfully fooled his father.

FERREIRA, JOSÉ LEMOS

In September 1957 Captain José Lemos Ferreira, along with Sergeants Alberto Gomes Covas, Salvador Alberto Oliveira and Manuel Marcelino, was on a routine flight from Ota Air Base, Portugal.

Ferreira relates that during the flight he noticed a very bright star with a coloured centre, to the left of the aircraft. It was also noted by other pilots of the flight. The centre of the star 'hazed' from green to red. Several times the object expanded and contracted. Apparently towards the end of the flight the object suddenly dived and then accelerated towards the flight, causing it to break its formation.

The sighting had lasted over half an hour and the pilots were not of a mind to accept conventional explanations for their event. 'We have got no conclusions,' they said, 'except that after this do not give us the old routine of Venus, balloons, aircraft and the like which has been given as a general panacea for almost every case of UFOs.'

FIELD, ETHEL MAY

In September 1977, Ethel May Field of Poole, Dorset, was in her garden when she saw a grey saucer shape hovering overhead. She saw two entities in silver suits watching her from a dome inside the saucer and at one point they fired a blue beam at her. (The blue beam is reminiscent of many such reports across the world; see, for example, **Gulf Breeze**.)

When she ran indoors, the UFO disappeared. The hands she had put up to protect herself from the blue beam turned red and were sore for a considerable time.

FIGUERAS, SPAIN

In the early evening of a day in October 1958, Señor Angelu was riding his motorbike near Figueras in Spain and saw what he thought was a crashed aircraft in a nearby wood.

Concerned, he went towards the site to give assistance but found there a landed flying saucer. It was standing on landing legs, had a transparent dome, and was approximately twenty-five feet wide.

Nearby were two dwarf-like creatures with large domed heads collecting samples. Inside the dome was a third figure. The witness watched unobserved for some fifteen minutes until the entities boarded the ship which took off.

FINLETTER, SECRETARY THOMAS K.
On 8 May 1952 Air Force Secretary Thomas Finletter was briefed by Air Technical Intelligence officers regarding UFOs and it was left to Finletter to make a public statement. This he did on 4 June: 'No concrete evidence has yet reached us either to prove or disprove the existence of the so-called flying saucers. There remain, however, a number of sightings that the Air Force investigators have been unable to explain. As long as this is true the Air Force will continue to study flying saucer reports.'

FIREBALLS
One of the most common and mundane solutions to UFO sightings is that they are fireballs. These are generally larger meteors burning up as they pass through the sky, usually moving virtually horizontally.

There are, however, some 'fireball' UFOs which require a good deal more explanation and in particular the case of Peter **Day**'s film.

There is also a particular phenomenon of green fireballs which appears most common around large electrical output installations and which certainly gives rise to some UFO reports.

Green fireballs came to the public's attention in the 1940s when Dr Lincoln la Paz made a special study of them, rejecting the hypothesis that they were 'normal' meteors. Project **Twinkle** was set up to try to capture this phenomenon on film, but due to lack of funding and manning it totally failed.

FISH, MARJORIE
During the hypnotic recall of the encounter by Betty and Barney **Hill**, Betty recalled seeing a three-dimensional 'star map' presented for her study by one of the aliens. She had

drawn a version of the map from memory following the encounter. In 1969 Ohio school teacher Marjorie Fish used Betty's drawing as the basis for her own three-dimensional star map in an attempt to pinpoint the home planet of the aliens who had contacted the Hills. Certain assumptions were made regarding the correctly applicable stars, seeking out those likely to be able to support intelligent life.

If the three-dimensional model is correct, and it has been replicated on computer by an astronomy professor, Walter Mitchell, then the home world of the aliens who abducted Betty Hill is thought to be around the stars Zeta Reticuli 1 and 2. Many American Ufologists have firmly stated that they believe this to be the solution to the mystery of the Hill event and that it is confirmation that UFOs are extraterrestrial and originate at that star.

One of the world's most authoritative researchers into UFOs, Dr Jacques Vallée, has made several important points regarding the likely validity of the map. He questions whether or not different viewpoints in space would produce different correct matches for the apparent position of the stars recalled, and also what the effect would be if the star map was not drawn to scale, which clearly it was not. Vallée also points out that a star map on a spacecraft is obsolete even by our own standards of technology and if real 'must have been placed there for Betty Hill to see, not for the pilot to use'. If the map was real then Vallée suggests it may have been used for a different purpose, i.e. to divert Betty Hill's attention, to reinforce her belief that the visitors were alien, or some other purpose.

It has also been pointed out that the finding of a perfect match for the drawing Betty Hill made is in itself remarkably unlikely considering that she was drawing, under hypnosis, an object she had seen for a short period of time, at a time of some confusion and possible stress, years after the event.

The probability of being able to match a random pattern of roads with the only information being 'that they represent some pattern of roads somewhere on the planet Earth' under those conditions seems highly unlikely, and yet the size of space compared to the size of Earth obviously gives rise to infinitely more variation.

Real or otherwise it appears that the star map is unlikely to provide us with any detailed information on our extraterrestrial visitors.

FISHER, JIMMY
(See **Avery Estates, Louisiana**.)

FISHER, MAJOR-GENERAL W. P.
Major-General Fisher, the Director of Legislative Liaison for the Air Force, resisted attempts throughout the early 1960s to instigate official hearings on the subject of UFOs. He stated: 'Hearings would only benefit the sensation seekers and publishers of science fiction.'

FLATTER, GARY
Gary Flatter had an extraordinary entity encounter in October 1973 at Blackford County, Indiana.

He was a second witness to the entity encounter of Mr and Mrs **Donathan**. Like them he watched a pair of entities dancing in the roadway and turned his spotlight on them. When the light hit them they kicked their feet and lifted off the ground, just drifting away.

FLORENCE, KRISTINA
Kristina Florence reported that as a young girl she had discovered a hatred of ants' eggs and would search out and destroy ant hills. During hypnosis sessions, it appears Miss Florence compared the shiny skins of the ants' eggs to the skins of entities which had abducted her.

This is one of many examples where investigators have uncovered UFO abductions although there is no apparent UFO or abduction memory as source trigger for the investigation.

FLORES, LORENZO
In December 1954, in Venezuela, Lorenzo Flores and his companion Jesus Gomez encountered a disc-shaped object landing nearby. They were assailed by four dwarf entities apparently trying to drag them aboard. A fight ensued and in one instance Lorenzo hit one of the entities with a rifle, breaking it. He said later, 'It felt like I hit a rock.' When the two men were examined by police they were apparently covered in scratches.

FLYING ELEPHANT
Not all apparently exotic sightings of UFOs remain unexplained. In April 1979 there was a report of an orange flying

elephant seen by many passengers from the windows of an aircraft. Even the most uncritical UFO researchers might have thought that this was one case that belonged at the hallucination end of the spectrum but in fact investigation proved that the object was indeed a huge orange-coloured elephant balloon. It had been used to publicise a circus, had broken loose and was flying at 36,000 feet!

FLYING SAUCER, ORIGIN OF TERM
When Kenneth **Arnold** in June 1947 saw a formation of objects in the Cascade Mountains of Washington State, USA, he described them as moving 'like a saucer would if you skipped it across water'. A local reporter picked up on this phrase and coined the term 'flying saucer'.

It was a term which immediately attracted **media** interest and is probably the facet of the phenomenon most responsible for attracting public attention. It was just the right phrase for the mood of the moment; one of the most enduring advertising slogans in the world. Despite doubts about the product, it is still being 'bought' some forty years later.

BUFORA Vice-President Lionel Beer, at the Twenty-fifth Anniversary Meeting of the British UFO Research Association, made the humorous point that had Arnold's sightings been of elongated green objects and he had coined the phrase 'flying cucumber' the whole phenomenon may have taken much longer to come to the public's attention!

Although certainly correctly credited with attracting media attention to the term 'flying saucer', the Arnold sighting was not in fact the first time that the word 'saucer' had been used in connection with UFOs; it was the term used by a Texas farmer to describe an object seen over his farm in January 1878.

FLYING SAUCER REVIEW (FSR)
Flying Saucer Review was one of the first British magazines devoted to the UFO phenomenon and rightly deserved its considerable prominence in the 1960s and 1970s.

It did a great deal to promote the development of Ufology, focusing serious attention on those aspects hitherto considered 'untouchable'. For example, for many years it was acceptable to countenance the existence of flying saucers but not of alien pilots – *FSR* brought these claims 'into the open'.

The magazine also brought together many stories from other

countries, and as such was the first truly international UFO magazine.

FLYNN, JAMES W.

In March 1965 James W. Flynn was camping in the Everglades. After midnight he saw an object descending approximately a mile away; he believed it to be a plane in trouble. With this in mind he drove his swamp buggy towards the light – which remained visible through the trees – stopping approximately a quarter of a mile from the object and walking on foot the rest of the way. The vegetation prevented a closer approach in his vehicle.

When he got closer, he saw the object to be a large cone-shaped structure hovering near the ground; it was some 75 feet wide and 25 feet high. He observed rows of windows with light shining through them.

As he approached the object a beam of light struck him in the forehead, knocking him unconscious and temporarily leaving him partially blinded. The UFO then disappeared, leaving burned trees and other vegetation where it had been. Flynn's doctor also found impairment of muscle and tendon reflexes which he believed could not have been faked, and the **NICAP** investigation concluded that the account of the event was supported by the physical evidence.

FOGLE, LIEUTENANT EARL

In December 1952 an Air Force pilot given the name Lieutenant Earl Fogle (pseudonym) reported a blue UFO which deliberately raced head on to his F51 fighter but at the last minute flipped to one side and made off at speed. Fogle watched the object apparently dive back towards him, then circle Laredo Air Force Base before disappearing.

FONTENAY-TORCY, FRANCE

In October 1954, during the French UFO wave of that year, a couple in Fontenay-Torcy saw a cigar-shaped UFO. It dived towards them and landed nearby in some bushes. The witnesses were, shortly afterwards, confronted by an entity some three feet tall, wearing a helmet, and whose eyes glowed bright orange. There were many corroborative reports from the locality of the craft in flight.

1954 saw a wave of sightings across France, and perhaps the highest concentration of entity sightings then or since.

'FOO' FIGHTERS

During the Second World War British and American pilots reported tiny white balls of light pacing their aircraft. These became known as 'foo' fighters. It was thought at the time that they were secret German weapons but following the end of the war it was shown that the Germans had also been reporting the same sightings and indeed had believed them to be secret Allied weapons. Generally speaking they were observed around the outside of aircraft but on some occasions were noted to have entered and moved slowly inside the fuselage. A similar account of this phenomenon was noted in March 1963 on an Eastern Airlines plane flying from New York to Washington.

It has been speculated that the 'ball of light' 'foo' fighters might have been either **ball lightning** or some other form of plasma energy but no definitive conclusion has been drawn. The fact that UFOs, even balls of light, interacting with modern planes do not so frequently exhibit the same characteristics as the 'foo' fighters of the early 1940s (notwithstanding the Eastern Airlines case mentioned above) may indicate that the phenomenon was in some way related to the characteristics of the 1940s aircraft or their particular activities.

There were some reports of 'foo' fighters from the Pacific air arena at the end of the Second World War.

FORD, PRESIDENT GERALD

It was Congressman Gerald Ford, later President of the United States, whose pressure for congressional hearings on the subject of UFOs partly led to the setting up of the **Condon Commission**.

He stated, 'I think we owe it to the public to establish credibility regarding UFOs, and to produce the greatest possible enlightenment on the subject.'

FORD, HENRY, II

In April 1968 Henry Ford II, aboard a jet star belonging to his company, and in the presence of several of his executives, was flying at 35,000 feet near Austin, Texas. The pilot sighted a huge UFO overhead and noticed that it seemed to be pacing their plane. The speed of the object, approximately 600 miles per hour, ruled out the likelihood of its being a balloon; in any case, the witnesses estimated the object to be twice the size of a DC-8. It was seen by all the passengers.

FORRESTAL, SECRETARY JAMES V.

James V. Forrestal is reported to have been a member of the **Majestic 12** panel formed to investigate UFOs in the 1940s. Before becoming Secretary of Defense in 1947 he had been Secretary of the Navy. In 1949 he had a mental breakdown and committed suicide at the Bethesda Naval Hospital.

FORT ITAIPU, BRAZIL

At two o'clock on the morning of 4 November 1957 two guards at Fort Itaipu in Brazil saw a UFO above and descending fast towards them. It was apparently a circular orange glowing object some 100 feet wide, which they believed was under intelligent control. Despite what happened next the guards are adamant that they did not make any aggressive movements towards the object.

Suddenly they heard a humming sound and were hit by a blistering heat, giving them the impression that they were on fire, although in fact there was no physical flame. At the same time the base was blacked out and the power only returned after the UFO had streaked away. The guards were in a serious condition and were treated for burns in the medical centre.

No explanation has ever been offered as to why the UFO should have attacked them, if that was what happened.

FORT MEADE

In December 1953 a UFO was sighted at Fort Meade, Maryland, by Private Alfred De Bonise and Sergeant James Conley. The object was disc-shaped and glowing white, moving towards the north-east.

Some four months later there was a second sighting of an object over the same area.

FORT MONMOUTH, NEW JERSEY

In September 1951 the Army Signal Corps Radar Center at Fort Monmouth, New Jersey, reported a UFO on its radarscopes. The target was moving too fast for the radar to track; in other words, faster than any jet of the time. Over a forty-eight-hour period there were four such dramatic sightings; one apparently involved a target at 93,000 feet.

It is believed to be this incident which reactivated the almost dormant Project **Grudge** which within a few months was renamed Project **Blue Book**; the most famous project of official US UFO investigation ever undertaken.

FORT RILEY, KANSAS
Following the New Mexico crash retrieval of either **Roswell** or **Aztec** there was a report from a military policeman at Fort Riley that he saw several wooden crates being delivered to the base, covered with what appeared to be dry ice and apparently containing small figures approximately four feet tall. The sentry later heard that these were the bodies of the crew of a disc that had crashed in New Mexico, and it is reported that while he was on guard duty a general informed him to 'shoot anyone unauthorised who tried to enter'.

FORT WORTH AIR BASE
During the **Roswell** incident of 1947 Brigadier General Roger M. **Ramey** was commander of the 8th Air Force at Fort Worth. It was to Fort Worth that the recovered debris of the alleged disc crash was taken before it was sent to its final destination at **Wright Patterson Air Force Base** in Dayton, Ohio.

It was at Fort Worth that substitute debris belonging to a Rawin balloon was displayed as being the material recovered by the military exercise.

FORTENBERRY, SECOND OFFICER W. H.
(See **Nash, First Officer W. B.**)

FOSTER, J.
Deputy Sheriff J. Foster was co-witness to an incident in March 1966. (See **Bushroe, Deputy Sheriff B.**)

FOURNET, MAJOR DEWEY, JR
Major Dewey Fournet was a member of the **Robertson Panel** set up in 1952. (See also **Adams, Colonel William A.**)

FRANKEL, DR HENRY
Following the landing of a UFO at **Socorro** some metal fragments were recovered from the landing site. These had apparently scraped off the UFO's landing legs when it was touching down. Dr Henry Frankel of the Space Craft's Systems branch of NASA headed the examination of the particles.

It is alleged that the researchers who provided the material to NASA asked for half of the fragments to be retained for their own use but that the whole rock had been scraped clean of metal before it was returned to them.

It is alleged that Frankel confirmed verbally that the metal did not seem to be of terrestrial origin and, 'This finding definitely strengthens the case that might be made for an extraterrestrial origin of the Socorro object.' However, when pressed to put his statement in writing, it appears that the earlier statement was retracted and the sample declared to be a simple silicate.

FRAPPIER, FRANCIS AND MRS
Evidence of interaction between high-flying UFOs and ground-based observers comes from the case of Mr and Mrs Francis Frappier in July 1967. Together with former radar operator Gary Storey, the Frappiers saw a UFO making several passes over Newton, New Hampshire. They saw five lights flashing on and off in definite sequence. Storey took a torch and fired a series of flashes at the UFO which retraced its path and returned the signals.

Before anything else could happen, Air Force jets apparently drove the UFO up and out of sight.

FRASSINELLI, BRUCE P.
Bruce Frassinelli was editor of a newspaper in Easton, Pennsylvania. In March 1973 he reported seeing rounded masses some ten times the size of Venus in the night sky. The UFO emitted a blue-white, occasionally red, glow.

In the ten minutes of his observation he watched the UFO stop and hover, indicating what he believed may have been surveillance.

FRAUDS
All UFO investigators are well aware that the material they study contains a percentage of frauds and the precise calculation of that percentage is unknown. Some frauds are self-confessed – usually many years after the incident; others are perhaps never uncovered.

For the UFO investigator, frauds are still a valid part of research as they have two effects on the phenomenon; firstly, they give researchers an outsider's view of what the UFO phenomenon is all about and, secondly, they influence others – including possible future witnesses – in reinforcing imagery of the UFO phenomenon.

UFO investigators have an obligation to root out frauds, mainly to prevent an overall distortion of the understanding of the phenomenon and also to prevent exotic frauds perpetrated for financial gain becoming the staple diet of the silly season tabloid press and thereby reducing the credibility of all UFO research.

Obviously in seeking out a fraud the credibility of the claims of the witness is important, and claims which seemed tailored to bring the witness fame and fortune must be regarded as suspect. The rule is not absolute, however, as it would be improper to suggest that a witness who had gone through a strange experience should in some way be prevented from profiting from it. However, witnesses who clearly do not profit, either in terms of fame or fortune, are likely to be more credible unless more complex psychological motives can be uncovered.

While not actually fraudulent, researchers are also aware of what is called 'me too' syndrome; that when a sighting in a locality becomes known, a host of other witnesses come forward to say 'we saw it too'. Some of these people are corroborative witnesses, but many are often ascribing strangeness to sightings of airplanes, planets, etc. that they would not normally pay any attention to. In a similar way, any heightening of awareness of the UFO phenomenon – the release of a high-profile film like *Close Encounters of the Third Kind*, perhaps – also has the effect of increasing UFO reports beyond the 'normal' level.

FREEDOM OF INFORMATION ACT (FOIA)

The Freedom of Information Act became law in the United States on 4 July 1974 and has been used by many American UFO researchers and research groups, and particularly CAUS (**Citizens Against UFO Secrecy**) to force the release of many documents previously held secret by government agencies.

However, matters relating to **national security** are still withheld from Freedom of Information Act requests and there have been many cases of documents purporting to relate to UFO incidents which are almost totally censored by the time they are released; censorship on the grounds of national security interests.

Australia has a Freedom of Information Act which has assisted researchers on that continent to access government files, but unfortunately the United Kingdom – a Ufologically rich country – does not.

FRODSHAM, CHESHIRE

In January 1978 four men on the banks of the river Weaver near Frodsham in Cheshire witnessed the landing of a silver balloon-shaped object in a nearby meadow. Entities apparently emerged and paralysed a cow in the meadow, placing it in a cage, possibly to measure it.

The men, quite reasonably, panicked and ran off, no doubt considering the possibility that the next cage would be for them. They had noticed a blue-green glow around the area and one man developed some sunburn-like marks on his leg.

FRY, DANIEL W.

In 1954 Daniel Fry wrote his book *The White Sands Incident* (see References and Background Material), an account of his contact with extraterrestrials. It followed very closely on the heels of George **Adamski**'s claims, as did many contactee claims of the locality at the time, though it had features peculiar to itself.

Fry had been working at the White Sands Proving Ground in New Mexico when he saw a huge flying saucer land nearby. About to touch the hull of the saucer, a voice from inside warned him: 'Better not touch the hull, pal, it's still hot!'

The alien who eventually contacted Fry was apparently named **A-Lan** though he later simplified matters by calling himself Alan. In what amounts to a 'standard' for the contactee claims of these years, A-Lan took Fry for a journey in the space craft and then asked him to tell the world in a book of his experiences so as to warn people not to encourage a possible nuclear war.

Fry was able to photograph the saucer, which was a fairly classic shape with banded rings around the rim.

FUND FOR UFO RESEARCH (FUFOR)

Operating from **Mount Rainier**, Washington State, United States of America, and headed by US Navy physicist Dr Bruce Maccabee, the Fund for UFO Research is a financial support aid for American and other research groups. Amongst its many operations, it gave $16,000 as part of a project to verify the authenticity of the MJ 12 documents (see **Majestic 12**).

G

GAETANO, PAULO

On 17 November 1971, in the early hours of the evening, Paulo Gaetano and a companion, Mr E. B., were driving near the town of Bananeiras, in Brazil. During the drive the car started to malfunction and eventually stalled near an object beside the road.

Gaetano was abducted by the 'flying saucer'; a beam of light apparently fired at the car, opening the door, and entities grabbed the witness, taking him on board the saucer. He was subjected to a medical examination leaving him with a cut – later to be used as evidence of the occurrence – and was given what appears to have been an implied warning that the town of Itaperuna would be destroyed by nuclear explosion. He was later helped home by his companion, in a confused state.

Of particular significance was the fact that Mr E. B. did not see the flying saucer but only a *parked bus*. This raises the question of whether Gaetano had a bizarre fantasy based on a mundane event, i.e. he had seen a bus and fabricated a strange story around it because of some particular state of mind he was in, or whether the object really was a flying saucer and the entities it contained implanted the image of a bus into Mr E. B. in order to cover up their activities from him while they went about dealing with Gaetano.

There have been many cases of so-called **screen memory**, where the aliens are held to have replaced 'normal' memory with another image, either to protect the witness or to conceal the details of the abduction.

GAIA

The Gaia concept speculates that the Earth is a living, conscious entity. It is theorised that our failure to understand many so-called paranormal activities is a failure to recognise this fact.

With regard to Ufology it is speculated by some UFO

investigators that the UFO phenomenon may be that manifestation of the Earth's consciousness which man cannot interpret at his present level of development. It is further speculated that the manifestation is designed to bring us to a new, higher, level of understanding that *will* enable us to understand this planetary consciousness.

GALLEY, ROBERT
France's Minister of Defence Robert Galley is quoted as saying in a 1974 interview: 'If your listeners could see for themselves the mass of reports coming in from the airborne gendarmerie . . . then they would see that it is all pretty disturbing.'

GAMMIE, BERT
In 1964 Bert Gammie, driving in Canada with his mother and daughter, was buzzed by a huge UFO. The significance of the case was the 'official' reaction that followed. When visited by an officer of the Royal Canadian Air Force whom Gammie had telephoned, and whom he knew personally, the officer stressed that he would publicly deny having had any involvement in the investigation.

GANSU, CHINA
On 11 June 1985 the captain of a Boeing 747 flying from Peking to Paris witnessed a UFO over Gansu Province in China. The UFO apparently crossed the path of the airliner at incredibly high speed, causing the captain to consider making an emergency landing. The most significant aspect of the sighting was the estimated size of the UFO – six miles wide!

GARDIN, CAPTAIN W.
Flying from Adelaide to Perth on 22 August 1968, along with Captain G. Smith, Captain W. Gardin had a potentially frightening encounter with UFOs. The pilots were flying an eight-seater Piper Navajo at 8,000 feet, Smith asleep in the back and Gardin at the controls.

Suddenly, ahead of them Gardin could see a formation of UFOs with a central large craft and several small objects around it: throughout the sighting the UFOs were milling about one another in strange manoeuvres.

Gardin contacted Kalgoorlie Communication Centre and was informed there was no traffic in the area. At that time there seemed to be some electro-magnetic interference as the radio was not functioning well, one of the very few cases of UFO interference relating to aircraft though it is a very common phenomenon with road vehicles.

The sighting lasted some ten minutes, during which time Gardin woke Smith and asked him to come forward to confirm the sighting, which he did. When the UFOs left, the radio resumed normal functioning.

GARDNER, NORMA

Mrs Norma Gardner had worked at **Wright Patterson Air Force Base** as a civilian and retired for health reasons in 1959. Apparently dying of cancer, Mrs Gardner made some extra-ordinary confessions on the grounds that 'Uncle Sam can't do anything to me when I'm in my grave'.

She stated that in 1955 she had undertaken the job of cataloguing UFO-related, retrieved material and had processed over a thousand items, including dismantled parts of a recorded disc, all items of which had been photographed and logged. She also said that she had seen two retrieved discs in a hangar, had witnessed the movement of humanoid bodies, and had worked on their autopsy reports.

GATAY, GEORGES

One of the most notable cases of the 1954 wave of UFO sightings across France occurred at Nouatre in September of that year. At around four o'clock in the afternoon Georges Gatay, a member of a construction team, found himself strangely tired and wandered away from his group.

Suddenly he found himself facing a man wearing grey overalls and boots with an opaque glass visor covering his face. Gatay noticed a metal object in his hand and a light projector on his chest. Behind the entity a shining bone-shaped object floated above the ground. Suddenly the man vanished. The object rose vertically and then also disappeared.

Gatay found himself paralysed throughout the confrontation and subsequently. Apparently the other members of the con-struction team were also similarly paralysed and all of them, afterwards, were able to confirm Gatay's sighting.

There is no report of any '**missing time**', though possibly no inquiries were made at the time, but Budd Hopkins has detailed several cases where mass **paralysis** has been a factor in one person's abduction – the others powerless to interfere.

GDYNIA HARBOUR, POLAND

The source documentation for this case must be regarded as somewhat dubious as Polish researchers working for **BUFORA** were unable to come up with documentary evidence to support the claims. However, the details have become quite famous throughout the world and therefore are reported here as they are generally stated.

According to the claims, a UFO crashed into Gdynia harbour on 21 January 1959. (The actual date is not always given consistently.) Shortly afterwards, a small humanoid in a space suit was found wandering around on the seafront in a confused state and was taken to a local clinic for observation. It took metal shears to remove his one-piece suit and they also removed a bracelet from his wrist, after which he died immediately. A post-mortem on the entity apparently revealed an abnormal number of fingers, a strange arrangement of internal organs and a spiral circulatory system around the inside of the body.

According to the story, the hospital was sealed off and a refrigerated lorry took the body to a research institute in Moscow.

GEPAN

France is one of the few countries which have taken the UFO phenomenon seriously at an official and semi-official level. For example, it has been noted that the gendarmerie are instructed to take UFO reports seriously. A section of the Centre National d'Études Spatiales (CNES), the equivalent of the American NASA, studies the phenomenon under the name of GEPAN (Le Groupe d'Étude des Phénomènes Aérospatiaux Nonidentifiés).

At commencement GEPAN was headed by Dr Claude Poher, Director of the Rockets Division of CNES, and it was given access to scientific resources across the nation.

However, it has been suggested that the most exotic UFO reports do not go to GEPAN but are suppressed by other government agencies. Certainly the current status and future of GEPAN are in question and there are fears that if it is revived fully it will be as a public front for official UFO research – not to put such work into the public domain but rather to bluff the public and conceal the most exceptional cases. The precise, current status of GEPAN is not known even by French researchers.

GERLA, MORTON

Morton Gerla was President of the New York Section of the American Rocket Society, and stated: 'UFOs are capable of performances beyond our technological ability.' Gerla believed it was important that we learn the secret of the alien machines, a statement he made to **NICAP**.

GHOST ROCKETS

One of the earliest manifestations of the UFO phenomenon, in the 1930s, was that of the ghost rockets first reported around Sweden and Norway.

Lights were seen behaving like aircraft lights although craft were not known to be in the area at the time. By January 1934 over forty reports were being received per day.

Even today there are no clear answers to the mystery; certainly some of the sightings will have been misidentifications of stars, planets, etc. but that would not explain all of the cases on record.

There has been a suggestion that the ghost rockets may have been the testing of some form of early cruise missile. The further suggestion that these might have been of an extraterrestrial nature would seem unreasonable; a terrestrial nation would be a more likely source. It should be noted, however, that cruise missile technology is not known to have existed at the time.

One of the most interesting cases was the crash of an object into Lake **Kolmjärv** in the north of Sweden in July 1946.

Erik Reuterswärd is credited with taking the first photograph of a ghost rocket although it is generally accepted that he may have photographed a meteor.

A report from August 1946 suggests a pre-**Arnold** era saucer; a Swedish Air Force Lieutenant and his flight observer observed a cigar-shaped or disc-shaped object during a training flight from Västeraas. When they attempted interception in their craft, the object sped away beyond their capability to follow. Had this sighting occurred in the days after the Kenneth Arnold sighting, when the phrase 'flying saucer' was coined, then it would almost certainly have been listed as such, and not as a ghost rocket.

The ghost rockets were reported all over Europe in those years, with many reports from as far south as Greece.

GIABOWSKI, CONSTABLE FLORIAN

Constable Florian Giabowski of the Ontario Provincial Police was involved in a puzzling UFO encounter in 1953 when, from his patrol car, he watched a UFO disintegrate. The sighting was corroborated by a nearby pilot and tests by the Defence Research Board showed abnormal radioactivity where the debris had fallen.

GILL, REVEREND WILLIAM

During 1959, Papua New Guinea was in the middle of a UFO flap. The most extraordinary encounter of the time is that of the UFO and related entities seen by members of the Boianai mission of Reverend William Gill. At around six o'clock in the evening Annie Borewa, a Papuan medical assistant, called Reverend Gill to come and see a UFO in the sky over the mission buildings. They witnessed two small UFOs and a larger, apparently structured, object hovering nearby.

The **structured object** was described as circular with a wide base and a narrower upper deck with something resembling four legs protruding from beneath it. Occasionally a shaft of blue light was seen firing up into the sky from the object at a 45 degree angle, and there were reports of portholes or panels around the rim of the object.

As the witnesses from the mission, totalling no less than thirty-eight in all, watched the object, four figures appeared on the upper deck and seemed to be manipulating equipment there. Father Gill waved to the figures who all started waving back, to the considerable surprise of the terrestrial observers.

Gill followed up his waving by flashing a series of torchlight 'dashes' at the UFO, and believes the UFO responded by swinging in pendular motion.

In many ways the next part of the story is the most extraordinary of all. Despite the obvious significance of the encounter the entities on the UFO apparently got bored and turned away from their waving, and Father Gill went in for his dinner! When he re-emerged some half an hour later the UFO was still visible though much more distant; eventually it disappeared.

It is perhaps noteworthy that some hours later there was an ear-splitting explosion outside the mission house though nothing was seen and it is only conjecture that links the two events.

GILLIGAN, GOVERNOR JOHN

John Gilligan, Governor of Ohio, apparently witnessed a UFO during the October 1973 flap across the United States, thus making him one of many high officials to report such events. He and his wife apparently watched a vertical-shaped orange object for some half an hour while driving near Ann Arbor, Michigan. He was sure that it wasn't – to quote the report – 'a bird or a plane' (and presumably not Superman either!).

GIULIANA, HÉLÈNE
In June 1976, Hélène Giuliana was returning home late one night from the movies when her car cut out crossing the bridge at Romans, France. She saw a huge orange glow in the sky which then suddenly vanished and she drove on.

By the time she arrived home she realised she had missed some considerable period of time and subsequent regression hypnosis revealed that she had been abducted by small figures, tied to a table and examined around her abdomen. It is one of a few cases not from America which none the less has all the 'classic' details revealed by regression hypnosis following commonly reported symptoms, including **missing time**.

GLASS, LIEUTENANT HENRY F.
Lieutenant Henry F. Glass, along with Captain Jack E. Puckett, is reported to have made a small piece of UFO history in August 1946 when flying a C-47 transport plane from Langley Field to MacDill.

On route the pilots saw a large cigar-shaped UFO speed across their course; they estimated it to be twice the size of a B22 bomber and trailing fire in an apparent rocket stream behind it. They estimated its speed at 2,000 miles per hour.

However, the most important point of the sighting was that they were the first people to report a UFO with rows of windows. The implication of windows or portholes was that living creatures might be aboard; it would be many years before entity reports would be 'acceptable' even to mainstream UFO researchers.

GLOVER, OFFICER FLANNING
During the October 1973 wave of UFO sightings across the United States, Officer Flanning Glover of Collier made a self-critical report after seeing orange and white UFO lights while in the company of others. He said, 'I know it sounds fantastic but it's true. If I was by myself, I would say I was nuts.'

GODFREY, PC ALAN
In the early hours of 29 November 1980 Police Constable Alan Godfrey at Todmorden, Lancashire, experienced a UFO and abduction event.

Driving his police car Godfrey encountered what he at first thought was a bus which had slid sideways across the road. As he approached to within 60 feet of it he realised it was more anomalous; some 20 feet wide and 14 feet high, and shaped like a diamond. He recognised a bank of windows in it and the bottom half of it was rotating. Most significantly, he noticed it was hovering at approximately five feet off the ground.

The object seems to have cut out his police car radio so, unable to report the object, Godfrey sketched it on his clipboard.

There appears to be a strong suggestion of **missing time** and spatial dislocation as Godfrey then found himself approximately 100 yards down the road and the UFO was gone. Under hypnotic regression Godfrey recounted a strange and exotic story of having been abducted aboard the UFO.

On board the UFO he apparently found himself in a room on a table with a tall bearded man looking down at him. He reported other creatures of bizarre appearance in the room and also the entry of a large dog. There was some evidence of examination by the entities before Godfrey found himself back in his police car.

One interesting point arose in regression; he referred to the tall human-like entity as 'Joseph'. Aliens generally do not give their names to their **abductees** (unlike the claims of the **contactees**) and it is worthy of note that one of the investigative team undertaking the regression hypnosis was named Joseph, suggesting there may have been some leak from external influence into subconscious recall. To be fair to the investigative team involved, it must be stated that they do not share that opinion.

Godfrey displays an intelligent and unbiased attitude towards the incident, stating that he remains uncertain as to what actually happened to him during the period of missing time, and he admits that some of the abduction material may be fantasy. None of this suggests that the event or experience was unreal, but is indicative of honesty and reasonableness on Godfrey's part.

GODFREY, ARTHUR

Arthur Godfrey had his UFO encounter in June 1965. At the time he was a well-known national figure in the United States, an experienced pilot having flown for the Navy and the Air

Force as well as commercially, and a colonel in the Air Force Reserve. During his own nationwide programme broadcast Godfrey disclosed the details of a UFO encounter which had occurred when he had been flying a private plane with his co-pilot Frank Munciello.

An object cane in near to the right-hand side of the plane, causing Godfrey to bank to avoid collision. The UFO then took up position close to the left wing and in fact matched Godfrey's manoeuvres throughout. After some time the UFO veered away. Godfrey admitted that he and his co-pilot were concerned by the UFO encounter.

This particular incident was reported at a time when the United States Air Force was **debunking** UFO sightings, on the basis that observers were either incompetent, hoaxers or deluded. However, in Godfrey's case the Air Force was well aware of his sharp temper and the fact that in his position he could make a nationwide response to any adverse comments.

They apparently decided discretion was the better part of valour.

GOLDWATER, BARRY
It has been suggested that US Senator Barry Goldwater had made failed attempts to visit **Wright Patterson Air Force Base** to examine crashed saucer debris and alien bodies reportedly held there. Goldwater apparently wrote in March 1975: 'The subject of UFOs is one that has interested me for some long time . . . I made an effort to find out what was in the building at Wright Patterson . . . I was understandably denied this request . . . It is still classified above top secret.'

GOMEZ, JESUS
(See **Flores, Lorenzo**.)

GONZALES, MAYOR VALENTIN
(See **Riva Palacie, Governor Emilie**.)

GOOSE BAY, LABRADOR
(See **Howard, Captain James**.)

GORMAN, LIEUTENANT GEORGE
In October 1948 Lieutenant George Gorman of the North Dakota Air National Guard found himself in something of a

dog fight with a UFO. Piloting an F51, Gorman approached the airport at Fargo, North Dakota, at around 8.30 in the evening. While taking landing instructions from the tower he was informed that there was a light aircraft nearby which he visually sighted. Shortly afterwards he was distracted by another craft near his right wing and contacted the tower requesting details. The tower had no details to offer.

Gorman saw the UFO as a ball of light some eight inches wide and 'making a pass at the tower'. Gorman tried to catch the object which then turned towards him. As they were about to collide at 7,000 feet Gorman went into a dive and the light passed over the top of the plane, circling above him; he then gave chase a second time.

From the control tower there was visual confirmation of the object with one witness watching the aerial combat through high-powered binoculars. The contact lasted approximately half an hour and Gorman reported, 'I am convinced there was thought behind the thing's manoeuvres.'

The official explanation of this event was that Gorman was seeing a lighted balloon for some of the time and a mirage of the planet Jupiter for the rest.

GOUDSMIT, DR SAMUEL A.
Dr Samuel Goudsmit, an expert in atomic structure and statistical problems, was one of the members of the **Robertson Panel** convened in 1953 to examine UFO reports. His appointment demonstrates the wide-ranging skill base of the panel members.

GRAND RAPIDS FLYING SAUCER CLUB
It is thought that this organisation, founded in 1951 but sadly no longer in existence, holds the honour of being the world's first private flying saucer research group.

GRAVES, SELMAN E.
Selman Graves claimed to be a witness to the recovery of a crashed disc at Paradise Valley, Arizona, in 1947.

He was to go on a hunting trip with friends but was told that the Air Force had restricted the area and they would not be able to do so. Graves went to the location anyway and apparently found a vantage point from which he could see the activity. He saw a large, aluminium, dome-shaped object approximately 36 feet wide surrounded by tents and watched by moving personnel. Graves observed the activity for some twelve hours.

He apparently saw no sign of humanoid bodies although he was told by another informant that some had been recovered. Graves also believes that there was a considerable cover-up of the retrieval to the extent of changing the local topography of the area to make access to the site more difficult and to disguise its exact location.

GRAY, GORDON L.

Gordon Gray is reported to have been a member of the **Majestic 12** panel formed to investigate UFOs in the 1940s. Gray was Assistant Secretary of the Army at the time, becoming Secretary in 1949. The following year he became Special Assistant to President **Truman** and was apparently involved in psychological warfare strategy.

GREAT CHINESE BLACKOUT

In September 1979, a story very similar to the **Great North-East Blackout** of the United States of America, brilliant UFOs were seen over the cities of Xuginglong and Huaihua in Hunan, China.

There was power failure across the cities, known to have been associated with the UFO sightings. This report led to rumours of other power blackouts suppressed by the government and associated with other UFOs, prior to this event in Hunan.

The Chinese government has not been forthcoming in making available information about these blackouts.

GREAT NORTH-EAST BLACKOUT

The most spectacular of all UFO-related blackouts is the Great North-East Blackout which took place on 9 November 1965. 80,000 square miles of the north-eastern United States of America, encompassing six states, parts of Canada and the whole of New York City were blacked out. A total of 26 million people were affected by the event, many of them in frightening circumstances in New York City, where hundreds of thousands were trapped in the underground subway system, in elevators, etc. Airports across the north-eastern United States had to be shut down and flights redirected across the continent.

A complex series of cut-outs had been installed in the grid system and the Americans had already been assured that a serious breakdown was impossible. The breakdown when it came appeared to start at the Clay power substation which channelled the power from Niagara Falls into New York City. **Fireball**-like objects were seen above the substation shortly before the blackout and many UFOs were seen and photographed from New York during it. There is no definite correlation between the UFO sightings and the blackout itself, although no satisfactory explanation for the blackout has ever been published. The only 'explanation' offered by one official was that vast amounts of electricity had been 'lost' from the system, although he could give no further details – a far from satisfactory answer to the mystery.

GREENHAW, POLICE CHIEF JEFF
During the October 1973 wave of sightings across the United States, Police Chief Jeff Greenhaw at Falkville, Alabama, encountered a UFO following a report from a citizen that an object with flashing lights was landing near the town. Greenhaw, armed with a Polaroid camera, drove to the scene. Just outside the town he encountered a six-foot tall entity standing in the middle of the road, dressed in a silver suit. Greenhaw got out of the car and took four photographs of the entity, got back in the car and turned on the blue lights. The creature then turned and ran down the road. Greenhaw chased him in the patrol car but couldn't catch him, the 'man' apparently able to run at some forty miles an hour. Eventually the car spun off the road, the entity having vanished.

Greenhaw's experience following this is an extreme form of that experienced by many UFO reporters; he lost his car, his home, his job and his wife, following what appeared to be some form of campaign against him.

GREENVILLE, SOUTH CAROLINA
Major Donald E. **Keyhoe** refers to a report sent to him by Air Technical Intelligence Center from four astronomers at Greenville, South Carolina, who in May 1952 all witnessed four saucer-shaped UFOs flying in diamond formation. The objects were glowing yellow and passed overhead, making a wobbling motion. All the astronomers agreed the shape was like that of a disc on its side.

GROENDAL RESERVE, SOUTH AFRICA
Just before noon on 2 October 1978 four young boys in the Groendal Reserve in South Africa had a sixty-second sighting of

strange entities which left them feeling distinctly uneasy.

It started when they saw a silver object between the trees and then saw two (and later three) silver-suited entities gliding up the hills, a motion they distinguished from normal walking. In fact, the legs of the entities were very indistinct and the witnesses described their appearance from the knee down as being 'like a fin'. At the top of the hill they were gliding up they suddenly disappeared and the UFO was also gone.

GROTH, ARNE
(See **Anders**.)

GROUND SAUCER WATCH (GSW, USA)
An important UFO research organisation is the Arizona-based Ground Saucer Watch Inc.

Two notable aspects of its varied work have been the instigating of a law suit against the **CIA** for failing to obey **Freedom of Information Act** requirements to release certain documents, and also its pioneering work in photographic analysis and **computer photographic enhancement**.

GRUDGE, PROJECT
In December 1948 Project **Sign**, which had always been nick-named Project Saucer, was replaced by Project Grudge. It is believed that this name came from Captain Edward **Ruppelt**'s feeling that UFOs were a nuisance.

The way in which Project Grudge dealt with its UFO investigations differed in some ways from its predecessor; in particular the project relied more heavily on local Air Force officers where the sightings had occurred and did not use civilian experts where scientists and other analysts under Air Force contracts could be used instead.

In March 1952 Project Grudge became the much more famous Project **Blue Book**, the United States Air Force's apparently final UFO investigation of the period.

GUÉRIN, DR PIERRE
Dr Pierre Guérin of the French Institute of Astrophysics made statements in an interview with British researcher Timothy Good (reported in Good's book *Above Top Secret* – see References and Background Material) that suggest he shows a much more reasonable and balanced attitude towards the subject of the UFO phenomenon than many of his colleagues across the

world. He stated: 'Scientists are not only embarrassed by UFOs; they are furious because they don't understand them.' He also said, 'In science there is no proof of any phenomenon if no scientific model for it exists. The observation of the facts is not the actual fact.'

Guérin also believes that, 'nobody has the fundamental explanation [for UFOs]'.

GULF BREEZE

The Gulf Breeze encounters are a contemporary UFO event of extraordinary nature. They have taken place in and around the area of Florida near Pensacola known as Gulf Breeze. The principal witness is Ed **Walters**.

This particular case is extraordinary for the following reasons:

1. It is the first case where an extensive series of distinct photographs apparently supports close encounters (and a possible abduction).
2. It is a multiple photograph case studied as it unfolded.
3. It is a multiple witness case, possibly including independent photographers to the same event sequence.
4. There are multi-vehicle photographs and video film.
5. Extraordinary photographic techniques such as three-dimensional photography and stereo photography have been used.

The case commenced in November 1987 when Walters observed a UFO and took five photographs of it. During the encounter he was paralysed by a blue beam of light and physically lifted into the air. At the time of the incident Charles and Doris Somerby also apparently spotted the same UFO in the sky. Mr Somerby is a former editor of the local newspaper (and his wife is the present editor's mother) and it was to this newspaper that Walters presented the photographs. This was the event which triggered the investigation. The blue beam was also seen by a Mrs **Zammit** who reported this to the newspaper in response to the article which was published along with the photographs.

Over the next six months Walters had many encounters and photographed a great many of them. They were often preceded by a buzzing noise in his head, which it has been speculated may have been caused by an **implanted device** put there for the purpose during an early abduction.

As the UFO investigation was proceeding, several steps were

taken to try to authenticate the photographs. Two Polaroid cameras were fixed at a given distance apart with a broom handle projected between them and into the field of vision of each camera so that two pictures of each incident could be taken to give some sense of perspective. Later, a three-dimensional camera with four lenses was given to Walters by **MUFON (The Mutual UFO Network)**. The camera was apparently sealed and when the film was developed UFO pictures were apparent. During the time of the sightings Walters undertook a **lie detector** test and the result was that the examiner believed that the witness 'truly believes that the photographs and personal sightings he has described are true and factual to the best of his ability'.

The events ended for this witness in May 1988 when it is speculated that he was abducted (there was a **missing time** period during the UFO sighting) and the implanted device removed. After that time Walters did not hear the humming noise nor see the UFOs, except one somewhat distant sighting some months later. It has been speculated by investigators for MUFON that the fact Walters was to undergo medical analysis to locate and identify the putative implanted device may have become known to the aliens who removed it to prevent detection.

The case has caused some considerable controversy in the United States with UFO groups and investigators lining up in a polarized argument. Broadly speaking, some groups fully support Walters' claims, believe him to be utterly sincere and that the photographs are proof positive of UFO intervention, while others believe the entire case is a hoax.

Since, like the best wine, UFO cases need to 'mature' before many of the underlying facts are revealed it is possibly too early at this stage to comment on the validity or otherwise of the case but there is no question that the final analysis of Gulf Breeze will have considerable repercussions for both American and global Ufology.

GU YING

In April 1968 Gu Ying was working on an irrigation project in the North Gobi Desert when he encountered a UFO. He described it as a disc of light, glowing red, which landed on the desert. Inside the light he could see a harder luminous point; the object was less than a kilometre away. When troops on motorcycles tried to approach it, the disc disappeared into the sky, leaving burn marks on the ground.

H

HAGENAU, GERMANY

On 22 December 1944 a pilot of the 415th Night Fighter Squadron was completing a mission over Hagenau, Germany, when he encountered **'foo' fighters**.

It was six o'clock in the morning and he was flying at 10,000 feet; both the pilot and his radar operator saw two large orange glows climbing rapidly towards them. The glows apparently levelled off and paced the aircraft, even when it was put into a steep dive to try to evade them. The lights apparently continued to pace the plane throughout several complex manoeuvres before they peeled away from it – seemingly under control – and then disappeared from sight.

HALL, ALAN N.

Alan N. Hall became director of **NICAP** in 1979, replacing Jack **Acuff**. Alan N. Hall was yet another retired **CIA** agent and there is much made by researchers in America of the involvement of CIA operatives in this organisation. It is generally assumed that the CIA's involvement was more to direct public opinion than to subvert knowledge, though of course the two could go hand in hand.

HALSTEAD, DR FRANK

Dr Frank Halstead of the Darling Observatory, Minnesota, stated in 1957: 'Many professional astronomers are convinced that saucers are interplanetary machines.'

HALT, LIEUTENANT-COLONEL CHARLES

Probably the most important witness in the **Rendlesham Forest** encounter in Suffolk in 1980 was Lieutenant-Colonel Charles Halt, the Deputy Base Commander of **Woodbridge RAF/USAF Base** and a Lieutenant-Colonel in the United States Air Force.

His initial involvement appears to have been the making of a report to the British Ministry of Defence in January 1981 describing the way in which a security patrol from the base had investigated lights in the nearby forest, believing that there might have been an aircraft crash. In his report Halt summarises the findings of the patrol: that they encountered a triangular-shaped metallic object approximately 9 feet wide and 6 feet high, displaying a variety of red and blue lights and glowing generally white. The object was apparently standing on short legs or hovering near the ground, and Halt's report indicates that the patrol watched the object moving through the trees, disturbing animals nearby and leaving ground traces thought to be the impression of legs, i.e. three depressions in the ground approximately 17 inches wide. He reports also that readings were taken indicating peaks of radiation in the ground traces.

Lieutenant-Colonel Halt's report was released under the **Freedom of Information Act** in America following a request from CAUS (**Citizens Against UFO Secrecy**).

Despite a report from this very senior officer, the British Ministry of Defence, through Lord **Trefgarne**, then Parliamentary Under-Secretary of State for the Armed Forces, replied to an inquiry from a former Chief of the Defence Staff, Lord **Hill-Norton**, that the event had 'no defence significance'.

Lord Hill-Norton appears to have been unimpressed by this reply, pointing out that, 'Unless Lieutenant-Colonel Halt was out of his mind, there is clear evidence in his report that British airspace . . . [was] intruded upon by an unidentified vehicle . . . and that no bar to such intrusion was effective.' Lord Hill-Norton went on to say that if Halt's report was untrue, then evidence of such serious misjudgement by such a high-ranking officer would itself be of defence significance.

HALTER, SECOND LIEUTENANT BARTON
(See **Hemphill, First Lieutenant Oliver**.)

HAMILTON, ALEXANDER
In April 1897 Alexander Hamilton, a farmer in Kansas, was woken by an extraordinary attack on his cattle. He saw an airship descend over his ranch which he described as being cigar-shaped, approximately 300 feet long and with a transparent undercarriage. He also reported seeing six entities, 'the strangest beings I ever saw'.

Apparently the airship dropped a thick cable around one heifer's neck and flew off with it while Hamilton and farm workers watched in amazement.

Worse was yet to come. The following morning a local neighbouring rancher found the hide, head and legs of the butchered animal in his field. Prudently enough Hamilton commented: '. . . I don't want any more to do with them [the entities].'

Here is a most extraordinary example of **cultural tracking**: not only is the UFO apparently some sort of **airship** design similar to airships that would soon be flying in the United States but even the abduction method matches the methods of the time, i.e. a lasso to restrain an animal. Apparently the airship was not equipped with the sort of levitation beam that future UFOs would soon be using!

HAMMARSKJÖLD, KNUT

Just when the United States Air Force was comfortably **debunking** UFOs, Knut Hammarskjöld became Director-General of the International Air Transport Association. Addressing a meeting of aviation writers, Hammarskjöld stated that on becoming head of the organisation he had been given a huge number of UFO reports, hundreds of verified encounters by air crew members of the body. Coming from trained observers, Hammarskjöld became convinced that there was substance to the reports that 'the UFOs were probably observation machines from outer space'.

The United States Air Force refused to comment on his claims, presumably because it had no way of making a positive reply and because any **debunking** or negative reply could have encouraged Hammarskjöld to reveal what it was he had in his files.

HANGAR 18

Hangar 18 is the title of a film based on UFO **crash retrieval** stories. It was made in 1980 and has stood the test of time with regard to its main theme; indeed, the alleged reality put forward by some UFO researchers makes the film story line almost pedestrian by comparison.

Hangar 18, the hangar, rather than the film, would appear to be the equivalent of the so-called **Blue Room** at **Wright Patterson Air Force Base** where UFO artefacts are examined.

Prominent American UFO researchers were consultants to the film.

HARRISON, HENRY

In April 1879 Henry Harrison made an early UFO report following telescopic observation of the night sky. He sighted an object which he first supposed to be a planetary nebular at approximately 8.30 on the evening of 13 April. However, its behaviour became extraordinary and he asked friends to verify his observations. They confirmed that the sighting was not a meteorite, comet, star or cloud and made notes of its shape, diameter, density and luminosity. The object was observed for some three and a half hours before Harrison retired to bed. At approximately two o'clock in the morning he awoke feeling curious about the object and saw it disappearing beyond the horizon, more brilliant than ever before.

HART, MAJOR C. R.

In 1962 Hart was an Air Force spokesman for the Pentagon. He revealed that official UFO investigations involved a large number of Air Force intelligence officers, many scientists working for various government agencies, and commercial outwork when required.

HART, MR AND MRS LEWIS

In November 1960 seven occupants of a trailer camp in California witnessed UFOs for an extended period of some quarter of an hour. Mr and Mrs Lewis Hart were amateur astronomers and prominent witnesses to the event who submitted a report to the United States Air Force. The Harts commented, 'It was unquestionably some kind of intelligently controlled air or space vehicle.'

HARTLAND, EDWIN S.

In his book *The Science of Fairy Tales* (see References and Background Material) Edwin S. Hartland relates many tales of fairy folklore dating from the nineteenth century and earlier, many of which are comparable to modern day UFO and abduction accounts. For example, he recalls the tale of a man living in Wales who went up a mountain to look after his cattle and returned three weeks later, after his wife had believed him dead. He insisted that he had been away only three hours. His **missing time** period apparently occurred when he was surrounded by little entities looking like men who closed him into a tight circle, entranced him with song and dance and shared their food with him. There is a remarkable similarity between this and the story of Joe **Simonton**'s UFO encounter.

HARVEY, LUIS

In July 1962 a UFO, described as perfectly round, approached Camba Punta airport in Argentina at high speed, stopped and hovered for some three minutes. Apparently to facilitate the meeting, Airport Director Luis Harvey ordered the landing strip cleared. No interference with the object was suggested but unfortunately witnesses running towards it to make a closer inspection apparently caused it to make a hasty retreat.

A similar event took place at **Ezeiza International Airport** in South America.

HATHAWAY, LIEUTENANT-COLONEL E. U.

Lieutenant-Colonel E. U. Hathaway was one of three American officials who encountered a UFO while travelling in Russia in October 1955.

They sighted two flying disc shapes while travelling between Atjaty and Adzhijabul. They reported that the discs were beaming searchlights. During the sighting the rail staff of the train in which they were travelling blanked out the windows and refused permission for them to continue observing.

A report was apparently sent to the **CIA**.

HAUT, LIEUTENANT WALTER

On 8 July 1947 it was Lieutenant Walter Haut, the Public Information Officer for **Roswell** Army Air Base, who apparently issued, without authorisation, an extraordinary admission that the US Air Force had recovered a crashed flying saucer.

The report read: 'The many rumours regarding the flying disc became a reality yesterday when the intelligence office of the 509th Bomb Group of the 8th Air Force Roswell Army airfield was fortunate enough to gain possession of a disc through the co-operation of one of the local ranchers and the Sheriff's office of Chaves County. The flying object landed on a ranch near Roswell some time last week. Not having phone facilities, the rancher stored the disc until such time as he was able to contact the Sheriff's office, who in turn notified Major Jesse A. **Marcel** of the 509th Bomb Group intelligence office. Action was immediately taken and the disc was picked up at the rancher's home. It was inspected at the Roswell Army Airfield and subsequently loaned by Major Marcel to higher headquarters.'

Apparently having been promised a promotion to Captain, which he got, Haut resigned his commission in 1948 when he learned that he was about to be transferred.

HAV-MUSUVS: PAIUTE INDIAN LEGENDS
UFO reports are not confined to the modern times nor to technologically advanced cultures. The Paiute Indians of California believe that their land was once the home of the Hav-Musuvs who were warriors whose principal achievement was to travel through the air in silver 'flying canoes'.

The warriors also pre-dated UFO weaponry; they used a small tube which could inflict **paralysis** on their enemies, in a manner reminiscent of very many modern UFO reports.

HAWKINS, ROSEMARY
Rosemary Hawkins was one of three women who experienced a UFO event in July 1981 in Shrewsbury, Shropshire. The other witnesses were Viv Hayward and Valerie Walters.

They were returning from an evening out, driving towards Telford New Town in the early hours of the morning. During the drive they saw peculiar red and white lights across fields near them and they could apparently identify a **structured object** to which the lights were attached. The lights were apparently pacing their car.

There seems to have been some interference with their car as it lost power when they tried to speed up to put the object behind them; they also noticed that there was no other traffic on the road. However, the lights dimmed, vanished, and the car apparently regained its power. The women drove immediately to the local police station. They commented that the drive seemed to take an awfully long time.

From the apparent time of the event to the time taken to reach the police station there would appear to be a period of **missing time** of approximately twenty minutes or more.

Hypnotic regression sessions were undertaken by Dr Joseph Jaffe and Leslie Davis, a homoeopathic doctor.

Under hypnosis Viv Hayward recalls the car being taken up into the air and seeing a white cloud around her; her companions were apparently not with her as the car was drawn into the underside of a UFO. She was apparently removed from the car and subjected to some medical examination on board the UFO by creatures approximately four feet tall wearing green cloaks. After a gruelling physical examination Ms Hayward was then returned to the car and the car returned to the road.

There is some corroboration from Rosemary Hawkins of this account as she recalls being taken from the car and also recalls that her companions were not with her. Apparently she was examined by robots on wheels but was not subjected to the same gruelling physical examination as her companion.

Valerie Walters was examined by Dr Albert Kellar who found a different uncorroborative story in her recollection. During her recall the car was apparently stationary and Ms Hawkins was missing. Ms Walters left the car, leaving Ms Hayward alone. She has no recollection of the UFO but does feel that she was floated into a room and encountered entities wearing green cloaks but these are of quite different proportions to the entities Ms Hayward encountered. They were tall with dark shoulder-length hair, blue eyes and white skin. Ms Walters apparently believes that something gynaecological in nature occurred but has no recollection of what (a claim which would ring true in later years with the predominant modern theory of human/alien hybrid breeding).

Although sensibly cautious about the objective reality of the recall of these women, all the doctors involved appeared to have been impressed by their sincerity, with Leslie Davis stating that the women were telling him 'the truth as they saw it'.

HAYASHI, COLONEL FUIJO
Air Force involvement in UFOs has not been restricted to any one country. In the 1960s Colonel Fuijo Hayashi, the Commander of the Air Transport Wing of Japan's Air Self-Defence Force, stated that 'UFOs are impossible to deny'. He added, 'It is very strange that we have never been able to find out the source for over two decades.'

HAYWARD, VIV
(See **Hawkins, Rosemary**.)

HEALEY, JOHN
Staff Sergeant John Healey was one of the witnesses, along with Captain Lawrence J. **Coyne**, to the famous Coyne helicopter encounter of 1973.

HEATON, PETER HENNIKER
Perhaps the most concise criticism of the **Condon Report** was made by Peter Henniker Heaton, staff writer for the *Christian*

Science Monitor, who commented: 'Read as a whole, the report could not conceal the considerable body of evidence which pointed to an important and inexplicable phenomenon. But the introductory summary of the report performed a hatchet job on flying saucers that has rarely been equalled in the field of scientific scholarship. And as everyone knows, when a scholar and a scientist picks up a hatchet, he does a job of it with unparalleled effectiveness and ferocity.'

HEFLIN, REX
In August 1965 highway inspector Rex Heflin photographed a UFO near Santa Ana, California. Shortly after this he was visited by an alleged official of United States Air Force Intelligence who took the prints away, never to return them. Stories like these, of which there are many, add weight to the belief that governments seek to cover up some aspects of the UFO phenomenon, and may have been responsible for several '**Men in Black**' stories of early years.

HEILAND, DR CARL A.
It is alleged that Dr Carl A. Heiland, a geophysicist and head of the Colorado School of Mines, was one of a team of scientists who are alleged to have recovered the virtually intact saucer and alien bodies at the **Aztec** crash site in New Mexico in 1948.

HELEN
Jacques Vallée, in his book *Dimensions* (see References and Background Material), relates the abduction of a witness he refers to as 'Helen'.

In the summer of 1968 she, together with three others, was returning in the early hours of the morning to Los Angeles when they encountered a white light approaching the car. The object was apparently large, silent, and may have had windows. Beams of light emanated from the object, encapsulating each of the four witnesses. An abduction seems to have taken place which is more similar to an **out of body** experience.

Under regression hypnosis Helen apparently recalled being drawn on board a 'saucer' and meeting a man who showed her a motor mechanism. It has become Helen's mission in life to replicate that motor mechanism although according to our own present-day physics it would not, apparently, be functional. The other witnesses corroborate the encounter.

HEMPHILL, FIRST LIEUTENANT OLIVER
On 15 October 1948 First Lieutenant Oliver Hemphill and his radar operator Second Lieutenant Barton Halter encountered a UFO exhibiting neither wings nor tail and emitting no exhaust flames or vapour trail, over Fukuoka, Japan. They made six attempts to close into the UFO, which was returning a radar echo on the plane's radar. However, each time the plane attempted to engage it the UFO would streak out of range and eventually dived so fast they were unable to stay with it.

When Lieutenant Hemphill contacted ground control he was informed that there were no other aircraft around them.

HENDERSON, MAJOR PAUL W.
Major Paul W. Henderson was the author of a report in the files of the 100th Bomb Wing, Strategic Air Command Pease Air Force Base, New Hampshire, which confirms that the object seen by Betty and Barney **Hill** had been detected by radar at the Pease Air Force Base.

The Hills' encounter is a very important one of UFO study and whatever the true details of the abduction, this report confirms at least their claims of a UFO sighting.

HENDRIX, ALLEN
Savannah Beach Mayor Allen Hendrix was one of several senior officials who witnessed a UFO apparently plummet into the ocean off Tybee Island, USA, during the 1973 flap.

The Coast Guard was so unimpressed with the witnesses' report that he refused even to send out a craft to investigate the encounter, despite Hendrix's position in the community. This seems a rather strange reaction considering the possibility that the object was terrestrial and in grave peril.

HESSDALEN, PROJECT
Between 1981 and 1985 Project Hessdalen in Scandinavia became the centre of an extraordinary prolonged study of UFOs.

The first reports came from the Norwegian valley of Hessdalen, south-west of Trondheim. Hundreds of witnesses described variously shaped illuminated 'objects' including fast- and slow-moving lights, Christmas tree shapes, and so on.

Over a period of years an investigative team 'staked out' the valley and took many photographs and much film of the lights. In June 1983 this stimulated the formation of Project Hessdalen formed between UFO Norway, UFO Sweden, Finnish Ufological groups and the Society for Psycho Bio Physics.

The project was directed by Leif Havik, Odd-Gunnar Roed, Hakan Ekstrand, Jan Fjellander and Erling Strand. A great deal of equipment was used during the observations, including Atlas 2,000 radar, seismographs, magnetometers, spectrum analysers, infrared viewers, geiger counters, and all forms of camera devices.

There was some indication that the lights were interactive with the investigators, and the suggestion has been made that they were some form of intelligence though such conclusions are highly speculative at this time.

What Project Hessdalen serves to confirm without doubt is that there is a UFO phenomenon, i.e. a phenomenon of genuinely unexplained events. It also showed that co-operation between researchers could produce impressive results when there was a significant duration of sighting involved.

HETZEL, JOSEPHINE

During the 1952 **Washington 'flap'**, DC, USA, Mrs Josephine Hetzel, together with witness Frank Gonder, reported a V-formation of objects over Staten Island, New York, showing that the activity was not purely localised. She described them as silvery in colour with red rims, and like five large dinner plates flying through the sky. Gonder reported that they gave off a glow but made no sound.

HIBBARD, ROBERT

In March 1897 Robert Hibbard became a potential abductee from one of the **airships** of the wave of sightings at that time. He was a farmer living near Sioux City, Iowa, and when he encountered the airship an anchor hanging from it attached itself to his clothes and dragged him for some considerable distance until it released him. There was a report from a farmer whose cattle had been similarly, crudely, abducted and which ended up in a nearby field horrifically mutilated, so perhaps Hibbard had a very lucky escape.

HIBBS, DR ALBERT

Not all scientists automatically welcome contact with extraterrestrials, whether as a product of the UFO phenomenon or otherwise. One of the most expressive comments on record came from Dr Albert Hibbs of Caltech's Jet Propulsion Laboratory. On being

Photograph taken by George Adamski allegedly showing a mothership and six attendant scout flying saucers seen over Palomar Gardens, California on 5 March 1951. (*Mary Evans Picture Library*)

Photographed in 1982, this is one of many photographs and films taken of the series of repeating lights which occurred in the Hessdalen valleys in Norway and were the subject of long-term study by ufologists. (*Mary Evans Picture Library*)

Researcher Leif Havik at Project Hessdalen in 1983. Extensive equipment was used to monitor the ongoing sightings of light phenomena. (*Project Hessdalen*)

Aerial photograph of a circular trace in the maize field at Castions de Zoppoca, Italy, taken in August 1985. In more recent years, elaborate patterns of cornfield circles have been subject to major controversy, particularly in the southern United Kingdom. (*Maurizio Verga*)

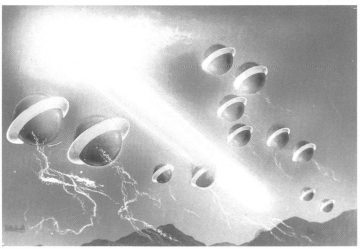

Artist's impression of Saturn-shaped UFOs seen on 17 October 1952 in Oloron, France. Witnesses reported a fall of 'angel hair' from the objects. (*GEOS*)

This photograph was allegedly taken on 21 March 1968 at Kanab in Utah by Fritz van Nest. (*Mary Evans Picture Library*)

Photograph taken on 23 May 1971 in Belgium by Rudi Nagor. (*Mary Evans Picture Library*)

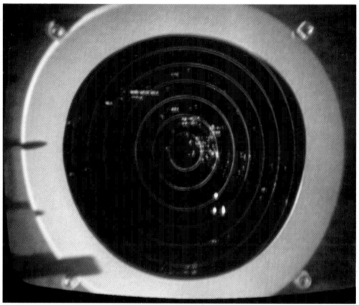

Many UFO reports are radar-confirmed or initially radar-sighted. There are many corroborative reports of sightings in aircraft which have been confirmed by ground and aircraft radar suggesting some physical presence behind the report. (*Mary Evans Picture Library*)

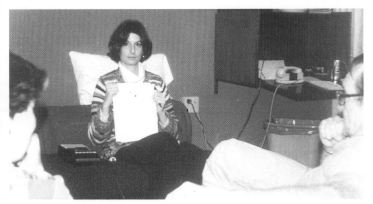

Dr Alvin Lawson's imaginary abductee experiments were an important step in understanding some of the mechanisms of UFO abduction recall. The photograph shows one of Dr Lawson's colleagues, Dr McCall (right), with two subjects: Robyn Morgan (left) and Joy Marsden (centre). Ms Marsden is holding up a drawing of an imaginary entity recalled under hypnosis. (*Alvin Lawson*)

The leading light of ufology for over three decades was Dr J. Allen Hynek. Originally 'drafted' by the United States Air Force to debunk UFOs as part of Project Blue Book's investigation, Hynek became convinced of the reality of the phenomenon and went on to lead one of the most serious civilian scientific research bodies of its time, the Center for UFO Studies. (*Dennis Stacy/MEPL*)

Betty Cash (right) and Vicky Landrum, together with Vicky Landrum's grandson Colby, suffered horrific injury after exposure to a UFO in 1980. They are pictured here with their attorney, C. V. Ford Jr, and a financial backer supporting their legal claims against the United States government. (*John Spencer*)

Australian researcher Paul Norman at Moorabbin Airport, from which Valentich flew in the 1978 Bass Strait case. Norman is standing next to a Cessna similar to the lost aircraft. (*Paul Norman, VUFORS*)

Some of the earliest forms of UFOs, reported during the 1940s, were the ball of light phenomena known as 'foo fighters', as depicted here. (*Soucoupes Volantes/Biscottes DOR*)

asked how we should reply to a message from another world, he replied: 'Hang up! Look what happened to the Indians.'

HICKSON, CHARLES
Charles Hickson was one of the two principal witnesses in the **Pascagoula, Mississippi**, case.

HIGDON, CARL
When oil driller Carl Higdon went hunting elk on 25 October 1974 in Wyoming, USA, he could have had little idea what was about to happen to him.

Having found a suitable beast with its companions in a clearing, Higdon pointed his rifle, took aim and fired. He watched incredulous as the bullet slowly floated out of the end of the gun and fell gently to the ground fifty feet away. Higdon was surrounded by a cone of silence and became aware of a tingling feeling; he was approached from the left by a man he thought might be a hunter, like himself.

He was not! In fact, the 'man' seemed not to be human. He had no chin or jaw and his face extended down to his throat; he had yellow skin, no lips but large teeth, small eyes and no ears, and, incredibly, antennae protruding out of his forehead.

A cube-like UFO was parked nearby and Higdon believes he was somehow teleported into the object which also contained the five elk he had been shooting at. They were 'frozen' in a compartment beside him.

Higdon was wired up to some machinery and shown the home planet of the aliens, presumably by some form of advanced image-making.

A search party eventually found Higdon in his truck stuck in the middle of a ravine.

Regression hypnosis revealed that Higdon had apparently seen ordinary human beings in the aliens' world, apparently acting normally and contentedly. The suggestion would seem to be that they felt they belonged there and were therefore not captured humans but humans bred by the aliens on their planet. This would support the current theory that UFO visitations relate to genetic manipulation and hybridisation programmes between aliens and human beings. Higdon believes that he was rejected by the aliens and thinks this may have been because he had had a vasectomy and was therefore of no use in any breeding programme.

HIGGINS, JOSÉ

In July 1947, in Brazil, José Higgins was one of a group of surveyors who witnessed a disc-shaped craft land near them. Three entities in shiny translucent suits emerged from the saucer and apparently indicated to the witness that they came from the planet Uranus. They were approximately six feet tall with large bald heads and huge eyes.

HILL, BETTY AND BARNEY

One of the most important and significant UFO sightings and abductions in UFO lore is the abduction of Betty and Barney Hill.

In September 1961 the Hills were returning from a holiday in Canada to their home in New Hampshire. During the drive late in the evening, near Indian Head, they noticed a bright light in the sky ahead of them and over a period of time noticed that it appeared to pace their car and get much closer. A radar report at the nearby **Pease Air Force Base** confirmed that there was something moving in the air at that time.

They stopped the car and examined the light through binoculars, believing the object to be **structured** and with various flashing coloured lights.

At a later point in the drive the object came much closer and Barney left the car, walking across a field to within close proximity. Through binoculars he gained the impression that there were people looking back at him and became afraid that he was going to be captured by them. He ran back to his car and rejoined his wife; they drove off in haste.

They arrived home apparently some two hours later than they should have done.

Some two years after the event they began a programme of regression hypnosis under Dr Benjamin **Simon**, a Boston psychiatrist, to relieve tensions which they attributed to this encounter.

Under regression hypnosis the couple revealed that they were stopped by the UFO, removed from their car, taken aboard a landed flying saucer and subjected to various forms of medical examination before being released.

Any full analysis of the case must take into account the fact that Betty Hill, in particular, had shown great interest in UFO material in the years intervening between the event and the regression hypnosis sessions, and that this material may have affected the recall. Dr Benjamin Simon insisted that any analysis of the event should take account of the fact that under regression hypnosis the subject will tell a story which is the truth *as it appears to the witness* but which may not necessarily be an objective truth.

However, any analysis of the case also has to take into account the radar trace at Pease Air Force Base.

During the encounter Betty Hill reported seeing a '**star map**' and based on this, researcher Marjorie **Fish** reconstructed a three-dimensional representation of stars in proximity to Earth which would seem to indicate that the aliens came from Zeta Reticuli 1 and 2.

During regression Betty Hill also revealed that she had been examined by way of a needle through the navel. This is significant because at the time there was no such recognised medical test, whereas in subsequent years such a test has become prominent.

In subsequent years Betty Hill has been a **repeater witness** of many encounters and in an interview with John Spencer (editor of this encyclopedia) stated that there was a period in her life when she could not go outside her house without being followed by UFOs in the sky. It has been revealed that in addition to this Betty has a long history of paranormal experiences, including some particularly impressive precognitive dreams about the violent deaths of friends and acquaintances.

Her case was brought to the public domain by journalist John G. Fuller in his book *The Interrupted Journey* (see References and Background Material) and it remains one of the most impressively documented cases to date.

HILL, PAUL R.

In July 1952 aeronautical research engineer Paul R. Hill, with some thirteen years' practical experience behind him, witnessed an apparent rendezvous of UFOs over Chesapeake Bay. Two UFOs moving at approximately 500 miles per hour were revolving around each other and were met by a third UFO 'falling in' several hundred feet below, creating a V-shaped pattern. A fourth UFO joined the group which then flew at speed towards the south.

Hill's qualifications and practical experience make the sighting an important one, particularly given that the Air Force concluded that its own aircraft were not in the area at the time.

HILL-NORTON, LORD

Admiral of the Fleet, Lord Hill-Norton, former Chief of the Defence Staff between 1971 and 1973, has been prominent in pressurising the government to make public UFO data.

It was Hill-Norton who responded with apparent astonishment to Lord **Trefgarne**'s comment on the **Rendlesham Forest** close encounter that it had 'no defence significance'. Hill-Norton believed that intrusion into UK air space and territory, or alternatively a misleading report by a senior officer of the American Air Force, constituted 'defence significance' in one way or another.

Lord Hill-Norton was a member of the **House of Lords, All-Party UFO Study Group**.

In a letter to John Spencer (editor of this encyclopedia) Hill-Norton stated: 'The more pressure that can be put on governments about UFOs the better.'

HILLENKOETTER, VICE-ADMIRAL ROSCOE H.

Vice-Admiral Roscoe H. Hillenkoetter was the first director of the **CIA**, which was established in 1947.

He was also on the board of **NICAP (National Investigation Committee on Aerial Phenomena)**, which appears to have suffered considerable CIA infiltration throughout its life. Hillenkoetter apparently stated that, 'Through official secrecy and ridicule, many citizens are led to believe the unknown flying objects are nonsense.'

HINGLEY, JEAN

Jean Hingley is the witness in the **Rowley Regis** case.

HIRANO, LIEUTENANT-GENERAL AKIRA

In September 1977 Lieutenant-General Hirano, Chief of Staff for the Japan Air Self-Defence Force, stated: 'We frequently see unidentified objects in the sky. We are quietly investigating them.'

HIX, COLONEL GUY F.

During the ill-fated flight of Captain Thomas **Mantell** in 1948 over Louisville, Kentucky, when Mantell encountered a UFO and died in an attempt to investigate it, the Commanding Officer at Godman Field, Fort Knox, Kentucky, Colonel Guy F. Hix, also observed the 'flying saucer' for some time and confirmed that a National Guard flight had been sent to investigate the sighting.

HOAX REPORTS

No compilation of UFO events would be complete without referring to the number of hoax reports received by researchers, the media, etc. There is virtually no limit to the hoaxes received, from fraudulent witness testimony, through prefabricated photographs and other physical traces, right to the other end of the spectrum with the total prefabrication of complex encounters, usually 'revealed' to the world by way of high profile, high print run books.

The reasons why people hoax are varied: certainly they would include the desire to be 'something special' to the hoaxer's friends, local community or the world at large, also a pandering to personal fantasy, and will almost certainly include the same complex psychological motives that cause people to give hoax reports of fires to the fire services, crimes to the police force, etc.

However, it is reasonable to assume that the simplest motive for creating a complex hoax is the acquisition of fame and fortune and this has almost certainly been the case in several high profile claims in past years. Although it cannot be regarded as an absolute truth, a researcher has more reason to doubt a claim which is guaranteed to produce fame and fortune for the claimant than one which brings the claimant difficulties, loss of status, and possibly loss of employment. (See also **Frauds**.)

HODGES, JOHN

John Hodges was the principal witness of the **Dapple Grey Lane, California**, encounter in August 1971.

HOLLOW EARTH HYPOTHESIS

One of the more absurd theories for the origin of UFOs is that they originate from within the Earth and enter and exit from their domain by way of huge holes in the North and South Poles. At least a part of this bizarre idea appears to have originated from an American satellite photograph of the North Pole clearly showing a large circular black area at dead centre; however, there is apparently no mystery to this as the photograph was a compilation of snapshots taken by a satellite while in orbit around the Earth and the field of the camera lens simply did not reach the North Pole, so when all the photographs were put together a gap originated which seems to have sparked off some imaginative thinking.

Despite its 'science fiction' attraction there is absolutely no evidence to substantiate this idea and a great deal of basic physics to refute it.

HOME GUARD (SWEDEN)
Official or even semi-official bodies are generally reluctant to become involved in UFO cases and it speaks volumes for the strength of a case when they do so.

In the **Vallentuna** wave of UFO sightings in March 1974, in Sweden, the local Home Guard, an active semi-official body, was so concerned by the number of reports being received that they organised **sky watches** with the local UFO groups. The initiative was led by the local Home Guard chief, Hardy **Broström**, and was particularly remarkable in that Home Guard officials outnumbered UFO investigators by over three to one. It was a well-organised programme of events, supported by a good deal of back-up equipment, and it is notable that there were many **LITS** (Lights in the Sky) reports even from the officials, confirming that something was happening in the skies over Sweden at that time.

The Home Guard officials were also involved in the abduction case that arose during the wave of sightings (see **Anders**).

HONTZ, JEFFREY
In March 1973 State Trooper Jeffrey Hontz of Saylors Lake, Pennsylvania, was called by witnesses Alan and Shirley **Pfeiffer** to a multiple UFO sighting.

Hontz reported that: 'I was there for about thirty minutes and saw four objects passing from west to east. My first assumption was that they were aeroplanes, but I didn't hear any noise coming from them. And they were so close to the ground that we should have been able to hear something if they had been conventional aircraft.'

Hontz described the objects as looking like flying Christmas trees displaying white and blue lights. The 'Christmas trees' analogy is one that arose several times during the investigation of light phenomena in Norway at Hessdalen valley (see **Hessdalen, Project**).

HOOKS, TEXAS
Occasionally a report is received which is every serious UFO investigator's nightmare but some of them, while raising

incredulous eyebrows, can also raise a smile.

During the American flap of 1973 two women from Hooks, Texas, reported seeing a UFO with red and white flashing lights. They had no difficulty in identifying this as such as the object had the letters 'UFO' printed along one side!

HOOVER, J. EDGAR

J. Edgar Hoover was, of course, the long-time Director of the **FBI** and is credited with having made a most extraordinary notation to a memo which, if true, gives further weight to the argument that the United States government had recovered crashed flying saucers. Apparently Hoover wrote: 'I would do it [aid the Army Air Force in its investigations] but before agreeing to it we must insist upon full access to the discs recovered. For instance in the LA case the Army grabbed it and would not let us have it for cursory examination.'

However, J. Edgar Hoover's public attitude towards UFOs was quite different; he wrote: 'For your information, the investigation of unidentified flying objects is not and never has been a matter that is within the investigative jurisdiction of the FBI.'

HORNER, RICHARD E.

In 1958 Richard E. Horner was Assistant Air Force Secretary and made a nationwide television broadcast to state, 'The Air Force is not hiding any UFO information. And I do not qualify this in any way.'

In the light of over thirty years' experience, and the release of information under the **Freedom of Information Act**, we can only presume that Mr Horner was carrying out orders.

HOUGH, PROFESSOR GEORGE W.

During the 1896/7 wave of **airship** reports across the United States of America, where many witnesses reported seeing **structured craft**, illuminated cabin-like structures, and even entities, Professor George W. Hough of the Deerborn Observatory at Northwestern University stated that the sightings of 'visitors' were likely to be misinterpretations of the star Alpha Orionis.

Readers should turn to the entry **Hamilton, Alexander**, where they will discover that the star Alpha Orionis threw a lasso around an animal's neck and carried it away into the sky!

HOUSE OF LORDS, ALL-PARTY UFO STUDY GROUP

This was formed by Lord **Clancarty** (formerly the author Brinsley Le Poer Trench) in June 1979. It received presentations from many prominent Ufologists – and particularly from officers of **BUFORA** – though it has fallen into abeyance in recent years.

In January 1979 the Study Group initiated a House of Lords debate on the subject of UFOs which was greeted with such enormous interest that copies of *Hansard* were sold out in record time.

HOWARD, CAPTAIN JAMES

One of the most famous early UFO encounters was that of Captain James Howard in command of a BOAC flight from New York to London in June 1954.

While it may be unconnected to the UFO sighting that was to follow, it is worth noting that early in the flight, above Rhode Island, Captain Howard was asked to hold his position. No reason was given by the air traffic controllers for this instruction but so long passed that Howard was forced to remind them that his fuel was being depleted. Traffic Control allowed him to proceed, but changed his flight plan via Cape Cod. In view of what was to follow there has been speculation that his plane was being held because the Traffic Controllers were showing UFOs on their radar.

At 34,000 feet Captain Howard sighted UFOs over the St Lawrence estuary. He counted seven objects moving at the same speed as the aircraft and parallel to it. The group apparently changed formation throughout the sighting and consisted of one large object and six smaller satellites. He and his co-pilot Lee Boyd radioed Goose Bay, Labrador, with the information who then instructed an F94 fighter to intercept the UFOs. The objects disappeared at the approach of the fighter.

There was some corroboration from the ground when a similar report was received from witnesses.

On landing, Howard and his crew were questioned at length on the sighting by United States Air Force Intelligence at Goose Bay. They admitted that they were not surprised by the sighting report as they had received many others from the area.

HOWARD, KATHRYN

In April 1969 Kathryn Howard and two companions, 'Harvey' and 'Martin' (pseudonyms), had a UFO experience which may well turn out to provide UFO researchers with the bridge between 'abductions' and benevolent 'contacts'.

One important point to note is that throughout it seems that Kathryn and 'Martin' experienced the same events, whereas 'Harvey' apparently experienced nothing. This suggests one of two possible explanations: either 'Harvey' was not intended to be a part of the contact and was 'switched off' to allow the abduction to take place unhindered (there are many such cases of this in recent UFO reports) or, alternatively, the experience was one which required a certain state of mind which was being shared by Kathryn and 'Martin', but not by 'Harvey'. Kathryn seems to believe that this latter possibility is more likely since she and 'Martin' had a very good rapport which 'Harvey' did not share.

Although Kathryn is certain that some aspects of the experience were **nuts and bolts** physical events there is also a good deal that is obviously non-physical imagery, suggesting a more complex nature to the UFO phenomenon than some researchers would seem to believe.

The event occurred in Sweden in the middle of a bright day in early spring. Much of its detail was suppressed until 1985 when Kathryn underwent **hypnotic regression**. Until that time she appears only to have recalled an uplifting, revelation-style event. There was considerable **missing time**; from the middle of the day there is no conscious recollection until eleven o'clock that evening when the companions found themselves in one of their houses.

Of the event itself it appears that Kathryn and her companions were sitting in a meadow talking about such problems as the Vietnam War and the Biafran Famine when an object appeared in the sky above them. It was oval-shaped and appeared to have legs drawn down from it. At that point the sky apparently disappeared and the witnesses experienced a vision of the moon as if from very close. Kathryn had the impression of sitting in 'the Universe'. There was much more imagery of this type, suggesting an interplay between physical abduction, out-of-body type dislocation and telepathic contact.

The first mention of fear being experienced came during the regression hypnosis sessions.

It appears that Kathryn was pulled inside the object, drawn up in one of the cylindrical legs. From inside the UFO she could look down at the Earth.

Since that time Kathryn has experienced many prophetic dreams, many of which she has not yet related. In a letter to

John Spencer (the editor of this encyclopedia) she states: 'Ever since that day, I have felt strongly that there is a message I have to get out, that I know how to get people to open their eyes in a way that they have never done before, that everyone wants to express their hidden desires and secrets with me, and on and on I could write about these things.'

HUFFMAN AIR FORCE BASE

This Texas base is thought to have been in some way involved with the close encounter of Betty Cash, Vickie Landrum and Colby Landrum (see **Cash**, Betty). The event took place close to this base, and involved American military helicopters, suggesting they were using that installation.

HULL, CAPTAIN W. J.

Captain W. J. Hull of Capital Airlines is one of many prominent and qualified pilots to report seeing UFOs. In November 1956 Captain Hull and his co-pilot spent several minutes watching a manoeuvring UFO during a flight. The object apparently executed incredible manoeuvres and 'lazy eights' before disappearing at fantastic speed.

HUMAN INDIVIDUAL METAMORPHOSIS

This is a cult group headed by a couple known as Bo and Peep which appeared in California in 1975. Bo and Peep are actually M. H. Applewhite and Bonny Nettles, the former a patient at a psychiatric hospital and the latter his nurse. It amounts to a fringe religion offering physical ascension by UFO and structured much like any other cult based around a channel and a purpose.

HUMANOIDS

Humanoid is the term used to refer to aliens, i.e. non-humans, who have broadly human form.

It is worthy of note that the vast majority of extraterrestrials are described as humanoid in appearance, though given the variety of non-humanoid life on Earth alone, there is no obvious reason why this should be the case.

It may be that the humanoid form is the highest level of development and one that advanced races would arise in. However, we have much data on Earth that suggests high intelligence in non-humanoid forms such as dolphins, and it may be that the predominance of humanoid forms in UFO reports reflects an interpretation rather than a physical reality, i.e. the phenomenon presenting itself in 'acceptable' form. In the **Beit Bridge** case in Africa, the alien who appeared as a humanoid indicated this ability to the witness who recalled, 'The being told me I would see the being only as I wanted to see it. If I wanted to see the being resemble a duck, it would look like a duck! If I wanted the being to look like a monster, it looked like a monster!'

HUMBERT, PIERRE

One of the most extraordinary twists to the **airship** wave of sightings across the United States in 1896/7 was the apparent SOS dropped from one of the craft by three individuals including Pierre Humbert of Boston, Massachusetts, and a C. D. Novina. The note was placed in a small container and thrown towards a person on the ground. It stated that the occupants of the airship had not been able to touch solid earth for two weeks following a short rest in Kansas. They appeared to have lost control of their vehicle and had run out of food and provisions and feared that they would not survive the flight.

Precisely what the ground-based witnesses were expected to do, given that this incident occurred before any form of aerial rescue would have been possible, is uncertain. There is no later confirmation that the airship eventually grounded with or without a crew.

HUNGARIAN GOVERNMENT (VIEW OF UFOS)

The Hungarian government in 1954 came up with a simplistic explanation of UFOs. They announced that UFOs did not exist because all flying saucer reports originated in the bourgeois countries, where they were invented by the capitalist warmongers with a view to drawing the people's attention away from their economic difficulties.

It must be said that this has a familiar ring to it – the first reaction of most countries to UFO reports is to blame them on other country's activities.

By an odd coincidence, however, in these more recent days of *perestroika* when the Soviet Union is releasing details of UFO reports, I spoke to Dr Lapidus of the BBC's World Service who suggested to me that Russian UFO reports tend to come in from areas where 'the salt and sugar are running out'. Seemingly, they are designed to take the people's attention away from their economic difficulties!

HUNSAKER, DR JEROME C.
Dr Jerome Hunsaker is alleged to have been a member of the **Majestic 12** panel formed in September 1947. He was head of the Department of Mechanical and Aeronautical Engineering at Massachusetts Institute of Technology and chairman of the National Advisory Committee for Aeronautics.

HUYTON, MERSEYSIDE
In January 1977 two witnesses, Barbara and her twelve-year-old son Robert (surnames withheld), encountered an extraordinary and apparently corroborated event. Robert went into the garden of their house to dispose of rubbish in the dustbin but rushed back saying he had seen a light. His mother, on going out to investigate, apparently saw a tall silver-suited figure floating in the bushes nearby. The woman ran back into the house and over a period of several hours other neighbours arrived to confront the entity. The entity was apparently unimpressed by attacks with brooms and knives, giving no reaction to either, although it took the trouble to examine the knife. During the event Barbara and her cousin Don, one of her visitors, felt tranquillised by the experience and have a memory of walking down the stairs in a trance. There may have been some time lapse element to the event.

Eventually two police officers arrived and approached the entity which vanished in front of their eyes, leaving them somewhat shocked!

HYNEK, DR J. ALLEN
Perhaps the single most significant figure in the study of UFOs over the past forty-odd years has been Dr J. Allen Hynek.

Hynek was Professor of Astronomy at Northwestern University in the United States. In 1948 he first became involved in the study of UFOs when he was engaged by the United States Air Force to conduct investigations for them and, from their point of view, hopefully to debunk the claims of witnesses. Hynek was consultant to Project **Sign**, Project **Grudge** and Project **Blue Book**, being the three predominant USAF investigations for over twenty years. Far from conclusively dismissing the subject, Hynek became convinced that there was a real mystery to be studied and on the closure of Project Blue Book in 1969 he and many other scientists who had worked with him created the **Center for UFO Studies (CUFOS)**, the first UFO group dedicated to a scientific analysis of the phenomenon.

From that point onwards, up until his death in 1986, Hynek dedicated his life to the serious study of UFO research and was very much a guiding light for those who advocated a serious scientific approach to the subject. On his death the foundation was renamed the J. Allen Hynek Center for UFO Studies.

During nearly forty years' work on the subject Hynek worked on every kind of case from **LITS** (Lights in the Sky) to complex abductions, and was involved in virtually every major event, particularly in the United States. His death left a void which has not yet been filled and the pretenders to his throne have proved to be pretenders indeed. In the United States his death also seems to have left a lack of direction and a great deal of internal conflict which may take some time to resolve.

There have been many epitaphs for Hynek but perhaps the most telling comes from British researcher Hilary Evans: 'Many of us knew him personally, as a friend as well as a researcher; but even those who knew him only from his writings and public appearances knew that he embodied all that is best in UFO research – his persistence, but also the lack of dogmatism; the confident belief in the importance of his cause, but also the willingness to listen to the ideas of others. Almost single-handed he showed how UFO research, though it might not constitute a science in its own right, could and should be conducted on scientific principles. We were fortunate, and privileged, to have such a man among us at such a time.'

HYPNOTIC REGRESSION

Hypnotic regression is the technique used by many UFO investigators to take a person back in their minds to the time of an encounter in order to elicit further information about the event, or possibly release memories blocked either by trauma or by the alleged deliberate interference of extraterrestrials.

There is considerable debate as to the effectiveness of this technique, as regards the validity of the data uncovered. Generally speaking, the medical profession takes the view that the technique is highly effective as a spur to memory. It is a tool used by psychologists for relieving tension in subjects (in a wide field, not exclusively UFO research), and skilled psychiatrists can then feed back the memory to the witness in order that they can face their fears and conquer them.

However, the medical profession is equally adamant that the memories revealed are highly unreliable; they represent the truth *as it is understood by the witness* and not necessarily an objective truth. In a simple example, where a witness has seen an apparently disc-shaped flying saucer nearby, they may have had fears and fantasies of extraterrestrial beings abducting them. When the case is examined by regression hypnosis some two or three years later (as is often the case) then these fears and fantasies could be recalled with the same strength and emotion as objective data, with very little chance for the investigator to differentiate the truth from fantasy.

Because of the exotic nature of UFO events and our inability to verify much of the data revealed by regression hypnosis, it is regarded as a highly unreliable tool and there is much criticism of researchers for accepting at face value extraordinary stories revealed under regression hypnosis.

In many cases the regression hypnosis takes place many years after the event and during that time the initial event, which may have been relatively mundane, may have inspired the witness to read a great deal of material on the subject of UFOs. This would undoubtedly have the effect of distorting at least some of the recall of the witness.

There are further problems associated with this technique; principally it is accepted that a person undergoing hypnosis is in a suggestible state and repeated questioning on a point by an examiner can have the effect of reinforcing this as reality into the mind of the witness – a particularly destructive by-product of the technique since the witness then becomes unable to distinguish memory from fantasy. In addition there is the difficulty of an investigator putting 'leading questions' while seeking their own truth based on their own role model of what they believe the case is likely to reveal. This last factor is compounded by the recognition of psychiatrists that in a state of hypnosis the relationship between the patient and the hypnotist is such that the patient will tend to give answers that please the investigator.

It has been alleged that the use of regression hypnosis, while not creating the abduction phenomenon – which certainly stands as a genuine phenomenon in its own right – may have the effect of apparently standardising data which is not as uniform as would seem to be indicated, simply because of the vast store of knowledge held not by the witnesses but by the investigators themselves.

It would however be simplistic to dismiss the technique completely, for several reasons; firstly, good researchers are aware of the problem of leading questions and avoid them;

secondly, there are many stories where the details of several witness accounts are so identical that there is every indication of a real event being recalled; and thirdly, whether or not the technique produces reliable data it is unquestionably useful in releasing the fears and anxieties of the witnesses. This concern is of paramount importance to serious researchers. One of those, Budd Hopkins, has made clear that for him it is the witness and not the data that counts. By releasing the near-suicidal anxiety of one witness, Kathie **Davis**, using this technique, Hopkins has clearly demonstrated its value in this regard at least.

As he put it at a lecture in London in 1990: the 'big picture' may be a long time coming together; these people need help now.

I

ICUR (INTERNATIONAL COMMITTEE FOR UFO RESEARCH)

A UFO group for UFO groups. Individuals cannot be members but research organisations in various countries of the world form the membership of this international coordinating network.

The administration of ICUR moves around the world from country to country. For a number of years it was based in Sweden and at the time of writing is currently based in the United Kingdom, 'housed' principally by **BUFORA**.

The main aims of ICUR are to provide an internationally compatible database of computer-stored data relating to UFO events, and to promote international cooperation in the research of the phenomenon.

It was formed in 1973 and has been the prime mover behind recent international congresses in London in 1987 and 1989.

IDENTIFICATION, PROJECT

Project Identification was headed by Dr Harley D. Rutledge and began with the investigation of anomalous lights in the area of Missouri in the 1970s. The project was scientifically based and had considerable technical support.

It was the opinion of Dr Rutledge that some of the lights may have displayed interactive responses with the observation team, including himself. This is a suggestion put forward by the much longer term observation at Project **Hessdalen** in Norway.

IDENTIFIED FLYING OBJECTS (IFOS)

The object of the UFO investigator is to turn UFOs into IFOs. In short, he attempts to explain what a witness has not been able to explain. Obviously investigators are not 100 per cent successful in this regard or there would be no UFO phenomenon but it is important to note that over 90 per cent, possibly

95 per cent, of UFO reports received are turned into IFOs and explained satisfactorily. While the remaining percentage still amounts to a significant number of unexplained sightings, the enormous percentage of IFO reports shows the degree to which we can misperceive otherwise everyday objects.

For some time it was considered that the IFOs were a 'nuisance' factor to be eliminated but current research makes considerable use of them, because of what they can tell us about witness reliability.

IMAGINARY ABDUCTEES

In 1977 Alvin Lawson and his colleagues set up an experiment to discover the nature of the UFO **abduction** experience. They proposed to examine the differences in testimony between those people who claimed they had had genuine UFO abduction experiences and those who were deliberately faking the testimony from their imagination.

The 'imaginary abductee' test subjects were selected as not having a high degree of knowledge of the UFO subject, and were given the basic outlines of an abduction with no particular detail. They were then hypnotically regressed and asked to 'recall' their abduction experience. In doing so, they produced a great deal of imaginary information which had not been input by the examiners.

What was remarkable, however, was that much of the detail given by the imaginary abductees matched the detail of real reports and suggested at the very least that those who wished to fake UFO reports had the capacity within them to do so.

Lawson's experiments were criticised on the basis that in the 1970s in California there would be few people who would not have knowledge of the UFO phenomenon. While this is true, the criticism seems to overlook the fact that that same truth must apply to those who claim the genuine experience. The study may therefore indicate that while the experience is genuine, detailed recall may be flawed and based on culture and background beliefs.

There was one major difference between the recall of the genuine and imaginary abductees: emotional response. The genuine abductees displayed considerable emotion during recall, while the imaginary abductees related their account as if talking about a television programme they had seen. However, it is unlikely that this will give us a way of identifying genuine abductees. It merely indicates that those who claim the genuine

experience also genuinely believe it to have happened and are
therefore potentially frightened of it, whereas those who do not
claim the experience have nothing to fear. But the belief of an
individual does not necessarily reflect the reality of his experience.

Whatever the flaws of Lawson's work it represents one of the
most important attempts to experiment with the data from a
subject otherwise based largely on uncorroborated testimony.
To some degree these experiments have been repeated in
certain cases and have produced less successful results; one
researcher, Budd Hopkins, relates the story of an attempt he
made – obviously with the witness's agreement – to get an
abduction story out of a witness who appeared not to have been
abducted (though his companion had been). The witness was
unable to produce data similar to 'real' claims and ended up
describing '10 per cent Star Trek and 90 per cent his last visit to
the doctor'.

IMJÄRVI

In January 1970 Aarno Heinonen and Esko Viljo were skiing
north-west of Heinola at Imjärvi in southern Finland. They
saw, approaching from the north, a very strong light and heard a
buzzing sound. The light was surrounded by a luminous mist
and as this drew closer they could see that inside was a
saucer-shaped object some nine feet wide. It came so close that
one of the witnesses stated, 'I could have touched it if I had
reached with my ski stick.'

From the base of the object a tube of light descended to the
ground, and the witnesses saw an entity standing in the light
holding a black box in its hands. The entity was thin and pale
with a hook nose, small ears and pointed head. It was wearing a
light green coverall and dark green boots. The visitation lasted
only a few seconds before the beam and the entity were taken
back into the craft which disappeared.

One of the witnesses reported that at the time his right leg
which had been nearest the light felt as if it was anaesthetised.

On returning to his home Esko's face was red and bloated
and Aarno, when he urinated, described its colour as like black
coffee; this symptom continued for a number of months.

Aarno also complained of aching joints and a headache,
numbness and tiredness. His memory also suffered badly to the
extent that he seemed to lose short-term memory, forgetting
even where he was going during the day.

Six months later the two witnesses revisited the site together with a Swedish journalist, a photographer and an interpreter; Aarno had to leave the site suffering from a severe headache and all three of the visitors suffered swollen red hands.

In the two years following the incident Aarno claimed some twenty-three further UFO sightings and has made contact with extraterrestrials which match very much the descriptions of the early 1950s **contactees'** claims of California.

There were also corroborative reports by farmers in the locality of seeing a light at the exact time of the first encounter.

IMPLANTS IN ABDUCTEES

There have been many suggestions that during abductions the abductees are implanted with devices by the aliens for some purpose. It is speculated that these implants are inserted into the brain, either through the nasal passages or through the ears, by long thin probes, and that they may represent some form of tracking or communication device.

One case suggested that the implant may have been a device to heighten extrasensory powers.

Despite the obvious physical properties of such an implant, and the capacity for exposure, there have been few claims of recovery of such a device. At the time of writing one American UFO group was studying – along with some specialist laboratories – what they believe to be a recovered device. In 30,000 × magnification the device shows what appears to be wiring.

In the case of the **Gulf Breeze** principal witness, Ed **Walters**, it is speculated that he had an implant in his head for many years but shortly before the UFO research team were able to get him to a local hospital to have the implant area scanned, he was abducted and the device removed. Investigators were quick to speculate that the aliens may have been able to monitor the investigation team's own methods and retrieve the device before it could be recovered. After the device was removed the witness claimed no further close contacts with the aliens.

INDIAN HEAD CASE
(See **Hill, Betty and Barney**.)

INSTITUTE FOR COSMIC RESEARCH

Founded in Michigan in 1967 by 'Gordon', this group of enthusiasts came together to construct a flying saucer which they called the 'Blue Bird'.

Gordon had certain attributes useful in UFO cults; he had apparently arrived in his mother's arms clad in white while a UFO hovered above them, an extraordinary birth no doubt reflecting his personal contact with extraterrestrials from the Jovian system.

Excessive hatred on Earth had apparently caused the Inter-galactic Council, based in the Jovian system, to give Gordon the mission of re-educating us.

The group lasted some seven years before it disbanded.

INTERPLANETARY PARLIAMENT

For those tired of Earth politics it must be daunting indeed to hear from so many UFO cults and groups that there are any number of galactic or interplanetary governments waiting to minister to Earth. Perhaps the most famous of those is the Interplanetary Parliament which contacted former London taxi driver George **King**. It informed him that he would become their voice on Earth and led him to create the **Aetherius Society**.

INTERPLANETARY PHENOMENON UNIT (IPU)

It is alleged that in 1947 General George **Marshall** set up a crack unit of UFO investigation scientists within the scientific and technical branch of the counter-intelligence directorate of USA Army Intelligence. This was known as the Interplanetary Phenomenon Unit (IPU) and is believed to have been dis-banded in the early 1950s when its records were handed over to the Air Force's Project **Blue Book**.

It is alleged that the IPU, which operated out of Camp Hale, Colorado, was a form of 'quick reaction force' to retrieve crashed flying saucers. It has been described as Ufology's equivalent to a SWAT or SAS team, supporting the backroom boffins of **Majestic 12**. (See also **MacArthur**, General Douglas.)

INVISIBLE COLLEGE

The 'invisible college' is a phrase used to refer to the large number of scientists researching into UFOs who have preferred to keep their interest separate from their public image and careers. Originally the expression was used when Dr J. Allen **Hynek** left the Air Force consultancy position he had held throughout Project **Blue Book** and formed the **Center for UFO Studies (CUFOS)**, bringing his scientific colleagues into the open with him.

Since then the expression has been expanded somewhat to refer to the very considerable effort put into the UFO subject by scientists throughout the world.

The term 'invisible college' was originally used in the 1600s by scientists who had to meet in secrecy for fear of being suspected of being in league with the devil.

IRWIN, GERRY

In February 1959 Private Gerry Irwin was driving from Idaho to his barracks at El Paso, Texas, when, at Cedar City, Utah, he observed a glowing UFO.

He was of the opinion that he might be watching a crashing aircraft and made an immediate attempt to aid any survivors. He left a note in his car requesting that anybody reading it should call the police. On the side of his car he wrote the word 'Stop' in shoe polish to direct people to the note.

The Cedar City Sheriff and others eventually found Private Gerry Irwin unconscious, some hour and a half after the sighting. There had been no aeroplane crash.

He re-awoke in the hospital, puzzled by the UFO sighting and also by the disappearance of his coat. It was some six weeks after the incident that he returned to the site and recovered his coat. He then reported to the Cedar City Sheriff, apparently having come out of some sort of trance and being unaware of all that had happened to him since the night he had been returning to barracks. In August Private Irwin failed to report for duty and was listed as a deserter.

He has never been seen again.

ISHIKAWA, GENERAL KANSHI

In 1967 General Kanshi Ishikawa, the Chief of Air Staff of Japan's Air Self-Defence Force, stated: 'UFOs are real and they may come from outer space . . . UFO photographs and various materials show scientifically that there are more advanced people piloting the saucers and motherships.'

ISLA DE LOBOS, URUGUAY

On 28 October 1972 the garrison of a remote lighthouse on the Atlantic coast of Uruguay, Isla de Lobos, witnessed the arrival of UFO entities.

Just after ten in the evening one of the garrison, Corporal Fuentes, left his four companions to inspect the generators at the base of the lighthouse some 150 feet from garrison headquarters.

Fuentes noticed something parked next to the lighthouse on top of a terrace. He returned to garrison headquarters, collected his gun, and made his way towards it. Next to the object Fuentes saw three **humanoid** figures, who apparently saw him. He raised his gun but was somehow prevented by the entities from shooting at them; a simple man, he was never able to explain what it was that prevented his doing so but described the effects as 'like a vibration'.

The entities boarded the UFO and took off.

Although Fuentes was the only witness to the event the other four members of the garrison were witness to his state of mind and were 'impressed' by the agitation that he suffered, not typical of a man of his kind. Psychological testing indicated that Fuentes was an uncomplicated person not prone to flights of imagination or fantasy, with a tendency to react aggressively – which very much bears out his initial reaction to the UFO.

ISTRANA AIR BASE

It is alleged that in November 1973 a UFO landed at Istrana Air Base near Venice and two entities emerged. Ground traces were apparently seen at the landing site.

Few details of the case are known as military authorities at the base have successfully kept them top secret; what information is available comes from one newspaper account.

IVANOFF, AINO

In April 1980 Aino Ivanoff, in Finland, was surrounded by mist while driving her car and apparently transported to a room where she was examined by small entities.

The abduction appears to have been more of a **contactee** experience with the entities concerned to explain to us that we should not be conducting war.

They also made reference to their inability to have children which has been interpreted, rather loosely, as supporting the theory so prominent in America that UFO aliens are abducting people for hybrid breeding purposes.

J

JACKS, MAJOR MASTON M.
When police sergeant Lonnie **Zamora** reported his close encounter at **Socorro**, New Mexico, it was a natural case for the Air Force to debunk. In a remarkable and uncharacteristic statement Major Jacks, a spokesman attached to the Office of the Secretary of the Air Force, indicated that Zamora had observed 'an unidentified vehicle'. It was a long way from their normal stance of denying such things altogether, though it failed to mention the two **humanoids** that Zamora also reported.

JACKSON, MAYOR W. C.
Convinced that one problem that had not been addressed in the UFO phenomenon was the question of hospitality towards the aliens, Mayor W. C. Jackson of Palacios, Texas, made an announcement that: 'It just occurred to me that no one has ever made those fellas welcome', and on this basis published the proclamation by town council vote to greet the flying saucers. To date, they have disappointed Texas hospitality.

JACOBS, DR ROBERT
In January 1965 Dr Robert Jacobs of the United States Air Force (now an Assistant Professor of Radio, Film and TV at Wisconsin University) was responsible for the filming of Vandenberg Air Force Base missile launches.

During one of the launches a UFO apparently buzzed one of the missiles, and was recorded on film seemingly 'attacking' it with beams of light before disappearing.

Shortly afterwards the missile malfunctioned and crashed into the Pacific Ocean, off course.

Jacobs was informed by his commanding officer, Major Mannsmann, 'You are to say nothing about this footage. As far as you and I are concerned, it never happened.'

JANAP DIRECTIVES

Concern over military personnel releasing details of UFO sightings came to a head with publication of a report by the Joint Army/Navy/Air Force Publication (JANAP). The JANAP directives indicate that anybody discussing their sightings with the media or the public could be liable to imprisonment for up to ten years and/or a fine of $10,000. They came into force in February 1954.

One such directive, JANAP 146, relates to **CIRVIS** (Communication Instructions for Reporting Vital Intelligence Sightings). One pertinent section states as follows: 'All persons aware of the contents of the service report are governed by the Communications Act of 1934 and amendments thereto, and espionage laws. CIRVIS reports contain information affecting the national defense of the United States within the meaning of the espionage laws, 18 US Code 793 and 794. The authorised transmission or revelation of the contents of CIRVIS reports in any manner is prohibited.'

While these directives clearly failed to prevent UFO reports being made, they almost certainly reduced the level of reporting, and delayed some reports until they were valueless from the point of view of on-site investigation.

JANOS PEOPLE, THE

A 'routine' abduction in June 1978, in Oxfordshire, became the subject of a book by Frank Johnson, *The Janos People* (see References and Background Material).

Husband John, wife Gloria, their own daughters and John's sister were driving towards the Gloucester area when they saw a UFO. They experienced strange imagery: a house that apparently does not exist, repeated sightings of strange scenery and time distortion. Their car seemed to take control of itself. (All of these are familiar components of other abductions and particularly the case at **Beit Bridge** in South Africa.)

When the witnesses reached home they had suffered a one hour **missing time** period. Under regression hypnosis it appeared that the family were taken aboard the UFO by tall, fair-skinned entities who conducted a medical examination on them. They drank a salty liquid (another common feature of both UFO abductions and folklore stories) which they were told would help them by suppressing their memories.

The Janos People were the aliens involved in the case, and the book featured a letter from them to Earth asking for our acceptance of them. They themselves had lost their planet, it having been destroyed by their moon.

Frank Johnson made an offer to the Janos People which, while seemingly generous, may not have gone down well in the southern hemisphere. He suggested that the people of New Zealand clear off the island to give the homeless aliens a place to live!

JANSEN, TRYGVE
In 1956 Mr Trygve Jansen and a neighbour were driving through a forest near Oslo, Norway, early in the evening when they encountered a shining disc with wings circling their car.

The disc hovered over the road directly ahead and Jansen was 'compelled' to stop the car. Both witnesses suffered a burning sensation and Jansen's watch was damaged, apparently from exposure to a strong magnetic current.

Perhaps the most surprising event was that on arriving home Jansen found that his dull brown car had turned a shiny green. Even more surprising, the car resumed its normal colour the following day.

JANZEN, POLICE CHIEF LAVERN
In March 1969 Police Chief Lavern Janzen of North Dakota became one of the great number of police and other officials to report a close UFO encounter.

'The whole damned car lit up,' Janzen reported of the brilliant light which surrounded him. Above he saw a domed greenish-blue disc hovering some 700 feet up and rotating. The blinding light was beaming down from its base. Janzen said, 'I was real scared.'

During the ten or fifteen minutes of the encounter the police radio was inoperative; it was restored when the UFO put on a high burst of speed and disappeared.

JEAN, NOEL
In December 1973 Noel Jean and his father, fishermen at Carteret on the Normandy coast, were collecting their catch early in the morning when they saw a brilliant UFO over the sea. It was approximately 8 feet long and 5 feet high, and the witnesses saw it directing a beam of light downwards. When the light disappeared it left a green globe that eventually flew away.

Noel Jean had had other UFO sightings, in the same area, of various formations of lights. A result of this sighting is that his father refuses to leave his house and no longer goes fishing.

JENKINS, BRIAN
In April 1967 eight coast guards, including Brian Jenkins, reported a sighting through binoculars, at Brixham in Devon, of a cone-shaped UFO which they described as 'shining brilliantly'. Their description indicates they believed it was made of metal. There appeared to be some sort of hatch on the underside.

Jenkins reported the sighting to RAF Mountbatten who in turn contacted the Ministry of Defence.

The Ministry offered the explanation that the object was 'something like the reflection of car headlights'.

The coast guard station commander, Harry Johnson, seemed less than impressed with the Ministry of Defence's efforts, referring to their **debunking** attempts as 'silly'.

JENNINGS, LIEUTENANT-COLONEL PAYNE
The involvement of Lieutenant-Colonel Payne Jennings in the so-called **Roswell Incident** might have gone unnoticed but for the circumstances of his disappearance.

Shortly after the alleged retrieval of a crashed flying saucer from the New Mexico desert, the Commander of Roswell Air Base, Colonel William **Blanchard**, suddenly went on leave and could not be contacted by the press. Lieutenant-Colonel Payne Jennings took over temporary command of the base. Shortly after these events Lieutenant-Colonel Jennings' aircraft disappeared in the **Bermuda Triangle** and he has never been heard of since.

JEROME, MAJOR EDWIN A.
United States Air Force Major Edwin A. Jerome criticised the UFO cover-up and suggested, 'The national policy should be to educate the public.'

As he made the statement in 1962 there has been speculation that this, and other pressure in a similar vein, led the government to undertake such a policy. There is a belief that the slow release of UFO data is a form of public conditioning. This is held to explain why there is much inconsistency in the activity of the Air Force, with some strict cover-ups and other apparently incredible releases of information.

There is another theory, and a much more likely one, that the fact that some sections of the Air Force were releasing information while others appeared to be covering it up was simply an indication that the military left hand does not know what the military right hand is doing!

JEZZI, LIEUTENANT ARRIGO D.

Lieutenant Jezzi was one of the witnesses in the **Coyne** helicopter encounter.

JIANMING, WANG

In December 1979 in the early hours of the morning Wang Jianming, together with a co-driver, Wang Dingyuan, were driving in separate trucks when they encountered a beam of light on the highway in front of them. The light contained two entities. At first the entities disappeared when the trucks stopped but they reappeared again shortly afterwards. This time Wang Jianming got out of the vehicle with a crowbar in his hand and both the light beam and the figures prudently vanished.

JINDABYNE ABDUCTION

On 27 September 1974 a nineteen-year-old man and an eleven-year-old boy were in the Snowy Mountains near Jindabyne, Australia, when they saw a bright white light on the horizon. It would be nine years before the boy had dreams which indicated a possible abduction memory.

The dreams were of being floated inside a UFO and given an examination by tall thin grey creatures measuring the electromagnetic field around his body; according to the boy's memories, his companion was subdued to prevent his interfering.

Whether or not this was a psychological or a real event cannot easily be determined but the fact that they also saw the same bright light for one and a half hours the following night indicates the possibility of a psychological event implanted over a mundane sighting with possibly the intervening years of memories distorting the recall.

Alternative possibilities would include the light on the horizon being a **screen memory**, or the fact that their psychological reaction to a mundane event 'opened' their minds to accept a message which they interpreted as abduction. There are cases in UFO literature which would support either of these possibilities.

JOHANNIS, PROFESSOR RAPUZZI LUIGI

In August 1947 Rapuzzi Johannis, an Italian artist, was walking in the mountains between Italy and Yugoslavia. Ahead of him he saw a glowing red saucer-shaped object approximately thirty feet wide attended by two dwarf-like entities. The dwarfs were short with large heads and green faces, similar to those of fish. This impression was heightened by a circular ring around each eye.

It appears that one of the entities struck Johannis with an electrical ray, leaving him weak if not paralysed.

Following this, the entities appear to have ignored him and left.

JOHNSON, DAVE
A friend of the 'first' reporter of UFOs, Kenneth **Arnold**, Dave Johnson, the aviation editor of the *Idaho Statesman*, sighted a large round UFO in July 1947. It was to perform a series of manoeuvres before disappearing out of sight.

Like Arnold before him, he made what attempts he could to verify the sighting, such as pulling back his plexiglass canopy to observe the object through clear air.

JOHNSON, HARRY
(See **Jenkins, Brian**.)

JOHNSON, RONALD AND DUREL
(See **Delphos Ring Case**.)

JOHNSON, FLYING OFFICER T. S.
In November 1953 RAF Officer T. S. Johnson and his co-pilot Officer G. Smythe in a vampire fighter over their base, RAF West Malling in Kent, encountered a stationary glowing object above their flight position. The object appears to have made a sharp turn towards them before moving off at incredible speed.

They routinely reported the incident to their commander and were somewhat surprised to end up being interrogated for over an hour by intelligence officers from the RAF.

JOHNSON, DEPUTY VAL
In August 1979 Deputy Val Johnson of Marshall County, Minnesota, was involved in an encounter, the full extent of which has never been discovered.

While driving at night he encountered a light ahead of him which suddenly engulfed the car. Apparently the alarmed officer crashed his vehicle. He recovered some time later with the car slewed across the road. Johnson was suffering from severe soreness in his eyes.

Sheriff Denis Brekke investigated the crash site and noted considerable damage to Johnson's vehicle although he could not account for it from objects in the immediate vicinity.

There was also the strange fact that the car clock and Johnson's watch agreed with each other but were both fourteen minutes slow.

Investigation of the vehicle by the Ford Motor Glass Division suggested that the damage caused to the windscreen required the simultaneous raising of pressure inside the patrol car and the lowering of it outside.

There has been no regression hypnosis and no analysis of what may have happened to Johnson during the half hour of his unconsciousness, and no conclusion has been drawn as to what it was he encountered.

JONES, AIR MARSHAL SIR GEORGE
Many top-ranking officials exposed to the UFO phenomenon through their work end up becoming serious and valuable researchers in the UFO community. One such example is Air Marshal Sir George Jones, who was Australian Chief of the Air Staff between 1942 and 1952. In 1930, as a Squadron Leader of the Royal Australian Air Force, Jones investigated UFO sightings around **Bass Strait** (later the scene of some extraordinary encounters including the death of pilot Frederick **Valentich**). In October 1957 he had a UFO sighting of his own, observing a globe-shaped object moving at the speed of a jet.

On retirement he became a member of the Victorian UFO Research Society, **VUFORS**, one of Australia's most prestigious UFO research organisations.

K

KAIKOURA, NEW ZEALAND

On 21 December 1978 Captains Verne Powell and John Randle were flying from Blenheim to Christchurch in an Argosy cargo aircraft, en route to Dunedin, when they became witnesses to several radar and visual sightings of UFOs. At one point there were five strong radar targets where none should have been, according to known traffic movements. Throughout the flight there were several UFO sightings of objects apparently pacing the plane and Captain Randle commented that although he had seen one or two unusual things in his twenty-eight years of pilot experience, they were 'nothing as irrational and inexplicable as these latest ones'.

Ten days later, on 31 December 1978, Channel 0 in Melbourne decided to retrace the Argosy's flight in a plane of its own which it chartered for the purpose. There was a film crew on board whose purpose was to film background material for a documentary on the earlier sighting. They were going to get more than they bargained for!

As the film crew were in the loading bay filming background material, the crew suddenly spotted lights in the direction of Kaikoura and radioed Wellington control who told them that there were 'targets' in that position, though they kept appearing and disappearing.

Wellington radar, shortly after midnight, reported another target which the Argosy was able visually to confirm with the comments: 'It's got a flashing light.' Twelve seconds of film were taken of this object which has since become world famous.

Throughout the remainder of the flight there were many other sightings. On the return leg an hour later, now past two o'clock in the morning, another bright UFO was seen and filmed from the aircraft.

Despite the film footage there has never been a final conclusion drawn on what exactly was seen.

KALIZKEWSKI, J. J.

J. J. Kalizkewski was working for the Navy on cosmic ray study in 1951 at Minneapolis. He and another engineer were flying near Minneapolis to examine a cosmic ray research balloon in the sky. Suddenly they saw a bright UFO moving at terrific speed crossing their plane's path. It slowed for a short time, circled, and then accelerated away towards the east.

A few minutes later a second UFO did the same and Kalizkewski called the ground technicians, asking them to investigate. One of the men on the ground managed to observe the object through a theodolite for a short time; he described it as 'strange' and 'cigar-shaped' but it was moving so quickly he could not track it. All of the witnesses maintained that the device appeared to be 'controlled'.

Kalizkewski commented, 'I can't say whether they were spaceships, saucers or what. I have never seen them before. They were strange, terrifically fast. I think the government should set up a twenty-four-hour alert with radar, telescopes, sky cameras, and other instruments.'

KARTH, JOSEPH E.

In May of 1961 it looked as if the United States government was going to reveal what it did know about the UFO phenomenon. Open hearings were suggested by the House Space Committee and a sub-committee was to be headed up by Congressman Joseph E. Karth of Minnesota. He was already on record as criticising censorship of the UFO phenomenon and therefore it seemed that openness was to be the order of the day.

The Air Force resisted this on the grounds that, 'Hearings would only benefit the sensation seekers and publishers of science fiction.' However, although there had been resistance by Congressman Brooks of the **Science and Astronautics Committee** he eventually agreed that he would hold the meetings as requested and asked Vice-Admiral **Hillenkoetter** and Major Donald E. **Keyhoe** to begin producing their evidence for the sub-committee.

Unfortunately just before the conference was due to take place, Congressman Brooks was taken ill and died and his successor, Congressman George Miller, bluntly announced that he would not order the hearings.

KARYAKIN, LIEUTENANT-COLONEL OLEG

In June 1980 there were reports of UFOs in Moscow. One such report was filed by Lieutenant-Colonel Oleg Karyakin, who reported a flying saucer hovering over his house. When he attempted to approach the object, Karyakin was apparently prevented by a force field.

There were corroborated sightings from local people in the area; other reports include one **humanoid** entity report.

KEECH, MRS MARIAN

Mrs Marian Keech was a contactee who received messages from space beings known as The Guardians. She received the messages in the form of **automatic writing**; as she put it, 'Without knowing why, I picked up a pencil and a pad that were lying on the table near my bed. My hand began to write in another handwriting.'

The Guardians explained to her such concepts as life in the beyond; one of their 'elder brothers' was Mrs Keech's personal guardian and communicator.

A sect grew up around Mrs Keech, following the messages that were being received through her as the channel.

The legendary details of the successes of The Guardians are perhaps held to be of more substance than is strictly justified. For example, on one occasion the group predicted the landing of a flying saucer at a military base and went to the area to see this. They were approached by a man who gave them an eerie feeling and who suddenly disappeared but no one had seen him leave.

Predictably, the group became a pseudo-religious sect, turning in on itself. It forecast a disaster, a massive flood on a biblical scale, from which believers in The Guardians would be taken away by flying saucer to safety. The group published its warnings in newspapers. However, sociologists infiltrated the group, studying the nature of the sect.

They wrote up their findings of what was occurring in Mrs Keech's group in the book *When Prophecy Fails* (see References and Background Material) which is a very important analysis of the sociological reactions to belief in UFOs and particularly extraterrestrials.

For a time the apparent failure of the group's predictions was held to reflect success; when no flood wiped out the United States then the sect took the credit for having averted a disaster. Eventually, however, without a target aim the sect fell apart and the flying saucers did not come to save it.

The feelings of the sect are perhaps typified by the comment of one member as he began to acknowledge some disillusionment. He said, 'I've had to go a long way. I've given up just about everything. I've cut every tie. I've burned every bridge. I've turned my back on the world. I can't afford to doubt. I have to believe.'

KEIRN, MAJOR-GENERAL DONALD J.

In April 1959, the head of the United States Air Force nuclear engine development programme, Major-General Donald J. Keirn, stated of UFOs: 'It is entirely possible that some of them may have passed through our stage of evolution, and may have already achieved a higher level of social and technological culture than our own.'

KELLY, MAJOR-GENERAL JOE W.

In 1957 Air Force Major-General Joe W. Kelly admitted the involvement of the Air Force in UFO pursuits. He stated, 'Air Force interceptors still pursue Unidentified Flying Objects as a matter of security to this country and to determine technical aspects involved.'

The implication would seem to be that the Air Force was strongly considering a physical, perhaps extraterrestrial, explanation for the reports.

KELLY-HOPKINSVILLE CLOSE ENCOUNTER

Considering the strange, not to say unique, details of this case, had it been reported by a single individual it would not have received a high credibility rating. In assessing the case it is therefore worth bearing in mind that there were eleven witnesses aged between seven and fifty (with eight adults over twenty) and that in the thirty-five years since the event none of these has publicly retracted their extraordinary claims, though in fact to have done so in the early days would have alleviated the public ridicule with which they were met.

The event happened on the night of 21/22 August 1955 in a small group of houses at Kelly, near the town of Hopkinsville in Kentucky.

At seven o'clock that evening one of the witnesses, Billy Ray Taylor, went outside to collect water from a well and saw a huge shining UFO, with an exhaust 'all the colours of the rainbow', landing in a dried-up riverbed near his farm. Although he told others in the house about the landing no one believed him and no one investigated the landing site. Whether this landing has anything to do with the subsequent events is therefore not proven.

It was approximately an hour later when the Taylor family and friends were alerted to something by the barking of a dog in the yard. Elmer Sutton and Billy Ray Taylor went to the kitchen door to see what was causing it. They were greeted by a unbelievable sight. A creature was approaching the farmhouse with its arms stretched high in the air. It had enormous eyes and was glowing as if from within. The creature was short, approximately 3–3½ feet tall, had a round egg-shaped head, completely bald, huge eyes placed on the side of its face, an enormous crack-like mouth stretching from ear to ear, and elephant-like ears. The arms ended in long claw-like hands and the whole body emitted a silver glowing shining colour, except the eyes which glowed yellow.

The two witnesses took a rifle and a shotgun and fired at the creature; it somersaulted backwards and scurried away into the trees around the farm. But the encounter was not over yet by a long way.

After hearing a sound on the roof they ran out into the yard and found one of the creatures moving on top of the house. Again they fired at it and it floated gently down to the ground in the backyard. When the witnesses fired again, the creature disappeared into the scrub.

The family and friends gathered inside the house and bolted the doors; for a time they watched the creatures roaming around outside. By eleven o'clock they were frustrated and decided to make a run for it, to end the siege. They dashed out of the house and into two cars, then drove the ten miles to the local police station for help. The idea of hardened, proud country folk running from their house, the ordeal of cramming themselves into two cars and then 'high tailing' it to the police, speaks volumes for the sincerity of the report.

When they returned to the farm it was with the Hopkinsville Chief of Police, Russell Greenwell, his deputy George Batts, four other officers and the photographer from a local newspaper.

Although not necessarily directly connected to the event, while they were on the Kelly road out of Hopkinsville they saw and heard two sounds passing overhead 'with a noise like artillery fire'.

The police examined the area. They found the bullet holes but no trace of the UFO or the creatures. Greenwell made the point that these were not the sort of people who ran to the police normally and therefore 'something frightened these people, something beyond their comprehension'.

And still the encounter was not yet over.

The police returned to Hopkinsville, planning to investigate more fully in daylight. At 2.30 in the morning Elmer Sutton's mother, Glennie Lankford, saw one of the creatures looking in her bedroom window. She called softly to the family and when Elmer Sutton ran into the room he ignored his mother's pleas for peaceful communication and shot through the window at the creature. The creatures continued milling around the farmhouse until just before sunrise that morning.

Following the event the witnesses insisted on telling the truth as they saw it, refusing to protect themselves from ridicule by holding back the more extraordinary details. As a result they were forced into the spotlight of public attention, were accused of religious hysteria, and became the focus of sightseeing tours.

Theories as to what lay behind the Kelly-Hopkinsville siege have been varied. One suggestion was that because a circus had passed through Hopkinsville that day, some monkeys may have escaped, but this does not hold up since obviously the physical description of the creatures does not match that of monkeys, and in any case no monkeys were reported missing. Furthermore, whatever the creatures were, if they were vulnerable in the normal way then there ought to have been at least one body lying around after a night-time of 'shoot-out carnage', yet no creatures were ever found.

There was some corroboration from a neighbour who had seen lights moving around on the fields near the Sutton farm that evening, but he believed only that some animals might have escaped and the Suttons were rounding them up. As he said: 'I am glad I didn't go out there [to help] – I might have been shot.'

KERRINGER, ROBERT E.

Department of Justice Inspector Robert E. Kerringer was driving on patrol near Lynden, Washington, just after midnight on 12 January 1965. Suddenly a bright glow lit up the ground; it was so powerful that even buildings in the distance were illuminated. As Kerringer began to slow the car down an enormous object swooped down right over him. It was about thirty feet wide and apparently round but the glare prevented Kerringer seeing any details. It stopped just above the road some fifty feet from him and it was apparent that no matter how quickly he braked he was going to hit it. Suddenly, at the last minute, the UFO shot up out of the way. Kerringer stopped the car, jumped out and aimed his .357 Magnum revolver but did not fire it.

For some three minutes the object hovered above him and Kerringer got a strong feeling of 'I was being watched'. He reached in for his radio mike to call headquarters and the disc began to move. Suddenly it climbed faster than any jet and disappeared into the clouds.

Other Department of Justice investigators corroborated the sighting and Blaine Air Force Base tracked it on radar. As Kerringer summed up his encounter: 'The Air Force is making a bad mistake trying to hide this. It could blow up right in their faces. People should be warned that such things can happen. I didn't believe UFOs were real. I had to be shown, and believe me, it was a rough way to learn.'

KERRYVILLE, TEXAS
On 11 January 1953 a huge oval-shaped UFO, glowing orange red, was seen by witnesses at Kerryville, Texas, and it was reported that it created a very peculiar interference with television reception. It came at the beginning of something of a minor wave of sightings which lasted throughout that month and into February.

KERVENDAL, GENDARMERIE CAPTAIN
It was acknowledged by Captain Kervendal of the French Gendarmerie that because of the force's social, political and military position throughout France they were in a unique position to assist in UFO research. He commented: 'Something is going on in the skies . . . that we do not understand. If all the airline pilots and Air Force pilots who have seen UFOs – and sometimes chased them – have been the victims of hallucinations, then an awful lot of pilots should be taken off and forbidden to fly.'

KEYHOE, MAJOR DONALD E.
An important figure in American UFO research in its early days was United States Marine Corps Major Donald E. Keyhoe, a

director of **NICAP (National Investigations Committee on Aerial Phenomena)**.

Keyhoe made no secret of his strongly held belief that UFOs were probably of an extraterrestrial origin. He expressed this view unwaveringly in his public statements and several books.

Because of his sensitive position within the United States Marine Corps he was frequently subject to censorship, including one incident on a live television programme in 1958 when he was taken off the air seemingly 'in the interests of **national security**'. He was trying to state that a congressional investigation could prove that UFOs are 'real machines under intelligent control'.

Keyhoe's books (see References and Background Material) were often challenged in official circles, in one case on the grounds that they were 'too near the truth'! Based presumably on the high degree of apparent infiltration of NICAP by the **CIA** (NICAP's controlling body at one point included a former director of the CIA) it has been suggested that Keyhoe was in fact an official outlet for educating the public to accept UFOs in a joint military/CIA long-term programme of conditioning.

Keyhoe was removed as NICAP's director in December 1969 by John **Acuff**, who himself has been linked with the CIA, and who in turn was replaced by a former CIA employee. It is held that Keyhoe's removal from the board was instigated by its chairman, Colonel Joseph **Bryan** III who was a former chief of the CIA psychological warfare staff.

KIDD, CAPTAIN J. L.

In October 1953, while flying an American Airlines DC-6 towards Washington DC, Captain J. L. Kidd was forced to make drastic manoeuvres to avoid collision with a UFO over Maryland. Such was the force of the manoeuvres that several passengers were injured and the plane had to radio ahead for ambulances and doctors to be on standby for its arrival. It would be remarkable if an experienced pilot caused such injury without what must have seemed very good reason at the time.

The UFO appeared to be as large as the aircraft although there were no reports of any other activity in the air at the time, according to the Civil Aviation Authority.

KILBURN, FLIGHT LIEUTENANT JOHN

Flight Lieutenant John Kilburn at RAF Topcliffe, in September 1952, in the company of four other RAF personnel, watched a

UFO following a Meteor jet heading towards RAF Dishforth in Yorkshire.

The object was described as silver and circular. During its descent it apparently exhibited '**falling leaf motion**' but at one point stopped in the air, rotating around its own axis but maintaining position.

Witnesses were convinced that the object was solid, approximately the size of a Vampire jet, and they believe that it accelerated to an 'incredible speed' before disappearing. Duration of the incident appears to have been about twenty seconds.

KILBURN, STEVEN

Steven Kilburn had not had a UFO event that he could recall nor had he any conscious memory of an abduction; in fact, his only concern was that he had a bizarre fear of a particular stretch of road and sought out help to investigate the reason for this.

Using regression hypnosis, the investigators determined that the fear had been caused by Kilburn having encountered a UFO and having been abducted by short dwarf-like entities at that particular point on the road; his fear reflected his trauma. In fact Kilburn's abduction case is protracted and extraordinary and probably the first time when such a detailed case has arisen from no self-reporting of a UFO on the part of the witness. However, it must be remembered that Kilburn sought out a UFO investigator, and as such Kilburn therefore seems to have pointed in the UFO direction by choosing that investigator.

There has been concern that the technique of regression hypnosis, which is known sometimes to be unreliable and inaccurate in cases of such trauma, may have contributed to some of Kilburn's memories. There are, however, also many similarities with other UFO cases, implying corroboration.

KILLIAN, CAPTAIN PETER W.

On 24 February 1959 American Airlines Flight 713 was flying from Newark to Detroit. It was piloted by veteran Captain Peter W. Killian and co-piloted by First Officer James Dee.

As the airliner cruised at approximately 350 miles per hour over Bradford, Captain Killian became aware of three glowing objects to the south of his route and above his altitude. They were flying in a direct line together.

He was able to ascertain that they were not stars, having first believed them to be the belt of Orion but then being able to identify that constellation separately; he also recognised that these unknown objects were larger and brighter and more distinctly coloured.

As the aircraft entered Erie, Pennsylvania, air space one of the objects left the formation and flew towards Captain Killian's DC-6. It then slowed down and returned to its original formation.

Captain Killian made one error of judgement; he told his crew and passengers of the objects, unfortunately causing some panic in at least one of the passengers who had to be reassured that there was no threat to his safety.

Killian radioed other aircraft to find out whether he was the only one seeing the phenomenon and received one response from an American Airlines colleague: 'We have been watching the formation for ten minutes.' There were other corroborative sightings to this event which for Killian had lasted three quarters of an hour. There is therefore no question of the accuracy of this report.

According to the Air Force, the explanation was that a flight of KC-97 tankers refuelling three E47 bombers had taken place in the vicinity at the time and the refuelling operation had been conducted at 17,000 feet, well above the flight level of the DC-6. Captain Killian, however, was not impressed by this explanation saying he knew full well what such a refuelling operation looked like. He heartily embraced the extraterrestrial hypothesis, saying, 'I am sure there are people on other planets and they have solved the problem of space travel . . . I sincerely believe that their vehicles are coming close to the Earth.' Major Donald **Keyhoe** of **NICAP** stated that when the UFO had broken away from formation and headed towards the craft, 'Killian knew now it was a UFO – some unknown machine under intelligent control.'

KIMBALL, SECRETARY DANIEL
In the first quarter of 1952 one UFO chose a prominent target. Navy Secretary Daniel Kimball was flying to Hawaii when his aircraft was 'buzzed' by a flying saucer. A second Navy plane was following and Kimball's pilot radioed back asking for information; they were told that the saucer had buzzed the second plane also but so swiftly that no one had been able to assess its shape with any accuracy.

Shortly after this Air Force instructors in New Mexico also reported a huge shining oval craft some six times the size of a B-29. Speculation had it that this was the mother craft and that Kimball's plane may have encountered a surveying scout ship, assuming of course that the sightings were connected.

KIMBERLEY, LORD
During the 1979 House of Lords debate on the subject of UFOs a former Liberal spokesman for aerospace, Lord Kimberley, stated, 'The people of Britain have a right to know all that the governments, not only of this country but others throughout the world, know about UFOs.'

KING, 'SIR' GEORGE
Former London taxi cab driver George King became the founder of the **Aetherius Society** after a voice told him he was to become spokesman for an interplanetary parliament.

KING, JOHN T.
On 23 March 1965 John T. King took the law very much into his own hands when he encountered a UFO. He was driving near Bangor, Maine, when he encountered a huge domed disc hovering over the road. As he drove towards it his lights dimmed and the radio stopped and King believed he was in danger. King had a Magnum pistol in the car with him and opened fire on the UFO. With the third shot the disc took off 'at tremendous speed'.

KINROSS AIR FORCE BASE
On 23 November 1953 a UFO was detected by radar from Kinross Air Force Base. A multi-role jet fighter piloted by Lieutenant Felix Moncla was scrambled to intercept and observe the phenomenon. Radar controllers clearly saw the F-89C fighter converging on the unknown blip on the radar and then saw both blips merge into one another. It was as if there had been a collision.

The last radar contact with the jet had been 160 miles north-west of Soo Locks at 8,000 feet. The Air Force put out a statement that the F-89C had identified the UFO as a Royal Canadian Air Force C-47 transport travelling to Ontario and that having identified it the jet had returned to base.

However, **NICAP** investigations seemed to indicate that mention of this mission had been eliminated from the records.

There is speculation that no trace of the jet has ever been found since the Air Force *also* put out a statement saying, 'It is presumed by the officials at Norton AFB Flying Safety Division that the pilot probably suffered from vertigo and crashed into the lake.'

The Air Force seems either not to know what was going on on the US/Canadian border or knows very well and would prefer the public not to have the information.

KLARER, ELIZABETH

It was on 27 December 1954 that Elizabeth Klarer had her first **close encounter** but she had had two prior involvements with UFOs. In October 1917 she and her sister had watched a meteorite seemingly about to collide with the Earth but being deflected by the power of a metallic object which came in near to the meteorite, apparently protecting the planet. In 1937 while flying from Durban to Baragwanath, Elizabeth Klarer watched as a blue-white light streaked towards her plane. When it levelled out and paced the aircraft she could see that it was a circular object, changing from blue-white to gold and eventually to red. Shortly after this the craft shot high above her aircraft and disappeared.

At 10 a.m. in the morning of 27 December 1954 Elizabeth Klarer was drawn out of her farmhouse in the foothills of the Drakensberg in South Africa by a commotion from the farmhands. Elizabeth ran to the hill on which she had had her sighting in 1917 and saw a brilliant flash of light in the clouds above her. An enormous saucer-shaped craft some fifty-five feet wide descended towards her.

The object stopped some twelve feet above the ground, hovering near her, and although she was afraid she resisted the temptation to run. The whole of the ship was flat and rotating around a squat dome. Three portholes faced her and in one of them she could see a **humanoid** looking out. He seemed to view her nonchalantly while she was attracted to his good looks. No interaction took place and the craft took off.

In April 1956 Elizabeth had a compulsion to return to the farm and to her 'flying saucer hill'. When she reached it the spacecraft was resting on top as if waiting for her. This time the humanoid was outside the craft. He was tall with a deeply lined face and clear grey eyes, high prominent cheek bones and white hair. He wore a one-piece cream-coloured suit.

As he took Elizabeth's hand he said, 'Not afraid this time?'

and she felt she trusted him. Elizabeth allowed herself to be taken on board the saucer which took off, giving her a view of the Earth from 1,000 miles above. The saucer took Elizabeth to the mothership which was peopled by many like Akon, the name of her contact. She was also shown pictures of the alien's home planet, known as Meton. The people there are apparently vegetarians, there is no politics and no money, no arguments or war and no diseases. They can travel anywhere in our galaxy but cannot move between the galaxies.

Akon's main reason for his meeting was to recruit Elizabeth for a breeding experiment but his approach was with love and compassion rather than the clinical or aggressive approaches of most such contacts. In this case Elizabeth fell in love with Akon, became pregnant by him and spent the last four months of her pregnancy – up to and including the birth of her son – on Akon's home planet where the child now lives with his father.

Elizabeth Klarer has written her own story in her book *Beyond the Light Barrier* (see References and Background Material).

KNIGHT, COLONEL GORDON B.

Responding to a specific inquiry by Congressman Thomas N. Downing, Chief of the Congressional Enquiry Division, Colonel Gordon B. Knight stated, 'There never has been an Air Force or Air Technical Intelligence Center top secret estimate of the situation which declared that UFOs were interplanetary.' This directly contradicts the findings of some civilian UFO groups in the United States who believe that an estimate of the situation revealed just that, but was then withdrawn due to potential public concern.

KNOWLES FAMILY, NULLARBOR PLAIN, WESTERN AUSTRALIA

Mrs Knowles and her three sons were driving from Perth towards Mundrabilla when they saw lights ahead of them on the road. As they approached they realised that they were hovering above the ground just off the main road and indeed hovering over another vehicle. They turned their car round and chased back towards where the sighting had occurred; unfortunately, the light changed *its* course and came back to meet them. They met when something making an audible noise landed on the roof of their car.

The car was apparently dragged upwards and there was some consternation and agitation amongst the witnesses. Suddenly the vehicle was dropped back to the ground where it burst one of its tyres; where the object had been attached there was damage to the roof. Once the car was back on the ground the family leapt out and hid in the bushes until the UFO had gone. From their observation they described the object as a white light about the same size as their car, making a sound like electrical humming.

Throughout the incident the radio of the car had been malfunctioning though subsequent investigation by Paul Norman of **VUFORS** indicated that it was undamaged. Examination of the tyre indicated that it was ripped in a most extraordinary way all around its edge.

Subsequent investigation revealed a great many more UFO reports on the Nullarbor Plain on that night.

KÖLMJÄRV, LAKE

Just before noon on 19 July 1946 one of the famous Swedish 'ghost rockets' made its appearance in the far north of the country in what is probably the best documented of such cases. Farmer Knut Lindbäck and Beda Persson were working on the shore of Lake Kölmjärv when suddenly a humming sound could be heard in the sky. They looked up and saw what appeared to be something like an aeroplane or rocket-like device diving towards the lake.

The ash grey projectile fell into the water approximately one and a half kilometres away from them and a tall cascade of water splashed up from the impact. Lindbäck said, 'I am sure it was a solid object. It was two metres long and had a snub nose while the stern was pointed. I thought there were two wing-like protrusions on the side but I am not sure, everything happened so quickly.'

On another shore of the lake a further witness, Frideborg Tagebo, also saw the impact and noticed that when the thing went under the water it was like a bomb detonating.

The next morning soldiers under the command of Lieutenant Karl-Gösta Bartoll cordoned off the site and searched the lake; that search was to last for the next two weeks. Despite this, there is no confirmation that anything was recovered though, as it was pointed out, some of the guidance system and electrical circuits ought to have survived even if a light-weight body had disintegrated.

KOMURA, MAJOR-GENERAL HIDEKI

Major-General Hideki Komura, in 1977, was an adviser to the Cabinet Research Office in Japan which is that country's equivalent of the American **CIA**.

He stated that there were high level official Japanese UFO investigations based on the American Project **Blue Book** and cooperating closely with the United States government investigations.

He refers to these investigations having been conducted in the 1950s and comments that the system collapsed because of the garbage reports being received alongside more credible data.

KOPEIKIN, MAJOR ANTON

On 27 April 1961 a group of hunters watched the very close approach of a UFO during the early morning; the sighting was of a near crash landing. The object was egg-shaped and approximately the size of a commercial aircraft and was travelling very low and very fast towards an inlet of lake **Onega** in the Soviet Union. It came in so low that it struck the ground, making a tremendous noise and causing considerable damage before regaining forward and upward motion and disappearing from sight. Apart from the impact noise there was no sound associated with the sighting.

The collision had created three gouges into the vegetation and rock surface and there were a number of traces left from the impacts. There was something like a green ice which analysis indicated contained such elements as aluminium, calcium, barium, etc. although there was also an unknown organic compound. There were metallic-like particles which were very resistant to temperature and acid, and were not radioactive, and there were thin foil-like substances of great durable strength.

Major Anton Kopeikin, an engineer of the Soviet Army, was in command of the military side of the recovery and investigation and it was he who subsequently sent all of the recovered material to the Leningrad Technological Institute for study.

KURZ, SHANE

During the opening months of 1968 there were several UFO sightings around New York State where Shane Kurz lived. Several of these were seen by Shane Kurz and her mother who filed reports about them.

On 2 May Ms Kurz had been outside the house watching UFOs, after which she had then returned to bed and fallen into a deep sleep. She was awoken by her mother who was concerned that Shane was lying on top of the bedspread in her slippers and dressing-gown with her legs and clothes covered in mud. There were muddy footprints leading into the house from outside.

In the following days Shane suffered menstruation difficulties, migraine and other pains and felt that she must find out exactly what had happened to her on that mysterious night of which she had no memory.

It was not, however, until many years had passed that she was able to follow up her events with regression hypnosis. Under hypnosis she recalled being drawn to the window by a telepathic voice calling to her and then outside the house and towards a landed UFO nearby. It was when crossing a muddy field towards the UFO that Shane had become caked in mud. Somehow she was drawn inside (one of the commonest factors of UFO abductions is the lack of specific knowledge witnesses have about how they get on board the UFOs). She was taken into what appeared to be a hospital-like operating theatre where a medical examination took place, including many procedures which have been recorded by other abductees over the years.

Although many abductees recall being used for artificial insemination purposes, in this particular case Shane was physically raped by the leader of the aliens whom she described as humanoid though generally more slender than normal humans. Many of her worst fears about the encounter ended nine months after the event, suggesting some connection to pregnancy. Other American cases, notably those investigated by Budd Hopkins, might shed light on this, suggesting that perhaps a further abduction had taken place when the hybrid alien offspring was removed.

One interesting feature was the fact that Shane stated she had enjoyed the sexual encounter with the alien but possibly only because of a substance smeared on her body beforehand. This was exactly the same claim made by Antonio Villas **Boas** in 1957.

L

LA ROCHELLE, AFRICA

La Rochelle is part of the Nyabara Forest training school and is a tourist attraction. The estate used to belong to the Courtauld family.

At approximately half-past six in the evening of 15 August 1981 Clifford Muchena saw a ball of light near the tea room on the estate, a sighting which was corroborated by others.

It reached the estate's observation tower and seemed to roll up it and into the room at the top. Although it gave the appearance of setting fire to the tower it later left the building and rolled back down towards ground level, leaving no searing or burn marks where it had been. Apparently it was not hot nor did it contain heat within itself.

The ball of light moved across the lawns and into the 'Fantasy' building, which was an orchid house once used by Lady Courtauld. Again, it looked as if the building was filled with flames though subsequent investigation showed no such damage.

Clifford stopped ringing the fire bell and went across to the building; it was at this time that he saw three men standing on the lawns. At first he believed they were the estate's wardens, including Mr Andrew Connolley, and indeed Clifford called out Mr Connolley's name.

The entities turned around very slowly. They were wearing shiny silver coveralls and there was a brilliant light shining from them which blinded Clifford. He fell to his knees, possibly from fear or possibly because of something emanating from the entities. He stated, 'There was a power coming from them.'

Other witnesses on the estate saw the ball of light and also the men. It was considered by Clifford that they might be the ghosts of his ancestors, an alternative interpretation to extraterrestrials and not necessarily a less realistic one. When asked why they were wearing silver suits and not the furs and skins that his ancestors would probably have worn, Clifford said, 'Yes, but you know times change.'

It is not clear when either the men or the ball of light left, though one of the witnesses thought that the men had disappeared first and the light afterwards. Whether there is any connection between the two sightings is unclear but certainly something strange was happening on the estate and it would be remarkable if two such extraordinary events were independent of one another.

LANCASHIRE, ALBERT
In September 1942 Albert Lancashire was on guard duty at New Biggin, England. He saw a light appear out at sea and witnessed what appeared to be a black cloud moving towards the coast. Lancashire went outside; he was struck by a beam of light and felt a floating sensation. He later awoke, dazed and confused, lying on the ground. He had no memory at this time of what had happened to him but in 1963 made comments to people that he had 'been inside a UFO'.

In October 1967 there was a wave of sightings across Britain and these triggered Lancashire's memory of his 1942 event. Apparently in a series of dreams he recalled waking up in a room, presumably after being struck by the beam of light from the UFO, and seeing an oriental woman lying on a bed. He was given goggles to protect his eyes. Lancashire's recall is more of a semi-religious nature than pure abduction though there are abduction characteristics in the case.

The considerable time since the event makes thorough investigation impossible now, but if he was abducted then his was one of the earliest cases we have on record.

LANDRUM, VICKIE AND COLBY
(See **Cash, Betty.**)

LANGFORD BUDVILLE, SOMERSET
On 16 October 1973 Mrs A. (witness identity withheld) suffered **vehicle interference** when she was driving near Langford Budville in Somerset. She got out of the vehicle to examine it, and instantly fainted after she was touched and turned to see a huge robot standing behind her.

When she came around she found that she and the robot were standing next to a domed UFO parked in a field, the lights from which had already caused her concern during the drive but which she had not at that time identified. This proved too much and she collapsed again, coming around to find herself tied naked to a metallic table where three humanoid figures were conducting a physical examination on her. Even more extraordinarily, one of them sexually assaulted her, causing her to faint again.

The next time she came round she was back inside her car and three hours had passed.

She reported the event to her husband but kept the story generally under wraps for fear of ridicule. It was four years later before they were prepared to discuss the matter and even then Mrs A. was not prepared to undergo regression hypnosis.

There are obviously many parallels in this case with others across the world though it is clearly also rich in symbolism; whatever the truth, it appears that Mrs A. is sincere and her reluctance to involve herself in unwanted publicity says much for the sincerity of her claims.

LAREDO AIR FORCE BASE
On the night of 4 December 1952 a United States Air Force pilot (name withheld) was flying to Laredo Air Force Base, in Texas. Twelve miles out he watched as a strange blue UFO streaked directly towards his plane and only avoided collision by flipping aside at the last minute. The pilot had watched it climb vertically, turn and sweep back towards the plane as if attacking. He switched off his lights and dived.

The UFO also dived to 2,000 feet, missed the F51 plane, circled around the Laredo Air Force Base and then turned away swiftly, disappearing into the night on a straight vertical climb.

When he landed, the Air Force pilot was visibly frightened by his encounter and made a report to United States Air Force intelligence officers.

LAYNE, MEADE
A director of the Borderland Sciences Research Foundation in California, around 1949 he wrote memos relating to information received concerning crashed and retrieved flying saucers. It was a subsequent director of the foundation, Mr Reilly Crabb, who released one of the memos, quoted in the book *The Roswell Incident* by Charles Berlitz and William Moore (see References and Background Material). The memo states that a disc 'was shaped like a turtle's back, with a cabin space some fifteen feet in diameter. The bodies of six occupants were seared and the

interior of the disc had been badly damaged by intense heat.'
The memo goes on to add, 'An autopsy on one body showed
that it resembled a normal human body except in size.'

LEE, JOHN
In March 1984 Major Sir Patrick **Wall**, MP, (now President
of **BUFORA**) tabled a question to the then Secretary of
State for Defence regarding landings of UFOs between 1980
and 1983.

His reply came from John Lee, the Defence Under-Secretary
for Procurement, who stated that landings were not separately
identified from other reports, though there had been over 1,500
overall in the years concerned reported to the Ministry of
Defence. He went on to add, 'The Department was satisfied
that none of these reports was of any defence significance and,
in such cases, does not maintain records of the extent of its
investigations.'

LEMON, GENE
A glowing UFO was seen by thousands of people crossing the
state of West Virginia on the night of 12 September 1952. At
Sutton several witnesses thought that they had seen it land on a
nearby hill. They were Mrs Kathleen May, her three young
sons, and a seventeen-year-old National Guardsman, Gene
Lemon.

They climbed the hill towards where they believed the object
had landed and Lemon turned on a torch to sweep the area.
They noticed a malodorous, suffocating smell. As they
approached the spot where they believed the landing to have
taken place they saw two shining eyes and turned the torch on
them, thinking they would discover something like a racoon in a
tree.

In fact what they saw was a huge creature nine feet tall with a
glistening red face and protruding eyes a foot apart. The
monster glowed dully green and started moving towards them,
making an odd hissing noise.

The witnesses fled down the hill and immediately phoned the
local sheriff. They soon noticed that some oily, unpleasant
substances had covered the boys' faces and their throats began
to swell up. During the night Gene Lemon became seriously ill,
suffering the same inflamed throat as the other boys but also
went into fits and convulsions. Later it was established that the
effects had been similar to an attack of mustard gas as used in

the trench warfare of the First World War.

The sheriff had been unable to investigate the claim as his dogs refused to go anywhere near the location. After sunrise that morning a strange machine was seen taking off from the hilltop and subsequent investigation found landing traces in the form of flattened grass.

Such a story may be difficult to accept, although it is worth bearing in mind that it is one of many, but the Air Force's own appraisal of the claims seems to stretch credibility even further; they believe that the glowing object seen across West Virginia and by the family was a meteor, that it only appeared to be landing when it went past the hill, that the glowing eyes seen by the group was a large owl perched in the tree, that the giant figure was an illusion given by the undergrowth, that the illnesses were brought on by fright and shock and that the grass landing traces were caused by the people who went to investigate the case.

LENTICULAR CLOUDS

Lenticular clouds are a perfectly natural cloud formation but can be so striking as to cause reports of UFO sightings. They are disc-shaped and often metallic grey and although quite often appearing singly can also appear in large clusters. They are an impressive sight, looking like hovering flying saucers.

The fact that they stay around for much longer than the average flying saucer usually identifies them and photographs of them, while remarkable, also pick out their cloud-like characteristics. However, if they are part of an overall experience which includes the witness's own agitated state of mind, then they can unfairly enhance a witness's report and indeed confuse the true substance of the claims.

LEON, DR PADRON

In June 1976 Dr Padron Leon was travelling by taxi to treat a patient in the early hours of the evening on the island of Grand Canary. In the taxi with him was the patient's son, Santiago del Pino.

As the taxi rounded a bend in the road they were confronted by a transparent globe hovering just off the ground. It seems to have been approximately thirty-five feet in diameter at this time, and inside two very tall entities were seen operating machinery.

The taxi's radio cut out and the witnesses experienced a

feeling of severe cold, Dr Leon reported in his statement to the Spanish Air Ministry.

The beings were described as approximately 9–10 feet tall, wearing tight-fitting red coveralls, black helmets and possibly black gloves.

An even more extraordinary event was yet to unfold; the globe expanded to the size of a twenty-storey building!

The witnesses fled to a nearby house, where the occupants commented that their television had recently blacked out, and watched the object from there. Emitting a high-pitched sonic whine the object apparently moved at high speed towards Tenerife.

LEWIS, STEVE

A former Air Force intelligence officer who spent a number of years investigating UFOs on behalf of the United States military.

Following his retirement from the service he stated that he was convinced that intelligent extraterrestrials were visiting the Earth. He gave no details of his work – apparently under restriction from the Air Force – but commented that very little of their accumulated information had been released. Asked why he had arrived at the conclusion he had, he replied, 'The records, the information I saw while in my job.'

He also commented that 'that movie *Close Encounters of the Third Kind* is more realistic than you believe.' There have been many suggestions that the Air Force sought to 'educate' the public gently to accept the reality of UFOs; and even that science fiction films were a deliberate part of that process.

LEYS (LEY LINES)

Ley lines, or leys, are straight lines which are held to connect the sites of ancient and often mystical locations. It is held that the leys carry extraordinary energy with which our ancestors were able to interact and that many ancient monuments, burial grounds, etc. are erected on particularly powerful points (often the intersections of ley lines) because those are the sites where extraordinary events occurred.

It is held by some Ufologists that the ley lines are also used by UFOs for one reason or another and that the intersection of the leys are points of high UFO activity.

Certainly various forms of energy lines, though not necessarily ley lines, are a significant part of UFO research in Scandinavian countries. The British interest in ley line study has been extended into Ufology in France where some research has been done showing that French UFO cases take place along straight lines (see **Orthoteny**).

Tabloid newspapers usually refer sarcastically to leys as 'flying saucer runways'.

LIDDELL, DR URNER

Dr Urner Liddell of the Office of Naval Research is the prominent author, or at least the original author, of the 'UFOs are all balloons' school of thought. After Captain Thomas **Mantell** died in a crash following a UFO chase, Dr Liddell claimed that UFOs were real but they were the Navy's 'Sky Hook' cosmic ray research balloons and went on to add, 'There is not a single reliable report which is not attributable to the cosmic balloons.'

This may have been a slight oversimplification.

LIE-DETECTOR TESTS (POLYGRAPH TESTS)

One of the frequently asked questions, posed mainly by sceptics, is what would happen if UFO witnesses undertook lie-detector tests? The implication of the question, of course, is that they would fail the tests because they are lying.

In fact, many witnesses *have* taken such tests and in many cases the results have been positive. What is not generally appreciated is that the tests are often suggested by the witnesses themselves because they recognise the unbelievability of their claims and seek to offer as much corroboration as possible. This makes no particular claim as to the 'reality' of UFOs, but speaks volumes for the sincerity of the witnesses.

In the case of the Travis **Walton** encounter, he and his brother Duane took lie-detector tests which they apparently passed (although there has been some controversy about a previously failed test). For the witnesses other than Travis Walton, taking the lie-detector test had become very important indeed; Walton had been missing for five days and they were beginning to be suspected of having murdered him.

Charles Hickson, who had an extraordinary encounter in **Pascagoula, Mississippi**, in 1973, took a lie-detector test, the conclusion of which was: 'It is my opinion that Charles Hickson told the truth when he stated: (1) that he believed he saw a spaceship; (2) that he was taken into the spaceship; (3) that he believed he saw three space creatures.' The statement was signed by Scott Glasgow, a member of the Louisiana Polygraph Association.

In assessing the reliability of these tests as tools of UFO investigation it must be remembered, however, that aside from the possibility of a successful liar getting through the tests (which must have happened from time to time in UFO cases as much as it must have done in criminal investigation cases), there is also the problem that the lie-detector test can only confirm that the person is telling the truth *as they believe it to be* and that does not necessarily have to be the same as an objective truth which any other person at the time would also have agreed with.

However, the use of lie-detector tests has indicated that the UFO phenomenon is certainly more than mere hoax, an unsupportable belief held nowadays mostly by the more blink-ered scientists and astronomers for whom the UFO phenom-enon not only *does not* but also *must not* exist.

LIFESTYLE, CHANGES IN, OF WITNESSES
Several witnesses, and particularly **abductees**, have self-reported changes in their lifestyle following their experiences. In other cases, associates, friends and family members have reported such changes. Generally speaking these have been changes for the good; i.e. people become more concerned about the welfare of the planet or of people generally, or people become more artistic and less materialistic. There are of course psychological or physiological effects from UFO encounters which I am not including in this category.

One very clear example of this is in the case of the witness 'Marianne' who – as a young girl in Sweden in the mid-1970s – saw a disc-shaped UFO and had several night light encounters, sometimes also in the presence of her father, and held these to be of special meaning specifically for her. She believed that the UFOs were there to awaken her to the ecological needs of the Earth and at the present time, now as an adult, she is greatly involved with many ecological projects across the world.

Whether or not the UFO can be held to be the direct cause of this or whether she would have developed such interests anyway is debatable, but it is significant that *she* believed the two to be linked.

One popular theory of UFOs, whether their origin be extra-terrestrial or terrestrial, is that they are seeking to direct the human race towards a higher plane of living and that their minor manipulations of individuals are part of an overall picture we cannot understand as they direct our thinking and our culture towards this enhanced existence. The belief that UFOs may be linked to the **Gaia** concept of a conscious, living planet is one example of a 'terrestrial' theory that arises from such observations.

It must also be remembered that UFOs are in any case a 'New Age' phenomenon and that there is often some tendency towards or at least sympathy for New Age views amongst UFO witnesses; again, it is not clear whether or not these views would have existed prior to these encounters, i.e. whether the encounter opens up a previously broad mind or whether it is only broad minds which are able to perceive UFOs.

LIGHT, GERALD
In April 1954 a person called Gerald Light wrote to the then director of the Borderland Sciences Research Associates (now Foundation), Meade **Layne**, claiming that he had gone to the **Muroc Air Force Base** in the company of a newspaper man, Franklyn Allen of Hearst papers, Edwin Nourse, **Truman**'s financial adviser, and Bishop McIntyre and during two days was allowed to see and study a retrieved flying saucer, as the letter says, 'with the assistance of permission of the Etherians [the aliens]'.

Unfortunately very little is known about Gerald Light and it is highly possible that the letter is a hoax. Investigators seeking to authenticate the letter have failed to identify Light with certainty and in any case it is rumoured that he died many years ago and subsequently cannot now be questioned.

Meade Layne had apparently described Light in an article he wrote as, 'A gifted and highly educated writer and lecturer', and pointed out that he was involved in clairvoyance and the occult.

LIMA, PERU
According to a Reuters report from Lima, Peru, on 12 September 1968 a flying saucer had emitted rays which doused a Peruvian customs official. He had been standing on the terrace of his house when violet rays had shone on his face. He had suffered from short-sightedness and rheumatism for some time,

and indeed had to wear very thick glasses for the former condition, but both conditions were completely cured following the event.

LINDSAY, JOHN V.
In 1961 the Mayor of New York, representative John V. Lindsay, stated publicly that UFO sightings were a matter of vital importance. 'The security of the United States does not always demand total secrecy . . . the American people are fully capable of understanding the nature of these problems,' he said. Pressure from him and other representatives resulted in the statement in mid-1961 that there would be an investigation (see **Karth, Joseph E.**).

LITS (LIGHTS IN THE SKY)
When Dr J. Allen **Hynek** tried to classify UFO sightings he devised a system based largely on the witness's approximation to the event (subdivided into the nature of the event itself), and LITS or 'lights in the sky' was one of the subdivisions of *distant* encounters, usually a night-time equivalent of 'daylight discs'.

For those who believe UFO reports are a rare event it is sobering to consider that several US state investigation sections of **MUFON** now receive so many UFO reports that LITS often go uninvestigated as a matter of policy, due to limited resources available and the sheer weight of even more extraordinary claims. (See **Classification of UFO Events**.)

LITTLE GREEN MEN
Probably the most famous description of extraterrestrials is as 'little green men'. Certainly this is the favoured description in science fiction with perhaps Dan Dare's Mekon as the stereotypical form. However, there have been very few genuine reports of green aliens, with perhaps the closest being the glowing green entity seen at **Vilvoorde** in Belgium.

In fact, the commonest description of UFO or extraterrestrial entities is of little grey men and the commonest slang description in the United States for extraterrestrials is 'the grays'.

LIVINGSTON, SCOTLAND
Forester Robert Taylor had an extraordinary encounter in the morning of Friday 9 November 1979 at Livingston in Scotland. He had left his house at ten o'clock that morning in a pick-up

truck to inspect the plantations near the M8 motorway which connects Edinburgh to Glasgow. He parked the truck at the end of a track and walked towards a clearing to inspect the trees there. As he rounded a corner into the clearing he was confronted by an extraordinary UFO.

It was a large, globe-shaped object hovering just above the ground. At first the colour was a uniform dark grey with a rough texture but as Taylor watched there were times when it hazed in and out of near visibility and he could see the trees behind it. He gained the impression that it may have been trying to camouflage itself.

The object was approximately 20 feet wide and 12 feet high. Slightly below halfway down was an extended rim like the brim of a hat from which protruded stationary 'bow tie'-like objects, and behind which on the main body something like dark patches, or possibly portholes, could be seen.

Shortly after seeing this incredible vision Taylor saw two small, spiked, mine-like spheres rushing towards him either from behind or underneath the main object. Their colour and texture were similar to the large UFO but their size was just a foot or two across. They rolled forward across the ground and grabbed Taylor by the legs, dragging him towards the object. His trousers were torn where the mines had attached themselves. At this point he was overwhelmed by a choking smell and lost consciousness.

When he opened his eyes he believes he heard a swishing sound and then found none of the UFOs was visible. His dog was now racing around him, barking wildly, and he found that he was unable to walk properly or to talk.

On getting back to his pick-up truck he ran it into soft ground and could not move it; consequently he had to walk the mile or so back to his home. He had a headache which lasted for several hours and a thirst that lasted for two days.

Although the object was seen very close to the M8 motorway those driving on that road would not have seen it as it would have been obscured by trees from their field of vision. However, any approach into the clearing by air that the object made ought to have been seen by somebody and yet no such reports were forthcoming. This suggests that if the object really existed, i.e. it was not an image internally generated by Taylor himself, then it must have approached the clearing in another way, either during the night or by materialising where it was rather than physically flying to the site.

Investigation of the site revealed marks on the grass which correspond to the places where the legs of the spiked mines had rolled; there was no lasting effect on the site, no burn marks or damage to vegetation.

Following the event Taylor took an interest in flying saucers, which had before that not been of interest to him at all. He now does believe that he saw a spacecraft and that robots attempted to abduct him.

LLANCA, DIONISIO

In the early hours of the morning of 28 October 1973 Dionisio Llanca was driving down a deserted road when he was struck by a yellow beam of light and paralysed.

Near him was a hovering saucer from which three entities emerged. They wore tight-fitting grey overalls, were of normal height and had long fair hair and large slanting eyes. They spoke in squeaky voices and took a sample of blood from his finger, whereupon he fainted.

When he came round he was taken by a passer-by to the hospital at Bahia Blanca. Hypnosis and sodium pentathol were used to probe into Llanca's memory; he recalled that he was taken into a bright room and that the aliens told him that they had been recording the progress of the human race. Recently they had decided to see whether the human race could be 'tampered with' so that if the Earth met a large-scale disaster, some components of the race could be saved by evacuation.

These events parallel many aspects of other abductions over the past decades, most of which would probably have been unknown to this witness.

LLANERCHYMEDD, WALES

On 1 September 1978 at Llanerchymedd in Wales, several boys playing just outside the village started shouting that they thought a helicopter was landing in a nearby field. When they went to look at it they discovered that it was a bullet-shaped object glowing red and that it was landing behind some trees. Other people from the village started coming towards the field to see the object and the boys persuaded two nearby adults to witness the event also.

Through the dim twilight they saw two six-feet-tall figures in grey one-piece suits walking across the field, apparently panicking horses that were grazing there. One woman became so scared she locked herself in the upstairs bedroom of her house; from there she claimed she had seen three such figures in the field.

Once the police had been called and started to investigate, neither the men nor the object could be located and no one knows when they disappeared.

The Royal Air Force was held to have investigated the case using helicopters but denied that it had done so. Apparent ground traces consisting of a circular flattened patch of wheat suggested a landing area but there is no definite corroboration of this.

LORENZEN, JIM AND CORAL
In 1952 Jim and Coral Lorenzen founded the **Aerial Phenomena Research Organization (APRO)**, which was one of the first and foremost private United States research organisations. Their work in the early years of the UFO phenomenon did much to promote an acceptance of the claims witnesses were making.

LOTTI-DANIELLI, MRS ROSA
(See **Arezzo, Italy**.)

LOW, COLONEL CURTIS
On 29 December 1952 Colonel Curtis Low of the United States Air Force was flying an F-84 jet fighter at 27,000 feet over northern Japan. He was listening to communication between the nearby Air Force base and an F-95 flying in the area at the time.

The event had started minutes earlier when the Air Force base had received a call from a B-26 plane reporting a UFO 'like a cluster of lights – red, white and green'. The Air Force had picked up the UFO on radar but the B-26 was too slow to intercept; at that point the F-95 pilot radioed in confirming the sighting.

Shortly after this Colonel Low's own wing commander sighted the red, white and green object and ground control asked him to attempt to intercept.

Colonel Low climbed and switched off his lights. At 35,000 feet and much closer to the lights, Colonel Low could see that it was a saucer-shaped object revolving in a counter-clockwise direction at something between eight and twelve times a minute. Although there was this movement there was also the stability of three white, constant, unmoving beams and it appeared that only part of the saucer was rotating. Colonel Low pushed his plane up to full power, something like 500 miles per hour, but the saucer easily pulled away and disappeared within thirty seconds.

Five minutes later the wing commander spotted the object again, this time moving parallel with the F-84. Colonel Low left his lights on and tried to close in but the object fled again.

LOW, ROBERT J.

Robert J. Low was the project co-ordinator of the **Colorado (University) UFO Project**, the investigation into UFOs. On 9 August 1966 he produced a memorandum of instruction which has called this official investigation into question ever since. It stated, 'Our study would be conducted almost exclusively by non-believers, who, although they couldn't possibly prove a negative result, could and probably would add an impressive body of evidence that there is no reality to the observation. The trick would be, I think, to describe the project so that, to the public, it would appear a totally objective study but, to the scientific community, would present the image of a group of non-believers trying their best to be objective, but having an almost zero expectation of finding a saucer.'

It is difficult to decide which of the above extraordinary phrases is most significant considering that the investigation was supposed to be scientific, but perhaps the most telling expression is 'the trick'.

LOWMAN, DR PAUL

Dr Paul B. Lowman Jr, a NASA scientist at the Goddard Space Flight Center, was sensibly critical of persistent rumours that NASA had uncovered proof of the extraterrestrial origin of UFOs, particularly on some of the Apollo moon flights and notably the *Apollo 11* flight. He stated, 'I am continually amazed by people who claim that we have concealed the discovery of extraterrestrial activity on the moon. The idea that a civilian agency . . . operating in the glare of publicity, could hide such a discovery is absurd. One would have to swear to secrecy not only the dozen astronauts who landed on the moon but also the hundreds of engineers, technicians and secretaries directly involved in the missions and the communication links.'

LOWRY, BILLY

On 1 September 1983 Billy Lowry was motorcycling from Brighton to Blackpool. At 11.45 in the evening he telephoned his friends to give them an estimate of his likely arrival time while he was near Whitchurch in Shropshire. He drove on, noticing a bright light in the sky. When he got out into the open country near Warrington he noticed the light seemed to be coming towards him. He felt that he was being watched and stopped his motorbike in the middle of the road.

He considered photographing the object but for some reason decided not to do so, feeling this was perhaps by instruction. In fact, he turned out his lights and was all the more able to appreciate the dark object in the sky with lights all around it that was now hovering directly above him.

Car headlights appeared ahead of him and the object moved away; Lowry suddenly realised it was dangerous to be where he was in the middle of the road and drove off; he discovered that he was just outside Chester on the wrong road and it was some two hours after the time he had stopped.

No attempts have been made to unlock the missing two hours of memory using either regression hypnosis or various other visualisation techniques.

LUBBOCK LIGHTS

A pattern of V-shaped lights is frequently seen near Lubbock, Texas, for which no concrete explanation has been given. It is thought that they are a natural phenomenon though other suggestions have included flocks of birds illuminated from below and, inevitably, fleets of flying saucers.

They were photographed in August 1951 and those photographs have been shown all over the world, held up as proof of all sorts of possibilities.

I was told by one American colleague that the town of Lubbock had set up 'UFO watches' as part of a tourist attraction. As he put it, 'All Lubbock ever had was Buddy Holly and the lights, and now they've only got the lights.'

LURE, PROJECT

The Lure Project, or Operation Lure, was devised by the National Investigations Committee on Aerial Phenomena (**NICAP**), and particularly promoted by Major Donald E. **Keyhoe** in his book *Aliens from Space* (see References and Background Material).

The basis of the Lure was that it should be a landing site in an isolated area designed to attract the aliens' attention, with a view to interaction between aliens and humans.

It was based on a Canadian government attempt to create a 'UFO landing field' at **Alberta** in 1958. This earlier project is held to have failed because there was nothing to attract the aliens' attention.

The Lure was to be designed to attract alien attention by having displays clearly intended for them; dummy UFOs, items of particular interest to aliens, such as cars, planes, models of dams and reservoirs, etc. All of the base would then be covered by TV cameras and microphones connected to a Lure Control which would be an observation post for monitoring the responses of the aliens.

The Lure was based on the belief that the aliens are seeking interactive communication and that we should respond to their attempts to communicate with us.

Although revolutionary in its concept it is probably now outdated. Keyhoe's book was produced in 1973 when abduction or contactee claims were still treated with considerable suspicion by even mainstream Ufologists, let alone scientists, and this would have been seen as a rational and scientific alternative to abductions or contactees.

However, the upswell of such claims in recent years suggests that if aliens are involved in the UFO phenomenon then they are perfectly capable of arranging their own meetings as and when they seek to do so. Indeed, their abilities seem so wide ranging that the Lure begins to look like the equivalent of a child seeking to please his father by showing off a particularly nice building-bricks house and – as children do – believing that the father is receiving architectural instruction by looking at it.

Whatever the merits of the Lure, it is not a plan that has ever been put into operation, or at least no government has admitted doing so.

More recent statements by Ufologists and others suggest that the United States government and aliens have been working together for many years on a programme of acclimatisation towards an overall exposure of the truth. These statements are viewed with some suspicion, not least because each pre-appointed day of some revelation passes with no event happening and also because factors outside Ufology suggest that if the aliens were going to entrust a massive secret to anybody, the United States government might not be the first on the list!

M

MACARTHUR, GENERAL DOUGLAS

One of the most famous American generals, General Douglas MacArthur, is believed to have been involved in establishing the **Interplanetary Phenomenon Unit (IPU)**, allegedly formed to investigate crashed and retrieved flying saucers.

In 1955 he made an astonishing statement for somebody in his position, and one which has led to intense speculation that the Interplanetary Phenomenon Unit may have uncovered more than has been revealed. MacArthur stated: 'The nations of the world will have to unite for the next war will be an interplanetary war. The nations of the Earth must some day make a common front against attack by people from other planets.'

MCASHAN, LIEUTENANT-COLONEL JAMES

Lieutenant-Colonel James McAshan was one of a number of United States Air Force officers opposed to the official policy of **debunking** and cover-up. He stated, 'In concealing the evidence of UFO operations the Air Force is making a serious mistake.'

MCDILL AIR FORCE BASE, FLORIDA

In the stories of crash retrievals, i.e. the retrieval of crashed flying saucers and dead aliens by governments and particularly the United States government, it is generally held that the discs and bodies are stored at **Wright Patterson Air Force Base**. However, other locations have been given for the retrieval of other discs in the past and McDill Air Force Base in Florida is one of the more prominent of these.

It has been speculated that public pressure for disclosure about crash retrievals centred on Wright Patterson, caused the authorities to move the material to McDill Air Force Base where some researchers believe it is still held.

MCDIVITT, ASTRONAUT JAMES
During *Gemini 4*'s flight, astronaut James McDivitt reported seeing the appearance of a cylindrical-shaped object outside the spacecraft.

Although much has been made of this report, McDivitt has stated that it is not believed it was anomalous, i.e. that it was an 'ordinary' object he simply could not identify at the time.

MCDONALD, DR JAMES E.
In July 1968 there were congressional hearings on UFOs before the House Committee on Science and Astronautics and the atmospheric physicist, Dr James E. McDonald, reported of the **Great North-East Blackout** of November 1965: 'Just how a UFO could trigger an outrage on a large power network is however not clear. But this is a disturbing series of coincidences that I think warrant much more attention than they have so far received.'

Although the blackout in the north-eastern United States, engulfing as it did the city of New York, has received the lion's share of such publicity there have been many such reports from several countries of the world.

MCGILL, SIG
During a wave of sightings across the United States in October 1973 there were a number of reports of a silver and black UFO flying just 150 feet above a Santa Cruz road. One reporter was Sig McGill who was attracted to the object by the strange noise it was making. He watched it fly down Almar Avenue, turn right and disappear beyond some trees.

He telephoned the police and reported the UFO. The newspaper, the *San Jose News*, later stated that Santa Cruz and Santa Clara County Police received so many sightings from that evening that a special log was maintained for them.

MACKENZIE, DR J. C.
In January 1952 the Canadian establishment indicated its serious concern with the UFO phenomenon by a number of announcements. One was by Dr J. C. MacKenzie, the Chairman of the Atomic Energy Control Board and a former president of the National Research Council. He said, 'It seemed fantastic that there could be any such thing. At first the temptation was to say it was all nonsense, a series of optical illusions. But there have been so many reports from responsible

observers that they cannot be ignored. It seems hardly possible that all these reports could be due to optical illusions.'

MCLEAN, J. D.

On 16 November 1952 a group of five glowing objects was seen to the north of Landrum in the United States. Four of the witnesses were J. D. McLean and his wife, and David S. Bunch and his wife. They used an 8 mm camera and telephoto lens to take forty feet of film of the objects. This film was then handed over to McLean's son who was the editor of the *Ingalls Ship Building Corporation News*. It was then further handed on to the United States Air Force for study.

It is known that the film was reviewed by a large group of Air Force officials including Major Donald E. **Keyhoe**, Albert M. Chop (the Air Force's Press Liaison Officer), several public information officers, Colonel William A. **Adams** and Colonel Wendell Smith.

The film clearly showed five glowing oval shapes below the cloud cover and was reviewed three times before Colonel Adams stated, 'That's enough, we don't want to scratch it. Have copies made as soon as you can.'

It was pointed out that proper analysis of the film would take months but eventually there was a release suggesting that the film showed some form of natural light effect.

MCLENORE, DEPUTY-SHERIFF

Along with Constable Sumpter, Deputy-Sheriff McLenore of Arkansas, on 6 May 1897 witnessed the apparent landing of an **airship** UFO during the wave of sightings taking place in that year. It appeared first as a brilliant light in the sky. The light then disappeared and reappeared later much lower towards the ground. The law enforcement officers were on horseback. They stopped the horses to watch the landing, which they then rode towards.

Approximately a hundred yards away from the object that had landed in the fields, the horses refused to go further and the officers drew their rifles and shouted: 'Who is that, and what are you doing?' to the people moving around in front of the landed object.

One of the people from the object, a man with a long dark beard, explained that they were travelling across the United States in an airship, which the officers could see was cigar-shaped and some sixty feet long. The officers asked why the

Artist's impression of the Gran Canaria 'soap bubble'. Witnesses on the road drove to a nearby house where they joined the occupants in watching the object as it grew to the size of a twenty-storey building, although its contents remained the same size as before. (*GEOS*)

An artist's impression of the mysterious and repressive Men in Black who appeared in the early days of the UFO phenomenon in America. (*Mary Evans Picture Library*)

Occasionally, natural cloud formations can take extraordinary symmetrical shapes which give rise to a number of UFO reports. This photograph was taken near Marseilles in France. (*Mary Evans Picture Library*)

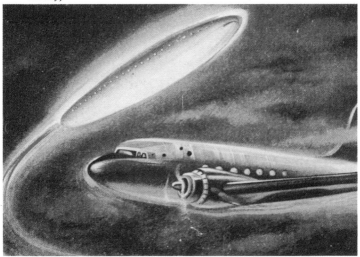

A depiction of the encounter reported by Captain Clarence Chiles and co-pilot John Whitted from an Eastern Airlines DC-3 over Alabama in July 1948. (*Soucoupes Volantes/Biscottes DOR*)

This photograph, taken by farmer Paul Trent and his wife at their farm near McMinnville, Oregon on 11 May 1950, was the only one that was not dismissed as easily explainable by the Condon Committee. (*Mary Evans Picture Library*)

Photographed on 16 July 1952, these lights seen at the Salem coastguard facility in Massachusetts have long been held to be visiting flying saucers. In fact, analysis indicates that it is highly likely to be a photograph of lights reflecting from inside the room in which the picture was taken. (*Seamus R. Alpert*)

UFO photographs are only of value in supporting credible witness testimony. They cannot stand alone as proof of UFOs when they can be faked so easily, as this picture, created by photographer John Shaw, shows. (*John Shaw*)

On 22 November 1979, Elsie Oakensen was abducted by a UFO in Northamptonshire, England. She is one of many witnesses whose honesty and credibility strongly support the reality of the UFO phenomenon, whatever its origins. (*John Spencer*)

Charles Hickson was abducted, together with Calvin Parker, at Pascagoula, Mississippi in October 1973 by extraordinary entities. Hickson (right) is photographed here at the 1990 MUFON UFO Symposium with the editor of this encyclopedia. (*John Spencer*)

After being contacted by aliens, French racing driver Claude Vorilhon set up the Raelian Movement, which achieved a considerable following in France and across Europe. (*Mary Evans Picture Library*)

A sample of the hundreds of UFO magazines and pamphlets published across the world each year by the hundreds of thousands of people involved in UFO research. (*John Spencer*)

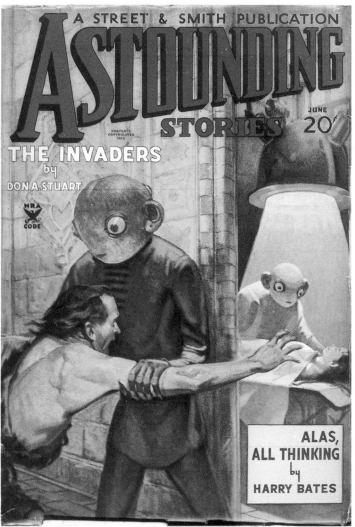

Those who believe that stories of abduction reported by witnesses must be literally true because there is no cultural image from which to draw the story should consider some of the early science fiction. This illustration from 1935 has all the main features of the abductions reported in the 1960s and beyond. (*Astounding Stories*)

light had been seen to be going on and off and it was explained to them that it took a great deal of their power and they only used it when they had to.

The officers had to hurry on their business, but some forty minutes later when they were able to return to the scene they could not see any sign of the craft though they had not seen it leave.

MCMINNVILLE, OREGON

On 11 May 1950 a UFO passed over the Trent farm near McMinnville in Oregon. Mrs Trent was outside feeding rabbits and she noticed the huge disc-shaped object flying towards her. She called her husband who brought their camera and the Trents were able to take two black and white photographs of the object as it passed silently across the sky.

Even the **Condon Committee** was forced to list these photographs as the only ones they were unable to dismiss and in their findings concluded that the photographs were consistent with the Trents' description of the UFO. The Condon Report conclusion was, 'This is one of the few UFO reports in which all factors investigated, geometric, psychological, and physical, appear to be consistent with the assertion that an extraordinary flying object, silvery, metallic, disc-shaped, tens of metres in diameter, and evidently artificial, flew within sight of two witnesses.'

In more modern times these photographs were subjected to complex computer analysis and those too confirm that the object appears to be large and distant. There was no evidence of supporting wires or other clues that the object may have been faked and it therefore remains a most thought-provoking image.

The photographs proved to be almost identical to a photograph taken by a pilot in Rouen, France, in the summer of 1954.

MAARUP, EVALD HANSEN

In the late evening of Thursday 13 August 1970 Danish police officer Evald Maarup, driving through the countryside near Haderslev, Denmark, encountered a brilliantly lit UFO.

Maarup found a fierce light beaming down on him, his car engine cut out, the lights of the car were extinguished and his radio was put out of action.

Beyond the light, above him, Maarup could make out a large, grey, soundless, circular object which he watched over a five-minute period. The light that had been surrounding his car was drawn up into the object which then moved rapidly, and still soundlessly, away. At this point the electrical systems of the car came back to normal.

Maarup described the object as thirty feet in diameter with an opening in the base some three feet wide which the light was beaming down from. There were domes on the underside similar to those reported in many other craft, including the famous **Adamski** scout ships.

Although Danish air tactical command suggested that Maarup had seen the landing lights of a T33 jet trainer (which Maarup denied), the Danish Air Force was complimentary to Maarup and said: 'We have the greatest confidence in the police officer, he is a trained observer, and we do not seek in any way to dismiss this kind of observation.'

Almost to the day three years later, on 14 August 1973, Maarup had a second similar encounter at almost exactly the same time and in the same place.

On this occasion he watched the object beaming down the light as it passed across fields, disturbing cattle and horses before knocking out the electrical systems of his car again. On this occasion he saw three domes underneath the object, just as in the Adamski photographs of the 1950s. Maarup took photographs of the object during the encounters but these show only indistinct points of light.

No particular conclusion can be drawn but the case suggests that Maarup was being specifically targeted, and with frightening precision.

MACEIRAS, VENTURA

In the late evening of 30 December 1972 Ventura Maceiras, living in a wooden shack in the Argentine countryside, noticed that the radio he was listening to was fading and creating a humming noise. When he looked up he saw that hovering above the trees around the shack there was an enormous purple and orange object. It had round windows and through them Maceiras could see two **humanoid** figures gazing at him. They wore dark suits and helmets but Maceiras could see their slanting eyes and thin mouth, and indeed could also see some of the instrumentation inside the control cabin.

Shortly before moving away and disappearing over the trees and behind a hill, the object fired a beam of light at Maceiras, temporarily blinding him.

For several weeks Maceiras had very severe headaches, diarrhoea, nausea and loss of hair. In addition, red sores appeared on his neck, and he had difficulty speaking and seeing.

Analysis of the site showed that the tops of the trees had been burned and there were a number of dead fish in the nearby stream.

But most remarkable of all was what happened to Maceiras approximately a year later. Although well into his seventies he suddenly began growing a third, and new, set of teeth!

MAGNET, PROJECT
Between 1950 and 1954 the Canadian government is believed to have investigated UFOs under the auspices of Project Magnet. Officially it was claimed that Project Magnet was a study of 'those phenomena resulting from unusual boundary conditions in the basic electro-magnetic theory', but documents released since that time include twenty-five UFO reports and the startling conclusion: 'It appears then, that we are faced with a substantial probability of the real existence of extraterrestrial vehicles.'

Project Magnet was discontinued in 1954 apparently because the publicity that it attracted was embarrassing the government.

Project Magnet has also been linked with the investigations into the **Bermuda Triangle**, an area off the cost of Florida where it is alleged that many planes and ships have been lost in mysterious circumstances. According to one reporter the Project had discovered 'peculiar magnetic forces' in the area. It has been suggested that the Canadian government was working with the US Navy, who were concerned about the loss of a flight (No. 19) of their aircraft in 1945, and who were concerned that the US Air Force would not share their knowledge of UFOs with them (UFOs have frequently been linked with the mysteries of the Triangle). The official releases of Project Magnet deny such a connection.

Whatever the true aims of Project Magnet it was hardly the top secret, undercover project that many hold it to have been; one of its aircraft was photographed with the words PROJECT MAGNET emblazoned on its tail.

MAJESTIC 12
It is alleged that following the retrieval of the crashed flying saucer in **Roswell**, New Mexico, in 1947, the government set up a highly secret investigative group known as Majestic 12. Its brief was to report its findings directly to the United States President.

The following were the members of the Majestic 12 group,

and brief biographies of each are given under their names in this encyclopedia: Dr Vannevar **Bush**, the head of the group and a former head of the Office of Scientific Research and Development which developed the first atomic bomb under the work of the Manhattan Project; Vice-Admiral Roscoe **Hillenkoetter**, a former director of the **CIA**; Lloyd V. **Berkner**, a former executive secretary of the Joint Research and Development Board; Detlev W. **Bronk**, one of America's most widely known and respected scientists; James V. **Forrestal**, a former Secretary of Defense; Gordon L. **Gray** who later became Special Assistant to President **Truman**; Dr Jerome C. **Hunsaker**; Dr Donald H. **Menzel**, a noted debunker of UFO reports; General Robert M. **Montague**; Rear-Admiral Sidney W. **Souers**, Executive Secretary of the National Security Council; General Nathan A. **Twining**, Commanding General of Air Materiel Command at **Wright Patterson Air Force Base**; and General Hoyt S. **Vandenberg**, Director of Central Intelligence.

All members of the Majestic 12 group are now deceased, making any direct verification of their involvement impossible. The existence of the group appears to be corroborated by documentary evidence now available in the United States but neither it nor the involvement of the aforementioned people can be definitely confirmed.

It is thought highly likely that many of the documents relating to Majestic 12 are faked, but even in that case the source of the fraud is uncertain. One theory has it that the documents were put on file by some part of the United States establishment as part of a conditioning process designed to educate the public towards the existence of UFOs. A further refinement of this theory suggests that the implications of Majestic 12 (i.e. confirmation of the reality of saucer **crash retrievals**) is so absurd that the US establishment placed the documents on file so that they would be discovered and would assist in **debunking** or at least reducing the credibility of UFO reports. The US government would presumably – according to this theory – be able to point to those UFO investigators who had been 'taken in' by the documents and condemn *all* such research by implication.

One unfortunate theory which certainly cannot be discounted is that the documents were falsely created by UFO researchers for their own obvious personal reasons. Although names have been attributed it would be unfair to state them here as this speculation is undocumented and – however possible – remains hearsay.

The **Fund for UFO Research (FUFOR)** run by Dr Bruce Maccabee gave $16,000 for research designed to verify the truth of the documents and many researchers believe they have been able to confirm their authenticity.

MALISHEV, ANATOLY

In May 1978 Anatoly Malishev was confronted by two entities as he walked near the shores of Lake Pyrogovskoye in the Soviet Union. They apparently wore dark suits and conversed with the witness by telepathy.

Malishev asked them to rid the world of evils which apparently they felt unable to do since they had a policy of non-interference.

During the counter Malishev was given a salty-tasting drink which is similar to that described by several other witnesses and may well have been designed to induce amnesia. There followed an exchange which British researcher Jenny Randles points out could well be the only example we have of an alien sense of humour. Malishev asked them why an advanced civilisation such as theirs did not drink alcohol and they replied, 'Perhaps if we did, we would not *be* such an advanced civilisation.'

Malishev appears to have been abducted and when he was able to return home he could recall parts of his experience as if in a dream.

Malishev, an officer in the Red Army, felt obliged to report his abduction to the authorities, particularly since the memory block given to him by the aliens had prevented him performing his assigned duties. The authorities were, however, unconvinced and threatened court martial. He was subject to **hypnosis** and **lie-detector tests**, and since the authorities could not conclude that he was fantasising or lying the court martial was abandoned.

MANIFOLD, ROY

The **close encounter** which appears to have killed, or permanently abducted, pilot Frederick **Valentich** over the **Bass Strait** in Australia in 1978 was seemingly corroborated by many witnesses reporting UFOs around the same time as Valentich's disappearance. One such witness, Roy Manifold, took photographs of anomalous objects just minutes before Valentich radioed in his sighting. The photographs show dense black anomalies over the sea, apparently stirring up the water.

Kodak examined the photographs and ruled out the possibility of film or processing defects.

The Royal Australian Air Force apparently took the line that the photographs showed cumulus cloud, which seems slightly to overlook the point made by Australian researcher Bill Chalker that for the cloud to have moved into view within the time sequence of the photographs stated it would have to have been moving at approximately 200 miles per hour!

MANNING, CAPTAIN ROBERT F.
(See **Adickes, Captain Robert**.)

MANNOR, FRANK AND RONALD
Forty-seven-year-old farmer Frank Mannor and Ronald, his teenage son, were among the first people to witness the so-called 'quilted' UFO at Ann Arbor, Michigan, which was to lead eventually to the **swamp gas débâcle**.

It was Sunday 18 March 1966 and they were two of the closest among a total count of over twenty-four witnesses. The UFO had a strangely quilted surface, with blue and white lights to the front and rear, a large central searchlight and a small cabin. It was being escorted by four smaller UFOs. Both Frank and Ronald confirmed from their position that the UFOs never actually landed but 'sat on a base of fog'. From their position – within 1,500 feet of the globular object – they saw that it was approximately the length of a car and was pulsating.

The sight was to be one of many and to lead to an investigation authorised by the Air Force's Project **Blue Book**, headed by Professor J. Allen **Hynek**.

MANTELL, CAPTAIN THOMAS F., JR
Described by many as the first martyr of Ufology. In January 1948 Captain Thomas Mantell was part of a flight of four P51 Mustang aircraft belonging to the National Guard and flying between Georgia and Kentucky.

Godman Air Force Base in Kentucky radioed the flight and asked them to investigate a UFO sighting near the base. Of the four pilots one, Hendricks, continued his heading and landed at Standiford Field while the remaining three pilots, Hammond, Clements and Mantell, climbed to 22,000 feet in pursuit. Apparently because of lack of oxygen, Hammond and Clements called off the pursuit and continued on their way, safely landing at Standiford Field some forty minutes behind their colleague.

Mantell continued the pursuit. It is alleged that he radioed the tower, 'It appears to be a metallic object, tremendous in size, directly ahead and slightly above. I am trying to close for a better look.'

A few minutes later Mantell was dead, his plane wrecked and strewn across the ground some two miles south-west of Frank-lyn, Kentucky.

The official report on the Mantell crash alleges that he lost consciousness while suffering from anoxia (oxygen deprivation) because of climbing too high, and it was likely he was 'chasing' the planet Venus. Another suggestion has been made that he 'locked on to' a rogue weather balloon. Speculation has always been intense that Mantell was engaged and destroyed by deliberate, intelligent intent.

The case has always been shrouded by mystery, much of it unwarranted. For example, it was alleged that his funeral was held 'closed coffin' because his body was not there! – having not been in the plane when it was recovered. There is no evidence for this and although an open casket before a funeral is traditional in some parts of the United States, that is rarely the case for plane crash victims for obvious reasons. Other stories report that the body was recovered and found to have extraordinary and inexplicable wounds. Again, there is no documentary support for this. Even the statement that Mantell reported the object as 'metallic . . . tremendous in size', while documented, could have been the result of his oxygen-starved perceptions.

That said, Mantell was an experienced pilot and it seems unlikely he could have been so swept along by the tide of flying saucer publicity that he died chasing Venus because of it.

MARALINGA, SOUTH AUSTRALIA

The British government used the Maralinga site in South Australia as a nuclear testing range during the 1950s.

After one test in October 1957 several servicemen at the base saw a large UFO hovering nearby. It was described as blue and shiny with portholes along the edge and of a clear metallic construction.

Although the object stayed for some fifteen minutes no photographs were taken as cameras had been forbidden at the base; investigation indicated there was no aircraft activity in the area at the time.

MARCEL, MAJOR JESSE A.

During the **Roswell** crash retrieval it was Major Jesse A. Marcel who was first sent to the farm where the saucer debris was alleged to have been found. He was ordered in by the 509th Bomb Group Intelligence Office, for whom he was a staff intelligence officer. He confirmed collecting the wreckage of the alleged saucer which was in small chunks which he loaded into the boot and back seats of his Buick car. Marcel was then ordered to load the wreckage on to a B-29, which he would then fly to **Wright Patterson Air Force Base** in Ohio. However, when he made an en route stop at Carswell Army Air Force Base in Texas, Marcel was returned to Roswell and the debris sent on without him.

Marcel confirmed that it was material such as he had never seen before, including objects with hieroglyphic markings, something like light wood which was unburnable, foil-like metal which could not be dented and paper-like substances that would not burn.

The wreckage of a Rawin weather balloon was paraded for public consumption in explanation of the crash but Marcel confirmed that he was well acquainted with the appearance of such balloons and that this was not what he had recovered. This is the basis of the well-founded suspicion that the US government lied about what exactly it had recovered.

However, he also confirmed that he did not see a full disc, only the small pieces of debris, and he did not see alien **humanoid** bodies, both of which were subsequently reported to be part of either the Roswell crash retrieval or an associated crash retrieval nearby.

MARCH AIR FORCE BASE SIGHTING

In September 1951 a round, silver UFO thought to be at approximately 50,000 feet flew over March Air Force Base in California. Two F-86 jets were scrambled and vectored in towards the object by ground control but the object passed high over the jets and kept circling them. Four more jets were scrambled, putting six in the air altogether, but none of the pilots was able to reach the UFO's altitude.

MARIANA, NICHOLAS

On 15 August 1950 Nicholas Mariana of Missoula, Montana, became one of the first people to produce a movie film of UFOs.

The owner of a local radio station, he was with his secretary looking over the facilities of a local sports field when two UFOs were sighted above. He took a 16 mm camera from his car and filmed the objects; 315 frames were exposed.

As he was watching them through the viewfinder the objects slowed to a halt and then picked up and moved off again along their original flight path; the movie film produced this image clearly.

The film was sent to the Air Technical Intelligence Center of the United States Air Force at **Wright Patterson Air Force Base** for analysis where it was stated that 'nothing decisive could be established'. The suggestion that they were balloons was dismissed though no further information was forthcoming.

Photographic analyst Robert M. L. Baker, Jr, for the Douglas Aircraft Corporation rejected the suggestion that the UFOs could have been jet aircraft; in fact he could not attribute any specific phenomenon to the images on the film.

His own interpretation was that they were 'bright circular points of light . . . confirming visual observation of discs with rotating rims'.

MARIANNE

Marianne is a **repeater witness** of several disc and night light sightings. The importance of her sighting is not in the interest that it generated in the UFO phenomenon but in precisely the lack of it.

During the 1974 flap in Sweden, and particularly **Vallentuna** near where Marianne lives, she was twelve years old. Her sightings during this time were of only short duration. She had a total of eighteen sightings. The closest and most significant took place on 27 April 1974, just a month after the abduction of **Anders**.

She was sitting at her desk and found that she had drawn a flying saucer which was a pleasing image and better than she had created before. She felt compelled to go to the window and there saw a silver disc moving across the field behind the house where she lived (and still lives today). It was approximately treetop height and, from where she was standing, around 112 centimetres at arm's length. When she went downstairs to see it through the living-room windows she decided it was not appropriate to go out of the house to see it closer and consequently lost sight of it and did not see it land, if indeed it did.

What is more important is that the sighting, along with the others that she had (some of which were corroborated by her father), did not inspire her to study or even take a great interest in the subject of UFOs. While she obviously accepts their existence, the importance of the sighting is not that it moved her in this way but rather in another.

She seems to have considered that the sighting was a form of 'awakening' designed to give *her* specifically a more spiritual dimension to her life. In the years since she has become an active ecologist, studying and protecting the natural Earth environment.

The question for Ufologists is whether the effects of their experience on the witnesses is an irrelevancy or whether it is in fact the very core of the subject. If UFOs are physical vehicles belonging to somebody or something, then presumably studying their flight patterns and movements is important. However, if they are a form of message alien to, but intended for, humanity, then what they *do* is not important but the effect they *have* is. Marianne, along with thousands like her, may hold the key to unlocking the UFO mystery.

MARS

No encyclopedia of UFOs would be complete without reference to the traditional home world of the aliens, Mars. If the expressions '**little green man**' or 'bug-eyed monster' are used then 'man from Mars' usually follows. That said, there is absolutely no proof whatsoever that any flying saucer or extra-terrestrial has ever come from Mars and a good deal of scientific evidence to suggest that they never could have and never will. However, Mars is firmly established in the mythology of UFOs for many reasons:

1. In 1877 the Italian astronomer Giovanni Virginio Schia-parelli referred to random streaks on the Martian surface as *canali*, an Italian word meaning channels (and therefore quite possibly natural), but the similarity between this world and the English word 'canal' (always artificial) implied a sugges-tion that the Martian landscape was riddled with artificial waterways, suggesting an intelligence living there. It must be admitted that Schiaparelli himself made the comment that some others believed that intelligent beings may have been behind the marks.
2. Science fiction has often centred on Mars as the home world of invading aliens, such as in *War of the Worlds* by H. G. Wells.
3. There seemed a certain logic in a migration from Mars since it appeared to be a planet that had lost the atmosphere

and vegetation that perhaps once it had and thus the inhabitants might be searching around for a lusher, greener planet to live on.

4. One of the moons of Mars, Phobos, has a peculiar orbit apparently violating usual natural laws. Phobos orbits Mars faster than the planet turns on its axis and this, with other factors, has led to the belief that Phobos is in fact a ten-mile-wide, hollow, artificial spacecraft or orbiting shelter which contains the Martians waiting to either return to Mars or colonise somewhere else.

5. There has been a suggestion that there is an unnatural bulge at the Martian equator which the more imaginative have suggested might be an artificial dome covering underground colonies.

6. Both the Martian moons, Phobos and Deimos, were discovered in 1877 by the American astronomer Asaph Hall. However, one hundred and fifty years before this the writer Jonathan Swift wrote a fictional account of the discovery of two Martian moons which turned out to be extraordinarily accurate when the discovery was finally made.

More directly associated with UFOs there have been suggestions that the spates or flaps of high UFO activity occur when Mars is nearer the Earth, though this has never been proved.

A recent photographic analysis of Mars has shown a rock formation that would appear to be a huge face carved into the surface – the face with the long chin and wide eyes so familiar to American abduction claims. Nearby are what appear to be pyramids. Clearly the assumption is being made that this is a message of some sort, bringing Mars back into the equation once again.

And of course, there has been the occasional claim by an extraterrestrial that Mars is indeed his home world.

MARSHALL, GENERAL GEORGE C.

Researcher Dr Rolf Alexander reportedly interviewed General George C. Marshall, the Chief of Staff of the United States Army during the Second World War and later Secretary of State for Foreign Affairs. He questioned him regarding UFOs.

According to Alexander, whom researcher Timothy Good describes as 'trusted and respected', Marshall stated that the UFOs were from another planet and that they were friendly, that there had been contact with the occupants of the UFOs and that there had been landings which had resulted in the death of the occupants.

However, considering the remarkable importance of such a statement and its significance for the world, it seems incongruous that Marshall also indicated that the reason UFO reports were denied or censored was that the United States believed its people should concentrate on the real menace of communism rather than a distraction such as extraterrestrial visitation.

MARTIN, JOHN

It is accepted that Kenneth **Arnold**'s use of the word 'saucer' was the beginning of the modern era of UFOs and was also the point at which the expression 'flying saucer' was coined, attracting the public's attention and giving an acceptable name to a phenomenon of great public interest.

However, it was not actually the first use of the expression 'saucer'; that honour goes to a Dallas newspaper reporting on the sighting of farmer John Martin.

The *Dennyson Daily News* of Texas in its 25 January 1878 edition, under the heading 'A Strange Phenomenon', referred to Martin's sighting thus: 'Mr John Martin, a farmer who lives some six miles north of this city, while out hunting, had his attention directed to a dark object high in the northern sky.

'The peculiar shape and the velocity with which the object seemed to approach, riveted his attention, and he strained his eyes to discover its character. When first noticed it appeared to be about the size of an orange, after which it continued to grow in size.

'After gazing at it for some time, Mr Martin became blind from long looking and left off viewing to rest his eyes. On resuming his view, the object was almost overhead and had increased considerably in size and appeared to be going through space at a wonderful speed. When directly over him it was about the size of a large saucer and was evidently at a great height.'

MARTIN, RONALD

In November 1957 there seemed to be a lot of attention around Route 116 near Levelland, Texas. There were at least half a dozen independent reports of a large object sighted on 2 November in that area, including several of a landing.

Ronald Martin was one witness to the landing, describing the object as extremely large, bright brown and red, and sitting on the road blocking his route. The electrical system of his truck cut out, the object turned bluish-green and took to the sky, reverting to red as it disappeared from sight.

Many similar reports were received within an hour or so of Martin's sighting, including several reports of **vehicle interference** as well as corroborated descriptions, suggesting very strongly that a genuine physical presence was in the sky that night. For several hours police were combing the highways trying to discover precisely what that presence was as there was considerable alarm amongst the neighbouring communities but no conclusion was ever drawn, despite the fact that two of those police officers, Sheriff **Clem** and Deputy McCulloch, also witnessed the object.

MASSE, MAURICE
(See **Valensole**.)

MAUNDER, E. W.
On 17 November 1882 E. W. Maunder was at the Royal Observatory in Greenwich watching an auroral display two hours after sunset when he saw 'a great circular disc of greenish light' appearing in the sky. It took approximately two minutes to cross his field of vision; it was moving smoothly but very quickly compared to any astronomical bodies he was observing.

As it passed just above the moon it seemed to elongate, suggesting that it was a disc changing its angle relative to Maunder's position.

There were many other observers of the object, spoken of as 'cigar-shaped', 'torpedo-shaped' or 'shuttle-shaped'.

Maunder stated, 'It appeared to be a definite body, nothing could well be more unlike the rush of a great meteor or fireball . . . than the steady . . . advance of the "torpedo".'

MAURY ISLAND, WASHINGTON
Just after noon on 21 June 1947 Harold Dahl and his teenage son, accompanied by his pet dog and two other crewmen, were piloting a boat in Puget Sound near Maury Island, just off Tacoma, Washington.

Dahl noticed up above them six UFOs of ring- or doughnut-shaped description. They seemed to be hovering at a height of around 2,000 feet; Dahl also noticed that five of the objects seemed to be circling around the sixth one, which was perhaps having difficulty maintaining its height. Eventually the drop in height arrested itself at a few hundred feet above the witnesses.

None of the witnesses was able to determine whether there were any protrusions, exhausts or other clues as to the objects' mode of operation; they were thought to be approximately 100 feet wide with something like a 25-feet-wide hole in the centre. They were metallic, golden and silvery, and had portholes around the perimeter and a near-black observation window in the underside.

Suddenly there was something like an explosion and the UFO that had apparently been having difficulties showered silver and aluminium flakes over the area. This was followed by a discharging of hot bulky slag-like material which crashed into the water, the beach, and fell on the boat, killing the boy's dog and injuring the boy himself on the arm. After this the five remaining UFOs gained greater altitude and disappeared from sight.

The crew members were unable to contact their patrol base as their radio was malfunctioning, attributed to the presence of the UFOs, but samples of the debris dropped on the boat were collected for analysis.

Dahl took the analysis and a film he had taken of the UFOs just before the explosion and handed these to Fred L. Crisman who was part owner of Dahl's boat.

After having the boat repaired, Dahl visited Maury Island the following day to inspect the debris and while he was there an identical UFO swept across the island in his full view. Crisman confirmed all the descriptions given by Dahl the previous day.

It must be said that many of the details of this case are conflicting: the date of the incident is variously given as 21, 22 or 23 June 1947 and the characters of Dahl and Crisman are shadowy to say the least.

It was on 24 June 1947 that Kenneth **Arnold** had his sighting in the Cascade Mountains of Washington State and became a national figure associated with flying saucers. He took on the job of investigating the Maury Island incident. It was the editor of a science fiction magazine, Ray **Palmer**, who asked Arnold to become involved but, to his credit, Arnold apparently would only do so provided he had credible support. This came in the form of military intelligence officers Captain William Davidson and Lieutenant Frank M. Brown, who flew to join him in an B25 bomber assigned to them. The significance of this will become apparent later.

On arriving in Tacoma, Arnold had some difficulty in finding accommodation for himself and was caught completely unawares when he telephoned the best hotel in the city and was told that it was already holding a reservation for him in his name. It has been subsequently speculated that military intelligence set the room up for him so that it could be 'bugged'.

Arnold and Dahl got together very quickly and Dahl told the story of a visitation from one of the '**men in black**', i.e. one of those shadowy characters that seemed to hover around UFO witnesses in the early years, who gave him a description of the incident as if he had been on the boat with Dahl and said, 'What I have said is proof to you that I know a great deal more about this experience of yours than you will want to believe.'

Dahl took Arnold to his home and showed him a chunk of the debris found on the Maury Island beach; it appeared to be similar to volcanic rock. Later Arnold and an airline pilot, Captain E. J. **Smith**, were able to examine more of the debris and it is believed may have examined the movie footage taken, though this has never in fact surfaced since and so whether it exists or not is indeterminate.

As this point Arnold called in Brown and Davidson who joined them later to inspect the material.

The story was told to the intelligence officers but they seemed remarkably uninterested and did not even seem keen to take away any of the material that they were offered. Nevertheless they did do so, even though they gave the impression that they thought the whole thing was probably some sort of hoax. The carton of debris was loaded upon the B25. The plane took off with Brown and Davidson aboard, was piloted by Master Sergeant Elmer L. Taff and also had a hitch-hiker aboard, Technician 4th Grade Woodrow D. Mathews (hitch-hiking in military planes by members of the services was a common practice at the time).

It has been suggested that one possible solution to the Maury Island mystery is that the UFOs were terrestrial, man-made, and in some way 'belonged' to the Atomic Energy Commission. They are alleged to have been over Maury Island to dump radioactive slag and unfortunately got caught doing so by the witnesses. The 'man in black' who approached Dahl is held to have been an agent of the Atomic Energy Commission. All of this is speculation and all possibilities are open to question.

Twenty minutes after taking off from McCord field the B25 exploded. Master Sergeant Taff and Technician Mathews parachuted to safety.

Intelligence officers Brown and Davidson apparently died in the explosion.

MAY, MRS KATHLEEN
(See **Lemon, Gene.**)

MAYS, GLEN
Glen Mays was one of very few witnesses to the death of Captain Thomas **Mantell**. He lived near Franklyn, Kentucky, and watched the Mantell plane flying high. He believed that it exploded in the air, which would of course be significantly important if correct. The generally accepted story is that Mantell ran out of oxygen chasing the UFO too high and therefore the plane would have simply gone out of control and come back to Earth, being destroyed on impact.

Mays' testimony suggests something quite different. According to him: 'The plane circled three times, like the pilot didn't know where he was going, and then started down into a dive from about 20,000 feet. About halfway down there was a terrific explosion.'

MEDIA
There is no question that the influence of the media has strongly shaped the public perception and, to an extent, the overall development of the UFO phenomenon. For example, in the case of Kenneth **Arnold**, he reported seeing unidentified objects over the Cascade Mountains in Washington State, USA, in 1947 and reported them because he believed they might be enemy weapons. The next day the media speculated that they could be of extraterrestrial origin although he had made no such suggestion; clearly, the media's own suggestion was based on speculation rather than evidence.

Certainly, the public perception of UFOs as extraterrestrial in origin is caused mostly by the media's concentration on this particular possibility and by its relative lack of interest in other possibilities, which are perhaps less newsworthy. As a consequence, the bridge between serious UFO research and the public perception of UFO research can be quite wide.

MEDINACELI ABDUCTION
On 5 February 1978 a witness known as 'Julio' was walking his dog when he realised that he had suffered a **missing time** period. Regression **hypnosis** was carried out and Julio recalled being taken by a blinding light into a room where he was confronted by tall, blond aliens who were more concerned to examine his dog than himself. A full medical examination of

both was eventually undertaken. Julio had returned suffering from painful eyes.

Interestingly, the witness had been told that there were two basic races visiting the Earth, the tall blond graceful people and the short dwarf aliens, who were concerned with genetic engineering.

This is a finding that many Ufologists have been making in their study of abduction cases over the past thirty years. Other cases have suggested not only that the two races are indeed visiting the Earth but that they interact with each other frequently; there are cases on record where both types of entities are seen in the same UFOs.

MEIER, EDUARD (BILLY)

In 1987 a **contactee** claim from Switzerland received a great deal of publicity. Farmer Eduard (Billy) Meier made a detailed claim of many meetings with beautiful long-haired extraterrestrials and backed up his claim by hundreds of good, clear photographs of the visiting spacecraft.

Although it has always been maintained that the Meier photographs 'baffled the experts', there have been many who have claimed they are clear fakes; it has been pointed out that many of the photographs are taken with a camera pointing directly at the sun, blurring detail and therefore potentially obscuring supporting struts or wires. Computer enhancement by William Spaulding seems to reveal some string holding up what would presumably be fake models. One of the original investigators of the case also claimed to have found the models in Meier's garage used to perpetrate the fraud though apparently these were explained as being made after the event as re-creations of the objects he had seen in the sky.

Because of the high publicity received by Gary Kinder's book on the subject, *Light Years* (see References and Background Material), the case has been the subject of considerable controversy amongst serious Ufologists.

'MEN IN BLACK' (MIBs)

The 'Men in Black' were a curious phenomenon of the early years of UFO stories in North America; typically they went around in twos and threes, were well dressed – always in dark suits – and looked not unlike **FBI** agents. There is a suggestion that they were in fact government agents suppressing stories of UFOs, and one of the more specific claims was that they were agents of the Atomic Energy Commission who were suppressing stories of an accidental leakage of radioactive material at **Maury Island**.

Of more interest is the theory that the 'Men in Black' were themselves alien and suppressing witnesses' stories in order to carry on conducting their own clandestine activities. There are claims that they wore bizarre make-up, with the men often wearing lipstick as if somehow not quite appreciating the difference between the sexes on Earth. Typically they would drive old cars that were in pristine condition, suggesting somehow that they had been 'created' for a specific purpose.

Although they have not completely gone away, the 'Men in Black' are now much more rarely reported, possibly coinciding with an era of much greater openness world-wide about the subject of UFOs.

MENGER, HOWARD

One of the celebrated contactees in America in the 1950s was Howard Menger of Brooklyn, New York. According to his claims, made after George **Adamski**'s revelations in 1953, Menger saw his first flying saucer in 1932 in New Jersey, when he was with his brother Alton. In a wooded glade near his home he met a beautiful long-haired girl wearing a translucent ski-suit who emanated love and whom he found physically attractive. The woman stated that she was contacting those of her own kind.

It was when Menger joined the Army ten years later that he saw saucers in the southern United States deserts and on one occasion was confronted by a tanned man with long blond hair who asked Menger to accompany him. Menger declined and later found out the man was one of the Space People.

According to Menger's contacts, the Space People had been involved in the development of the Aztecs and even older Earth civilizations. Shortly after this Menger, now in Hawaii, suddenly had an impulse to drive to caverns in the hills where he met another beautiful Space Woman wearing a pink translucent suit who also emanated the same love and physical attraction that his earlier contact had done.

At later times Menger met his Space Woman again; she revealed that she was five hundred years old and there were a number of rather ludicrous escapades such as his offering the Space People a bundle of bras which they rejected, saying they didn't wear such things.

Very helpfully the Space People also explained the power mechanism of their ship and enabled Menger to build a model of this, though there is no record of its ever having worked. Menger revealed his story in his 1959 book *From Outer Space to You* (see References and Background Material).

MENZEL, DR DONALD H.

Dr Donald H. Menzel was a specialist in astronomy and is world famous for his **debunking** of the UFO phenomenon. It is doubtful that anyone else has been as vociferous and forceful in putting forward mundane explanations for all UFO events than Menzel, often stretching credulity in his prosaic explanations to the same extent as researchers desperate to prove the 'extraterrestrialism' of their findings.

Dr Menzel is listed as one of the **Majestic 12** group which would seem to suggest that his debunking of UFOs was to protect the extraordinary knowledge that that group had obtained through working with retrieved crashed flying saucers.

However, it has been widely speculated that the documents alleging the existence of Majestic 12 are a fraud. Further it has been speculated that these documents were created by unscrupulous UFO researchers to bolster their own theories and sources of personal income. In that event the inclusion of Dr Menzel in the Majestic 12 group is an inspired piece of genius, poking fun at the man who has for years poked fun at them! To some extent the inclusion of Menzel on the list tends to add weight to the theory that these documents are the fraudulent result of UFO researchers' imaginations, and seems to represent a tongue-in-cheek jibe by American researchers.

If the Majestic 12 documents are genuine then Menzel's involvement is a most mysterious one.

MESSEL, DR HARRY

In 1965 Dr Harry Messel, Professor of Physics at Sydney University, Australia, stated that, 'The facts about saucers were long tracked down and results have long been known in top secret defence circles of more countries than one.'

METEORS AND METEORITES

A meteor is a particle of rock or dust which flares up brilliantly as it burns in the Earth's atmosphere and is usually destroyed by the heat. It only becomes a meteorite if it reaches the ground intact as some particular, larger, objects do.

They are frequently reported as UFOs since people are often not familiar with them but for UFO investigators there are certain characteristics of the reports which tend to indicate meteor activity. Firstly, there tend to be whole rashes of reports as many people see them; secondly they have a particular general downward motion; and thirdly, they are usually white though occasionally varied in colour, dependent on the component material.

MIBs
(See '**Men in Black**'.)

MICHAEL, DR DONALD N.
In studying the possible effects of a meeting with extraterrestrials NASA consultant Dr Donald N. Michael pointed out, 'Space beings may be ethical, moral, immoral, aesthetic or something different from us. Such beings may have ideas on proper relationships among creatures inhabiting planets which may or may not support our most cherished beliefs.'

He went on to say, of the proof of an intelligent extraterrestrial race, 'I would imagine this discovery would present real threats to the Pentagon.'

If all the peoples of the world were focused on an external invader then presumably they would not need to be focused on each other and most of our present defence characteristics would be obsolete. This is, however, in conflict with the alternative theory which suggests that UFOs are the product of government disinformation designed to focus us on an external invader rather than concentrate on fighting each other; in other words, to create a war atmosphere without the threat of casualty or disaster.

But if the extraterrestrials are real then these considerations are redundant and we would do well to consider Dr Michael's words.

MICHALAK, STEPHEN
Probably Canada's most famous UFO encounter is that of Stephen Michalak at Falcon Lake, Ontario, in May 1967.

At noon on 20 May, Michalak witnessed two red, cigar-shaped objects descending near him. One hovered in the air while the other landed. The hovering craft eventually picked up speed and flew away into the clouds while the landed craft apparently cooled down, its red glow diminishing to a gold shimmer. Michalak described the object as 35 feet in diameter and 12 feet high.

Michalak was an amateur geologist and was carrying protective goggles with him, used to shield his eyes from chips of rock when working. He observed the object through these goggles, watching purple light beaming out of openings in it. He also sketched the object and made notes of such details as the smell of sulphur, the noise of an electric motor, and warm air emanating from it.

When a door opened on the side of the object and Michalak heard voices within he walked over, requesting communication in various languages but receiving no response. Indeed, any occupants inside ignored him completely and 'shut the door in his face', leaving him to examine the outside of the craft. Michalak found it was still very hot; the glove he was wearing burned and melted when he touched its surface and at this moment a blast of hot air was forced out of an exhaust vent near him, catching him in the chest and causing him considerable panic when it set his clothes alight. Shortly after the craft took off.

Besides burns Michalak suffered many after-effects from the encounter, including nausea, vomiting and severe headache. In hospital, he was treated for first-degree burns and then released. For several days he was unable to eat properly and lost a considerable amount of weight. He suffered skin infections, hives and nausea, also numbness and swelling of the joints. Haematologists reported some imbalance in his blood.

Of particular interest was a pattern of burn marks on Michalak's chest which exactly matched the grid from which the blast of hot air had emanated, giving horrific and extraordinary corroboration of the encounter.

Over two dozen doctors examined Michalak over a period but none could fully diagnose the cause of his problems. One doctor indicated that Michalak might have received a dose of radiation that, had it lasted for a longer period of time, could have proved lethal.

MICROWAVES

As an alternative explanation to the classic belief that UFOs are extraterrestrial spaceships visiting the Earth, it has been suggested that they could be messages being beamed from some other source, perhaps interplanetary, in the form of microwave radiation. Experiments have suggested that microwaves can be beamed at the mind and can create sensory hallucinations; indeed, there is very little known about the effects of certain forms of radiation on the electrical circuits of the brain.

This would not, however, be sufficient to explain the whole phenomenon, particularly radar cases and physical traces. Like most forms of research in this subject, it remains open as an option for further investigation.

MILLBANK, CAPTAIN ROBERT

On the night of 29 December 1966 Captain Robert Millbank was flying Canadian Pacific Flight 421 from Lima, Peru, to Mexico City at 35,000 feet.

Suddenly his DC-8 was approached by an object with two lights at either end, divided by a strip of light something like the cabin lights of an aircraft. It paced his plane.

After it had maintained position for a short while it then dropped back and disappeared behind the DC-8.

MILLER, S. N.

Several passengers on the TWA DC-3 captained by Robert **Adickes** on 27 April 1950 confirmed that they saw the object that the pilots reported. One such witness was jewellery store manager S. N. Miller of St Paul who stated: 'The thing was the colour of a neon sign – just a big red disc. I used to laugh at saucer stories – but not any more.'

MILLINOCKET, MAINE, SIGHTING

On 29 January 1953 a very revealing statement was made by the pilots of jets attempting pursuit of a UFO. The chase took place near Millinocket, Maine, where a silver, oval UFO was seen by the crew of an F94 plane. The crew attempted to chase the object, which was flying at 23,000 feet, but called off pursuit when it appeared to be fruitless; however, two jet pilots from a different squadron sighted the object and began debating over the radio whether or not it should be pursued.

The two pilots decided against any attempts to pursue the object but one of them made one point which was overheard by ground control. He stated, 'I'll never admit I saw the thing.'

There was certainly a time when reporting UFOs was not a positive career move in the United States Air Force, and even when that was no longer a problem it certainly involved a lot of unwelcome attention by Air Force intelligence.

MILLMAN, DR PETER

Dr Peter Millman was the Chairman of Project **Second Storey**.

Fifteen years after the dissolution of this project, Millman stated of meteorites that they were the 'only proven thing that comes from outer space . . . after all, we have never had a piece of a flying saucer'.

MILTHORP, POLICE CONSTABLE RICHARD

In April 1984 several witnesses at Stanmore in Middlesex, near RAF Bentley Priory, witnessed a multi-coloured UFO apparently firing balls of light at the ground. Several police officers, including PC Richard Milthorp, were called to the scene and watched the object for approximately two hours. Milthorp sketched the object, described as circular with a dome on top and below.

In all, eight policemen, and others, witnessed the event, a full report of which was sent to both the Ministry of Defence and the Civil Aviation Authority.

At Harrow Police Station Chief Superintendent Ronald Poole confirmed that PC Richard Milthorp and the other officer who had made the report were 'two normal sensible men'.

MINCZEWSKI, WALTER A.

In April 1947, shortly before the Kenneth **Arnold** sighting of June that year, meteorologist Walter A. Minczewski in Richmond, Virginia, together with his staff, were using a theodolite to track their own balloon when suddenly they noticed a silver saucer-shaped object, apparently with a dome on top, through the theodolite. The disc was observed for some fifteen seconds before finally disappearing from view.

There were later occasions when scientists tracking balloons also saw UFOs which, given that the balloon was in the sky as an aid to comparison, suggests that it would be difficult to dismiss all UFO sightings as merely balloons, as has been suggested by some debunkers.

MINDALORE, SOUTH AFRICA

(See **Quezet, Meagan**.)

MIRACHI, DR ANTHONY O.

When the Office of Naval Research, in the person of Dr Urner **Liddell**, commented on Captain Thomas **Mantell**'s death, remarking that, 'There is not a single reliable report which is not attributable to the cosmic balloons', former Air Force scientist Dr Anthony O. Mirachi stated: 'The Navy report is erroneous. *It lulls people into a false sense of security*.' (Emphasis added.)

MISSING TIME
It is held by many UFO researchers that one of the classic signs that an abduction has taken place, and where it may be suppressed in the memory of the witness, is that of missing time.

In a typical scenario the witness may find that he has taken, say, two hours more to drive home than he would normally expect to do, and this – linked with other factors, particularly an otherwise mundane UFO sighting – may indicate a suppressed memory of an abduction experience.

It should be noted that in many cases the missing time has to be pointed out to the witness by the investigators, as appears to have been the case in the classic Betty and Barney **Hill** case in 1961. Where this is the case and the missing time period is not that striking, then researchers must consider that the lapse may be only the result of confusion or disorientation.

At the 1989 International UFO Conference in London representatives of major UFO organisations across the world laid down certain criteria for 'safe' (reliable) abduction cases and one of these was that the missing time period should be *self-reported* by the witness and not suggested by the investigators.

MJ 12
(See **Majestic 12**.)

MOCK SUN
A mock sun occurs when light reflecting on ice crystals in suspension in the air causes a hazy glow in the sky, often below normal cloud level. These are frequently reported as UFOs even by experienced observers, and of course by their transient nature it is often difficult to determine whether or not this has been the cause of a particular sighting.

MOIGNE DOWNS
Probably the most famous UFO sighting during the British wave of 1967 was the report by former RAF intelligence officer J. B. W. 'Angus' **Brooks**.

While walking his dogs in the early morning of 26 October at Moigne Downs in Dorset, he witnessed an object descending at phenomenal speed before abruptly levelling out at a height of approximately 250 feet, some quarter of a mile from where he was positioned.

Brooks described the object as a central circular body with a leading fuselage in the front and three separate fuselages at the rear. During the period of observation the three rear fuselages moved so that with the fourth fuselage they formed a cross shape. Brooks reported no obvious power units or noise and despite a very strong wind, up to Force 8, the object apparently remained motionless for over twenty minutes.

During the encounter one of Angus Brooks' dogs, an Alsatian, was very distraught and frantically pawed at him, disobeying his commands to sit.

A team of researchers from the Ministry of Defence, Dr John Dickison of the Royal Aircraft Establishment at Farnborough, Leslie **Akhurst** from **S4 (Air)** and Alec Cassie, a psychologist, interviewed Mr Brooks and offered their explanation; he had seen a vitreous floater, i.e. dead matter in the fluid of his eyeball, the sighting of which had become dramatic due to Brooks' falling asleep or entering a near sleep state and dreaming.

Brooks seems to have been less than impressed with the MOD's explanation and not least the idea that he had dozed off to sleep during a Force 8 gale with an Alsatian clawing at him.

MOLAVA, PHILIP

On 8 November 1954 thirteen-year-old Philip Molava, in Croydon, south of London, England, was in the garden in the early hours of the morning, feeding his pet rabbits, when a small disc-shaped UFO flew nearby.

The following day Philip vomited and was being treated for suspected food poisoning; he was lying in bed, paralysed and numb, when suddenly three entities materialised in the room out of a glowing mist. He cannot recall more details of the event but woke up the following morning fit and well.

He told the investigators that this experience had been the start of many psychic experiences such as ESP, **out-of-body experiences**, telepathy and clairvoyance, and stated: 'I wasn't awake until they came.' This question of being 'awake' is one which has arisen many times; Swedish witness **Marianne** commented that her UFO sighting had 'woken her up' to the needs of the world's ecology and similarly another witness to a Swedish abduction, Kathryn **Howard**, commented that 'awakening' was part of her UFO experience.

MONCLA, LIEUTENANT FELIX, JR
(See **Kinross Air Force Base**.)

MONTAGUE, GENERAL ROBERT M.
Reported to have been a member of the **Majestic 12** panel formed to investigate UFOs in the 1940s, General Robert A. Montague was Base Commander at Sandia Base, Albequerque, New Mexico.

MOONDUST, PROJECT
Officially Project Moondust is a programme of collection of missile and satellite debris centred at **Wright Patterson Air Force Base** in Dayton, Ohio. It has been speculated that it is also a cover for recovery of extraterrestrial saucers and that there are documents from various American agencies released under the **Freedom of Information Act** which indicate it is UFO-related.

MOORADUC ROAD, AUSTRALIA
On 5 July 1972 Mrs Maureen Puddy was driving along the Mooraduc Road south-east of Melbourne in Australia. Suddenly, from above and behind her, she saw a blue light approaching and stopped the car to get out and look. She became somewhat alarmed when she saw that hovering above her was a huge UFO at some twice the height of the telegraph poles and overlapping the road either side, making it approximately 100 feet wide. She described it as shaped like two saucers with no markings or signs of construction, and glowing intensely blue. Mrs Puddy noticed a faint humming noise, the only sound heard from the object. The sighting terrified her and she drove off as fast as she could, but it maintained an exact position with her for eight miles before streaking away.

On 25 July 1972, at more or less the same time and in the same place, she encountered the same blue light again and when she tried to escape found that the engine of her car had cut out. The vehicle rolled off the road inoperative. In real fear Mrs Puddy could see the blue light beaming down from above and heard messages such as 'We mean you no harm' and 'You now have control', at which point her car started up again.

One of the messages was 'All your tests will be negative', though Mrs Puddy could not be sure what this meant.

Other witnesses in the locality also reported seeing the streak of blue light which was presumably the object leaving Mrs Puddy.

On 22 February 1973 Mrs Puddy received a message indicating that she should go to the place of the contact to receive further messages from whatever was controlling the blue light. Mrs Puddy telephoned **VUFORS** and was accompanied to the site by their top investigators, Judith Magee and Paul Norman.

When Mrs Puddy met the investigators she was already in an agitated state; apparently a gold-foil-suited entity had appeared inside the car and then disappeared again.

While the three were together the entity reappeared again and began walking towards the car. In fact only Mrs Puddy could apparently perceive the entity; neither of the investigators did although they were convinced of her sincerity and personal alarm.

Mrs Puddy went through a complete abduction scenario, apparently being kidnapped from the car and taken aboard a UFO though in fact she never left the driving seat nor the sight of the investigators.

Apparently inside the UFO, she described a mushroom-like object with something like jelly moving about inside it which is thought to have been a possible entity.

Whether or not Mrs Puddy's encounters were internally generated or the product of a receptive mind receiving a particular message cannot be determined, yet analysis of this case must throw light on many like it; had Mrs Puddy been alone she would almost certainly have reported a physical abduction though in fact it did not take place. Can it be that Mrs Puddy was 'tuned in' to whatever intelligence it was that contacted her and that unfortunately the investigators were not?

MORGAN, COLONEL SAM
Colonel Sam Morgan is a former base commander of **Woodbridge RAF/USAF Air Base** and was apparently responsible for releasing a tape allegedly made on the night of the encounter at that location. The tape is said to have been made 'live' during an investigation of the landing area and includes an apparently live account of the contact.

Opinions vary about the tape's authenticity. Asked directly to comment on the authenticity of the tape Colonel Morgan stated: 'I do not think it is a hoax . . . those guys definitely saw something which cannot be explained. As for them fabricating it all and putting on an act, I do not think they could have pulled it off.'

(For what it's worth, I have heard the tape and it seems to me to be the product of ham acting, and very cheaply stage managed.)

MOSCOW, USSR, 1961 SIGHTING

During the construction of part of the famous Moscow air defence network there were reports of an enormous UFO 'mothership' together with a fleet of 'fledgeling' UFOs overhead. The battery commander instructed a missile salvo to be fired at the UFOs but all exploded well short of the objects, as did a second missile attack.

A third missile attack was ordered but never launched because suddenly the whole electrical system of the base cut out!

MOTH MEN, THE

During the 1960s, particularly in West Virginia, United States of America, there were many reports of Moth Men sightings. Various people claimed to see extraordinary-looking entities often described as headless or with glowing red eyes. One was described as the size of a small aircraft and terrorised witnesses.

Although it seems to have been a genuine phenomenon, publicised mostly by John A. Keel, an American researcher of great perception and extraordinary lateral thinking, it nonetheless seems to have been a limited, localised scare that eventually died down.

England had one Moth Man-type encounter on 16 November 1963 when courting couples in a remote lovers' lane were somewhat rudely interrupted by a grotesque headless black creature with webbed feet and wings like a bat. The witnesses did not stay around to provide any more information.

MOUNT RAINIER, WASHINGTON: SIGHTING

Mount Rainier in the Cascade Mountains of Washington State, USA, was the area where Kenneth **Arnold** had his famous sighting of 1947 which gave birth to the expression 'flying saucer' and very largely to UFOs as a public phenomenon.

MOUNTBATTEN, EARL LOUIS

Earl Mountbatten of Burma, Admiral of the Fleet, Supreme Allied Commander of Asian Forces in the Second World War, Chief of the Defence Staff and the last Viceroy of India, turned UFO investigator when, allegedly, a flying saucer and occupant landed on his estate at **Broadlands** in Hampshire in February 1955.

Lord Mountbatten himself investigated the report made by Frederick Briggs, a bricklayer employed at the estate, examining the marks in the snow which confirmed the claims of the witness. He stated of the witness, 'He did not give me the impression of being the sort of man who would be subject to hallucinations, or would in any way invent such a story. I am sure from the sincere way he gave his account that he, himself, is completely convinced of the truth of his own statement.'

MUCHENA, CLIFFORD
(See **La Rochelle**.)

MUFON (THE MUTUAL UFO NETWORK)

MUFON is an international scientific, non-profit-making organisation dedicated to a serious and scientific study of the UFO phenomenon. It was founded on 31 May 1969.

It has representatives in every state of the United States of America, and many overseas officers representing Ufology on every continent. It is the largest, most widely based such organisation in the world.

MUNCIELLO, FRANK
(See **Godfrey, Arthur**.)

MURDER OF EXTRATERRESTRIAL, LEGAL CONSIDERATIONS

The UFO phenomenon has inspired many controversies but one little considered aspect is whether or not our killing an extraterrestrial, whether an individual in self-defence or a government using its military might, would constitute murder. Inspired by reports of several people shooting at UFOs the American Department of Justice, in the body of Assistant Attorney General Norbert A. Schlei, stated, 'Since criminal laws are usually construed strictly, it is doubtful that laws against homicide would apply to the killing of intelligent man-like creatures alien to this planet unless such creatures were

members of the human species. Whether killing these creatures
would violate other criminal laws – for instance the laws against
cruelty to animals or disorderly contact – would ordinarily
depend on the laws of the particular state in which the killing
occurred.'

MUROC AIR FORCE BASE (EDWARDS)

On 8 July 1947 officers and airmen of the Muroc Air Base
(now Edwards Air Force Base) in California witnessed a
formation of three disc-like UFOs over the site. Approximately ten minutes later, at ten o'clock in the morning, a
single UFO was spotted by a test pilot testing an XP84
engine. When he saw the UFO he thought it might be a
balloon but realised it was moving in the opposite direction to
the wind; he described the yellow globular object as travelling
at approximately 200 miles per hour at a height of two miles.
(In the circumstances wind direction is irrelevant as it is
known that winds can move in different directions at different
heights.)

Nearly two hours later base technicians waiting for an observation test thought that it must have occurred earlier than
expected because suddenly they could see a round object high
above them. The object was lower than 20,000 feet and falling
at three times the rate of the test parachute which was ejected
some thirty seconds after the UFO had been spotted: like the
previous sighting it was moving against the prevailing wind (at
ground level).

At four o'clock in the afternoon a flat circular object was seen
over the base by an F51 pilot flying at 20,000 feet but he was
unable to climb to sufficient altitude to close in on it.

At the same time, in New Mexico, the **Roswell Incident** was
unfolding which would overshadow such sightings.

MURRAY, J. A. H.

In a letter to *The Times* in 1895 Mr J. A. H. Murray of Oxford,
England, told of his sighting of 'a brilliant luminous body' low
in the sky. It floated as if driven by a strong wind, many times
slower than a meteor and considerably larger than Venus. The
object dimmed as it approached the horizon and disappeared
beyond distant treetops.

MUTUAL UFO NETWORK, THE (MUFON)

(See **MUFON**.)

MYTHS
There is some debate as to whether the UFO phenomenon constitutes a modern day myth. Studies done, particularly by Dr Thomas 'Eddie' **Bullard**, in the United States, suggest that the UFO phenomenon is not a myth because of certain characteristics about its development which do not correspond to the development of myths such as Santa Claus and Cinderella. For one thing there appears to be little deviation across time and across the world, which is normally characteristic of the 'development' of myths.

However, it may be worth considering that the UFO phenomenon could be the first myth to have formed in a high tech, instant communication world and it may therefore be that the myth, if myth it is, has not had time to mutate in its transmission across the world – giving it uniformity. Dr Bullard has acknowledged that this is a consideration yet to be examined in more detail.

The likely truth is that there is a hard core of reality in the UFO phenomenon but that a very thick mist of myth surrounds that reality, generated primarily by wish fulfilment and media hype.

N

NAKAMURA, TOSHIO

In June 1974 Lieutenant-Colonel Toshio Nakamura and Major Shiro Kubuta were flying an F-4EJ Phantom jet on what they thought was a mission to intercept a Soviet bomber. Once airborne they were informed that they were in fact being launched to investigate reports of a bright-coloured UFO that had been visually observed and radar-tracked. (It is interesting to consider what was regarded as the excuse and what was regarded as confidential.)

At 30,000 feet they encountered a red disc-like object which Major Kubuta claimed even at first sight made him feel that it was 'made and flown by intelligent beings'.

Apparently aware of them, the UFO manoeuvred around the plane, forcing Nakamura to make violent dives and turns. This dogfight continued for some considerable time. Disaster was to follow; apparently the UFO struck the jet which crashed. Both Nakamura and Kubuta ejected but unfortunately Nakamura's parachute caught fire and he plummeted to his death.

NAMUR, BELGIUM

At 7.30 in the evening, on 5 June 1977, amateur photographer Monsieur Muyldermans took three photographs of a disc-shaped flying object near his car at Namur, Belgium. Studies of the photograph indicate that the object was probably some thirty-six feet wide and about a mile high.

The photos achieved considerable fame at the time though no firm conclusion could ever be drawn from them and many such photographs have been taken since.

NASH, FIRST OFFICER W. B.

During the 1952 flap in the United States, on 14 July a Pan Am flight from New York to San Juan, piloted by First Officer William Nash and Second Officer W. H. Fortenberry, encountered six glowing disc-shaped objects below their aircraft. They were in the vicinity of Langley Air Force Base, Virginia.

The objects were described as being approximately 100 feet in diameter and flying in formation. The discs performed bizarre bobbing motions and flipped up on edge before accelerating away in their original formation. They were joined by two other discs, climbed above the flight level of the Pan Am DC-4 and disappeared.

NATIONAL ACADEMY OF SCIENCES (NAS)
When Robert J. **Low** issued his memorandum regarding the **Colorado (University) UFO Project**, he added that it would look better if the National Academy of Sciences actually stood between the Air Force and the University so that the Air Force could distance itself from the project. The National Academy of Sciences was unwilling to do this though it did agree to review only the scientific methodology and not the conclusions or recommendations of the report.

The panel consisted of eleven scientists and on 15 November 1968 the National Academy of Sciences gave its unanimous approval to the report, giving the Air Force precisely the 'angle' that it required.

NATIONAL INVESTIGATIONS COMMITTEE ON AERIAL PHENOMENA
(See **NICAP**.)

NATIONAL SECURITY
Most of the governments of the world that have ever been involved in the UFO phenomenon have used 'national security' as their only criterion for investigation. They argue that provided they have no knowledge of a threat to national security then their job is complete, and it is not their role to investigate UFO claims on any other basis.

By the same token they have often refused to release detailed information about their own UFO investigations on grounds of national security – which would seem to contradict the oft-made claim that there is no national security problem with UFOs! The one argument which is valid is that their methods of data collection would be compromised if they revealed too many of their intelligence-gathering techniques, but it seems that this is a much overused argument. With regard to the

United States government which released documents under the **Freedom of Information Act**, these documents have often been abridged in such a way as to stretch the credulity of anyone believing that this alone could be the explanation.

Given the weight of testimony from people all over the world it seems highly unlikely that there could be no threat to national security from the UFO phenomenon as a whole, even if it is only the major unrest of the population. Presumably the counter-argument that would be used by governments, though they have never been able to verify it, is that their handling of the phenomenon is designed to allay that very unrest.

NAVAL PHOTOGRAPHIC INTERPRETATION CENTER

Donald **Menzel**'s analysis of the Tremonton, Utah, film taken by Warrant Officer Delbert C. **Newhouse** was that he had photographed birds. The **Colorado (University) UFO Project** stated that a thoughtless analysis gave 'a totally wrong impression' because the images were small and relatively sharp and it was the distance rather than poor photography which gave rise to identification difficulties.

The US Naval Photographic Interpretation Center stated that they believed the objects were a light source rather than reflected light, which would rule out any bird. As the estimate of speed of the objects was 3,780 miles per hour this would also seem to rule out even the Roger Bannisters of the aviary!

NEFF, DEPUTY SHERIFF WILBUR

During the night of 16 April 1966 Deputy Sheriffs Wilbur Neff and Dale F. Spaur were alerted by radio to a UFO report being made by a woman in Summit County, Ohio. She reported a UFO as big as a house flying over the area. The officers investigated.

They stopped their car and got out to investigate the area in woods near the caller's address. Suddenly they saw a UFO rising above the trees and coming towards them. It was glowing brightly and illuminating the area all around. The object was making a sound like an electrical transformer on overload. It stopped above the officers and was apparently generating some heat because one of the officers was moved to say, 'My clothes weren't burning or anything', suggesting he considered that a possibility.

One of the officers, Spaur, admitted he was petrified in the two minutes or so they watched the object. They got back into the car and then watched as the object moved away from them. The officers picked up the mike and reported, 'This bright object is right here, the one that everyone says is going over.' The radio controller replied, perhaps comically, 'Shoot it!' but the officers pointed out that this object was no toy and no joke. It was bright and as big as a house, just as the woman had reported earlier.

The officers were instructed to chase the object and did so, reaching speeds of over 100 miles per hour. They were joined by another officer, Wayne Huston, who also witnessed the object. In Pennsylvania, as the chase continued, Police Officer Frank Panzanella also witnessed the UFO which hovered near Pittsburgh Airport while a plane took off and then shot straight up and disappeared.

Like Police Chief Jeff **Greenhaw**, Dale Spaur was ridiculed after making his report; his home life was destroyed, he suffered poor health and had to leave the police force.

NEFF, FIRST OFFICER WILLIAM
(See **Ryan, Captain Raymond E.**)

NEW HAMPSHIRE, ABDUCTION
(See **Hill**, Betty and Barney.)

NEWHOUSE, WARRANT OFFICER DELBERT C.
In the late morning of 2 July 1952 Warrant Officer Delbert C. Newhouse and his wife were driving along a road seven miles from Tremonton in Utah when they spotted a formation of brilliant objects, clear against a bright blue sky. They were round and unlike any aircraft Newhouse had ever seen. As a Navy photographer, Newhouse was familiar with most aircraft forms.

Using a 16 mm camera and telephoto lens Newhouse shot forty feet of film of the objects and their manoeuvres. It was submitted to Project **Blue Book** for evaluation and for three months was studied by the Photo Reconnaissance Laboratory at Dayton, Ohio.

According to Major Donald E. **Keyhoe**, in his conversation with the Air Force Public Liaison Officer Al Chop, 'Fraud was completely ruled out. They tried every trick and method to duplicate the film but it couldn't be done.' Keyhoe believed that this perhaps constituted proof that the saucers were interplanetary, though obviously the Air Force would not confirm that.

While such a conclusion might be seen as somewhat premature, given the nature of the sighting and film, it is clear that the
film must have given the Air Force food for thought.

NEY, EDWARD
The comment which seems to have set the scene for serious
scientists has been attributed to the professor of astrophysics at
University of Michigan, Dr Edward Ney. He is alleged to have
stated, 'Respectable scientists don't even discuss UFOs in
serious terms.'

NIAGARA FALLS, NEW YORK, SIGHTING
In his book *Dimensions* (see References and Background Material) Jacques Vallée describes the case of a woman who, in
January 1958, was driving along the New York State thruway
near Niagara Falls in the early hours of the morning.

As she was driving she saw what appeared to be the debris of
an aeroplane crash on the road. A slim pole some fifty feet high
was apparently sticking out of the ground and from around it
two shapes were rising. They were like animals with four legs
and a tail but with feelers near the head, something like arms.
Suddenly the entities disappeared and a UFO rose into the air.
It was then she realised it was saucer-shaped; it spun and lifted
up into the air and disappeared from her view.

An investigation with a torch across the area showed a hole in
the melting snow, warm grass, but no artefacts.

NIAUX, FRANCE: PALAEOLITHIC CAVE DRAWINGS
There are many places in the world where prehistoric man has
left cave drawings and paintings which are thought-provoking in
imagery. Perhaps none is more so than at Niaux in France
where there is an image of two elongated and possibly disc-
shaped objects with domes on top, one actually showing a line
of dots behind which suggests an interpretation of movement.

While it is unwise to draw too many conclusions from images
which are not fully understood, they are nonetheless food for
Ufological thought.

NICAP (NATIONAL INVESTIGATIONS COMMITTEE ON AERIAL PHENOMENA)
The National Investigations Committee on Aerial Phenomena
(NICAP) was founded in 1956 by Navy physicist Thomas
Townsend **Brown**. For many years it was headed by US Marine

Corps Major Donald E. **Keyhoe** and, taking his general line, was an active and vociferous organisation in the United States, arguing a broadly pro-extraterrestrial line with regard to the origin of UFOs (i.e. that UFOs are likely to be extraterrestrial in origin). NICAP heavily criticised the Air Force, principally, and also other establishment organisations for their apparent cover-up of and conspiracy over the phenomenon.

NICAP was allegedly heavily infiltrated by the **CIA**, and certainly many of its prominent members were former or active CIA personnel, though whether this was by Agency design or simply the result of personal interest in the people involved is debatable.

Vice-Admiral Roscoe H. **Hillenkoetter**, a former director of the CIA, was a member of the NICAP board for many years, resigning in 1962 on the grounds that NICAP had completed what investigations it could carry out. Colonel Joseph J. **Bryan** III, a chief of the CIA psychological warfare staff, was also on the board of NICAP. A vice-chairman of NICAP in 1956 was Count Nicolas **de Rochefort** of the CIA psychological warfare staff; CIA briefing officer Karl Pflock was chairman of NICAP's Washington sub-committee; John **Acuff** who was alleged to have CIA affiliations took over as head of NICAP when Major Keyhoe was apparently ousted by the CIA in 1969 and he in turn was replaced by CIA agent Alan N. **Hall** in 1979.

Whatever conclusion is drawn about this it must be fairly stated that NICAP had for many years a formative influence on American, and therefore world, Ufology. That alone may well have given the CIA pause for thought.

NICAP was dissolved in 1973 and its reports handed over to Dr J. Allen **Hynek** for use in the **Center for UFO Studies (CUFOS)**.

NITEROI, RIO DE JANEIRO

Following a report of a UFO landing on a hill near Niteroi, a suburb of Rio de Janeiro in Brazil, police found the discovery of two dead men with their faces covered with lead masks. The suggestion was that the men were preparing to make contact with the occupants of a UFO but that somehow the contact went badly wrong. Laboratory analysis indicated no obvious cause of death, having ruled out poison, violence or asphyxiation. The police investigation was supervised by Inspector José Venancio Bittencourt of the Rio de Janeiro police force.

NOCTILUCENT CLOUDS

Rather like **mock suns**, noctilucent clouds are made up of ice and particles in the atmosphere and are often visible at night or at dawn or dusk because the sun's rays (or occasionally reflections from ground lights) illuminate them, causing them to appear as solid, shaped masses, often orange and red.

They are of course often reported as UFOs because of their nature but are otherwise consistent with cloud materials and generally can be identified because of their lack of or slow movement.

NORCROSS, CAPTAIN J. N.

(See *Caroline*, HMS)

NORWAY, CRASH RETRIEVAL

In June 1952 the paper *Zeitung* published a report of an alleged crash retrieval of a saucer near Spitzbergen.

According to the report, Norwegian jet fighters flying near Himlopen Straits had encountered radio interference and had seen an enormous blue disc lying on the snow beneath them. The disc was later investigated by the Norwegian Air Force. It was supposedly 125 feet in diameter, with a plexiglass dome, but otherwise of metallic construction and containing remote control equipment. No entities were associated with the saucer. It was held to be powered by forty-six jets which caused a rotating movement around the ring.

The disc had been dismantled and taken to Narvik where analysis indicated its flight range was over 18,000 miles and that it was equipped to carry explosives.

It must be admitted that this report is uncorroborated, and indeed part of the claim was that the instrument bore Russian notations. If true, this would indicate an early attempt to produce a flying saucer by the Soviet Union.

The Norwegian government deny knowledge of this disc.

NOUATRE, FRANCE

(See **Gatay**, Georges.)

NOVINA, C.D.

(See **Humbert, Pierre**.)

NOYES, RALPH

Ralph Noyes could be described as 'gamekeeper turned

poacher'. He has had a significant 'official' career within Britain's intelligence service; he was private secretary to Sir Ralph Cochrane, the Vice-Chief of the Air Staff from 1950 to 1952, was the head of the Ministry of Defence's **DS8** (which dealt with UFO investigations amongst other things) and retired in 1977 with the grade of Under-Secretary of State.

Since that time he has become an active contributor to the field of UFO research, is a consultant to **BUFORA** and has been responsible for a considerable body of official inquiries into the subject.

Although obviously frequently questioned at length, and asked to lecture about his Ministry connections, his interest in the phenomenon is very widespread.

Adding another string to his bow, he published the book *A Secret Property*, a novel loosely based on aspects of the UFO phenomenon.

NURJADIN, AIR MARSHAL ROESMIN
Air Marshal Roesmin Nurjadin was Commander-in-Chief of the Indonesian Air Force in 1967. He stated, 'UFOs sighted in Indonesia are identical with those sighted in other countries. Sometimes they pose a problem for our Air Defence and once we were obliged to open fire on them.'

'NUTS AND BOLTS'
A buzz term in Ufology expressing the belief that UFOs are physical, metallic entities, usually spacecraft from other planets. Although a nuts and bolts hypothesis is not widely adhered to across the world, it is strongly supported in America and is a cornerstone of the extraterrestrial hypothesis which is more strongly advocated there than anywhere else. (See also **structured object**.)

O

OAKENSEN, ELSIE

Mrs Elsie Oakensen is an **abductee** from Northamptonshire in England. She is very open about her experience, and feels that it is important she share it with others. Accordingly she has spoken at many UFO group meetings, has appeared on radio and television and given press interviews, and is an active member of a local UFO research group. The editor of this encyclopedia has known Mrs Oakensen for several years. She has accompanied him around the site of her abduction and gone over the case in detail with him. At the Sheffield UFO Conference in July 1990 he interviewed Mrs Oakensen specifically for this book. What follows is her story, in her own words, so that the reader may appreciate something of the feelings of witnesses.

'On 22 November 1978, when travelling along the A5 at Weedon in Northamptonshire, I saw a couple of very bright lights above the road, a red light on the left-hand side and a green light on the right-hand side. They were attached to a dumb-bell-shaped object which was grey, very smooth, and hovering about one hundred feet above the road. It was about fifty feet wide. I was unable to avoid this; I just had to travel underneath it. I felt compelled to stop but realised it was a busy road (and potentially dangerous to stop), so I carried on driving.

'When I got off the A5 the electrics of the car started to play up. I was able to travel a little further, until I passed underneath some trees. When I came out from under the trees I suddenly found myself in darkness, absolute pitch black darkness. As I sat in the car I could not see the road, buildings, trees or anything else.

'As I sat there, a circle of brilliant white light about a yard in diameter shone on to the road to the left-hand side of the car. It went off and it was dark again. Another circle came towards the front of the car, went off and then shone on and off, on and off, in a semicircle round the front of the car from left to right, then back again from right to left and again from left to right with the last one shining into the garden of the cottage at the side of the road. It was then as if the light was turned; it went in a circle up the front of the cottage and off over the top. Then everywhere went into darkness again.

'I sat in the car absolutely fascinated by this, thinking that someone was playing the fool, perhaps sitting with a bright torch at the top of the farm buildings. However, I realised that, had that been so, the light would have had an oval-shaped beam (because of the angle of strike of the beam). These lights were, though, completely circular, with no beams at all. As I sat there thinking about it I was absolutely fascinated by the whole thing. I said, "Good gracious" out loud.

'I then found myself in normal daylight about thirty yards further down the road, driving normally in third gear as I had been before this started. I travelled for about a hundred yards without being in control of the car. I think it was probably being driven by remote control.

'I went home, looked out of the window, saw a yellow flashing light in approximately the same position as the point where the incident had taken place. I thought, "This might be it. There might be some connection, but perhaps not." But whether that was anything to do with it or not I really don't know. I looked at the clock and I found that a fifteen-minute journey had actually taken me half an hour on that day. I suppose I lost fifteen minutes of time as I sat in the car while the lights were flashed round me.

'About seven o'clock in the evening I found that I had a tightening sensation around my head. This reminded me that the same thing had happened to me at lunchtime. Both times the sensation had lasted about a minute, and then stopped. Whether these were anything to do with it, at the time I didn't know.

'Nearly twelve years on (since the incident) and with a lot of time to think about it, I now believe that in some way, for some reason, I was selected by that UFO. I believe that it was in the area and at lunchtime when I had the tightening sensation around my head it was saying to me or to my subconscious, "Look, we are going to stop you on the way home, have a closer look at you but you will not be frightened in any way at all." I believe it was there over the road making sure that it saw me and that I saw it and that it knew, or the occupants (if there were some) knew, that I was fascinated by it. I think when the green light started to flash it was saying, "Right, you've seen us, here we come" and of course it tried to stop me when I went under the trees.

'I think it tried to stop me by the trees but the trees got in the way and then of course when I came out from under the trees it got me. I believe that perhaps some kind of barrier came down and excluded all light from the area, around the houses and everything, in which it controlled my car's movement for those hundred yards. I think that the lights were there not for any particular purpose other than to take my mind off what really happened.

'I would think that in that fifteen minutes there was some kind of examination and by that I don't mean necessarily a medical examination – it could have been a spiritual examination or something like that. I think that when I saw the yellow light it was just flashing at me to say "Mission accomplished".

'Of the tightening sensation around my head in the evening, I know now that it ties in with another sighting nearby when four ladies were driving in a car and saw red and green lights in the same configuration as mine. Apparently, the lights crossed the road and paced the car as they drove along, and then changed to a white light and went out. That is some kind of corroboration of my story.

'During 1989 and 1990 the type of people I seem to be meeting are healers and mediums. I have been told by seven people of this kind that I have the power to heal and that if I chose to develop it I could enter mediumship through healing. I am beginning to be able to do this with the help of a very good friend who is working with me and giving me additional power. Together we are working to heal the sick. I think that it is a gift that I have and I would be silly not to develop it if I can help people.'

OBERTH, DR HERMANN

Dr Hermann Oberth was one of the world's great rocket experts and the father of the V1 and V2 rockets of the Second World War. Although used as weapons of death they were conceived as tools of science. He was one of Dr Wernher von Braun's contemporaries during the birth of the American space programme.

In a press conference in June 1954 he stated, of UFOs, 'These objects are conceived and directed by intelligent beings of a very high order. They probably do not originate in our solar system, perhaps not even in our galaxy.'

As if that were not enough Oberth went on to make an astonishing admission: 'We cannot take the credit for our record of advancement in certain scientific fields alone; we have been helped'; and when pressed to explain who he referred to, he replied, 'the people of other worlds'.

OBJECTS SEEN FLOATING

Although the expression 'flying saucer' or 'unidentified flying object' is most commonly used for the UFO phenomenon, Charles Fort, who dedicated most of his life to collecting bizarre phenomena stories, referred to the phenomenon as 'objects seen floating' which, while perhaps less useful descriptively, does have a certain charm.

O'CONNOR, J. J.

While flying a private plane in Florida J. J. O'Connor, on 20 September 1966, encountered a huge UFO in his path. He was flying at 9,500 feet and was forced to reduce power and dive to avoid possible collision.

At 3,500 feet O'Connor saw that the UFO had followed him down; he became scared and at one point grabbed a revolver he had with him but realised that to use it would be both useless and dangerous.

Shortly after this the UFO circled upwards and disappeared, leaving him a shaken man.

OETINGER, DR LEON

Two days after the famous Kenneth **Arnold** sighting, in the wake of the event, on 26 June 1947, a medical practitioner, Dr Leon Oetinger of Lexington, Kentucky, together with three other witnesses, saw a large silver globe moving along the edge of the Grand Canyon. It was travelling at high speed and they were quite clear that it was not a balloon or similar object.

O'KEEFE, MAJOR-GENERAL RICHARD

According to Major Donald E. **Keyhoe**, at a private briefing of Air Force commanders by Major-General Richard O'Keefe, the acting Inspector General stated, 'What is required is that every UFO sighting be investigated and reported to the Air Technical

Intelligence Center at Wright Patterson Air Force Base.' Prophetically, Major-General O'Keefe also warned that sightings would increase, causing public apprehension, and suggested the appointment of 'UFO officers' who could conduct investigations correctly, with proper scientific and technical support.

Although this was stated in the mid-1960s there is no evidence that his suggestions have been firmly acted upon; alternatively some UFO investigators believe it was a statement of what was already happening and continues to happen.

OLD NEW MOON
Project Old New Moon is held to have been a successor project to Project **Blue Book**, a continuation of the United States Air Force's UFO investigation. The Air Force always maintained that it ceased investigation when it closed that earlier project and has never officially confirmed the existence of Old New Moon. The Project was apparently confirmed to Major Donald E. **Keyhoe** by former Army Intelligence officer Lieutenant-Colonel Lou **Corbin**.

OLÉRON, FRANCE, MOTHER-SHIP SIGHTING
On 14 October 1952 many witnesses at Oléron in France reported sighting a cigar-shaped UFO accompanied by a flotilla of disc-shaped objects. These UFOs were described as red with yellow rims around them, giving them a 'Saturn-like' appearance.

There is a report that the UFOs dropped **angel hair**, a substance similar to a spider's web often associated with UFO encounters. However, in a rather hysterical addendum to this there is a story of one man being trapped like a fly, confined by the filaments. No details are available of his fate, if indeed that part of the sighting is correct, and in any case angel hair that has been briefly examined *in situ* does not seem to have anything like the strength to ensnare a person.

ONEGA, LAKE
On 27 April 1961 twenty-five woodsmen watched as a UFO neared the ground at Lake Onega, near the village of Entino in the Soviet Union; it struck the lake shore causing a great deal of damage before recovering its height and flying away. The object was described as huge, oval-shaped and glowing blue-green.

The woodsmen called the local forest ranger, Valentin Borsky, who arrived the next morning to inspect the site. He found large grooves cut into the lake shore, damage to vegetation, and located some pieces of debris. These were described as black, artificial-looking, and metallic. They were examined at the Leningrad Technological Institute; no conclusion was drawn, except to state that they were not meteorite fragments.

ONEIDA AIR FORCE BASE, JAPAN
On the night of 5 August 1952 Oneida Air Force Base in Japan witnessed the close approach of a flying saucer. Operators in the control tower used binoculars to examine the object and described it as a bright light with a larger dark shape behind it.

The objects remained stationary for some minutes and the tower contacted ground control intercept, who picked up its track on radar. Strangely, the object broke into three parts and all three raced off at speeds of 300 knots.

GCI contacted a transport plane, a C54 in the vicinity, and vectored it in towards the saucers but it could not catch them with its much slower speed. The objects were not seen after this.

ORDOVAS, CAPTAIN JAIME
On 25 February 1969 Captain Jaime Ordovas, co-pilot Augustin Carvajal and engineer José Cuenca, crewing an Iberian Airlines flight from Mallorca to mainland Spain, witnessed a powerfully bright red UFO pacing the airliner.

At one point it descended towards the ground, climbed and disappeared out of sight. All three of the crew confirmed the sighting.

ORREGO, COMMANDER AUGUSTO
Augusto Orrego, a Chilean naval officer in command of an Antarctic base, reported that during one night in February 1950 he and colleagues had seen flying saucers moving above the base and manoeuvring at incredible speed. Photographs were taken but not released by the Chilean government as they were classified.

ORTHOTENY
French Ufologist Aimé Michel proposed the orthoteny theory of UFOs, which suggested that their appearance occurred along straight lines related to a number of factors. He charted such lines across France; other researchers have taken up his work across other countries.

It is difficult to determine, given the frequency of UFO

reports, whether or not it is a case of finding the patterns you are looking for or whether the patterns are genuinely there.

Either way no actual cause has been given for this possible effect.

OSBORNE, F. M.

In October 1969 the Australian Minister for Air, F. M. Osborne, stated of UFO reports: 'Nothing that has arisen from these three or four per cent of unexplained cases gives any firm support to the belief that interlopers from other places in this world or outside it have been visiting us.'

OSCEOLA, WISCONSIN 'METEOR SHOWER'

On 28 July 1952 Air Defense Command at Osceola, Wisconsin, reported that ground control intercept radar had tracked UFOs nearby. The UFOs were moving at 60 miles per hour but one of them shot off at over 600 miles per hour when jet interceptors pursued them.

One of the pilots visually sighted the radar-tracked objects from 25,000 feet and one of the ground observer corps on the base also saw them.

A suggestion was made that they were a meteor shower before information about their speeds and manoeuvrability was known, though an astronomer later correlated the data and declared this 'impossible'.

OSWALD, LULI

On 15 October 1979 Luli Oswald and a friend were driving from Rio de Janeiro to Saquarema. At the exact moment when Ms Oswald asked her companion what he would do if he saw a flying saucer, three UFOs appeared out at sea.

They became concerned about the sighting and turned inland. However, due to taking a wrong turning they found themselves back on the coastal highway and had to continue along it. Suddenly there were signs of **vehicle interference** and the UFOs were seen to climb into the air, pulling towers of water behind them and scaring both witnesses.

As the UFOs approached, the witnesses debated whether they would be safer hiding inside the car or running. Their memory of subsequent events disappeared.

Later, they were still in the car but now much further along the highway, and off on a side road. They pulled into a service station for refreshment and were amazed to discover that it was then two o'clock in the morning, over two hours since the time of their last memory recall.

Under regression hypnosis, Ms Oswald revealed a classic abduction story; the UFO had sucked the car up in a beam of light and the witnesses had been confronted by short gruesome entities with reduced facial features, long thin arms and dull grey skin. Ms Oswald was naked and the entities were taking hair samples, making a gynaecological examination and shining light beams which were painful to her. The entities rejected her as of no use to them. The research continued however; they then examined her companion and took biological samples from him.

Summing up the problem even Ufologists have with abductions Ms Oswald stated, 'It isn't real, but it happened all the same.'

'OUT-OF-BODY EXPERIENCES' (OOBEs)

An 'out-of-body experience' or 'near-death experience' is, broadly speaking, a perception of the soul, or 'personal self', leaving the mortal body and engaging in travel on what is generally known as an astral plane. Although not directly related to UFOs, there are many UFO experiences, and particularly abduction experiences, which have similar characteristics to 'out-of-body experiences' and 'near-death experiences'.

There have been several cases where witnesses have found themselves drawn into flying saucers while still seeing their own inert mortal body elsewhere, suggesting a direct interface between these phenomena.

P

PADELLERO, FRANCO
(See **Di Salvatore**, Attilo.)

PADRICK, SID
In January 1965, Sid Padrick of Watsonville, California, saw a landed flying saucer in the early hours of the morning. It was approximately seventy feet wide and sitting motionless in the dark near his home.

When he ran from it a voice from inside the craft said, 'Do not be frightened, we are not hostile. We mean you no harm.'

Rather trustingly, Padrick boarded the craft. On board, he met eight aliens, fully human in appearance, including one very pretty female. They had dark skin and eyes, angular features and full heads of long hair. They wore two-piece snow-type suits in blue-white.

One of the men spoke perfect English though explained he was the only one aboard who could. Padrick noticed that he delayed before replying to even the simplest question and believed this may have been due to the alien being in telepathic communication with his colleagues, in conference with them before replying to any questions. Telepathy is frequently reported as a means of communication by aliens, though usually it is used in communication with humans.

Aboard the craft, Padrick was able to take note of several rooms with instruments and machinery operating in them, including, rather archaically, one instrument with a physical tape moving within it rather like the feeder of a teletype. Padrick discussed the power system of the craft with the crew which was just as well because they were taking him for a journey, landing and allowing him to step out for a time some 200 miles away to the north-west of his home.

Discussing the home world of the aliens Padrick discovered – not untypically for **contactees** – that they came from a perfect world of no sickness, no crime and total equality. Their planet is somewhere in our solar system but hidden from the Earth; there are a great many such claims in contactee stories but the mechanism of 'hiding' a planet is never explained. There have been stories – from prior to the space age – of planets hidden behind the moon but these have never been located since people ventured into space. It has been speculated that the method of 'hiding' is that the planet is in another dimension. Any such suggestion is wild speculation, to say the least.

Rather unusually, even for the more religious contactee stories, Padrick was taken into a sort of on-board 'chapel' and given the opportunity to say some prayers.

Padrick makes one telling point. He was informed by the aliens that the purpose of their visit was 'for observation' but he believes that it was for Earth to observe them rather than the other way round; he noticed that they asked him very little about himself.

There was apparently an Air Force investigation on Padrick's return where the investigator made, according to the witness, several remarkable statements, including telling him that 'there was more than one group of UFOs visiting Earth'.

A few years after the event, Mr Padrick appeared to find the attention of UFO researchers unwelcome and disappeared from public view.

PAGE, DR THORNTON
Dr Thornton Page represented the sciences of astronomy and astrophysics on the **Robertson Panel** set up in 1953 to review UFO reports.

PAINE, THOMAS
Thomas Paine (1737–1809), author of *The Rights of Man*, seemed to suggest that belief in extraterrestrial life, by which some would also encompass belief in UFOs, could not be reconciled with belief in God. He wrote, 'To believe that God created a plurality of worlds at least as numerous as what we call stars renders the Christian system of faith at once little and ridiculous and scatters it in the mind like feathers in the air. The two beliefs cannot be held together in the same mind and he who thinks he believes in both has thought but little of either.'

PALMER, RAY
Ray Palmer became the managing editor of science fiction magazines and fantasy fiction magazines during the 1940s and

seems to have played a prominent if rather shadowy role in some of the development of the UFO mystery.

It was Palmer who promoted the Kenneth **Arnold** sighting in *Fate* magazine, a paper which he created. The magazine carried UFO stories continually after that date. Kenneth Arnold's book on his encounter, *The Coming of the Saucers* (see References and Background Material), was co-written by Palmer. He was also involved in the **Maury Island** mystery by being the person initially to contact Kenneth Arnold and involve him in the investigation.

Palmer did much to promote a particular view of UFOs, i.e. the **extraterrestrial hypothesis (ETH)**.

PARALYSIS, INDUCED BY UFOS

There are countless cases of reports of people witnessing UFOs, particularly at close quarters, where they report the onset of paralysis. There are many possible causes for this paralysis which rely on both components of the sighting, i.e. the UFO and the witness. Firstly, it is possible that at least in some cases paralysis is induced by UFOs or associated entities, and many times this is implied still further by the fact that the entity will draw what would seem to be some sort of weapon, point it and fire a beam, resulting in the witness's paralysis, as in the case of farmer Maurice Masse in **Valensole**, France, in the mid-1960s.

However, there are certain cases of paralysis where there is no obvious deliberate intent and yet the witness believes that it is induced by the UFO. We have only the witness's interpretation for this but obviously this is important and must be taken into account.

A further suggestion is that some cases of paralysis are caused by the shock of the encounter and are therefore psychological in origin.

In the case of some of the more extraordinary abductions, and particularly bedroom visitation abductions, the origin of the paralysis is less easy to determine. On many occasions witnesses of such encounters report that they were unable to move and to prevent the abduction. However, if the abduction comprises at least partially dream material, then paralysis is also a quite common factor in such dreams since they are often expressing frustration and inability to act.

These effects are not always one way; in the case of '**Dr X**' in France, his encounter left him cured of many previous injuries and ailments, including a partial paralysis. Of course there have been many people who have commented on the similarity between visions of UFOs and visions of the Blessed Virgin Mary (see **BVM Connection**), the latter of which are often associated with miracle cures of all forms of ailments.

PARAVICI D'ERBA, ITALY

On 20 October 1954, in Paravici d'Erba, Italy, one witness encountered a short, strange entity in a luminous suit, standing near a tree. The entity apparently aimed something like a torch at him and paralysed the witness. He freed himself by what seems to be an effort of will and made as if to attack the creature.

However, as he ran towards it, the entity rose from the ground and disappeared with a soft whirring noise. The witness suffered shock and fever. Local people who knew him described him as 'trustworthy'.

PARKER, CALVIN
(See **Pascagoula, Mississippi**.)

PARRISH, LEE

At 1 a.m. in the morning of 27 January 1977 Lee Parrish was driving home in the town of Prospect, Kentucky, when he was buzzed by a UFO, bright and perfectly rectangular in outline. Suddenly it sped away at great speed.

Once he arrived he discovered that the seven-minute drive had taken three quarters of an hour. His mother contacted a local UFO group with regard to the sighting. Investigations began immediately including a hypnotic regression session.

Apparently, while passing underneath the UFO Parrish had blacked out and had been transported inside the UFO, into an all white circular room some twenty feet around. Three entities surrounded him and he believed that they were living though in fact they all appeared machine-like rather than **humanoid**, a rare feature of abduction accounts. Parrish regarded himself as being examined rather like a laboratory rat.

The vast majority of UFO contacts appear to be with humanoid-type entities, i.e. creatures with two arms, two legs and a head carrying sensory organs at the highest point, but occasionally this is not so, as in this case.

It may be that these entities fit more into anti-machine age symbolism than physical reality. By the same token the encounter may reflect what is generally accepted as the 'absurdity of

UFOs', a factor of the overall UFO phenomenon which seems to suggest that probably we are simply not understanding the true mechanisms at work.

Though described as 'machine-like', one of the abductors was a huge black slab some fifteen feet tall. It has been compared to the Monolith in the film *2001 – A Space Odyssey*.

His captors subjected Parrish to some form of medical examination including a probe into his head, which he believed was analysing his chemical make-up.

PASCAGOULA, MISSISSIPPI

October of 1973 saw an extraordinary wave of UFO sightings across America but none so incredible as that of the abduction of shipyard workers Charles Hickson and Calvin Parker.

It was seven o'clock in the evening of 12 October when the pair were fishing from a pier at the Shaupeter shipyard. Suddenly they realised that there was something behind them – a machine making a buzzing noise. They saw an oval-shaped object with a blue light on it just behind them. The witnesses watched as a hatchway opened in the object and three bizarre entities floated out.

As Hickson described it: 'They didn't have clothes. But they had feet shape . . . it was more or less a round like thing on a leg, if you'd call it a leg . . . I was scared to death. And me with the spinning reel out there – it's all I had. I couldn't, well, I was so scared, well, you can't imagine. Calvin done went hysterical on me.'

The entities were described as ghostlike and pale with wrinkled skin, and conical projections where nose and ears would normally be.

Using crab-like pincers they apparently floated Hickson into the UFO. Parker had fainted. (Though there is some suggestion that in fact he, too, was conscious when they abducted him, his hypnotic recall is unclear on the point.) Inside the craft Hickson could not move though he believes he remained conscious. Hickson does not clearly remember leaving the craft but eventually found himself on the dock with Parker who was looking very agitated.

The UFO is described as something around eight feet tall and oblong, with an opening in one end and a blue light outside. Inside it was bright but with no obvious source of lighting. While inside the object, Hickson was examined by a 'roving eye' type of machine.

I spoke to Hickson in July 1990 and he confirmed that there had been many other strange occurrences to himself and his family in the years since and that he was assisting investigators with research to help make sense of the data.

In 1987 he stated: 'I was offered all kinds of money to let them do a movie. I declined. I am still declining. Making money is not what this experience is all about.'

Witness credibility is very important in such cases; when I met and spoke to Hickson and his son in 1990, I was instantly impressed by their obvious sincerity and honesty.

PATRICK, RONNIE
Resident of Tyler, Texas, Ronnie Patrick began a series of experiences in 1977. Firstly, two shadow-like figures were seen outside the door of his home one evening, floating off the ground.

Shortly after this, Patrick witnessed a silver disc-shaped UFO making extraordinary aerobatic manoeuvres.

It was two years after the first incident when while working at 3 a.m. in the morning he was touched by a sparkling ray of light which was beamed into him through the walls of a building he was in. His next memory was of waking up four hours later.

After this last event Patrick self-reported psycho-kinetic abilities and believed he had insight into the physics of space.

PATTERSON, LIEUTENANT WILLIAM
During the wave of sightings of 1952, pilot Lieutenant William Patterson had his encounter with a UFO arranged by his air traffic controller! The object had been picked up by Air Route Traffic Control and the jet was scrambled to intercept it. Patterson made visual contact with the object and went to afterburners to chase it.

However, just as he was approaching it, the radar controllers vectored him around and he quickly realised he would not be able to catch up with the UFO. Ultimately he lost visual contact as well.

His description of the encounter stated that he saw white lights but there is no other detail available.

PEASE AIR FORCE BASE
Although itself the location of one or two not very significant UFO sightings, Pease Air Force Base is most significant to Ufology in the case of Betty and Barney **Hill**. While there is

much in that case to suggest that the abduction story drawn out by regression **hypnosis** may have resulted from fear and absorption of UFO book and magazine material, the fact remains that at the time of the sighting Pease Air Force Base tracked an object on radar whose timing was later confirmed to correspond with the Hill UFO encounter. If the abduction was some form of internal 'fantasy', then at least we can be reasonably certain it was based on some genuine external event.

PECCINETTI, CARLOS

Carlos Peccinetti and colleague Fernando José Villegas were the subject of a car stop in September 1968 in the early hours of the morning, in Mendoza, Argentina.

Both men got out of the car to investigate the **vehicle interference** and found themselves paralysed and unable to move. In front of them were three entities, short with large bald heads and tight-fitting overalls; two more such creatures stood slightly further away across the road next to a hovering UFO. The creatures came towards the witnesses, as if walking on the air itself. The witnesses received an apparently telepathic communication, which basically stated that without the sun the solar system would not exist (hardly a revelation) and were then told that 'Mathematics is the universal language' (not much better).

The entities apparently scratched hieroglyphics all over the windows of the car and also projected images of the nuclear destruction of an otherwise beautiful planet, which might or might not have been their planet or the Earth. Before leaving, the entities pricked the fingers of the witnesses. They then turned and walked back into the UFO up a beam of light. The UFO rose and disappeared.

Subsequent investigation indicated that the witnesses did indeed have pin pricks in their fingers and that there were strange marks on their car.

The witnesses eventually claimed that this contact was a **hoax**.

However, even the claim that it was a hoax may have to be disregarded as it followed a statement by the police that those spreading rumours about UFOs would be subject to legal penalties.

While it cannot be ascertained for this specific case there have certainly been reports that have been withdrawn and denied by the witness because of fear of publicity or ridicule, where the witness has privately confirmed that they still hold the report to be true.

PEDLEY, GEORGE
On 19 January 1966 banana grower George Pedley, in Horseshoe Lagoon, Queensland, Australia, was driving his tractor early in the morning when he heard a loud rushing noise. Just a few yards ahead of him a grey-blue spinning UFO was rising into the air. He estimated it was about 25 feet wide and 9 feet high and at an altitude of about 60 feet, apparently disappearing at amazing speed.

On investigation Pedley discovered landing traces in the form of a circular area of flattened grass.

Such circular patterns of grass have become very frequently seen in modern times, particularly in the southern counties of England, but there are few reported connections between UFOs and such ground traces, which appear to be some quite separate phenomenon.

There are reports of **cornfield circle** formations being associated with orange glowing balls of light – thought to be caused by ionized air – giving some UFO connection, but that does not appear to be the case in Horseshoe Lagoon.

PEEBLES, RIKKI
Singer Rikki Peebles was the British entrant for the Eurovision Song Contest with the song 'Only the Light' which apparently describes a **close encounter**. He claimed that the song followed ESP resulting from a close encounter and that the lyrics had been dictated to him by the aliens.

They promised Peebles that he would win the competition in May 1987 – and proved themselves totally unreliable when he came thirteenth.

PENNINGTON, E. J.
Probably the most valid terrestrial explanation for the 1896/7 **airship** wave in America was that it was created by one E. J. Pennington. This idea was promoted by Dr Geoffrey Doel, of **BUFORA**. Apparently the Pennington airship was developed in 1891 in Illinois and matched many of the witness descriptions. At one time it was seen resting on the ground in Brown County, Indiana, by two farmers, Jeremiah Collier and William York.

Since there is a known ten-mile flight of an airship in 1901 by

Santos-Dumont it seems quite possible that other developments would have been taking place earlier.

Certainly Pennington's airship alone does not explain all of the reports made but the degree to which **mythology** has interfered with these reports is difficult to examine nearly a hundred years away from the event.

PEREGO, DR ALBERTO

In November 1954, on more than one occasion, Italian diplomat Dr Alberto Perego was among crowds witnessing formations of white dots in the sky, often moving very rapidly. At one point he realised he was looking at over a hundred of these objects at one time.

Dr Perego also appears to be one of the few witnesses to the formation of **angel hair** – a fall of thin fibrous filaments which dissolve after a few hours.

Dr Perego made a report to the Italian government but they replied that nothing had been tracked on radar.

PETROPOLIS, BRAZIL

There have been several cases of people's illnesses being cured by close encounters with UFOs and alien occupants but these have usually taken place in a very ambiguous way where mere close proximity to the object or beings somehow cures ills. This leads to some speculation that the healing is by will power, inspired by the sighting but not a direct result of it.

However, on 25 October 1957, in Petropolis, Brazil, an incredible story of a most extraordinary 'flying doctor' service occurred.

The subject was the dying daughter of a wealthy family, suffering from severe cancer of the stomach. On the night in question the girl was in some considerable pain when she saw a beam of light outside her home. Seven members of her family witnessed the room being filled with such light.

Outside the house a flying saucer with its hatch open was 'de-planing' its rescue mission. There were two entities somewhere around four feet tall with long, yellowish-red hair and bright green slanting eyes. The entities entered the house and approached the girl's bed and laid out medical instruments. One of the entities allegedly obtained details of the illness by telepathy from her father.

The entities shone a brilliant blue-white light on to the girl's stomach; her insides were made visible and the cancerous tumours could be seen. The 'surgeons' operated and removed the cancer. One of the entities handed the girl's father a globular tool box containing thirty small white pills, which were to be taken daily for a month.

Two months later the girl's doctor verified that she had been completely cured of the cancer.

PETSCHE, JOHN
Shortly after the Kenneth **Arnold** sighting and before the **Roswell**, New Mexico, crash retrieval, an electrician, John Petsche, together with other unnamed witnesses, reported seeing the apparent landing or low level descent of a disc-shaped object in the vicinity of Bisbee near the New Mexico border in Arizona.

PETT, SAUL
Media writer Saul Pett sighted a glowing orange saucer shape over New Jersey, United States of America, in 1953 and his reaction, although perhaps unusual for the time, was one that has been echoed many times since. He stated, 'I wasn't frightened at all because the thing looked so peaceful and serene. There wasn't any appearance of menace.'

Many similar encounters have led modern witnesses to move on to enhanced lifestyles, often non-materialistic in nature, but whether or not this can be directly related to the sighting is indeterminate.

PFEIFFER, ALAN AND SHIRLEY
Alan and Shirley Pfeiffer are credited with being amongst the first group of witnesses to the March 1973 UFO sightings around Saylors Lake in Pennsylvania. These were the sightings which 'kicked off' the 1973 wave across the United States which was to include many extraordinary encounters including that of Charles Hickson and Calvin Parker at **Pascagoula, Mississippi**.

They saw several aerial lights during the early evening, describing them as unknown circular objects, of various colours. They were apparently wheeling around the area at a height of approximately 2,000 feet.

PHOTOGRAPHIC EVIDENCE
Probably the most publicly known face of UFOs is in the photographic evidence. There have been many thousands of

UFO or UFO-related photographs over the years.

It has to be said that a great many are immediately exposed as frauds or self-confessed hoaxes, and many more after a passage of years when new techniques of analysis are available. By the same token many can be explained as mistakes such as camera flaws, film developing flaws, objects seen out of focus or otherwise misidentified.

Of the remaining photographs which might reasonably be called 'real' UFOs, again it has to be made clear that there are no unambiguous photographs. No one has photographed anything aboard a flying saucer; there are no reliable entity photographs; and the authenticity of the clearest saucer or object photographs has in every case been called into question at some time.

Investigators suffer, of course, from having no known credible photographs to use as a yardstick for establishing exactly what is and what could not be credible.

One important point to make is that photographs alone do not constitute a UFO case. They can only be used in conjunction with the testimony of a credible witness.

The earliest case of a UFO photograph is that taken at Zacatecas observatory (see **Bonilla**, José A. Y.); the most enduring credible photographs are the 1950 pair taken by the Trent couple at **McMinnville** in Oregon, which have withstood all analysis to the present day; and the most photographed case is the **Gulf Breeze** case of Florida, between November 1987 and May 1988.

PIERMAN, CAPTAIN S. C. 'CASEY'

During the 1952 **Washington 'flap'**, in the United States of America, Captain 'Casey' Pierman was one of several pilots who visually confirmed what was being tracked on radar. For several minutes he observed many objects with the appearance of bright lights. They were moving like falling shooting stars without tails, but Pierman indicated that they were moving horizontally. He said he hadn't the slightest idea what the things were.

PILKINGTON, ROBERT

Former RAF pilot Robert Pilkington confirmed that during a training exercise in 1952 over the North Weald in Kent, England, he was flying one of two Vampire fighters when they were vectored in to intercept a UFO that had been detected by radar ground control.

Pilkington witnessed the object at a flight level of 30,000 feet while he was flying at approximately 600 miles per hour. It was multi-coloured, and as the plane approached it flew off at high speed. One interesting description given by the witness is that shortly before flying off it changed from a cigar shape into a saucer shape, which could be just a realignment of the angle of the object to the witness's line of sight.

POPULATION DENSITY AND UFOs
Statistical analysis of the UFO phenomenon has generally proved to be quite useless for the purposes of research except in particular, and exceptional, circumstances.

One of the most studied statistics – and one which no Ufologists have yet been able to agree upon the meaning of – is the correlation between population density and UFO sightings.

If UFO sightings are random then it would be reasonable to expect that there would be more reports received from centres of high population than there would be from remote locations. In fact this is not generally the case and the studies that have been done indicate that in many areas and at many times there have been considerably more sightings per head of population in remote areas than in populated areas.

However, so many factors are unknown and may be influencing the position that little can be made of this statement. Firstly, there is the possibility, unproved, that UFOs prefer to operate in remote locations for whatever reasons and therefore are quite correctly more frequently seen there.

Secondly, there is the possibility that the social interaction of small widely spread groups is different to that of large urban groupings. It is possible that those in remote areas feel the need to report their sightings because otherwise no one else will, whereas many people in the towns and cities often ignore the phenomenon on the basis that 'somebody else will probably report it'.

Thirdly, there is the possibility that remote areas induce in certain people a form of **sensory deprivation** and **altered state of consciousness**. This makes them misinterpret mundane objects more easily than their city counterparts and report them as UFOs, whereas no such predisposition may exist in the towns and cities.

Fourthly, there is the point that local **media** and particularly local newspapers are often starved of material and will use UFO reports that are sent in, whereas the newspapers of large cities and towns may be swamped with offers of material and will leave UFOs out except at certain times, which they probably regard as the 'silly season'.

It should be noted that some remote areas have few or no sightings at all but this can almost always be explained by the fact that there is no one there nor anyone to report the UFOs to! Less technologically advanced areas may well be having exactly the same sightings – indeed *are* having the same sightings, when we do obtain reports – but have no one to report them to. It may also be that they do not associate their sightings with the UFO phenomenon and therefore report them in a way which does not come to the UFO researchers' attention.

PORT McNEILL, BRITISH COLUMBIA, CANADA

The Canadian government appears to have made several attempts to offer UFOs a means of identifying themselves, perhaps the most famous of which was the designation of 1,000 square miles of land over which aircraft were not permitted to fly in order that UFOs could land unmolested. This field in fact seems to have been part of the inspiration for Major Donald E. **Keyhoe**'s suggestion, Project **Lure**.

A slightly less ambitious attempt was instigated by the Defence Ministry of Canada at Port McNeill, British Columbia, where landing pads were prepared for the UFOs. Similar pads were set up also at St Paul, Alberta.

Unfortunately such advances were 'stood up' by the visitors.

POURNOY-LA-CHETIVE, FRANCE

On 9 October 1954 four children playing near the local cemetery in the early hours of the evening reported seeing a bright light nearby.

They identified it as a round object some eight feet wide and standing on tripod legs. An entity emerged from it; he had large eyes, a hair-covered face and was short, perhaps four feet tall. He was dressed in something like a black sack and spoke to the children in a tongue they could not understand.

They ran off in fear and when they looked back saw something bright and high in the sky, flying away rapidly.

PRICE, PATTY

Patty Price (pseudonym, also date and exact location of event withheld) was living in a house in the mid-western United States of America with seven children; she was divorced.

One night she believed that there was a prowler in the house and alerted the police after taking her children to a friend's home nearby. The following morning one of the children stated that it was a spaceman that had been in the house.

Under regression hypnosis, Patty Price recalled that two stringy dwarf humanoids had entered the house and that she and all her children had apparently been together in a UFO, surrounded by computers. Mrs Price was given a medical examination by the entities. It appears that they probed physically into her brain in what she believed was an effort to take her thoughts. One interesting fact was that there were two completely human-like creatures assisting the more alien forms.

Other investigations prior to the hypnotism indicated that one of the other children also had a conscious memory of something like a skeleton in his living room, and the child who had originally identified the entity as a 'spaceman' also told stories of a spaceship, apparently confirmed by the regression.

PUCKETT, CAPTAIN JACK E.
(See **Glass, Lieutenant Henry F.**)

PUDDY, MAUREEN
(See **Mooraduc Road, Australia.**)

PUGET SOUND, WASHINGTON
(See **Maury Island.**)

PUNCAS, N. D.
In the sighting by Captain Peter W. **Killian** one of the passengers was a Mr N. D. Puncas. Apart from providing third-party confirmation of the sighting, Puncas added credibility to it as he was an aviation expert and manager of a Curtiss Wright plant, and indeed was the person who first alerted the newspapers to the sighting.

Considering the calibre of the people aboard the plane, the sighting must be regarded as of high validity.

PUSHIE, JOHN
In December 1979, former Royal Canadian Mounted Police Officer John Pushie took four photographs of a UFO near his home in Nova Scotia, negatives of which were sent to the

Canadian National Research Council.

Despite the fact that Pushie is adamant that the UFO, having hovered stationary for some time, moved off at high speed, the Council returned his negatives to him having identified the sighting as photographs of the star Vega.

Vega is not usually known for its high-velocity movement!

Q

QUEZET, MEAGAN

On the evening of 3 January 1979 Meagan Quezet and her son André were walking up the road near their home in Mindalore, Johannesburg, South Africa. They saw lights ahead of them and as they got closer realised that they were emanating from an egg-shaped craft standing on landing legs, not dissimilar to the American lunar landing model and very similar to craft in many abductee reports, including those of Kathie **Davis** in the mid-United States a few years later.

Some five or six people stepped out of an opening in the craft and spoke to the witnesses in a strange accent. They were normal in appearance with thick hair and beards. They wore coveralls.

Meagan became afraid that something was not 'correct' and implored André to run and 'get Daddy'.

Suddenly the entities jumped back into the craft which rose into the air and took off. As the craft took off, André gave up running back to the house, turned around and ran back to his mother and together they went home.

Under regression hypnosis it appears that Meagan was lured into the craft but was not given a medical examination, as she managed to break free and jump out of the craft before this took place. It was at this point that she apparently shouted to André to go and get his father.

Meagan was hesitant about being regressed under hypnosis, which was apparently first suggested by a tabloid newspaper in America, though she later agreed. Her son has never felt able to use this technique and has rejected all investigation of the event.

QUINTANILLA, MAJOR HECTOR

Major Hector Quintanilla was one of the heads of Project **Blue Book**. He took over the post in July 1963 and apparently reported to Colonel Eric T. De Jonckheere who in turn reported to Brigadier-General Cruikshank. This was confirmed in a statement by Major Quintanilla on 29 March 1966.

In the 1960s Quintanilla had been one of three Air Force representatives – along with Dr Harold **Brown** and Dr J. Allen **Hynek** – to testify to the House Armed Services Committee inquiry into UFOs.

R

RACHELWILTZ, PRINCE DE

Prince de Rachelwiltz translated the eighteenth-dynasty writings of the court of Thutmose III of Egypt from around 1,500 BC, in which appears the following tantalising UFO report: 'In the year 22, third month of winter, sixth hour of the day . . . it was found a circle of fire that was coming from the sky . . . now after some days had passed these things became more numerous in the sky than ever. They shone more in the sky than the brightness of the sun and extended to the limits of the four supports of the heavens . . . after supper, these fire circles ascended higher in the sky to the south . . .'

RADAR-DETECTED ANOMALY (RDA)

In a bid to avoid the term UFO (unidentified flying objects), and also in a somewhat unsuccessful bid to claim that UFOs were not being reported, the United States Air Force began reclassifying such reports according to the way in which the sighting arose. Those detected by radar were therefore designated RDAs, radar-detected anomalies, just as visually observed anomalies were reclassified VOAs. There have been a whole host of other reclassifications that have been used by the Air Force and private investigation groups but the term UFO, as an all-embracing umbrella term, seems to be destined to last for a long time yet.

RADFORD, ADMIRAL ARTHUR

In April 1952, Admiral Arthur Radford was in a Navy plane following a leading plane containing Dan **Kimball**, the Secretary of the Navy. They were on their way to Hawaii when both planes became involved in a close UFO encounter.

RAELIAN MOVEMENT

The Raelian movement aims, amongst other purposes, to set up an embassy on the Earth free of the Earth's political strictures through which extraterrestrials can benevolently assist the development of the people of Earth.

The movement started from an incident that occurred on 13 December 1973 at Clermont Ferrand in France. Claude Vorilhon was driving through the mountains when a UFO descended near him. It was approximately twenty feet wide, dome-topped, with a red light below and bright white lights above.

As it hovered, an entity emerged. It was approximately three feet tall with long black hair and a beard and wearing a green, one-piece coverall.

The entity spoke to Vorilhon in French and told him that his race had been observing him for some time. He added that Vorilhon had been chosen as an emissary to spread their message to the people of Earth.

Over subsequent weeks they gave him many messages, which enabled him to write a book as an introduction to starting the Raelian movement. The movement now has a high public profile throughout the world.

RAINBOW, PETER

In February 1983 Peter Rainbow was driving, early in the evening, towards Little Houghton in Northamptonshire to visit his mother. The journey should have taken him approximately fifteen minutes – it was a route he was familiar with.

At Great Houghton the motorcycle he was driving cut out and he dismounted to repair what he believed to be a blown fuse. Taking out a new fuse, he was about to insert it when he noticed a globular, white, glowing light in a field near him; the light was oscillating gently. Suddenly it shot vertically away from him.

He instantly realised that the fuse was no longer in his hand – though it had not been put into the motorbike – and found that he was holding the ignition key, although he had previously left it in the ignition. He started up the motorcycle and went on his way, arriving in Little Houghton at 8.30, with an hour and a half's **missing time** period.

Six months prior to this incident, in August 1982, Rainbow had had another sighting of a dome-shaped UFO near his home, which had also been witnessed by his son. No regression hypnosis or other memory enhancing techniques have been undertaken to explore the missing time period.

RAINIER, MOUNT
(See **Arnold**, Kenneth.)

RAMAYANA
In the Indian manuscript *Ramayana* there is a story of contact between what we might well nowadays regard as a UFO and a girl, Sita:

> Unseen dwellers of the woodlands watched the dismal deed of shame,
> Marked the mighty armed Raksha lift the poor and helpless dame,
> Seat her on his car celestial yoked with asses winged with speed,
> Golden in its shape and radiance, fleet as Indra's heavenly steed . . .
> . . . then rose the car celestial o'er the hill and wooded vale.

This is one of many thought-provoking images in the ancient manuscripts of peoples from all over the world, suggestive of either UFO activity in ancient times, or at least of identical imagery in the minds of 'witnesses'.

RAMEY, BRIGADIER-GENERAL ROGER M.
In 1947, at the time of the **Roswell** crash retrieval, Brigadier-General Roger M. Ramey was Commander of the 8th Air Force District at Fort Worth. It was he who castigated Colonel William **Blanchard** for allowing the issue of a press release indicating the retrieval of a saucer, and it was he who directed that the Roswell wreckage be moved, presumably ultimately to **Wright Patterson Air Force Base** in Dayton, Ohio.

Furthermore, it was Ramey who explained to the public that the so-called crashed flying disc was in fact only a weather balloon, and indeed was photographed displaying weather balloon wreckage to the press. The officer who first collected the debris – Major Jesse **Marcel** – was quite certain, however, that it was no weather balloon.

In 1952 Ramey was chief of the Air Defense Command and issued the following statement: 'No orders have been issued to the Air Defense Command, or by the Air Defense Command, to its fighter units, to fire on unidentified aerial phenomena. The Air Force in compliance with its mission of air defence of the United States must assume the responsibility for investigation of any object or phenomenon in the air over the United States.

Fighter units have been instructed to investigate any object observed or established as existing by radar tracks and to intercept any airborne object identified as hostile or showing hostile interest. This should not be interpreted to mean that Air Defense pilots have been instructed to fire haphazardly on anything that flies.'

RANKEILLOUR, LORD

During the House of Lords debate in 1979 Lord Rankeillour summed up some aspects of the UFO phenomenon very well. He commented: 'Those who report seeing UFOs are taken to be misinformed, misguided and rather below par in intelligence.' He alleged that this was unfair and commented on the Ministry of Technology's own information on the subject, 'It is not false information: it is data reported by civil and Air Force pilots, policemen, sailors and members of the general public who have all had personal experience which has intrigued and/or frightened them.'

Lord Rankeillour went on to make an interesting speculation: 'I suspect that the British government do have a department studying UFO sightings.' It is presumed that Lord Rankeillour was referring to a department other than the division of the Ministry of Defence which acknowledges its role in the subject.

RANKIN, RICHARD

Although 'officially' credited with the birth of the modern UFO phenomenon, Kenneth **Arnold** was not the first to report the formations of discs that he sighted on 24 June 1947. One earlier report came from ten days before, in the early afternoon of 14 June 1947, when pilot Richard Rankin, flying from Chicago to Los Angeles, sighted ten objects approximately thirty feet wide flying at a calculated 560 miles per hour over Bakersfield, California. The objects were flying in a triangular formation.

In his description of flying saucer sightings around the time of his own encounter, Kenneth **Arnold** refers to the Rankin sighting and makes references to Rankin's alleged psychic capabilities.

RATCHFORD, DR J. THOMAS

When Dr Edward **Condon** headed up the **Colorado (University) UFO Project** investigation into UFOs it was funded by the Secretary of Defense. Condon was accountable to Dr J.

Thomas Ratchford who was attached to the **Air Force Office of Scientific Research (AFOSR)**; he was a civilian scientist working, basically, in nuclear physics and it had been he who had handled the negotiations between the Air Force and the University of Colorado. The Air Force had insisted on an intermediary so that they could be seen not to be directing the outcome.

REES, MERLYN
In the mid-1960s Merlyn Rees was Under-Secretary of State for Defence and answered several questions in the House of Commons on the subject of UFOs. In one particular exchange he indicated that official research is perhaps more thorough than the government usually admits, when he stated in a reply to a question as to whether or not scientists are consulted about UFO sightings: 'I can give that assurance. This is not just an Air Defence matter. We have access to scientists of high repute – they have been consulted on all these matters – and also to psychologists.'

REIDA, CAPTAIN ALVAH
In August 1944 Captain Alvah Reida, flying a B29 bomber in Sumatra, encountered a **'foo' fighter** while flying at approximately 14,000 feet at approximately 200 miles per hour.

The 'foo' fighter was a glowing red ball approximately six feet in diameter. Captain Reida attempted to outmanoeuvre the object but for some eight minutes it held position relative to the aircraft before disappearing at high speed into the clouds.

At the time Reida made his report he believed that the object might be some form of enemy weapon.

RENDLESHAM FOREST
Rendlesham Forest lies behind the back gates of **Woodbridge RAF/USAF Air Base** in Suffolk and was the location of a famous **close encounter**.

REPEATER WITNESSES
One who reports more than one, and usually a series, of UFO sightings or encounters during his/her lifetime.

In the early years of UFOs, repeater witnesses were regarded with great suspicion and often their claims were discounted. They were generally thought either to be attention seeking, or overly imaginative.

However, recent studies of UFOs indicate that the repeater witnesses are often highly credible people and many of them do not seek any publicity. As such, therefore, it has become accepted within the phenomenon that this is an aspect that requires study.

Researchers have shown through their work that the repeater witness is actually an essential part of the UFO phenomenon as the UFOs appear to be tracing particular witnesses throughout their lives. The evidence further suggests that the tracing continues to offspring, following blood lines into witnesses' children and other descendants for purposes about which we can only speculate, but which would seem to indicate some form of genetic study or hybrid/alien human development programme.

A quite different possible explanation for repeater witnesses is that the UFO event is somehow dependent on psychic abilities or at least an open-mindedness which applies only to certain people and not others, allowing them access to UFO sightings and experiences to which other minds are closed.

There are many cases where two (or more) people together should experience the same sightings but where only one does and one does not. This would seem to give some support to this second possibility though it does not rule out the possibility suggested by Budd Hopkins, who believes that the UFOs can specifically 'switch off' those whom they do not want involved in their activities.

RICKENBACKER, CAPTAIN EDDIE
First World War flying ace Captain Eddie Rickenbacker joined a great many other knowledgeable people in supporting the existence of flying saucers. He stated, 'Flying saucers are real. Too many good men have seen them, that don't have hallucinations.'

RIPLEY, BEN
On 17 March 1969, pilots Ben Ripley and Herman Slater, flying a Cessna 150 near Mount Buckskin in Arizona, sighted approximately twenty-five oval-shaped UFOs, estimated to be three times the size of a domestic car.

The objects were believed to be moving at approximately 300 miles per hour when they passed underneath the Cessna, disappearing near Lake Havas, Sioux City. One of the pilots indicated he thought that the UFOs were remote-controlled as they were 'undulating in precise union'.

RISSER, ROBERT
Formations of UFOs were seen above several states of the United States on 31 July 1965 and the Air Force was pushed to make an explanation. It explained that the objects were the planet Jupiter and the stars Betelgeuse, Aldebaran, Rigel and Capella.

Director of the Oklahoma Science Foundation Planetarium, Robert Risser, pointed out that, 'This is as far from the truth as you can get', as unfortunately none of the stars named were visible in the United States at the time of the sightings.

The Air Force was either scaling new heights of **disinformation** or plumbing new depths of incompetence.

RIVA PALACIE, GOVERNOR EMILIE
On 23 September 1965 the Governor of Cuernavaca, Mexico, Emilie Riva Palacie, together with many local residents, witnessed the close approach of a glowing disc-shaped object which caused electrical and light equipment to fail all over the town. The UFO hovered over the town for some time, completely blacking out electricity supplies. The lights came on again when the disc shot quickly out of sight.

There was no shortage of authoritative witnesses. Apart from the Governor the object was observed by the Mayor, Valentin Gonzales, and a military chief, General Rafael Enrique Vega.

ROBERTSON, DR H. P.
Dr H. P. Robertson was Chairman of the United States Office of Scientific Intelligence's UFO Review Group, the Scientific Advisory Panel, known as the **Robertson Panel**.

ROBERTSON PANEL, THE
Set up in January 1953 by the Office of Scientific Intelligence the Robertson Panel, a scientific advisory panel, was designed to review UFO research to date.

Its chairman was Dr H. P. **Robertson**, a physicist, and other members were Dr Thornton Page (astronomy), Dr S. Goudsmit (statistics), Dr Lloyd **Berkner** (geophysicist) and Dr Luis **Alvarez** (physicist). Advisory members of the panel were Dr J. Allen **Hynek** and Frederick **Durant** (the panel's findings are sometimes known as the Durant Report).

The panel interviewed many high-ranking officers including Brigadier William Garland, the commander of Air Technical Intelligence Center, directors of the Office of Scientific

Intelligence, Steven Possony of the Special Study Group, directorate of Air Force Intelligence, various Air Force intelligence officers, Edward J. **Ruppelt**, most notable as the head of Project **Blue Book**, and the Air Force Press Officer. During the review the panel studied film and photographs of UFOs and examined reports prepared by the Air Technical Intelligence Center.

The panel concluded that most sightings could be explained in terms of naturally occurring physical or meteorological phenomena, that there was no evidence of a direct threat to national security, that there was no evidence of hostility and no evidence of extraterrestrial visitation. The panel recommended that UFO reports should be debunked in order to reduce public interest and dampen possible hysteria. The panel also recommended that civilian UFO groups should be monitored because they represented a potential mass influence over the population and could be used for subversive means.

Dr J. Allen Hynek, an adviser to the panel, commented, 'I was dissatisfied even then with what seemed to be a most cursory examination of the data and the set minds implied by the panel's lack of curiosity.'

ROBINSON, TIMOTHY
Evidence of serious RAF involvement in the UFO phenomenon comes from the testimony of Timothy Robinson. In October 1967 at the age of thirteen, together with his family, he watched two Lightning Interceptors fly over the garden of his home in Winchester chasing a black mushroom-shaped UFO at high speed. Apparently the UFO outmanoeuvred the aircraft by climbing too steeply for the Lightnings to follow.

The official position was that no Lightnings had been over Winchester at the time and no explanation was given for the Robinsons' report by the Ministry of Defence.

RODEFFER, MADELEINE
In February 1965 Madeleine Rodeffer and the famous contactee George **Adamski** took cine film outside Madeleine Rodeffer's home in Maryland, USA, of the visitation of a flying saucer virtually identical to the saucers described by Adamski in his earlier contacts. The UFO performed a series of manoeuvres, including apparently complex manipulation of its landing gear. Madeleine Rodeffer believes she could make out figures

looking through the portholes of the craft before it finally disappeared from view.

It has been suggested that the film is a fake but Madeleine Rodeffer has commented that someone intercepted the transmission of the film to the developers and substituted obviously faked frames for genuine material, presumably with the aim of discrediting the film.

Analysis of the film is inconclusive since, unfortunately, the saucer never appears to be in a position where a proper perspective can be analysed. In one particular frame of the film the UFO is severely distorted and it has been suggested that this was due to the powerful gravitational field projected by the saucer during its activity.

Dr Paul Lowman of NASA suggested: 'My own strong impression is that these frames show a small object, perhaps up to two or three feet across, a short distance from the camera.'

RODRIGUES, SERGEANT JOSÉ FRANCISCO

In June 1977, Sergeant José Rodrigues of the Portuguese Air Force was flying a Dornier over Castelo de Bodedam. During the flight he saw a dark object approaching the plane and radioed ground control to find out if there was any other air traffic in the area. He was told there was not. The object closed in on his aircraft and he was able to see panelling on its lower side. Then, suddenly, the object vanished at high speed.

At this point Rodrigues nearly became a victim instead of a witness! The plane began to dive out of control and Rodrigues could not pull the aircraft out of the dive until he was almost at treetop height. Frightened, he only just managed to bring the plane down safely.

Upon examination afterwards Rodrigues was found to be so alarmed that he had difficulty in speaking. The Air Force offered no explanation for the event though researchers did locate ground witnesses who, although they were unable to confirm the sighting of the object, confirmed the near death dive of the aircraft and confirmed hearing the power surge when Rodrigues managed to regain control of the plane.

RODRIGUEZ, CARLOS ALEJO

Pilot and parachute trainer Carlos Alejo Rodriguez was flying near the Curbelo Naval Air Base, Uruguay, when he suddenly encountered a disc-shaped, domed UFO some 70 feet wide on an approach towards him. It stopped and hovered and

Rodriguez flew towards the object to examine it. However, he was forced to turn away when he became suffocated by a wave of heat apparently emanating from the disc. The temperature returned to normal when the UFO disappeared.

There have been several cases of heat being employed by UFOs to deter close witnesses, including several that have resulted in hospitalisation.

RODRIGUEZ, PETER
(See **Dapple Grey Lane, California**.)

ROERICH, NICHOLAS
In 1929 Nicholas Roerich published a diary of his journey through India, Tibet and China. He relates that on 5 August that year he saw 'in a direction from north to south, something big and shiny reflecting the sun, like a huge oval moving at great speed. Crossing our camp this thing changed in its direction from south to south-west. And we saw how it disappeared in the intense blue sky. We even had time to take our field glasses and saw quite distinctly the oval form with the shiny surface, one side of which was brilliant from the sun.'

ROESTENBERG, JESSIE
On 21 October 1954 Mrs Jessie Roestenberg and her two young sons were the subjects of a **close encounter**. The incident occurred at five o'clock in the evening and had been preceded by a feeling of uneasiness throughout the day prior to that. At the time, Mrs Roestenberg heard a sound and went outside to investigate; she saw a shiny silver disc with a large transparent dome on top. In the dome she could see two entities observing her and received the feeling that the contactee was compassionately motivated. The entities had long blond hair and wore blue one-piece coveralls and were fairly human in other ways.

Mrs Roestenberg apparently became somewhat 'suspended' and suffered a **missing time** experience; suddenly the UFO was gone. Mrs Roestenberg apparently became fearful and concealed herself and her sons in the house; when they looked again they saw the object disappearing through trees beyond their farm in Ranton, Staffordshire.

She said, in a phrase that has been similarly applied by many witnesses, 'This was something absolutely marvellous. The saddest part to me is that I have never been able to understand the greatness of this thing.'

Since then she says she has had 'great development of ESP'. Since that time she has apparently felt the presence of 'aliens' around her and believed that she has a deeper understanding of people and things. She believes that contacts were implanted in her mind and that the aliens are there for her when she needs them. She also believes that some of them live amongst us as humans.

Many aspects of the case are mirrored in other well-documented contactee accounts: there are, for example, considerable similarities between this encounter and that of Kathryn **Howard**.

An interesting detail is the feeling of unease which preceded the event; witness Elsie **Oakensen**, for example, reported a sensation earlier in the day of her evening encounter.

Researcher Jean-François **Boedec** has made a study of what he describes as a 'build-up' phase preceding abductions in his native Normandy.

ROGERS, DR BRUCE A.
Dr Bruce A. Rogers was, in 1970, a member of the Board of Governors of **NICAP (National Investigations Committee on Aerial Phenomena)** and at the time expressed concern that if there were advances to be made in scientific knowledge from UFO encounters then it was important for the United States that the knowledge he housed there. He stated, 'It could make a nation master of the world . . . possession of this knowledge could create the influence for the future of the United States and perhaps determine our survival.'

ROHRER, JOSEPH
In 1952 Joseph Rohrer, president of Pike's Peak Broadcasting Company, stated that he had information that seven saucers were being held by the United States government, three of them having been forced to crash in Montana, presumably by Air Force interception. Aliens had been recovered from the saucers and one was alive and for two years had been kept in isolation while he had been taught to read and write English.

Rohrer described the saucers as rotating discs with stationary cabins, some 100 feet wide and 18 feet thick, and claimed he had been aboard one. (This is a description which matches closely the details of the **Aztec** saucer.) According to Rohrer the atmosphere in the saucers was 30 per cent oxygen and 70 per cent helium; they used magnetic fields for power. Rohrer concluded that the government was keeping all of this information secret to avoid any potential panic.

These claims came at a time when entity reports were frowned on even by UFO organisations and would certainly have had little credibility then. Shortly afterwards entity reports began to become frequent and ultimately acceptable.

The Air Force apparently chose not to deny Rohrer's claim on the ground that this would give him more publicity, which it sought not to do.

ROMERO, BARTOLME
A martyr to the UFO phenomenon after a sighting on 6 October 1961. A huge UFO appeared over the town of Santa Rita in Venezuela and moved slowly over the nearby Lake Maracaibo, flooding light down on several fishing boats on the lake. In the ensuing panic many of the fishermen leapt overboard and swam towards the shore but Bartolme Romero drowned, presumably as a result of the fear induced.

ROSENWALD INSTITUTE, CHICAGO
Frank **Scully** and his wife, in the 1950 book *Behind the Flying Saucers* (see References and Background Material), which described a flying saucer crash retrieval in New Mexico, stated that they had been told that alien bodies retrieved from the crash had been transported to the Rosenwald Institute in Chicago for analysis.

Like so much of the crash retrieval mythology there is no substantial supporting evidence for this.

ROSMEAD 'TENNIS COURT' CASE
(See **Truter**, Harold.)

ROSS, WELDON
During the **Great North-East Blackout** in the north-eastern United States of America and parts of Canada, Flight Instructor Weldon Ross, approaching Hancock Airport, witnessed a huge, glowing, red, fiery object thought to have been about 100 feet wide and close to the ground. Both Ross and computer technician James Booking, who was on board the plane with him, were startled by the globe and after landing at the blacked-out airport reported the sighting to its deputy commissioner.

According to Ross's report the object would have been directly over the Clay power substation – which was thought to have been the centre of the blackout problem.

ROSWELL INCIDENT, THE
In July 1947 a rancher, William 'Mac' **Brazel**, reported that he had seen wreckage from an explosion scattered across part of his ranch. This was reported to the local sheriff who in turn reported it to the Roswell Army Air Base.

Brazel was apparently held by the military while a team under Major Jesse A. **Marcel** collected the debris from the ranch. The debris was then loaded on to a B29 aircraft to be flown to **Wright Patterson Air Force Base** on orders from the commanding officer, Colonel William H. **Blanchard**.

Marcel made very clear that chunks of material were found but no damaged or partially intact flying disc. Further, he did not see any alien bodies although these claims became part of the mythology of Roswell in later years.

The Roswell Army Air Base issued a statement confirming that they had recovered a flying disc, though it was later stated that the material recovered was of a weather balloon and indeed wreckage from a weather balloon was paraded before the media to support this claim.

Marcel made clear that this was not the appropriate wreckage as the material he had seen was thin and foil-like but would not dent, and included something like balsa wood that would not burn when a flame was applied to it. He described indecipherable hieroglyphics printed on some of the debris. The Roswell incident triggered a series of crash retrieval stories, virtually all of which have taken place in the United States.

Particular aspects of the Roswell incident are covered in other sections of this encyclopedia under the names of the people involved in the events.

ROUSH, REPRESENTATIVE J. EDWARD
On 29 July 1968 the Committee on Science and Aeronautics of the House of Representatives in the United States held its conference on the subject of UFO investigation by the government. Although the Chairman of the committee was George P. Miller it was Acting Chairman, Representative J. Edward Roush, who directed the bulk of the events and the proceedings.

ROWLEY REGIS
On 4 January 1979 Mrs Jean Hingley had just seen her husband on his way to work early in the morning when she went to

investigate a light in her garden. She thought that the car port light had been left on.

Suddenly three entities making a buzzing noise flew past Mrs Hingley into her lounge. They were approximately 3½ feet tall, very similar to the classic American alien with white pasty skin, large dark eyes, etc. but in this case they had wings and were able to fly.

The entities apparently 'floated' Mrs Hingley into her own lounge and she believes that they penetrated her mind with telepathy, something like an X-ray.

Apparently they had a discussion about Jesus since it was just after Christmas and the aliens said, 'We know all about Jesus.' They also pointed out that they came to talk to people but that people didn't seem to be interested in them – clearly they had not come down to talk to UFO research groups who would be only too willing to listen to them!

When they apparently fled from her – after she lit a cigarette – each of them took a mince pie with them, thus labelling the case for ever more as the 'Mince Pie Martians'. In her garden she saw them float into an egg-shaped object, which then took off with a flash.

Her dog, which had apparently collapsed shortly before the sighting started, recovered and Mrs Hingley called the local police.

UFO investigation indicated that the electric clock in the house had stopped, that cassette tapes had become useless and that Mrs Hingley had certain physical or physiological effects such as sore eyes and sickness.

The landed UFO apparently left a mark in the snow and some months afterwards when the snow had melted marks could still be seen on the soil.

RUDLOE MANOR (RAF)

In Timothy Good's book *Above Top Secret* (see References and Background Material) he comments that independent sources have indicated to him that British top secret research into UFOs is carried out by the Royal Air Force at RAF Rudloe Manor in Wiltshire.

Corroborative proof that this installation houses a UFO-monitoring unit has not been forthcoming though Good, together with former MOD official Ralph **Noyes**, tested the claim by telephoning Rudloe Manor late one night in May 1985 to offer a bogus UFO report. Before doing so they asked whether or not they ought to be phoning Whitehall. The duty officer at RAF Rudloe Manor confirmed, 'No, sir, you've reached the right place.'

RUPPELT, CAPTAIN EDWARD J.

For a time Captain Edward J. Ruppelt was Project Co-ordinator for UFO Investigations for the US Air Force. According to those who knew him, particularly Major Donald E. **Keyhoe**, his attitude towards the UFO phenomenon underwent a surprising reversal.

After transferring to inactive duty Ruppelt wrote his book on UFOs, *The Report on Unidentified Flying Objects* (see References and Background Material), which confirmed their existence and the existence of a cover-up. He wrote in letters to Major Keyhoe that he would not follow the Air Force line and would not be part of their cover-up; apparently he often gave Keyhoe valuable UFO leads after he had become Director of **NICAP**.

Keyhoe wrote that in 1959, 'This suddenly ended.' Ruppelt was working with an aerospace company which had many contracts with the United States Air Force and he suddenly became very critical of UFOs, ridiculed witnesses whom he had previously supported, rejected much strong evidence and stated that he now knew that UFO sightings were only illusions, mistakes and hoaxes.

Keyhoe speculates that Ruppelt was put under pressure from the Air Force on the grounds that his aerospace company would lose contracts if he did not retract the statements in his book.

Keyhoe comments that he believes that Ruppelt's premature death from a heart attack was partly the result of being forced to make statements he did not believe in and facing criticism that was not rightly due to him.

RYAN, CAPTAIN RAYMOND E.

On 8 April 1956, Captain Raymond E. Ryan and his first officer William Neff were flying from Albany, New York, heading for Syracuse.

At 2.20 a.m., at a height of 6,000 feet, the two observed a brilliant white light like an approaching aircraft with its landing lights on. They banked immediately to avoid collision and watched the object spin into a right-angle turn and hurtle past them.

Ryan estimated that the object had been moving at approximately 1,000 miles per hour, much faster than any jet of the day, and neither he nor Neff believed it was any conventional aircraft they had ever seen.

So shaken was Ryan that he turned on his landing lights in order to avoid any further possible collision. The UFO appeared – glowing orange – ahead of them.

The pilots reported the encounter to Griffiss Air Force Base and were told to turn off their lights. Once they did so the Air Force Base confirmed that they could see an orange object nearby and said they would be scrambling two jets to intercept. Apparently, and rather strangely, the base's radar equipment was not switched on. On board the aircraft the stewardess, Phyllis Reynolds, also witnessed the object.

Astonishingly, the Air Force then chose to override the Civil Aviation Authority and instructed this passenger plane to change course and pursue the UFO!

They never caught the object, which headed over Lake Ontario and towards Canada. Concerned by being considerably off his normal flight path, violating air safety regulations and losing communications with the Air Force base, Ryan returned to a course that would bring him back to Syracuse.

Apparently the sighting lasted over twenty minutes and a subsequent report indicated that interceptors had been scrambled but had not found anything; Ryan reported that he had not seen any interceptors in the air.

Four and a half months after the incident it appears that Ryan and Neff had been pressured into changing their testimony. Ryan stated, 'I did not deviate from course at any time. I did sight an object and it was witnessed.' The Civil Aeronautics Board confirmed that 'Captain Ryan stated most emphatically that he did not deviate from his prescribed course, nor was he requested to do so'.

Dr Donald H. **Menzel**, notoriously sceptical about UFOs but not always very imaginative, concluded that this sighting was of the planet Venus.

RYBINSK, USSR

Rybinsk forms part of the very effective Moscow air defences and in 1961 some missile emplacements were being set up there.

An enormous flying saucer appeared overhead, surrounded by small satellite saucers. The Rybinsk battery commander decided to fire missile salvos at the objects which all exploded before reaching the target.

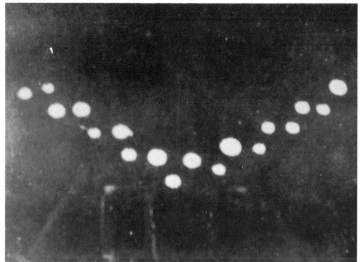

The Lubbock lights are an echelon formation of lights frequently seen near Lubbock in Texas. They have variously been attributed to natural phenomena, light reflecting off the underbellies of birds and fleets of flying saucers. (*Mary Evans Picture Library*)

A sketch of the humanoid seen in a walled garden at Vilvorde, Belgium in December 1973. It glowed green and was later seen taking off in a flying saucer from the other side of the garden wall. (*Mary Evans Picture Library*)

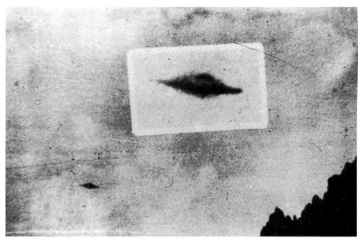

The Trindade Island photographs: Four photographs of this object were taken in January 1958 from the Brazilian naval ship *Almirante Saldanha*. Some fifty witnesses on board the ship saw the object. (*Mary Evans Picture Library*)

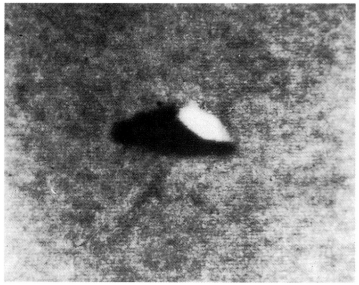

One of three photographs taken on 5 June 1977 by photographer Monsieur Muyldermans at Namur, Belgium. (*Mary Evans Picture Library*)

US Navy optical physicist Bruce Maccabbee analysed the many photographs in the Gulf Breeze case. Despite controversy, Maccabbee believed the photographs to be genuine. (*John Shaw*)

One of the most prominent people involved in abduction research in America is New York artist Bud Hopkins. His concern has always been primarily for the witness rather than for long-term information relating to the subject and as such his work has been mainly therapeutic, for which witnesses have expressed warmth and gratitude. (*John Spencer*)

Forester Robert Taylor encountered an extraordinary craft and robot-like entities at Livingston in Scotland in 1979. (*Mary Evans Picture Library*)

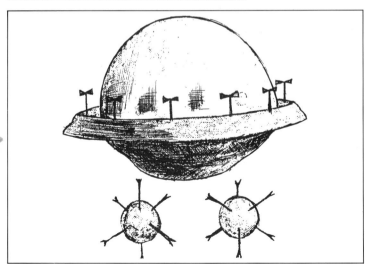

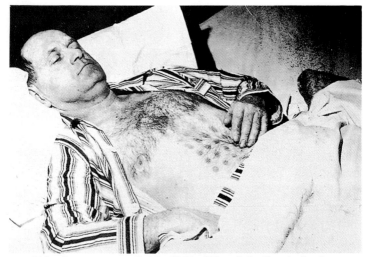

Following an encounter in May 1967 at Falcon Lake, Ontario, Stephen Michalak suffered burns from the exhaust vent of a landed object. As the picture shows, the burn marks on his body exactly matched the shape of the exhaust vent described. (*Mary Evans Picture Library*)

Patrolman Lonnie Zamora saw a landed UFO and related entities at Socorro in New Mexico in 1964. Investigator Dr J. Allen Hynek declared that this was the case that most clearly suggested a physical 'nuts and bolts' craft. (*Mary Evans Picture Library*)

Dr Donald H. Menzel was probably the foremost debunker of UFOs, often stretching credibility in his attempts to 'wish away' the phenomenon. (*Mary Evans Picture Library*)

The former head of the department of the British Ministry of Defence dealing with UFO reports, Ralph Noyes is now an active UFO investigator. (*Ralph Noyes*)

An MP for thirty years, Major Sir Patrick Wall pursued the question of UFOs in the House of Commons in a quest for more openness from the Government. Following his retirement from public life, Major Sir Patrick Wall became President of the British UFO Research Association. (*John Shaw*)

UFO SIGHTED . . . Schirmer points to where he saw saucer.

FLYING SAUCER . . . sketched by policeman; Schirmer, right.

Ashland Officer Makes Routine Report On UFO

By MILAN WALL
Star Staff Writer

Ashland — "2:30 a.m. . . . saw UFO at Hwy. 6 and 63 south sitting on Hwy—Believe it or not."

That entry in the "Officer's Daily Activity Report"—was

eight feet above the ground between two traffic signs on Highway 63 south of Ashland.

"When I first came upon it, the lights were still," Schirmer said, "But then I flashed my brights at it and the red lights inside the object started

ject disappeared he surveyed the area with a flashlight but could find nothing. On Tuesday, however, this piece of found a small, thin piece of what appeared to be molten metal at the scene.

Wlaschin said he planned to

Police patrolman Herbert Schirmer was abducted by a UFO in December 1967 at Ashland, Nebraska. His memories of his time aboard the alien craft are rich in extraordinary detail. (*Mary Evans Picture Library*)

The UFOs apparently stalled all the electrical apparatus of the base and only when they were safely out of range would it restart again; it seems that the craft effectively prevented any further attacks.

S

S4 (AIR)

S4 (Air) is a department of the Air Force division of the British Ministry of Defence which handles UFO reports from the public.

It operates at the same time as **Defence Secretariat 8 (DS8)** though with slightly differing briefs; generally speaking S4 (Air) only deals with low-flying cases.

SACRAMENTO, CALIFORNIA

Many hundreds of people, including the daughter of the Mayor of Sacramento, reported witnessing a huge radiant globe moving over Sacramento, California, on the evening of 17 November 1896. It was seen to be moving against the wind at an altitude of 300 or 400 feet and there was the impression of machinery behind the light, suggesting a huge dark object.

Coming as it did during the **airship** wave of the time, the report was received at the same time as sightings of propellers, gondolas, etc. There were also reports of voices heard within the craft and sightings of its crew.

The possibility of its being a prototype airship is high; however, there were several sightings during this wave that suggest a less prosaic explanation.

SAGINAW, AIRSHIP

The *Saginaw Courier and Herald* of 16 April 1897 reported an extraordinary encounter associated with the 1896/7 **airship** wave of sightings in the United States of America.

According to the report, at 4.30 a.m. on Wednesday 14 April an airship had landed near Howard City, Michigan, and a naked entity stepped from it.

He was 9½ feet tall and spoke in musical tones. One courageous farmer approached him but was kicked, resulting in his hip being broken.

According to reports the entity remained for days while sightseers came to view him.

The unlikelihood of this claim and the fact that there was no follow-up story suggest this may well have been a hoax on the part of the witness or the newspaper. If not, then the early UFO phenomenon was taking a strange new twist.

ST PAUL, MINNESOTA, BLACKOUT

On 26 November 1965, two areas of St Paul, Minnesota, were blacked out when power failed in their grid system. There were many reports from one area of UFOs overhead, and the power company offered no explanation for what had caused the blackout.

The second failure was apparently blamed on two power lines touching in high wind, causing a 'short', but it was noticeable that this explanation was not applied to the first area blackout, where the UFOs had been seen.

SALADIN, FLIGHT-LIEUTENANT JAMES R.

In October 1954, Flight-Lieutenant James Saladin of the Royal Auxiliary Air Force was flying over Essex, England, when he encountered three UFOs heading towards him. One came so close that it virtually obscured vision through the windscreen; Saladin described it as saucer-shaped with cupolas above and below.

Although armed with a gun camera Saladin did not have time to take film of the object.

Although he reported the sighting to the Air Ministry there was no response from them. The story came to light because he also reported it to an RAF intelligence officer, Derek Dempster, who was to go on to become the editor of the magazine *Flying Saucer Review (FSR)*.

Researcher Timothy Good described the report as 'one of the most important sightings to have been reported by an RAF pilot'.

SALAZ, JOE
(See **Saucedo**, Pedro.)

SALEM, LIEUTENANT-COLONEL GEORGE L.

In May 1969, Lieutenant-Colonel George L. Salem was chief of the Air Force Information Office in Los Angeles. When asked if the Air Force still chased and intercepted UFOs as had been believed in previous years, he stated, 'The Aerospace Defense Command takes whatever actions are necessary to identify objects appearing on defense radar scopes,' but he added, 'The US Air Force is not pursuing the investigation of UFOs today.'

There are many who would hold that this last comment was not totally accurate!

SALUTUN, AIR COMMODORE J.

Air Commodore J. Salutun of the National Aerospace Council of Indonesia, also a Member of Parliament for that country, gave the following confirmation of UFO events in the Far East: 'The most spectacular UFO incident in Indonesia occurred when during the height of President Sukarno's confrontation against Malaysia UFOs penetrated a well-defended area in Java for two weeks at a stretch, and each time were welcomed with perhaps the heaviest anti-aircraft barrage in history.'

Air Commodore Salutun also seemed to give weight to the possibility that UFOs are extraterrestrial when he stated, 'The study of UFOs is a necessity for the sake of world security in the event we have to prepare for the worst in the space age, irrespective of whether we become Columbus or the Indians.'

SAMFORD, MAJOR-GENERAL J. A.

In December 1951, Major-General John A. Samford took over as Director of Intelligence from Major-General C. P. **Cabell** and was briefed by Captain Edward **Ruppelt** and Colonel Dunn of Air Technical Intelligence Center regarding the Air Force's UFO programme. Samford delegated this work to Brigadier-General W. M. Garland and acknowledged that within the services it was the Air Force who was wholly responsible for UFO investigation.

By July of the following year Samford was holding a press conference designed, basically, to debunk UFOs. This is thought to have been one of the Air Force's most embarrassing moments since almost all of the people who ought to have been at the press conference were not; they were all involved in the extensive UFO activity that occurred during the **Washington 'flap'** of the same month. In particular, the official public relations man in respect of UFOs for the Air Force, Al Chop, was absent; he had been one of the people in the radar room on the night of the incidents.

SAN JOSÉ DE VALDERAS, SPAIN

On 1 June 1967 some extraordinary close-up photographs of a UFO were taken at San José de Valderas near Madrid in Spain.

The object was circular, some thirty-five feet wide, and was described as like 'two wash basins placed with their concave sides facing each other'. On the underside of the object there was an extraordinary sign similar to a mark seen on a UFO over a year prior to that, also near Madrid. The sign consisted of an H-shape with the four points of the H upright curved over and with a third upright dissecting the H along its vertical axis.

This UFO was seen by many dozens of witnesses and photographed by at least two of them. It flew off along the Estremadura highway and was seen to land for a short time on an open piece of ground near Santa Monica, some four kilometres from San José de Valderas.

It landed near a restaurant called La Ponderosa and the restaurant owner was alerted by people from the restaurant streaming on to the patio, declaring that they had seen an enormous ball of fire lowering three legs as if to make a landing.

Incredibly, mysterious metal tubes were also found at the landing site, one of which when opened exuded a liquid that evaporated. The tubes apparently had a mark on them similar to the mark on the underside of the UFO.

The recovered material was examined by the National Technical Institute for Aeronautics and space research in Madrid, who analysed the metal sample. They stated that it was made of nickel of an extraordinarily high degree of purity and the plastic part of the tube was a type of plastic not yet commercially available; it was believed to have been manufactured only by Dupont Nemours, who had produced it for NASA. This fact, reasonably enough, seemed to point to a terrestrial origin.

Researchers conceded the possibility that the device was an American test vehicle but others have also speculated that such development arises from studying captured or retrieved flying saucers.

SANDER, MAJOR GEORGE

During the mysterious **Maury Island** affair Captain E. J. **Smith** turned to Air Force Major George Sander, of S2 Army Intelligence Station at McCord Field, and told him the facts of the encounter. Sander gave the impression he believed the whole thing was a hoax but nonetheless was extremely thorough in gathering up every piece of the recovered material from the hotel room in which the discussion of the encounter had taken place. Shortly after this he took E. J. Smith and Kenneth **Arnold** to the Tacoma Melting Company to show them very similar material there. However, Arnold made the point that he did not believe the recovered material and that at the plant were exactly the same. The recovered material had a different 'feel' about it.

At the end of this part of the investigation Arnold was left with the feeling that Sander was either not all he should be or was 'a pretty smooth guy', but, Arnold added, 'He is not smooth enough for this point to convince me that these fragments aren't pretty important in some way.'

SANDERSON, COLONEL CARL

On 24 August 1953, Colonel Carl Sanderson was flying an F84 jet to Turner Air Force Base in Georgia. Flying at 35,000 feet, Colonel Sanderson sighted two circular, silver UFOs over Hermanas, New Mexico. One of them made an extraordinary right turn manoeuvre right in front of him.

At very high speed the objects disappeared, reappearing over El Paso, Texas; one was seen to climb very rapidly and the second joined in close formation, having passed close to Colonel Sanderson's plane.

Colonel Sanderson said, 'From their manoeuvres and their terrific speed I am certain their flight performance was greater than any aircraft known today.'

SARBACHER, DR ROBERT

Dr Robert Sarbacher was a consultant to the Research and Development Board and Chairman of the Washington Institute of Technology. He appears to have confirmed that stories of crashed flying saucers being recovered were factual and also that prominent individuals such as atom-bomb project consultant Von Neumann and Dr Vannever **Bush** were involved.

According to an interview given in 1950, Sarbacher confirmed that the analysis of UFOs was 'the most highly classified subject in the US.'

SAUCEDO, PEDRO

Pedro Saucedo and his friend Joe Salaz were driving on Route 116 near Levelland in Texas in the late evening of 2 November 1957.

They encountered a blinding radiation on a collision course

with their truck. The vehicle's lights and engine died and the pair leapt out of the vehicle and 'hit the deck' as whatever it was rushed over the top of the truck, making a sound like wind and thunder. It was apparently emanating considerable heat; there was some suggestion of flame. The object was shaped like a cigar some 200 feet long and moving at something like 800 miles per hour, according to the witness. This was the first of many reports at Levelland which were to go on through the night, and which were all similar in nature, apparently confirming that there was something in the air.

SAUCER, PROJECT
Project Saucer was a nickname for the American research Project **Sign**.

SAZANOV, ANATOLI
Astronomer Anatoli Sazanov was one of a dozen staff members of the Soviet Academy of Sciences who witnessed a huge UFO flying across the Soviet astro-physical station at Kislovodsk on 8 August 1967. Similar reports came in on 4 September and 18 October in the same year from other sites over Russia and were reported by astronomers.

General descriptions given for these kind of flying crescent craft were up to almost 2,000 feet wide and moving at over 11,000 miles per hour.

SCARBOROUGH, MAJOR CHARLES
Major Charles Scarborough was a Marine Corps squadron leader who encountered sixteen discs while flying over Texas in 1952. He was certain from their manoeuvring that they were listening to his air-to-ground transmissions and reacting accordingly; he was one of several pilots who made such statements.

SCHEMEL, CAPTAIN G. W.
During the 1951/2 intense wave of sightings in the United States, Captain G. W. Schemel of TWA was flying over Amarillo, Texas, in the late evening, at 18,000 feet when the lights of an object appeared less than a mile away from his plane.

The object flashed towards the plane at incredible speed, Schemel dived, and the UFO disappeared overhead in a burst of light.

The dive had been so steep and rapid that several passengers who were not wearing seat-belts had been thrown up against the ceiling and the passenger cabin of the airliner was described as 'a shambles'. Several passengers and crew were injured and there was a great deal of panic and hysterics. Schemel radioed Amarillo Airport, declaring an emergency landing and requesting medical attention.

The Air Force explained away the sighting as that of an ordinary aircraft which Schemel and his first officer had not recognised, but Schemel made it clear that the speed of the object made this quite impossible. Furthermore, civil aeronautics investigators showed that there had been no conventional aircraft within fifty miles, well beyond the good visibility that Schemel had. It also goes without saying that experienced pilots are unlikely to misidentify something so completely as to end up endangering their passengers and being forced to make an emergency landing.

SCHIRMER, PATROLMAN HERBERT

Ashland police patrolman Herbert Schirmer had an extraordinary encounter with a UFO on 3 December 1967, which was eventually to result in his having to leave the police force.

Schirmer was on patrol in the early hours of the morning and felt that something was amiss around the town, though admitted this amounted to policeman's instinct rather than any concrete grounds for concern. In a corral he saw a bull. It seemed very upset and was kicking and charging at a gate though Schirmer could see nothing out of the ordinary to upset the animal. As he left the town to patrol the outskirts he saw, reflected in the lights of the police car, an object on the highway which he first believed to be a broken-down truck.

Lights on the object began blinking faster and faster. Schirmer turned his car headlights on them and was stunned by what he saw. As he approached the object, he ensured he knew where his night stick and chemical 'Mace' spray were. Immediately, the flying saucer took off into the sky and disappeared.

But for Schirmer the experience had only just begun.

He completed his log of the evening's patrol and noted that there was a half hour time gap – unheard of in a police log since patrolmen are trained to be accurate in their timekeeping. Regression hypnosis was used which revealed an extraordinary encounter with the occupants of the UFO. The experience was a complete shock for Schirmer and very much against his background. As he stated, 'My father was an Air Force career man and I was raised as a service brat. My background just wasn't the kind that let you believe in spaceships from other worlds.' His own report on the sighting reflected this no-nonsense approach; it began: 'Saw a flying saucer at the junction of Highways 6 and 63. Believe it or not!'

The morning following the encounter Schirmer had a bad headache and a weird buzzing noise in his head. There was a red bruise over two inches long and a half inch wide running down the back of his neck. This type of mark has turned up in other **contactee** cases.

Under hypnosis, Schirmer revealed that he had been prevented by some unknown force from drawing or using his gun or his police radio. He could see entities approaching his police car. According to the entities, they were in Ashland to take electricity from the power lines but Schirmer could not explain precisely the need for this or the working of the spacecraft, despite the fact that it had apparently been explained to him.

One of the entities fired a green gas around the police car and paralysed Schirmer with a bright white light fired through the windscreen. (A white light fired at a vehicle was a significant part of the **Gulf Breeze** sightings by Ed **Walters**.) Schirmer was directed out of his car and taken up a ladder into the UFO. He noticed it was cold inside. The room was some 25 by 20 feet with red lighting and containing chairs and computers.

The implication of the contact was that the aliens were acclimatising people to accept their existence. One telling phrase which Schirmer related was, 'Everyone should believe in them some, but not too much.' Many researchers have speculated, on the basis of other such cases, that this is the purpose of the encounters.

Schirmer was deliberately given a cover story which was indeed the story he related until the regression hypnosis session, i.e. that he had seen a flying saucer which had immediately taken off. Schirmer was returned to his car to watch the craft leave. The session also revealed that the ship was made of pure magnesium (interesting when considered in the light of the **Ubatuba** recovery of pure magnesium made after a flying saucer apparently exploded). The occupants were described as being some 4½ to 5 feet high, muscular but wiry, with chests larger than would be expected and heads thinner than an ordinary human's. Schirmer described their eyes as something like cat's eyes or nearly oriental, and they had 'funny-looking' lips. (Both very common descriptions.)

Inside the saucer Schirmer was shown what he described as a 'baby saucer', a remote control observation device about the size of a hubcap. (There have been several reports of sightings of very small saucers – including years later some of the devices photographed at **Gulf Breeze**.)

The UFO entities were dressed in a one-piece silver-grey coverall with no zips or seams and wore a belt around the waist containing weaponry. Interestingly, Schirmer was able to determine that the entities were breathing our atmosphere as he could see their breath 'fog in the cold'. Schirmer was told that the UFOs had bases on Earth, in the **Bermuda Triangle**, under the sea off the Argentine coast and sites in the United States.

Schirmer asked if the UFO entities kidnapped people and he was told that there was a 'breeding analysis programme' and some humans had been used in such experimentation. This is very similar to many recent abductee claims but not something that would have been widely known in 1967. Schirmer did not pursue this line of discussion as he did not want to encourage them to kidnap him!

He was promised two more visitations by the UFO; repeat visits are another feature quite often reported by abductees.

Schirmer pointed out that he left the police force because he could no longer concentrate on his work and not because of any undue pressure. He had received some joking about '**little green men** from Mars' but accepted that with no difficulty; it was concern about what had happened to him that night that took his mind off his work and forced him to resign. He seems to be the kind of man who would rather not do a job if he cannot do it well.

In common with many abductees, such an encounter will undoubtedly dominate his world view. We can only assume that that also is part of the reason for such contacts.

SCHREIBER, BESSIE BRAZEL
Bessie Brazel Schreiber is the daughter of **Roswell** farmer William 'Mac' **Brazel**, the man who discovered the debris on his ranch in 1947.

Although only twelve years old at the time she recalled in an interview in 1979 much of the detail of the event.

She was able to confirm that hieroglyphics were found on some of the debris and that aluminium-like foil was recovered. She also confirmed that there was a lot of debris recovered, which other investigators have pointed out would be far too much for one balloon – the explanation for the debris given by the authorities. Bessie Brazel Schreiber said, 'No, it was definitely not a balloon. We had seen weather balloons quite a lot, both on the ground and in the air . . . this was nothing like that.'

She also gave testimony to the military's thoroughness in collecting up the debris by stating, 'We never found any other pieces of it afterwards – after the military was there. Of course we were out there quite a lot over the years, but we never found so much as a shred. The military scraped it all up pretty well.'

SCIENCE FICTION AND UFOs

There is undoubtedly a connection between science fiction and the reporting of UFOs. However, precisely what the connection consists of is difficult to ascertain.

Certainly we can point to science fiction films which are spin-offs from the UFO phenomenon itself. The most obvious of these would be *Close Encounters of the Third Kind*, which not only drew its imagery from UFO reports but which even contained a cameo appearance by Dr J. Allen **Hynek**, the head of the **Center for UFO Studies (CUFOS)** in America. The 1950s film *The Day the Earth Stood Still* clearly capitalised on the rash of UFO and flying saucer reports that had been filed in the few years prior to its making, as did *The Thing from Another World* and many, many others, mostly the black and white 'B' movies of American science fiction. When George Pal produced the film of H. G. Wells' *War of the Worlds* he updated it to include flying saucers rather than the 'walking engines' of the original book precisely because of the publicity caused by UFO flying reports.

However, the extent to which UFO reports arise from science fiction imagery is more difficult to determine. For example, in the 1950s film *The Day the Earth Stood Still*, the inside of a flying saucer consists of a circular corridor and a medical centre complete with platform bed. These were features first reported as real in the Antonio Villas **Boas** case and the Betty and Barney **Hill** case, and have subsequently been reported many, many times since, yet it would be simplistic to state that the witnesses' experiences arose purely from seeing such films and indeed would be dismissive of other considerable bodies of evidence. Even the aliens' cold and clinical attitude as reported by abductees mirrors their behaviour in many science fiction films; very few of the early movies depicted excitable, emotional, neurotic aliens – in fact, quite the opposite. Witness the aliens in their human disguises in the films *It Came from Outer Space* and *The Invasion of the Body Snatchers*; even the much loved Mr Spock of the *Star Trek* series only gets emotional once every seven years, so we are told!

One explanation which perhaps reconciles the similarity between science fiction aliens and real aliens as reported by UFO witnesses is that the witnesses are experiencing some extraordinary encounter or event which is unknown to their normal frame of reference. Having had the experience they then search their minds for something similar which they can liken the event to in order to seek to understand it and to explain it to others; as such they will often arrive at the imagery of the science fiction films they have seen and possibly standardise their report according to their exposure to science fiction material. This is not to suggest that the event is unreal or inspired by science fiction, only that the report may be distorted by the imagery of science fiction.

Just occasionally there are clear copycat cases: one woman watched a UFO abduction on the television and then quite seriously and sincerely reported exactly that event as her own experience. Clearly research into cases of this sort must lean heavily towards the psychological. In this case the connection was very clear and was easily determined. Many more are far from so obvious and a great many other factors, possibly external to the witness, must be involved.

SCIENTIFIC ADVISORY PANEL ON UNIDENTIFIED FLYING OBJECTS
(See **Robertson Panel**.)

SCIENTIFIC STUDY OF UNIDENTIFIED FLYING OBJECTS
(See **Condon Report**.)

SCOTT, STATE HIGHWAY PATROLMAN STANLEY
State Highway Patrolman Stanley Scott and colleague Charles Carson were two of many police officers reporting UFO sightings for an extended period on the night of 18 August 1960. As described in their official report, they were searching for a speeding motorcycle when they saw what they at first thought to be a huge airliner dropping from the sky. They quickly leapt out

of their car in order to get a proper bearing on the crash site.

On leaving the car they noticed that there was an absolute silence around them which they felt should not have been the case. They watched the object descend to within 100 feet of the ground when it suddenly recovered its altitude and flew back to some 500 feet, where it hovered.

They described the oblong object as surrounded by a glow with definite red lights at each end (reminiscent of the UFO description in the Betty and Barney **Hill** sighting). About five white lights were visible between the red lights which might or might not have been portholes.

They watched the object performing incredible aerial feats and radioed a sheriff's office requesting radar confirmation. The local radar base confirmed an object was on their radar but that it was unidentified.

There seemed to be some interaction between the object and the officers. The object 'swept' the car with a red light, and when Officer Scott turned on the red light on the patrol vehicle the object moved away.

As it moved slowly off in an easterly direction the officers followed in the car and, incredibly, saw that the object was met by another similar device. Finally both objects disappeared together.

In their official report the officers also commented that there was radio interference whenever the objects approached the vehicle. They had observed it for just over two hours. They described themselves as 'calm after our initial shock'.

SCOYEN, E. T.
Park Superintendent E. T. Scoyen of the Sequoia-Kings National Park in California reported seeing a large disc-shaped UFO from close proximity in the last days of July 1953.

The United States Air Force took the report very seriously and ordered a squadron of fighters to circle above the park on 1 August 1953 in case the disc should return. Just before midnight it did!

The pilots watched the disc slant down towards the park and paced it, shadowing it as closely as possible. They levelled out to prevent its being able to climb again; the pilots believed it would now have to land. A captured UFO seemed likely!

Suddenly, and with no deceleration, the UFO stopped in mid-air and the jets immediately overshot, going down below the object. Having out-manoeuvred the fighters, it immediately soared steeply away into the sky and disappeared.

There were other witnesses who reported seeing the jets diving towards the UFO.

SCREEN MEMORY

Sometimes known as a 'cover story' or a 'substitute image' the screen memory is alleged by some UFO abduction researchers to be a way in which the mind has the more traumatic details of an abduction covered up in order to protect the witness. Whether or not this is internally generated as a form of self-protection or whether it is overlaid on the abductee from outside is unclear but there are certainly particular cases where people have abductions uncovered using regression hypnosis, where the presence of alien faces is replaced by such images as deer or owls, etc. It is noticeable that the one prominent feature in these kind of aliens, and also in the screen memories, is that of very prominent eyes, which seems to be one of the main reporting features of the cases. Indeed, there is a certain similarity between the size and description of the eyes of such animals as deer and owls, and the eyes of the reported aliens.

There is speculation by some UFO researchers that these screen memories can be complex indeed; there are cases where the memory, which has later been revealed to have been an abduction by aliens into a spacecraft, takes the form of child-hood friends and strange houses or even shops and shopkeepers.

There must be some danger that the regression hypnosis seeks an abduction memory and interposes one where a normal memory already exists, but it would certainly be too simplistic to write off abductions on this basis alone. Whatever the true meaning, an understanding of the mechanism of screen memory is going to be important in understanding the true nature of abductions.

SCULLY, FRANK

It was writer Frank Scully who revealed to the world the details of the **Aztec** flying saucer crash retrieval in New Mexico. It is thought that this may have been a hoax played by or on Scully, though there is some indication that it may have been connected to the **Roswell** retrieval.

Frank Scully was a newspaper columnist. He told the Aztec story in his book *Behind the Flying Saucers*, published in 1950 (see References and Background Material).

SEAMANS, ROBERT C., JR

On 17 December 1969 Secretary of the Air Force, Robert C. Seamans, Jr., announced the end of Project **Blue Book** in Press Release No. 1077–69.

He stated that, 'The continuation of Project Blue Book cannot be justified either on the grounds of **national security** or in the interest of science.'

The decision to abandon Blue Book was the result of an evaluation of the UFO phenomenon by the University of Colorado under the guidance of Dr Edward U. **Condon**, who had then completed an eighteen-month study of the phenomenon.

The release went on to say, 'As a result of investigating UFO reports since 1948 the conclusions of Project Blue Book are:

1. No UFO reported, investigated and evaluated by the Air Force has ever given any indication of being a threat to our national security.

2. There has been no evidence submitted or discovered by the Air Force that sightings categorized as unidentified represent technological developments or principles beyond the range of present day scientific knowledge.

3. There has been no evidence that sightings categorized as unidentified are of extraterrestrial vehicles.'

Lastly, the release indicated that Blue Book's files would be given to the United States Air Force Archives at Maxwell Air Force Base in Alabama and that information relating to them could be obtained through the Secretary of the Air Force and the Office of Information in Washington DC.

SECOND STOREY, PROJECT

During the early 1950s, while Project **Magnet** was under way, the Canadian government also instigated UFO research under the title Project Second Storey. Very little is known about the work of this committee for which few minutes of meetings have been released but it appears that it was some sort of executive filtering body for the reports of Project Magnet, a function perhaps indicated by the choice of name.

SEITZ, DR FREDERICK

Dr Frederick Seitz was the president of the **National Academy of Sciences** which was charged with the task of reviewing the **Condon Report**, the Colorado University investigation into UFO phenomena.

It was made very clear from the outset that the National Academy of Sciences would not be able to examine witnesses or data but were to confine themselves only to the methodology employed by the university. Since the National Academy of Sciences was government-funded its objectivity was held to be in question though publicly it was said to be entirely independent.

There was some nervousness on the part of the project investigators but on 15 November 1967 their report was submitted to Dr Seitz.

Shortly afterwards the Air Force could presumably hardly believe its luck when it was pronounced that the Condon conclusions were highly creditable, the investigation was praised, and the Academy concluded with Condon that there was no evidence that UFOs were extraterrestrial or superior machinery.

SENSENBAUGHER, DR R. F.
A dentist from Silver City, New Mexico, Dr R. F. Sensenbaugher, reported sighting a UFO on 25 June 1947. It was over the town, and described as saucer-shaped and about half the size of a full moon.

This was the day after the Kenneth **Arnold** sighting had given widespread publicity to saucer sightings, and was shortly before the **Roswell Incident** in the same area of New Mexico.

SENSORY DEPRIVATION
Sensory deprivation refers to a situation where the mind is isolated from normal sensory input, i.e. sights, sounds, tactile sensations, etc. There have been many experiments over the past few decades examining the effects of sensory deprivation on the mind, generally by immersing the subject in a body temperature tank of water with no visual or audio input. The results have been extraordinary with many subjects experiencing what would seem to be hallucinations, fear, ecstasy, etc. All of these descriptions refer to the mind entering an **altered state of consciousness** which allows it to function as it would not normally in the outside world.

Some of the experiments have resulted in the subject's undergoing experiences similar to those of UFO abductees, and this may have considerable significance for the study of these claims.

In her book *Abduction* (see References and Background

Material), Jenny Randles speculates on the possibility that one such experiment by Dr John Lilly revealed material so similar that it appeared he could even have been abducted from his sensory deprivation tank. Since this is an unlikely possibility – and if we ignore the alternative that we are simply dealing with imagery – then we might consider the perhaps more likely probability that the state of sensory deprivation can itself 'open the mind' and make it receptive to the abduction experience, which may be more in the form of a message or a contact than a physical event. (This is a feature which is suggested by the Maureen Puddy abduction; see **Mooraduc Road**.)

Abductees prior to enduring abduction quite often report the onset of a 'cone of silence' around them which seems to isolate them from the real world, and this may be a form of sensory deprivation to enable the mind to accept the abduction message. As such, it may be self-induced or perhaps induced from outside in order to allow the message to get to the brain.

It is tempting to suggest that sensory deprivation experiments prove the abduction experience to be an internally generated event but in that case there would be considerably less consistency than there is. All people may fantasise, and they may even share some common images, but they would be unlikely all to share the same specific, small details. The consistency recorded suggests an external experience, at least external to the pure imagination, but the witness's state of mind must now be considered an important factor in such cases.

SETI (SEARCH FOR EXTRATERRESTRIAL INTELLIGENCE)

Although mainstream, conventional scientists are not willing to accept the existence of a UFO phenomenon and therefore the possibility of extraterrestrials visiting the Earth, they appear perfectly prepared to accept the possibility of their existence. Indeed, a very high budget programme called the Search for Extraterrestrial Intelligence (SETI) is underway to attempt to broadcast to, or receive messages from, civilisations far out in space.

Apparently, scientists find it acceptable to believe that aliens exist but must also believe that they are incapable of travelling across the vast gulfs of space; they point out that the physics involved simply makes it impossible to cross such distances, thus denying even the advances that have been witnessed in the last few hundred years.

SÉVÉRIN, ANTOINE

On 14 February 1975, shop assistant Antoine Sévérin, on Reunion Island in the Indian Ocean, reported witnessing the landing of a small domed object in a field at Petite Île. Several small entities some three to four feet tall left the object and fired a white beam of light at Sévérin, rendering him unconscious.

For several days Sévérin suffered poor vision and impaired speech, which a psychiatrist diagnosed as reaction to shock. When the police published their findings later, Commandant Alegros stated, 'It turned out that [the witness] is normally a well-balanced, well-behaved individual of excellent character and not given to the perpetration of hoaxes ... none of the persons who have testified to us believes Antoine Sévérin to have been hallucinating and they all take his statement seriously.'

They would have taken his report all the more seriously if they had had to hand the details of the encounter of French farmer Maurice Masse in 1965 (see **Valensole**) – his experience was very similar, and there are many other cases so alike that some mechanism must be at work which causes these reports to arise, be it extraterrestrial or otherwise.

SHAMANISM

The 'medicine men' of more tribal cultures, known as shamans, go through experiences very similar to abductees' in their acquisition of knowledge.

Quite often it is a light which begins the experience for the shaman, reaching inside his head and allowing him to acquire second sight. In abduction accounts there are many references to light; a light through which people are abducted on to a flying saucer; the brilliance of the light emanated by the saucer; and the strangeness of the light inside the flying saucer, which rarely comes from any particular source but seems to glow from the very machine itself.

Just as many abductees are taken into space and shown the Earth from above, so the shaman is often given exactly the same trip. Looking down from above the Earth, nothing is hidden from the shaman who can see every land and the soul of every person. This is all part of the knowledge that he must acquire.

In the **Anders** case in Sweden, the abductee was apparently pierced in the head during his abduction. By using rock crystal and a mineral, **yttrium**, in close proximity to the witness's wound, both the witness himself and the researcher believe that they enhanced his memory recall. In the Australian Aborigines' shaman stories, the shaman is visited by a supernatural entity who pierces the man's head and places a magic stone into the wound, giving great power and insight to the shaman.

There are those who would hold that the shaman is actually an abductee and forms part of the extraterrestrial interaction with humankind, and there are those who would simply state that these are human experiences translated in different ways, according to the culture in which they are experienced.

Certainly no complete understanding of the abduction mystery can be achieved until these parallels are understood.

SHARANOV, PROFESSOR VLADIMIR
It was the Soviet geophysicist Professor Vladimir Sharanov of the Leningrad Technological Institute who examined the Lake **Onega** crash retrieval. So interested was he that he visited the site personally. His analysis indicated he did not believe that the object recovered was a meteorite and that some material found was of artificial origin. He also stated that the object was not likely to have come from any kind of foreign object, i.e. American reconnaissance aircraft.

(See also **Kopeikin, Major Anton**.)

SHAUPETER SHIPYARD
(See **Pascagoula, Mississippi**.)

SHAW, SARA
(See **Tujunga Canyon**.)

SHINE, ANGELA
Occurring in the summer of 1942, but reported much later, a witness who is known only by the name of Bernard (to protect his identity the location is also withheld) reported an encounter which has great similarity to many **abduction** or **contactee** cases.

Aged about eleven or twelve, Bernard was with a girl called Angela Shine on a hillside when, as Bernard describes it, 'for the first and only time in my life I felt a sense of complete peace come over me'. They were lying on the grass, but were not asleep, when a man's voice interrupted them saying, 'Here they are.' The children sat up and saw two men who, during the conversation, often spoke to each other in a strange way.

Bernard describes the men as very handsome and giving off an aura of pure peace and tranquillity. The men were able to describe what was going to happen to the children in the future but warned them not to tell anyone that they had seen them. The men also promised that they would see the children again. When asked where they came from, one of the men said, 'I come from a long way away' and was rather pointedly looking at the sky. The children were then told to go to sleep and were aided in this by a brilliant light and a heat which surrounded them, after which they may have slept before they set off to walk back home.

When they got home the children believed they had been away for a couple of hours but in fact had caused considerable consternation by being gone for one whole day and night. Both Bernard and Angela noticed that they had identical bluish puncture marks on their elbows; such marks are not uncommon in the case of **abductees** and, of course, **missing time** is one of the principal indicators of some sort of **altered state** experience such as the abduction experience.

SIGMA, PROJECT

There is a claim, backed by only very dubious evidence, that the United States Air Force undertook a project, named Sigma, to communicate with visiting extraterrestrials and that the project met with some success when USAF officers met with aliens in the New Mexico desert.

Freedom of Information Act requests for documents relating to Project Sigma have not met with success.

SIGN, PROJECT

One of the United States Air Force's series of UFO investigations was Project Sign in the 1940s. It was also nicknamed Project Saucer. It was set up by Air Force Intelligence to investigate reports, and produced a startling conclusion. On the basis that the UFOs had to be some kind of technology, Project Sign ruled out Earth-based technology and therefore effectively concluded the UFOs had to be extraterrestrial in nature.

Sign was immediately shut down and its conclusions rejected. It is probably an indication of the Air Force's attitude towards this conclusion that its replacement was known as Project **Grudge**.

SIMON, DR BENJAMIN

Dr Simon was the Boston psychiatrist to whom Betty and Barney **Hill** were referred in order to relieve the stresses arising from what they believed to have been a UFO experience. During regression hypnosis sessions, the story of the first and archetypal abduction was drawn out. Dr Simon was not convinced this stemmed from an actual occurrence and felt that it could have been the product of their fears and fantasies.

Simon pointed out that the witness tells the truth as he or she sees it, but that does not have to be the truth as it really is, or as it would be appreciated by an outside observer.

SIMONTON, JOE

At approximately eleven o'clock in the morning of 18 April 1961 a peculiar rumbling noise attracted the attention of sixty-year-old farmer Joe Simonton. He went out into his yard and saw in front of him a bright shining saucer-shaped object hovering close to the ground. It was approximately 12 feet high and 30 feet wide and there was a hatch open through which Simonton could see three entities inside.

The entities were approximately 5 feet tall and 'resembled Italians'. They had dark hair, darkened skin, and wore black outfits.

One of the men held up a jug, apparently requesting water, and obligingly Simonton took the jug into the house, filled it and returned it to the men. On returning, he discovered that the men inside the saucer were having some sort of barbecue, cooking food on a grill inside the ship. Around them Simonton also noticed something like computer panels in operation.

Simonton indicated that he wanted some of the food and they gave him three pancakes each some three inches wide. After about five minutes the entities closed the hatch and the object rose into the sky; it then took off at high speed towards the south with such force that the passing of the object bent nearby pine trees.

Simonton took the pancakes to the United States Department of Health Education and Welfare (food and drug laboratory) who analysed them. The pancakes were made of terrestrial material but were totally lacking in salt. This has been held to be of some interest in comparing such cases to abductions by fairy folk and 'little people' of the Celtic faiths, where they too never take salt and often request pure water of their 'contactees'.

Those who had known Simonton for years stated that he 'obviously believed the truth of what he was saying'.

There has been no final resolution to this case and the only concluding statement at all was by Simonton, who ate one of the pancakes. 'It tasted like cardboard,' he said.

SKYWATCHES

Skywatches were basically a phenomenon of the 1960s in England though they tended to occur later in other European countries. Broadly speaking, groups of dedicated Ufologists collected together at high isolated points (Cradle Hill and Starr Hill around Warminster were much favoured) to spend the night surveying the sky in an attempt to see UFOs.

From the point of view of conclusive UFO evidence, the skywatches were totally useless. No reasonable or even dramatic cases arose from them that have added any real understanding to the UFO mystery.

However, those who spent their time on skywatches watching not the skies but the people themselves learned a great deal about the motivations and objectivity of UFO investigators. The objective and more healthily sceptical UFO investigator of today was a rare commodity in those days and many of the people at the skywatches were devoted, almost cultist, supporters of alien spaceships.

On one skywatch I attended (north-west of London) the group leader was so obsessed he logged every aircraft light going into Heathrow Airport as a UFO. He went on to log as anomalous lights what the rest of us could see were underground trains 'sparking' as they crossed the points to enter local stations. Eventually he was lost to sight running over a hill, apparently chasing a UFO entity which the rest of us thought bore a remarkable resemblance to a rabbit!

There were indeed many dedicated UFO researchers scanning the skies on that night, but it also has to be said that many of these skywatches arose because of the new youth freedom of the 1960s and were part of that liberated, 'swinging' culture. Not all of the nocturnal activity was directed towards the heavens!

SLATER, HERMAN
(See **Ripley, Ben**.)

SLAYTON, DONALD
In 1951 Donald Slayton, later to be one of the United States astronauts, and one of the original seven Mercury astronauts, encountered a UFO over Minneapolis.

He was flying a P51 fighter aircraft when he encountered a disc-shaped object moving away from him although he himself was flying at over 300 miles per hour. This fact alone would seem to eliminate any possibility that he was observing a weather balloon, which was his own first tentative consideration.

The object went into a steep climb, accelerated away and disappeared.

SLEPPY, LYDIA
Lydia Sleppy was the teletype operator for New Mexico radio station KOAT in July 1947. She received a call from reporter Johnny McBoyle that he wanted her to broadcast on the teletype machine some information relating to a saucer retrieval to which he had been a witness.

She typed a few sentences out and the machine stopped, interrupted by an incoming transmission.

That incoming transmission was 'Attention Albequerque: do not transmit. Repeat do not transmit this message. Stop communication immediately.' When Miss Sleppy asked McBoyle what to do, he replied, 'Forget about it. You never heard it. Look, you are not supposed to know. Don't talk about it to anyone.'

SLOAN, MARK
In July 1947 Mark Sloan was operator of the **Carrizozo** flying field and together with several other pilots witnessed a flying saucer at some 4,000 to 6,000 feet, moving at anything up to 600 miles per hour, and passing over the field. The sighting lasted approximately ten seconds.

This was reported at the same time as the **Roswell** crash incident occurred.

SMIT, BENNIE
On 26 June 1972, at Fort Beaufort, South Africa, Bennie Smit, the owner of Braeside Farm, and one of his labourers, Boer de Klerk, had an extraordinary **close encounter**.

De Klerk had been sent to examine the farm's reservoir and returned to Smit agitated and speaking of a ball of fire seen nearby. Smit went with de Klerk to the site and also saw the fiery red globe spitting out flames from treetop height. When de Klerk shouted at the object it appeared to back away.

Smit left de Klerk to monitor the object while he returned to collect a rifle and call the police. They returned with him to the site, where all together, and with other labourers, they watched the object, even shooting at it. Investigation the following day showed burn traces and there were other corroborative sightings by members of the town's council.

On 8 July, just a few days later, loud explosions were heard from the reservoir which was then discovered to have been shattered. Chunks of cement were found lying some sixty feet from the site. Smit attributed this to the action of another UFO he had seen earlier.

SMITH, CHARLES ABBOTT
On 11 August 1896, a patent was granted to Charles Abbott Smith for the production of an **airship** which he intended to have ready for April 1897. The airship in many ways matches the description given by witnesses to the 1896/7 airship wave and suggests that even if Charles Abbott Smith was not responsible (there is no concrete evidence that he ever constructed his design), then at least the design was not inconceivable for the time.

It could, of course, be a case of **cultural tracking** where 'alien' technology seems to match that of the Earth. However, cultural tracking itself has never been satisfactorily explained.

SMITH, CAPTAIN E. J.
Around the time of the Kenneth **Arnold** sighting, and indeed involved with Arnold, was a sighting reported to him by Captain E. J. Smith of United Airlines.

Smith had landed at Boise, Idaho, in the early hours of the evening and took off shortly afterwards to complete his flight. Oddly enough, shortly before take-off someone had asked Smith if he believed in flying saucers and he had stated, 'I would believe them when I saw them.'

Eight minutes after take-off he did! At 7,000 feet over Emmett, Idaho, Smith saw nine such objects, the same number as Arnold had reported just two weeks prior to that in June 1947. The objects were flat and circular and did not appear to be aircraft. Smith contacted the Civil Aviation Authority at Ontario, Oregon, and asked them visually to confirm what he was seeing. They saw nothing. The objects apparently performed strange manoeuvres, disappearing and reappearing, merging together, and so on, before vanishing completely. These sightings were confirmed by Smith's co-pilot, Ralph Stevens, and also one of the stewardesses, Martie Morrow.

Smith was adamant that 'I positively know that they were nothing from the ground in the way of fireworks, reflections or smoke. I know they were not aircraft that I am familiar with. I don't know how fast they were going but we all saw them.'

SMITH, MAJOR GERALD
On 14 September 1972 a UFO was sighted at West Palm Beach International Airport; the FAA supervisor, George Morales, also viewed the object with binoculars. Very shortly afterwards the UFO was reported by an Eastern Airlines captain, police and various citizens. Miami International Airport and Homestead Air Force Base also tracked it on radar.

At 6 a.m. Major Gerald Smith in one F106 interceptor, together with a second jet, were scrambled under orders from NORAD (North American Air Defense Command).

Smith visually sighted the UFO but it disappeared before he could close in. Although initially the Air Force attempted to cover up the scrambling of the jets, eventually they conceded that they had indeed reacted in this way and Major Smith was able to tell pressmen that there was 'something definite in the sky'. He added, 'If it had proved hostile we would have destroyed it.'

SMITH, CAPTAIN GORDON
(See **Gardin, W.**)

SMITH, BRIGADIER-GENERAL SORY
According to Major Donald E. **Keyhoe**, the Deputy Director of Information for Air Defense Command, Major-General Sory Smith, confirmed to him that the Air Force had long realised that UFOs were extraterrestrial spacecraft and that they were determined to capture one of the machines.

SMITH, WILBERT B.
Wilbert B. Smith was one of Canada's most prominent scientists, and a senior radio engineer with the Canadian government's Department of Transport. He commented, 'We believe that we are on the track of something which may well prove to be the introduction to a new technology. The existence of a

different technology is borne out by the investigations which are being carried on at the present time in relation to flying saucers.'

Smith recommended the setting up of a study group which led to the formation of Project **Magnet** in 1950. It was he whose Project Magnet reports included statements such as, 'If, as appears evident, flying saucers are emissaries from some other civilisation . . .' and 'It appears, then, that we are faced with a substantial probability of the real existence of extraterrestrial vehicles . . .'

It must be pointed out that the Canadian government took great pains to distance itself from these comments, and Smith obligingly admitted that they were his personal feelings and not representative of an official view.

Smith made it clear that he had been involved in direct contact with extraterrestrials.

He went on to become a prominent UFO researcher whose very significant contributions to the subject were regrettably curtailed when he died of cancer in 1962.

SNOWBIRD, PROJECT
Project Snowbird was allegedly set up in 1972 to test fly a recovered and repaired crashed saucer. It is alleged that the project was conducted in the Nevada desert in the United States of America and continues to this day though, obviously, no documents have been released regarding this and the claim remains highly speculative.

SNOWFLAKE, ARIZONA
(See **Walton, Travis**.)

SOCIAL STIGMA
It is a popular belief of sceptics that UFO witnesses, and particularly abduction witnesses, seek notoriety and publicity and for this reason make hoax claims. Undoubtedly some people do make such claims for such reasons but all serious UFO researchers know that a very large proportion, a figure of 70–80 per cent is probably reasonable, of those making claims not only seek no publicity but make it quite apparent that their case and name should not reach public knowledge or even be anonymously quoted in books. It is quite apparent from talking to these people that their sole aim in discussing these events is to try to find some meaning to them and to take comfort from

the fact that they are not alone.

There are many social pressures arising from UFO reporting, few of which are beneficial. There are cases of people in authority, such as police officers, who have made public their claims only to either lose their job or find that peer pressure makes it impossible for them to continue their work. There are several cases where people have been vilified by their local community, accused of religious fanaticism, been the subject of arson attacks and of general character assassination.

For some people it appears that the more frightening content of UFO reports is best dealt with by ridicule and the alarming subject is thus dismissed.

A very few people have made some financial gain from their UFO reporting and there are clearly some who enjoy the publicity and attention that it brings; for the majority, even the smallest amount of publicity and attention is unwelcome.

Critics of those reporting abductions should bear in mind that these people are undergoing a trauma not dissimilar to rape where victim support is necessary (the Americans call this the 'buddy system'), where kindness and understanding are often essential, and where one of the major duties of the UFO researcher is to provide or obtain some form of therapy to obviate the witness's fears.

It is the simplistic view of UFOs and abductions which results in many witnesses remaining 'in the closet'; a full exposure of all abduction material on UFO researchers' files would undoubtedly cause this view to be reconsidered.

Those considering the wisdom of repressing a full disclosure of information about the UFO phenomenon, usually on the basis that it could cause widespread panic, might consider what damage a little information can do. In Sinceny, France, during the French wave of entity sightings in 1954, one potential witness became alarmed at what he thought was the sight of a Martian repairing his flying saucer in a field near his home and opened fire on him. Unfortunately, the 'Martian' was the man's own neighbour repairing his motor car. (Luckily only the car was damaged by the shots.) Presumably, if people had valid information instead of only silly season stories from the tabloid newspapers, such panic would be less likely.

SOCORRO, NEW MEXICO
(See **Zamora, Lonnie.**)

SOMERBY, CHARLES
In the **Gulf Breeze** sightings the first period of photographic contact came on 11 November 1987 when the witness, Ed **Walters**, took five photographs of the UFO near his home.

There was some independent witness corroboration of this when Charles I. Somerby and his wife Doris apparently reported seeing the same UFO in the sky at the time of this photographic encounter. Their description of the UFO is very similar to the objects on the photographs. Unfortunately, the independence of their testimony is somewhat clouded by the fact that Ed Walters sent the photographs to the local *Sentinel* newspaper of which Mr Somerby is a former editor and his wife the present editor's mother.

It must be said, however, that the sheer weight of evidence in Gulf Breeze has convinced many top American Ufologists of the validity of this case.

SOTCHEVANOV, DR NIKOLAI
On 16 August 1960 Leningrad University Professor of Geology Dr Nikolai Sotchevanov, part of an expedition in Kazakhstan in the USSR, saw a bright disc-shaped object in the sky which he described as being of an apparent diameter something greater than a full moon's.

SOUERS, REAR-ADMIRAL SIDNEY W.
Rear-Admiral S. W. Souers is reported to have been a member of the **Majestic 12** Panel formed to investigate UFOs in the 1940s.

He had been the first director of Central Intelligence in 1946 and, when appointed to Majestic 12, was Executive Secretary of the National Security Council.

'SPACE BROTHERS'
A phrase generally used to describe the benevolent aliens who contact Earth people, usually with a view to guiding us towards a better future. Generally speaking most claims of such meetings have been discredited in the past, perhaps unfairly.

SPAUR, DEPUTY SHERIFF DALE F.
(See **Neff, Deputy Sheriff Wilbur**.)

SPITZBERGEN, NORWAY, CRASH RETRIEVAL
(See **Norway, Crash Retrieval**.)

STADVEC, ERNEST

Former Air Force bomber captain Ernest Stadvec in the Second World War became the proprietor of a flying service in Ohio. One night while in flight with two pilots as passengers he witnessed a bright UFO apparently intent on diving directly at his aircraft. Just before seemingly inevitable collision the object stopped and climbed away at incredible speed, leaving all three pilots stunned.

Without even asking Stadvec or the other pilots for their account, the Air Force commented that Stadvec had been alone and had been frightened by the sighting of the star Capella. Apart from pointing out that he had two other pilots with him, he stated, 'I have been flying nineteen years, thousands of hours at night, and I am certainly not going to be scared out of my wits imagining some star is diving at me.'

'STAR MAP'

(See **Fish, Marjorie**.)

STATUS-INCONSISTENCY

Anamnesis (life profile) studies of close encounter witnesses have revealed that generally speaking they are a normal cross-section of the population. This reduces the possibility that UFOs are somehow an internally generated product of a particular state of mind. However, certain factors did seem to recur in the anamnesis studies and the most prominent of these was status-inconsistency in respect of UFO reporters.

Status-inconsistency refers to the fact that many UFO reporters hold jobs or other social status positions inconsistent with what might be expected of them. Generally speaking, they tend to hold jobs which are much lower in a career structure than they might be expected to hold, i.e. people with many A-levels and even university degrees working in low paid labour-intensive jobs, which would seem to reflect either some under-achievement or lack of social confidence on their part.

It must also be said that some status-inconsistency is quite the reverse with some people holding successful social positions that would not necessarily be assumed for them from their education or background, though this occurs much less in UFO reporting.

STAVANO, JOHN

On 28 June 1965 an Ohio farmer, John Stavano, found a circular mark on the ground at his farm following a series of explosions. The crops that had been planted there appeared to have been 'sucked out'; there was no substantial trace discovered from analysis of the soil.

This event has certain similarities to the Charlton Crater (see **Blanchard, Roy**).

STERN, DR MARVIN

A concern about the UFO phenomenon, particularly in its early years, was that misidentifying UFOs as the product of hostile terrestrial enemy action could result in an accident of war. Although not specifically mentioning UFOs, the Assistant Director for Research and Development at the Department of Defense, Dr Marvin Stern, stated, 'We are not giving enough consideration to the factors of stress and coincidence that might lead to war by accident.'

Major Donald E. **Keyhoe** stresses that UFOs were known to be 'a major part of the accidental war danger'.

STIGMATA

Many UFO witnesses, and particularly abductees, have marks on their body which are regarded as physical evidence of their encounters, in particular scars, apparent radiation burns, and other specific wounds. The circumstances of many cases indicate that these are indeed real injuries but there are occasions when it appears that a traumatic event may have produced stigmata, i.e. psychosomatic wounding as a product of the experience. In one celebrated case a dream of a UFO experience by one witness resulted in what appeared to be a mark on his lower arm spelling out in blood the letters U F O. Since it is highly unlikely that UFOs set out to leave such an obvious calling card, this is classified by some researchers as evidence of stigmata. The extent to which abduction scars may be stigmata has never been fully explored.

STOLYAROV, MAJOR-GENERAL PORFIRI

In October 1967 a UFO research division of the Soviet Union's Committee on Cosmonautics was chaired by Major-General Porfiri Stolyarov, a retired officer of the Soviet Air Force. One of his close advisers was Dr Felix **Zigel** who was a key figure at the Moscow Aviation Institute and a member of the UFO Investigation Commission. It was through Zigel that much of the early USSR UFO information was released, though no official pronouncements have ever been made through Major-General Stolyarov's commission.

The semi-official committee was designed to investigate UFO reports although the Soviet Air Ministry denied it access to official material. This left the Committee in a position where its members had to appear on television asking for reports to be submitted from private citizens. They were inundated with such reports within just a few days.

STONE, STAFFORDSHIRE
On 1 September 1936 the daughter of a farmer near Stone in Staffordshire, England, witnessed the very close approach of a cigar-shaped UFO moving almost at ground level and only a few feet from her. It was brown in colour and displayed five portholes along its side. The approach scared the girl so badly she felt paralysed and after it had left she discovered she had drawn a pail of water from the well she was standing by though she could not remember doing so.

STOREY, GARY M.
(See **Frappier, Francis**.)

STRIEBER, WHITLEY
Whitley Strieber is an American novelist who self-reported an abduction and a series of UFO sightings in the late 1980s in his books *Communion* and *Transformation* (see References and Background Material). These books have produced enormous publicity for the UFO phenomenon, not to mention enormous fame and fortune for Strieber, and have been the subject of much controversy across the world.

Strieber became more deeply immersed in the UFO phenomenon when he produced the fictional book *Majestic*, based on the stories of crash retrievals.

His first book about his abduction, *Communion*, has been made into a film starring Christopher Walken.

Strieber has sought to isolate himself from the UFO community for the most part; in his book *Transformation* he stated, 'To approach any meaningful answers to such questions as why the visitor experiences are often so hard and what it ultimately means is going to take a substantial effort by better minds, quite frankly, than those that cluster in flying saucer study groups.'

STRUCTURED OBJECT

One of the problems UFO researchers face is that they seek to classify and categorise phenomena whose varied characteristics are not known or understood. As such, there is a broad division between those UFOs which appear to be anomalous atmospheric phenomena and are therefore not solid in the physical sense, and those UFOs which have the appearance and characteristics of solid objects. Where the latter category appears to be artificial, be it terrestrial or extraterrestrial, then a general term 'structured object' is usually applied as part of the descriptions to differentiate between these and unstructured, or non-solid, 'objects'.

STURROCK, DR PETER

Dr Peter Sturrock wrote the *Report on Survey of the Membership of the American Astronomers' Society Concerning the UFO Problem* in 1975, and quoted one astronomer who remained nameless as saying, 'I find it tough to make a living as an astronomer these days. It would be professionally suicidal to devote significant time to UFOs.'

The 'professionally suicidal' part of this quotation is an underlying theme of many mainstream scientists' reluctance publicly to examine this phenomenon, despite the obvious need.

SVERDLOVSK, USSR

In 1961 an Antonov AN-2P with seven people aboard was flying from Sverdlovsk to Kurgan. The aircraft disappeared from the radar screen some 100 miles from Kurgan and a search party was dispatched. The plane was recovered undamaged immediately but none of the crew was then or has ever been found. The plane was apparently in a densely wooded forest in a small clearing – conditions which completely precluded the possibility of a runway landing.

Just a little way from where the aircraft was found there was a 100-feet-wide circle of scorched grass.

SWAMP GAS DÉBÂCLE

In March 1966 there were reports of objects flying near Ann Arbor, Michigan, and one report of a landing.

Dr J. Allen **Hynek**, then the United States Air Force's consultant for UFO research, was dispatched to the area to investigate the case.

Its significance turned out to be not in the event itself but in the extraordinary social reaction to the investigation. Hynek was placed under pressure to release some sort of preliminary statement for the news media; the only statement he could make was that he believed *some* people *might* have seen swamp gas. He also made the point that a much more thorough investigation was still required.

However, the press decided to latch on to only the first part of his statement and declare that the expert had called into question the common sense and abilities of the local people. Indeed, one of the backlashes of the fiasco was the local press's determined whipping up of the population into believing in flying saucers and Martians simply to put down Dr Hynek's so-called explanation!

It was a further reminder to Ufologists, if one was needed, that the press has been all too influential in the development of the UFO phenomenon, and more importantly in presenting its more frightening aspects to the public.

SWEDENBORG, EMANUEL

Swedish philosopher, theologian and mystic Emanuel Swedenborg, in the early part of the eighteenth century, gave extraordinary **contactee**-like details of the lifestyles of the inhabitants of various planets in the solar system. He described Mercurians as wanderers, whose spirits can even pass out of this solar system into others; Jovians as educators of their children, an expressively gentle and sweet people; Saturnians as exceedingly humble; Venusians as divided into two orders, one mild and human and the other savage and brutal; and the people of the moon as dwarflike beings appearing as children of seven years old.

Swedenborg went on to add that there were other solar systems and other earths in immense numbers throughout the universe.

SWIMLEY, LIEUTENANT D. A.

Lieutenant D. A. Swimley of the United States Air Force had always dismissed the idea of flying saucers as nonsense and must therefore have been particularly shaken when on 3 August 1953, at Hamilton Air Force Base in California, he saw two silver discs racing through the sky. The two saucers circled the base locked in an aerial ballet as jet pilots on the ground watched them. He took a pair of binoculars and could apparently plainly see their round shapes, though the discs were too high for detailed observation.

GCI radar also picked up the saucers, and local civilians phoned in reports.

Six more discs joined the others and interceptor pilots were scrambled in F86s to engage them.

Before the jets could reach them, the machines, now in a diamond formation, had vanished. Swimley said, 'And don't tell me that they were reflections. I know that they were solid objects.'

Apparently, for some, seeing is believing.

T

TAMAROA BLACKOUT

The first reported power blackout caused by a UFO in the United States was at Tamaroa in Illinois on 14 November 1957. An area of four miles was blacked out for ten minutes while witnesses reported seeing a hovering UFO above the town.

Eight years later the **Great North-East Blackout** was to be one of the most spectacular of its kind.

Despite the number of blackouts that have occurred since this first event, no one has conclusively explained why they happen, and whether or not they are deliberate or a by-product of something else.

TASCA, ANTONIO

On 14 December 1983, radio announcer Antonio Tasca was abducted by pale-skinned entities described as having oriental eyes. According to Tasca, a message had been planted in his mind which he would never forget, his mind having been chosen because it was 'cosmic'.

According to reports, Tasca has lost interest in material things since the encounter.

Medical studies indicate that he had marks on his back which were burn-like in appearance but not in nature; they remain a mystery.

Many of the components of this case are familiar from other encounters; the description of the entities, the physical marks on the witness and the after-effects of the experience on the witness's lifestyle.

TAYLOR, ROBERT

(See **Livingston, Scotland**.)

TAYLOR, SANDRA AND PETER

At two o'clock in the morning of 17 August 1972, Peter Taylor and his wife Sandra were returning from one of Sandra's dancing engagements, driving through the Yorkshire Dales. On the way to Harrogate they encountered a melon-shaped object by the road. It had a fluorescent door that seemed to be opening. One of Sandra's dancing colleagues was dozing in the back of the car and did not observe the object, though this may have been due to poor eyesight.

Shortly before they saw the UFO the radio had filled with static; according to a reconstruction of the event the object that had caused this and which was seen by the couple landing near the road was some 30 feet high and 60 feet long.

As the door appeared in the object Sandra indicated that the couple entered some sort of 'cone of silence' where not even normal night-time noises could be heard, a commonly reported feature of such sightings.

Sandra became drawn towards the object, left the car and started to walk towards it, but Peter tried to drag her back.

Ahead of them on the road had been a police car but they could not remember passing it or where it had gone, suggesting some possible **missing time** period. When they arrived home a police car near the house 'checked them out', presumably due to the time of the morning. The police officer suggested that perhaps they had been drinking, which was likely to be because of their state of shock, the witnesses thought.

The Taylors made a report to the police the following morning though both the witnesses believed that the police already knew the story that they were being told. Possibly their own police car that had been on the road had filed some report of a sighting.

Incredibly, it appears that the police gave the story to the local press and, following this, the national press soon besieged the house, although Sandra had by then left for an engagement abroad.

Sandra apparently self-reported other types of clairvoyant activity and reported dreams of holding conversations with a small leathery man with piercing blue eyes and a slit-like mouth; dreams not dissimilar to many reported by abductees.

A year after the sighting Peter was driving alone when his car stalled and cut out. Suddenly he found himself driving on a different road, forty miles north of Daresbury in Preston, and discovered that he had a one-hour missing time period which has not been investigated.

TEJADA, CAPTAIN FRANCISCO LERDO DE

In November 1979 Captain Francisco Lerdo de Tejada was flying from Austria to Tenerife in a Super Caravelle with in excess of a hundred passengers abroad.

He encountered a UFO the size of a jumbo jet with powerful red lights beaming from it. It hurtled towards his aircraft at incredible speed and then took up position nearby, apparently playing games with the aircraft from just a half mile or so away.

Tejada's impression was that the aircraft was making movements 'quite impossible for any conventional machine to execute'.

One elderly passenger apparently collapsed on the plane as a result of witnessing this aerial activity and the pilot became so concerned that he requested permission to make an emergency landing at Valencia, which he did. The UFO was still visible in the air and was confirmed visually by the airport director, Señor Morlan, and several of the ground personnel with him.

Air Defence Command scrambled two Mirage jets to intercept the UFO and apparently they made visual contact including close approaches by the UFO. No official release was made about the event.

TELEPATHIC MESSAGES

The precise medium of communication between alleged extraterrestrials, or any other external force, and contactees or abductees is unclear. There are many instances when it appears that the communication is of a telepathic nature. Communication has often taken the form of the witness's own voice or of colloquialisms attributable to the witness's own vocabulary, which would seem to suggest a more direct approach to the brain than normal verbal communication.

Since the subject of communication between humans and non-humans is still very speculative, any more detailed discussion is pointless. As most such contacts occur in isolated situations with no third party witnesses it would in any case be very difficult for many witnesses to determine whether they were hearing voices or receiving telepathic impressions.

TELEPHONE TAPPING

Many people involved in the UFO phenomenon believe that at some point or another their telephones have been tapped by government agencies, presumably to discover precisely what information may be being withheld from the government. There must of course be times when this is true, but there is certainly a degree of paranoia about some of these claims. Precisely what information Ufologists are thought to have that governments are being denied is unclear, and to the best of my knowledge all significant information that comes to Ufologists' attention is disseminated reasonably quickly. The only information which is held on files not released tends to relate to the personal circumstances of particular witnesses, particularly those involved in contactee or abduction type cases, and is withheld only to protect those people from ridicule or unwarranted attention.

TEMPLE, OKLAHOMA

On 23 March 1966 an employee of Shepherd Air Force Base was driving to work in the early hours of the morning when just before the intersection of Route 65 and Highway 70 he encountered what he thought was a broken-down truck.

In fact the object turned out to be a cigar-shaped, aluminium-like craft with no obvious wings or protrusion. Kneeling next to it and nearly touching it was what happened to be a perfectly ordinary Army mechanic in military fatigues. He was of fairly normal build.

Shortly after this the object lifted up vertically and took off at considerable speed but with no obvious means of propulsion.

Clearly here there is some interface between the type of objects reported as UFOs while the 'entity' is perfectly human. The resolution of this apparent contradiction has yet to be found. There may be some validity to the suggestion that the 'normal' human was a **screen memory** covering up a more exotic encounter, but such a suggestion would be purely speculative, and based only on other cases and not the facts of this sighting as they are presently known.

TERAUCHI, CAPTAIN KENJU

An astonishing report, in terms of size at least, came from Captain Kenju Terauchi of Japan Air Lines who was flying over Alaska in November 1986. During final preparations for landing at Anchorage Airport, Terauchi and his crew on the cargo transportation flight noticed lights accompanying their Boeing 747 'jumbo' jet.

Terauchi had only a short while to examine the silhouette of the object which appears to have been partly saucer-shaped but more or less spherical and at least twice the size of an aircraft carrier.

The encounter was tracked by radar, and air traffic control instructed the pilot to make certain turns, possibly to avoid the object, which continued to pace the plane for over half an hour before disappearing.

Terauchi speculated in the most humorous way on the possibility that the encounter was extraterrestrial. He stated, 'We were carrying Beaujolais from France to Japan. Maybe they wanted to drink it.'

On 11 January 1987 Terauchi had a second encounter with a UFO but he described this as quite different, with lights that appeared three times below his craft and occasionally behind it.

THORNHILL, JAMES
James Thornhill of Marion County Civil Defense reported that at the same time as the **Pascagoula, Mississippi**, encounter involving Charles Hickson and Calvin Parker, his radar detected a UFO. At first he thought it was an aircraft but the reading then became stationary; shortly afterwards the radar system was knocked out.

Thornhill said: 'I've never seen anything quite like this, except perhaps during the Second World War.'

When the UFO reading returned later, the radar unit developed faults again.

TIENTSIN AIRPORT
On 16 October 1980 the radar crew at Tientsin Civil Aviation Airport were monitoring Flight 402 on radar when they lost track of the plane for approximately seven seconds. Subsequent checks indicated they had not been watching 402 at all, which was actually on a different course. When Flight 402 was on the radar at a later point, the unexplained radar return arose and then vanished again.

The object reappeared while Flight 404, a second aircraft in the area, was flying nearby but moving in the opposite direction.

Aircraft crew and radar personnel heard radio interference during the sighting but could not identify the source.

TIRMAN, COLONEL ROBERT M.
On 14 March 1969 the pilot and crew of a KC-135 Air Force tanker based in Thailand had a close encounter which was reported by their flight surgeon, Colonel Robert M. Tirman.

Tirman had been at the rear of the plane when he heard the pilots' astonished voices on the intercom. He went to the flight deck and was amazed to see, holding position near their plane and larger than the tanker aircraft, a huge cylindrical machine.

The plane's pilot asked the United States Air Force base nearby for interceptors but the base merely called back for more details. In order to facilitate this the pilot banked towards the object, which then veered away and disappeared in seconds. The pilot had not been able to see any sort of power source, windows or other details.

There is no report that interceptors were sent in response to the request.

TODMORDEN, WEST YORKSHIRE
(See **Godfrey, PC Alan.**)

TRANCAS, ARGENTINA
The occupants of a remote farmhouse near Trancas, Argentina, on 21 October 1963 found themselves besieged by six flying saucers which landed around their home. The saucers took up positions which also successfully blocked the railway lines, implying a military purpose to their positioning.

There were several entity reports of figures moving around the discs though the witnesses were not near enough to see them clearly; the siege ended without any apparently significant events.

Precisely why this farmhouse should have been designated for such treatment is unclear. There are similarities in the siege of the **Kelly-Hopkinsville** farmhouse in America where a remote farmhouse was surrounded – in that case by entities – and again where no obvious motive ever became apparent.

TRASCO, JOHN
On 6 November 1957, in the early evening, John Trasco stepped outside his house in Everittstown, New Jersey, to feed his dog.

Hovering off the ground just in front of a barn he could see a brightly lit, egg-shaped object and between him and it there was a small entity about three feet tall with a pasty-coloured face and large bulging eyes. The entity was dressed in green with something like a beret with shiny buttons. It said, 'We are peaceful people. We only want your dog.'

Trasco made his refusal quite clear. The entity ran away and the object took off.

From inside the house Trasco's wife did not see the entity but was able to confirm a sighting of the UFO.

Her husband had tried to arrest the entity but it had got away from him, leaving some green powder on his hands. There is no record of any scientific analysis of this substance.

Apart from the fairly classic design of the UFO, all the other components of this story are virtually unique, not least the extraordinary dress of the creature.

TRECUL, M. A.
On 20 August 1880 a member of the French Academy, Monsieur M. A. Trecul, reported a sighting of a glittering, golden, cigar-shaped object which dispatched a smaller craft – a sighting very much in the style of later, more modern, accounts. Cigar-shaped motherships were frequently reported in the 1950s.

TREFGARNE, LORD
During the incident which allegedly took place at **Woodbridge RAF/USAF Air Base** in 1980, where an apparently landed and possibly damaged UFO was seen at extremely close quarters by several military personnel and a close encounter report filed by a most senior American officer, it was Lord Trefgarne, then Parliamentary Under-Secretary of State for the Armed Forces, who stated: 'The events to which you refer were of no defence significance.'

TREMONTON, UTAH
(See **Newhouse, Warrant Officer Delbert C.**)

TRENT, MR AND MRS PAUL
(See **McMinnville, Oregon.**)

TRINDADE ISLAND SIGHTING
On 16 January 1958 a ship belonging to the hydrographic and navigation service of the Brazilian Navy, the *Almirante Saldanha*, was anchored at Trindade Island with around fifty people aboard. Trindade Island is some 750 miles from the Brazilian coast.

Among the people on board was Almiro Barauna, a professional photographer who had been taking underwater film at the time.

Just after noon a bright Saturn-shaped object was seen approaching the island and Barauna was called on to deck to photograph it. He took six photographs within fifteen seconds, of which four captured the object in motion. The photographs show a hazy flattened globe surrounded by a central ring. The haziness looks to be a factor of the photograph although apparently it corresponds to eye witness testimony. This fact has been used to suggest that the object may have been less a structured machine, and more a manifestation of energy (natural or artificial).

Captain Bacellar, the commanding officer of the ship, ordered that the film be developed immediately in a converted washroom on board. In order to authenticate the film he also insisted that Barauna strip to his swimming trunks before going into the darkroom, to prevent his taking an already exposed film in with him. Given these precautions and nearly fifty witnesses, it is not surprising that when the Brazilian Navy requested analysis of the film it was pronounced genuine and released to the press by the President of Brazil, Mr Joscelino Kubitschek.

The Trindade Island photographs are some of the most famous in the world, despite which they have never been held to provide conclusive proof of any aspect of the UFO phenomenon.

TRUMAN, PRESIDENT HARRY S.
At a press conference on 4 April 1950 President Harry S. Truman made the extraordinary statement: 'I can assure you that flying saucers, given that they exist, are not constructed by any power on earth.'

TRUTER, HAROLD
Harold Truter was the principal of Rosmead Junior School in South Africa in November 1972. On Friday 10 November he locked up the school and attendant tennis court and left for the weekend. When he returned on the evening of Sunday 12 November he had a distant light sighting of something in the sky; there had been a number of UFO reports across that weekend from many people, including police officers.

On examining the tennis court it was discovered that there had been enormous damage to the surface which was broken up. Tar and coal ash had been lifted and scattered up to 600 feet away up into the hills nearby and there seemed to be a pattern of symmetrical holes around the damaged surface. Bluegum trees just outside the tennis court had been badly burned and shortly afterwards died. The tennis court gates were still securely locked.

Connecting the damage with the UFO reports it has been speculated that the tennis court may have been a landing site, but investigation of the damage proved inconclusive.

TSEKHANOVICK, LYUDMILA
Astronomer Lyudmila Tsekhanovick sighted a UFO in the Caucasus mountains near Sukhumi in the summer of 1965. According to Tsekhanovick, the UFO had windows in the side which emitted light.

TÜBINGEN, GERMANY
The 1594 edition of Pierre Boaistuan's book recording many strange phenomena gives a description of what appears to be a mass landing of UFOs near Tübingen, Germany, on 5 December 1577.

Early that morning something appeared out of the clouds, described as 'resembling large, tall and wide hats and they landed in great numbers and in a variety of colours'.

Further, these landings were associated with entity claims.

TUJUNGA CANYON
Although revealed in 1975 the Tujunga Canyon abduction apparently relates to 1953 and therefore predates most of the major abduction cases.

Two witnesses were involved, known as Sara Shaw and Jan Whiteley (pseudonyms). They were two women in their early twenties living in the remote canyon in California. Sara was awoken by a light outside her bedroom window, which she considered might be the headlights of a motorcycle gang with evil designs on the isolated women. However, the smooth movement of the lights ruled out this possibility as there would have been a degree of bouncing motion on the rough roads. Jan Whiteley was now awake and Sara noticed it was 2 a.m. on the clock.

In a most extraordinary example of **missing time** and 'sealed memory' it seemed to be just the next instant when Sara and Jan realised it was now 4.20 a.m. and that over two hours had gone missing.

Regression hypnosis revealed an abduction story of capture and medical examination, though many researchers believe that the story reflected sexual tensions between the two who may have had a lesbian relationship.

Some cases have indicated that the heightened emotions of sexual energies and tensions may be a factor in creating the UFO 'state of mind' that allows the experience to manifest itself – assuming that it is accepted that a certain state of mind is relevant. There is debate between researchers on this point.

TUNGUSKA METEORITE

At seven o'clock in the morning of 30 June 1908 an enormous explosion was heard from the isolated forests of Siberia, particularly the Tunguska region.

Subsequent investigation revealed that there had been a great many hunters and fishermen in the area who had seen an object travelling through the sky. It was described as more brilliant than the sun and heading towards the site of the explosion.

So great was the impact that even 800 kilometres away one train driver stopped his train in the belief that his own cargo had exploded. There were shock waves over a great distance, and the event was recorded all round the world including London, England.

In the 1920s an expedition to the region discovered that there had apparently been something like an airborne explosion, rather than the meteorite impact that the team had expected to find. The debris in the forest was very similar to the debris at Hiroshima following the airborne explosion of an atomic bomb in 1945. In other words, there was total devastation radiating out from one central point, but at the point of 'ground zero' the destroyed trees were still standing while the others radiating out from that central point were felled.

A meteorite would not have caused such devastation, and of course in 1908 there could not have been atomic blasts, leaving the speculation that the Tunguska explosion was due to an extraterrestrial nuclear-powered craft exploding in the air. However, there may be other more natural explanations which have not yet been fully understood by science, i.e. some particularly destructive form of **ball lightning** or plasma energy.

TURNER, HARRY JOE

On 28 August 1979, at almost midnight, truck driver Harry Joe Turner was driving through Virginia. Suddenly the lights and radio, CB radio and engine of his truck cut out. He saw bright lights in his rear view mirror and something dark flew across the top of the vehicle.

Although the truck was apparently still coasting at over 70 miles per hour an entity ripped open the door, jumped in and grabbed Turner's shoulder. Turner was not diplomatic in his response; he pulled out a revolver and fired a bullet into the entity, causing it no harm whatsoever. Turner passed out.

When he came round he was in a parking lot at Fredricksburg some seventeen miles away although apparently there was over a hundred miles' worth of fuel gone from the truck. One of his radio aerials was burned and another sheared off, and there was apparently a thin film of material covering the cab. The witness passed out on his way home again and came to in a local hospital.

No **hypnotic regression** was needed to fill in the missing time; his memory came back unaided. After he had shot at the entity the truck had apparently been lifted into the air and into a hovering craft above. On board, Turner encountered humanoids dressed in white clothes and caps covering their ears. He was apparently operated on and a device implanted into his left side which gave the aliens control over him. It seems that he was taken on a tour of space, was able to examine Neil Armstrong's footprints on the moon and saw cities on planets orbiting the star Alpha Centauri.

After this experience he claimed he had gained psychic powers and had many more contacts with the aliens, he took an interest in religion and apparently made a determined effort to understand his own experiences.

Analysis of the physical traces relating to the encounter proved inconclusive; there was nothing that could not have been done deliberately and there was some controversy surrounding Turner himself with some of his colleagues believing him to be hoaxing to be 'bigger than he is' and others believing he was honest.

TWINING, GENERAL NATHAN A.

General Nathan Twining is reported to have been a member of the **Majestic 12** Panel formed to investigate UFOs in the 1940s.

General Twining was a prominent Second World War commander in both the European and Pacific areas of operations and in 1945 was appointed Commanding General of Air Material Command at **Wright Patterson Air Force Base**.

General Twining sent a memorandum to the Pentagon stating, 'The phenomenon reported is something real and not visionary or fictitious.' The remainder of the memorandum indicated analysis of physical objects. Significantly, Twining also reported that there was 'a lack of physical evidence in the shape of crash recovered exhibits' although by this time he was alleged to have examined the **Roswell** debris.

TWINKLE, PROJECT

One of the subsets of the UFO phenomenon in the late 1940s was the appearance of a great many green fireballs which became the subject of concentrated study. Many sightings were reported across the southern United States and were studied particularly by Dr Lincoln La Paz, an American expert in meteors.

Project Twinkle was set up to examine these so-called fireballs. It required three movie camera locations in New Mexico, which would photograph such objects, enabling their speed and height to be determined.

Project Twinkle was a total failure as it was never properly manned, only one camera made available, and the Air Force did not provide funds for finance. Throughout the period of the survey, nothing was seen by even the one camera operating.

Project Twinkle may have gone away but the green fireballs have not. They continue to be reported, exhibiting characteristics unusual for normal meteors.

U

UBATUBA, BRAZIL

In September 1957 there was a report from Ubatuba in Brazil that a flying saucer had crashed and exploded, scattering material.

Some of this was recovered and analysis indicated that the object had been made of a magnesium so pure as to be beyond the capabilities of our own production. For this reason, an extraterrestrial origin has been suggested for the craft sighted.

There have been several indications from other cases that UFOs are made of pure magnesium, which makes the Ubatuba retrieval all the more interesting. However, despite the fame of this incident no conclusive data has materialised from it, and all the fragments of the object are now believed to have been lost.

UFO

It is perhaps the most extraordinary fact of the UFO phenomenon that in an encyclopedia defining UFO events the one entry that cannot be stated in definitive terms is that for 'UFO' itself.

One quite factual definition of UFO, though quite unsatisfactory for most people, is 'that stimulus which creates a UFO report'. We must remember that we do not study UFOs, we study UFO reports and the UFO is the stimulus for this.

However, in a book I edited along with Hilary Evans in 1987, *UFOs 1947–1987* (see References and Background Material), Dr Richard Haines made a brave attempt to pull together the many definitions that had been made and some of these I list below.

1. The United States Air Force in 1966 defined the UFO as 'Any aerial object which the observer is unable to identify'.
2. In 1969 the **University of Colorado UFO Project** defined a UFO as 'The stimulus for a report made by one or more individuals of something seen in the sky (or an object thought to be capable of flight but seen when landed on the Earth) which the observer could not identify as having an

ordinary natural origin, and which seemed to him sufficiently puzzling that he undertook to make a report of it to police, to government officials, to the press, or perhaps to a representative of a private organization devoted to the study of such objects'.

3. Carl Sagan in 1972 defined a UFO as 'A moving aerial or celestial phenomenon, detected visually or by radar, but whose nature is not immediately understood'.

4. In 1972 Dr J. Allen **Hynek** defined a UFO as 'The reported perception of an object or light seen in the sky or upon the land, the appearance, trajectory, and general dynamic and luminescent behaviour of which do not suggest a logical conventional explanation and which is not only mystifying to the original percipients but remains unidentified after close scrutiny of all available evidence by persons who are technically capable of making a commonsense identification, if one is possible'.

Dr Haines went on to analyse these various factors and gave his own offering at the end as follows:

Manifestations of the UFO phenomenon are found among reports of the perception of indirect awareness of an object, light source, or presence of something in the sky, upon the land, or beneath the surface of a body of water, the appearance, trajectory and general dynamic luminescent or reflective qualities of which do not suggest an explanation that conforms with current conventional or logical explanations and which remains unidentified after all evidence surrounding the sightings has been studied by technically capable persons including the field investigator involved in the case and have applied both commonsense identification as well as intuition to their analyses.

It must also be said that defining the UFO fails to define the UFO phenomenon. The UFO phenomenon has so many interactions with paranormal and other psychic fields, particularly when dealing with abductions and 'high strangeness' cases, that the day may well be approaching when 'UFO' as a term and 'UFO phenomenon' as an expression are redundant. Instead, a wider recognition may have to be given to the fact that the UFO phenomenon is part of an overall paranormal experience. Some researchers are talking openly about the 'death of Ufology', in that the narrow field that started the ball rolling has widened so much that the phenomenon is now a recognisable collection of so many different 'sets' of data that one term cannot embrace the range adequately.

UFO INCIDENT, THE
One of the few films to be directly derived from a specific UFO encounter was *The UFO Incident*, a dramatisation of the Betty and Barney **Hill** encounter of 1961. Though not widely seen outside the United States, it has been frequently shown on that continent and may to some extent have helped to perpetuate a stereotype image of UFO abductions (see **Science Fiction and UFOs**).

UFO STATE OF MIND
Many researchers have indicated that there appears to be a 'UFO state of mind' which applies to the more exotic UFO experiences. In short, not anyone at any time can experience the UFO phenomenon; it tends to be a product of a particular state of consciousness. Such a state can apply to anybody but only at defined periods of time. In particular there are many cases where more than one witness sees a UFO but where only one has a more exotic experience. Whether this means that it is internally generated by that witness is debatable, particularly given physical traces often supporting the more exotic claims. What may be the case is that the UFO phenomenon is a consciousness with which mankind has basically lost contact but which at certain times the particular state of mind of certain people enables them to 'tap into'.

The idea that UFOs are 'merely' spacecraft visiting the Earth in the same way we send probes to the moon is too simplistic to encompass the whole spectrum of reports, even adjusting for psychological and sociological influences. It suggests that particular states of mind enable one to be receptive to something one would otherwise not be open to, which could presumably be caused by illness, self-trance, hypnosis due to sensory deprivation or highway hypnosis, close focus on the UFO phenomenon or psychic contact with people whose states of mind are already open to the phenomenon.

To determine whether or not the experience is internally generated, i.e. some form of hallucination, or externally generated in the sense that it does not derive entirely from the witness's mind is difficult, but the enormous range of reports from across the world from different people reporting very similar incidents suggests some external event overlaid on particular mind sets.

UFOCAL

A popular name for what are also known as 'window areas', i.e. areas where there is a high focus of UFO attention. For example, in Britain, Warminster in Wiltshire in the 1960s was a noted UFOcal; in 1952 the capital of the USA, Washington, was a UFOcal; and there have been many others for short periods of time in different parts of the world.

UFOCAT COMPUTER CATALOGUE

One of the earliest and most comprehensive catalogues of UFO reports was compiled by David Saunders for **CUFOS**. However, it was not a catalogue of UFO sightings so much as a catalogue of sources of information and took much information from media sources, where statistical studies would be unreliable. One of the main drawbacks of UFOCAT is that it cannot distinguish between IFOs and UFOs, i.e. identified and unidentified objects, which prevents its statistical use for most purposes.

UFOLOGY DEFINED

The term 'Ufology' has been coined to define the study of the UFO phenomenon. It is not a science, though many in the field would like to ensure scientific principles are applied, and it is unlikely ever to be a science since true understanding of the phenomenon is likely to reveal that it is in fact several 'sciences' rather than one thing.

Conventional scientists have criticised the use of the term Ufology as if 'Ufologists' are trying to make themselves seem scientific when they are not, but this has never been the purpose of the term; it has always been a simplistic usage designed merely to describe an overall study field.

UMMO

The UMMO stories relate to a series of complex messages arriving on Earth from the 'Cosmic Federation of Planets', which has been a feature of Spanish and French Ufology for some years. According to these messages they originate from a planet UMMO around the star IUMMA, which we call Wolf 424. Much detail has been provided but in essence the UMMO affair is a contactee message with no substantial supporting evidence.

UNCORRELATED TARGETS (UCTS)

Just occasionally some sections of the military get a bit over 'cute' in their denial of witnessing UFO activity. They may hold out that they do not encounter UFOs or file UFO reports.

This is of course nonsense as UFOs have been tracked on radar from ground control and airborne radar many, many times but becomes technically true when it is explained that radar operators refer to UFOs as either uncorrelated targets (UCTs) or **radar-detected anomalies** (RDAs).

UNDERWATER UNIDENTIFIED OBJECTS (UUO)

Although unquestionably 'UFO' has become the umbrella term to explain such anomalous phenomena, subsets of the phrase have been set up to try to categorise particular aspects. For objects seen under water the term UUO or Underwater Unidentified Objects has been applied.

UNEXPLAINED AERIAL OBJECTS (UAO)

The biologist Ivan T. Sanderson designated a subset of the UFO phenomenon Unexplained Aerial Objects or UAO where it was obvious that the objects displayed solid-like characteristics. These could then be differentiated from UAP or **Unidentified Atmospheric Phenomenon**, which displayed no such solid characteristics.

UNICAT, PROJECT

The Project UNICAT was undertaken by American researcher Dr Willy Smith. It was started in 1984 by Smith and Dr J. Allen **Hynek** and was designed to establish whether or not the UFO phenomenon was real and deserving of scientific consideration. Firstly, there had to be criteria designed to eliminate identified flying objects (IFOs), and it had to be certain that the sample represented the repeatable characteristics of UFO reports. This obviously meant that there had to be some subjective input to the system but the selection of the parameters was widely discussed before being implemented.

A full analysis of Project UNICAT is not appropriate in this encyclopedia but one example serves to show its usefulness.

Taking particular parameters such as LR (lonely road) and DR (driving) and also EM (electromagnetic problems), two scenarios were created. The first was HEPDRIL which stood for having electromagnetic problems while driving in an isolated location, and the second CLINROP which stood for craft landed in lonely road or place. Analysis of the reports fulfilling these criteria indicated that there were differences in the alien/human interaction, and in particular that abductions may be planned. In other words, when a witness accidentally came across a craft in a lonely road or place the aliens would often beat a hasty retreat, whereas they were obviously more prepared for abductions that they seemed to have themselves set up.

UNIDENTIFIED ATMOSPHERIC PHENOMENON (UAP)
For those classifications of the UFO phenomenon which do not display apparently solid characteristics, the term Unidentified Atmospheric Phenomenon is often used.

UNIDENTIFIED FLYING OBJECTS
(See **UFO**.)

UNITED STATES: A SPECIAL CASE
By any reasonable yardstick, the United States has a special place in Ufology. It is not that the UFO phenomenon is essentially American; indeed, reports from all over the world indicate that it is very much a global phenomenon with identical characteristics on all continents, in all countries.

However, there are certain characteristics about the phenomenon, social, psychological and mythological, which cannot be understood without analysis of the subject's greater acceptance in the United States.

There is considerable evidence that the United States Air Force and other defence agencies have made more intense UFO investigations than similar agencies in other countries.

There is a much greater preponderance of civilian UFO research groups in that country than in any other, even adjusting for the respective size and population of other countries.

There is a greater acceptance of such theories as the **extra-terrestrial hypothesis** amongst the general population of that country than any other country.

Possibly because of the above facts, there are far more numerous reports of sightings in the United States than any other country, even adjusting for population and size.

One notable factor about the UFO phenomenon is that no particular subset such as abductions, even disc sightings, etc. have been widely accepted across the world until they have been widely accepted in the United States. For example, the Antonio Villas **Boas** abduction in South America was the first and was published in the UFO press but did not make any impact on the media until the Betty and Barney **Hill** abduction in 1961 in North America commanded great **media** attention and brought the subject of abductions to the fore.

Similarly, there had been UFO-type sightings across the world, and particularly across Europe, since the turn of the century but it was not a global phenomenon until it had been christened 'flying saucer' by the sighting of 1947 by Kenneth **Arnold** in Washington State. It seems as if the world requires American sanction before it can go public with its UFO phenomena – or alternatively, perhaps more cynically, we all wait to see if America makes a fool of itself before we are prepared to as well!

There are also certain aspects to the phenomenon which are virtually unique to America and to this extent a proper understanding of those subsets, and possibly the whole UFO phenomenon, will not be possible until the particular characteristics of the American experience are understood. In particular, crash retrievals occur almost exclusively in the United States although there are similar sites in, say, Australia and Africa, where no significant reports have been received. Indeed, the one alleged crash retrieval report in the United Kingdom took place on an American air base.

UNIVERSITY OF COLORADO UFO PROJECT
(See **Condon Committee/Condon Report**.)

URD, PROJECT
Project URD was founded by researcher Bertil Kuhlemann and run by the International Project URD Foundation in Stockholm in Sweden. It set out to give a clear-cut answer to the question, 'Is there really something which is well worth allocating resources to?' In other words, Project URD was designed to determine, like Project **UNICAT**, that the UFO phenomenon was real and deserving of serious treatment.

The project determined, by analysis of over 1,500 cases, that the phenomenon existed by any reasonable scientific parameters and was deserving of scientific study. The basis of this was the repeatability of the phenomenon, i.e. similarity of unrelated reports, which could be determined by statistical analysis of well-defined cases.

UZUNOGLU, BASIL
In August 1966 Dr Basil Uzunoglu, a physicist and electronics researcher, was driving not far from Washington when he suddenly saw a UFO hovering some 18,000 feet above the road. It descended until he lost sight of it; he was then astonished to find it hovering just some 200 feet from a house nearby. He thought about stopping to get a better view of the object but apparently changed his mind, raced away, and admitted later that he had been very shaken by the encounter.

V

VÄDDÖ, SWEDEN

On 9 November 1958 a UFO apparently landed near Väddö in Sweden and was witnessed by two local people. After the object departed the witnesses were able to recover a small metal artefact which was warm to the touch. Subsequent analysis indicated it was made of tungsten carbide, cobalt and titanium. There was uncertainty in the witnesses as to whether the warmth indicated a UFO-origin for the fragment or not; either it came from a warm body, or was already lying on the ground and was warmed up by its close encounter.

VALDES, CORPORAL ARMANDO

On 25 April 1977 Corporal Armando Valdes was on night duty on the plateau above the town of Putre in Chile. Just before four in the morning the sentry, Pedro Rosales, alerted him to two purple lights descending towards them.

The lights became clearer as they approached, moving below the pair down the slope of the plateau. There was a central, large light with smaller lights either side. Valdes ordered his men to take cover and leapt over a wall, moving straight towards the object which soon disappeared. Fifteen minutes later Corporal Valdes reappeared, walking as if entranced and muttering, 'You do not know who we are or where we come from but I tell you we shall return.' He then collapsed into unconsciousness.

What followed seemed to be the most amazing story of time travel yet recorded in UFO lore. According to Valdes' watch it was showing the date of 30 April, five days in the future, and Valdes had several days' growth of beard acquired in the fifteen minutes he had been missing!

A local school teacher was alerted by the soldiers and journalists besieged Valdes, but the Army ordered him not to give out information; indeed, even six years later it was instructed that Valdes could only be approached through presidential order of President Pinochet.

Corporal Valdes indicated that he could not remember what was in his mind but, 'I shall talk one day.'

VALDIVIA, LUIGI
(See **Valinziano**, Giuseppe.)

VALENSOLE, FRANCE

On 1 July 1965, in the early hours of the morning, French farmer Maurice Masse at Valensole was attracted to the sight of a landed object in his lavender field by a strange high-pitched sound.

The object was shaped like an egg with a cupola on top and was approximately fifteen feet wide. It was standing on six legs in a manner reminiscent of a spider, according to the witness. The door of the object was open and within it Masse could see two seats.

Near the object were what Masse took to be two young boys apparently taking lavender plants; they turned out to be entities from the object about four feet tall and clad in green ski suits. When they noticed Masse approaching, one of them levelled a rod towards him which immobilised him.

On further examination the entities appeared to have large bald heads, big slanting eyes, pronounced chins and small lipless mouths; in fact, very much the description given by many American witnesses. They made guttural sounds.

This style of entity is often recounted by Americans under hypnosis in most fearful terms but Masse's conscious recall remembers them as good-natured and bringing a sense of peace to him. It is interesting that many American cases involving these entities combine fear with a great longing to be with the creatures, whether or not that emotion is 'engineered'.

While Masse was still immobilised, the entities returned to their craft and took off, with the landing legs retracting. It was some considerable time before Masse was able to move. Four days after the event occurred he fell into a deep sleep and members of his family fought to wake him up, believing that otherwise he would have slept for a very extended period. Usually Masse slept only five or six hours a night but for months after the event he needed at least twelve hours' sleep.

The most remarkable of the ground traces was that no lavender plants would grow at the landing site for ten years.

VALENTICH, FREDERICK

Certainly one of the most thought-provoking and tragic UFO cases on record is the encounter of Frederick Valentich over the Bass Strait, Tasmania, in October 1978.

Valentich had taken off from Moorabin Airport, Melbourne, and had flown for some three quarters of an hour in the early hours of the evening when he reported by radio to Melbourne Flight Service Unit that he had sighted an unidentified aircraft.

The Flight Service Unit indicated that they had no aircraft in the air that they were aware of and requested a description from Valentich. He confirmed it was a bright object that had just passed over his aircraft some 1,000 feet above him and was circling round and re-approaching him. Valentich radioed that he believed the aircraft was 'playing some sort of game'. On being further pressed by the Flight Service Unit Valentich attempted to describe the object but stumbled in trying to find the right description. What he did describe was that it was a large shiny metallic-like object with a green light. The object could not be seen for a time, but shortly before the end of the recorded transmission between Valentich and the Flight Service Unit Valentich confirmed that the object which had earlier disappeared from sight was again hovering above him. The Melbourne Flight Service Unit controller Steve Robey who had been in communication with Valentich believed that at the end of the transmissions Valentich was 'definitely concerned for his safety'.

At the same time as Valentich's encounter there were many other UFO reports received in the same area, including sightings of green lights, and in one case a photograph was taken showing a dense object rising up from and interfering with the sea (see **Manifold, Roy**).

Shortly after Valentich's last transmission that the object was 'not an aircraft' his microphone remained open but there were no further transmissions.

Search and Rescue was instigated when the aircraft did not land at its designation; an intensive air, sea and land search was maintained for five days but no trace of the aircraft or its pilot was ever found or has ever been found since.

There were rumours that the plane had been seen by divers under the **Bass Strait**, but since they were asking for $10,000 even to show the photographs they had taken it was considered that the claim might be a hoax. No money was paid and the matter was dropped.

VALINZIANO, GIUSEPPE

On 2 December 1896, at the beginning of the American **airship** wave, two fishermen near Pacific Grove, San Francisco, Giuseppe Valinziano and Luigi Valdivia, watched a small aircraft-type object glide down and come to rest on the beach near them. Three occupants stepped out and carried the craft across the sand into the woods.

The two fishermen took their boat to the shore to follow the men, but one of them quickly came back and suggested they should stay where they were. Valinziano, described as an aggressive and confident fellow, insisted on examining the craft and was eventually granted the right to come within fifty feet of it.

After necessary repairs had been undertaken on the vehicle it took off during the hours of darkness and the fishermen went home. Valinziano speculated that the captain had delayed their leaving so that they could not tell anyone else of the whereabouts of the ship before it was flying again.

They described the object as sixty feet long, cigar-shaped with wings folded against the sides, despite which it was apparently carried by only three people. (Whether that is meant to tell us something about the craft or the people, or both, is unclear.)

The following night such an airship was seen travelling over Twin Peaks. It crashed and the crew was recovered, injured.

There was no suggestion from either incident that the crew was other than terrestrial. Indeed, one was named as Mr J. D. de Gear.

VALLENTUNA, SWEDEN

One of the most extraordinary waves of sightings to have occurred was centred around the Vallentuna area of Sweden, just north of Stockholm, around 1974.

During the wave there was a well-documented abduction case, referred to as **Anders**, and within a few hours of this sighting many corroborative reports from independent witnesses in the area. Within a couple of months of the abduction there were up to thirty good reports of sightings and over the year to eighteen months around the abduction some one hundred good UFO reports from the same localised area.

So concerned were the local officials that the **Home Guard** was persuaded to make a stake-out on three hills around the area and they were able to field 50 personnel against 15 Ufologists, probably the only time that a **skywatch** has been conducted by more non-UFO personnel than UFO devotees. Even they were bringing in some anomalous lights reports from the area.

The abduction account became itself almost unique when an independent and unaffected witness reported seeing the same cone of light into which Anders had been abducted but unfortunately was unable to see Anders himself from her particular position.

Reports throughout this **UFOcal** of limited location and short period of time included a whole range of UFO phenomena.

VAN GRAAN, DANIE

Danie Van Graan was walking over a high earth bank, which is the flood protection for his village of Loxton in South Africa, when he saw below an oval-shaped object parked in a field. Inside, moving as if in slow motion, were four small thin entities with fair hair, slanting eyes and high cheek bones – a description that immediately brings to mind the female abductor of Antonio Villas **Boas**.

Van Graan could hear a humming sound, and as he approached one of the entities looked up at him. A beam of light hit him in the face, causing him impaired vision and a nosebleed. The machine apparently took off fast and disappeared.

No **missing time** period was apparently reported though nosebleeds have been seen by some American researchers as indicating part of the medical examination which often takes place during UFO abductions; no such investigation was conducted in this case and the witness has since died.

Investigation of the landing site showed hard baked soil and damage to the vegetation; nothing would grow on the spot afterwards.

Further investigation indicated that there were footprints around the site which did not match the farm workers', and possibly Van Graan encountered the entities after they had already done some fieldwork. This would correlate with a noise heard by a second witness, Jan Van Der Westhuizen, who heard a humming sound some twenty minutes before Van Graan arrived, which could well have been the landing of the craft, giving the entities twenty minutes to do some survey work.

VANDENBERG, GENERAL HOYT S.

General Hoyt S. Vandenberg was reputed to be one of the **Majestic 12** Panel formed in the 1940s to investigate UFOs.

He was Director of Central Intelligence.

In August 1948 the Air Technical Intelligence Center produced an 'estimate of the situation' which suggested that UFOs might be interplanetary. Vandenberg, who was Chief of Staff for the Air Force at the time, decided that this could cause widespread panic and ordered the document destroyed. Furthermore, its very existence was denied.

VEHICLE INTERFERENCE

One of the most frequent effects of UFO close encounters is vehicle interference, particularly in cars and trucks. In the vicinity of hovering or landed UFOs such vehicles are prone to cut out, their engines die, their lights and radios are extinguished and become generally inoperative. In many cases when the UFO moves away the car spontaneously starts up, or indeed in some cases the driver finds that he is now driving again although often cannot remember restarting the vehicle. There has been much speculation about what causes vehicle interference and many years ago **BUFORA** commissioned a special study and published its *Vehicle Interference Report*. The basic theory is that electromagnetic forces from the UFO, be they natural or artificial, interfere with the normal circuits of such vehicles. Whether or not this is deliberate on the part of any controlling intelligence is undetermined but there would certainly seem to be cases where cars have been selected out of several unaffected vehicles, presumably for abduction purposes.

Such vehicle interference appears to be selective also because there are very few cases of close encounters with aircraft where they have been similarly affected and where of course the results would be disastrous. The majority of electrical malfunctions in aircraft seem to be coming from Asia, particularly the Soviet Union and China. Some studies have indicated that diesel-powered cars are less prone to vehicle interference, possibly because of the ignition mechanism not being so affected by the forces unleashed.

Specific cases of vehicle interference are mentioned in the case histories in this encyclopedia.

VENUS (AS EXPLANATION OF SIGHTINGS)

One of the most brilliant planets in the sky, in evening and morning, is Venus and it causes many UFO reports. It is often brilliant blue-white, appears to be hovering and, if you happen to be moving in a car when observing it, can appear to be pacing the car in a quite unnatural way.

Any sighting report filed at a time when Venus is so visible is always checked against such. Other planets, of course, cause similar confusion and most researchers use the astronomical charts available to eliminate such mistakes.

There is at least one case on file of a woman who became very agitated when driving because she seemed to be being paced by a bright light. The following day the investigators were able to satisfy her that it was indeed Venus she had seen, but her reaction had been relatively extreme.

VERONICA, ARGENTINA
On 17 July 1952 hundreds of residents of Veronica in Argentina watched six discs manoeuvring and circling above the town before disappearing into the night. This report came within hours of a report from a Captain Paul Carpenter of a sighting near Denver of a similar saucer formation. Carpenter estimated the speed had been 3,000 miles per hour, making the saucers' appearance in both locations quite possible.

VICTORIAN UFO RESEARCH SOCIETY
(See **VUFORS**.)

VIDAL, DR AND MRS GERARDO
During the South American wave of sightings in 1968 Dr Gerardo Vidal, an Argentine lawyer, and his wife were driving from Chascomus to Maipu near Buenos Aires when they apparently disappeared.

Relatives and friends searched the area but could find no trace of the couple. It was two days later when Dr Vidal telephoned his family to tell them where he was – 4,000 miles away in the Argentine Consulate in Mexico City!

Apparently on leaving Chascomus the car had been enveloped by a dense fog across the road and the Vidals had found themselves, when they next became conscious, sitting in their parked car on an unknown road. They felt that they had slept for some time, they both had similar pains in their necks, their watches had stopped and the surface of the car had apparently been scorched as if by flame.

No regression hypnosis or other studies have been conducted into the forty-eight hours of missing time and the case is therefore left open with a wealth of mystery potentially undiscovered.

Dense fog as part of an abduction mechanism has been reported in several varied cases across the world.

VILLEGAS, FERNANDO
(See **Peccinetti, Carlos.**)

VILVOORDE HUMANOID
On 19 December 1973 a witness (name withheld) went into his kitchen in the early hours of the morning, and heard a noise and saw a green glow from his small walled garden.

Peering through the curtains the witness saw that at the end of the garden was a **humanoid** about three feet tall wearing a shiny one-piece suit and, incredibly, glowing green. The entity seemed to be sweeping the end of the yard with some kind of device like a Geiger counter or vacuum cleaner.

The witness flashed his torch at the humanoid who turned fully round to face him in jerky and uncomfortable-looking movements. It seemed as if the creature could not turn his head on his neck but was forced to point his whole body in the direction of sight.

At this point the witness noticed that the humanoid's face contained pointed ears and large, yellow, oval eyes. In what could well have been a rather extraordinary intergalactic gesture, the entity stuck two fingers up in a V-sign before turning away and walking towards the back garden wall.

In a curious manner the creature walked up and over the wall, treating every surface as if it were flat and always remaining at 90 degrees to it in the same way as a human would normally walk along a road – a further example of its stiffness and awkwardness of movement.

Shortly afterwards the witness saw a small round object take off from just beyond the wall. The witness was far from troubled by the sighting; he went on to make himself a snack in the kitchen.

VINTHER, CAPTAIN LAWRENCE W.
On 20 January 1951 Sioux City Airport control tower requested Captain Lawrence W. Vinther, flying a Mid-continent Airlines flight, to change course and manoeuvre towards a strange bright light above the airport. Vinther did so and the light dived towards the airliner, a DC3.

The UFO flashed above the plane, reversed direction and paced Vinther for several seconds; Vinther and his co-pilots confirmed the sighting and described the object as bigger than a B29.

VON POPPEN, BARON NICHOLAS

According to Gray Barker in his 1977 UFO report 'America's Captured Flying Saucers – Cover-up of the Century' (see References and Background Material), Baron Nicholas Von Poppen, a refugee from Estonia who had designed a system of photographic metal analysis, was called in by the United States military to photograph and examine a retrieved flying saucer.

Von Poppen was apparently taken to an air base, probably Edwards Air Base, where he stayed for several days filming and photographing the saucer.

According to reports Von Poppen stated that the machine was about 30 feet wide with an interior cabin of some 20 feet and curved ceiling. Von Poppen reported seats and control boards with levers and push buttons.

Even more extraordinarily, Von Poppen reported that still strapped in the four seats were the four dead bodies of its pilots, all white and wearing black one-piece outfits. They were some 2–4 feet tall and generally complied with the usual descriptions of such entities.

Von Poppen was not encouraged to examine the crew or to photograph them but did attempt to steal an artefact from the craft; he was caught and stopped from removing anything. There was a rumour that Von Poppen had kept one negative away from the military which he would use if he were ever put under pressure from them but after his death at the age of ninety in 1975 no trace of this photograph was ever found.

VORILHON, CLAUDE
(See **Raelian Movement**.)

VORONEZH, USSR

According to a Soviet news agency report a UFO landed in October 1989 in a suburban park some 300 miles south of Moscow, at Voronezh.

The object was described as a sixty-feet-wide glowing globe which apparently left landing trace evidence on the ground. Two entities were associated with the sighting; giants with small heads (almost the exact opposite of what is reported across most of the rest of the world, and certainly in the United States of America, where the majority of reports are of dwarf entities with big heads).

The Veronezh landing occurred as part of a wave of sightings in the area.

VUFORS

VUFORS, the Victorian UFO Research Society, is the most prominent civilian research group in Australia. It is based near Moorabin Airport, near the **Bass Strait**, which has seen one of the world's most active concentrations of UFO activity.

VUFORS has played a major part in UFO research on that continent; in particular it did a great deal of work on the case of Frederick **Valentich** who disappeared while flying over the Bass Strait.

W

W. A., 1896 'MARTIAN' LETTER

On 24 November 1896 the *Sacramento Bee*, a local newspaper, published a letter from a Martian known only as W. A. which explained all that was needed to be known about **airship** waves.

'The Lord Commissioner of Mars has evidently sent one of his electric aircraft on an exploring expedition to the younger and larger worlds. The airships are constructed of the lightest and strongest fabrics and the machinery is of the most perfect electrical work. Aluminium and glass hardened by the same chemical process that forms our diamonds contribute the chief material of their most perfect airships. When in use these vessels at a distance have the appearance of a ball of fire being operated wholly by the electric current generated on such vessels. The speed of our Martian ships is very great and can be regulated to the rapidity of 1,000 miles a second. In fact, with the Martian inventions space is almost annihilated. These aerial craft can so adapt their courses that when they desire to rest they can anchor within certain degrees of latitude and wait for the revolutions of the Earth, for instance, to bring any particular locality desired much nearer them without the necessity of any aerial navigation.'

Since the writer refers to 'our' Martian ships, it was assumed that he claimed to originate from that planet.

WALKER, JOSEPH A.

In May 1962 Joseph Walker, a top NASA test pilot, admitted to having twice filmed UFOs while in flight but commented, 'I don't feel like speculating about them.'

NASA indicated that the objects were identified as ice flaking off his X15 aircraft.

WALL, MAJOR SIR PATRICK

Major Sir Patrick Wall, now retired from a long political career as Conservative MP for Humberside, spent over thirty years in the House pursuing the cause of serious UFO research amongst his colleagues.

He was a consultant to NATO which gave him a particular interest in the security concerns of the UFO phenomenon.

Since retiring from politics Major Sir Patrick Wall has become a keen and active member of the UFO community, continuing to voice his very pertinent questions around the world. In 1989 he became President of **BUFORA**.

WALSH, ROBERT C.

At the very beginning of the **Great North-East Blackout** in the United States and Canada one of the first reports of a UFO that may have been associated with the blackout was made by Robert C. Walsh, the Deputy Aviation Commissioner of Syracuse. Amongst other witnesses, Walsh was on a plane that had just landed at Hancock Airport and had seen something resembling a huge fireball ascending from low altitude.

It was seen over the Clay sub-station which is often said to have caused the blackout. The nature of the fireball remains unknown.

WALTERS, EDWARD

Ed Walters is the real name of the principal witness of the **Gulf Breeze** sighting, although for a long time he was known only by the pseudonym of 'Mr Ed'. His wife Frances has also admitted that she is a close participant in the case although originally she retained her anonymity and refused to be drawn into the publicity for the sake of their family and home life. Ed and Frances Walters have now published a book on the Gulf Breeze sightings, *The Gulf Breeze Sightings* (see References and Background Material), and have made many public presentations on the events and are therefore now fully in the public domain.

Walters is a specialist house designer who lives in the Gulf Breeze area of Pensacola, Florida, where he took the extraordinary series of photographs. He maintains a relatively laid-back attitude towards what he saw and experienced, not trying to push particular interpretations but accepting any possibilities. He is made angry only by the 'debunkers' who have made his life very difficult; attempts to discredit him (arising from the politics of American Ufology rather than the case itself) have resulted in many personal attacks on his character which he and the **MUFON** investigators believe are quite unwarranted.

WALTON, TRAVIS

On 5 November 1975 a seven-man wood-cutting gang was contracted to remove trees in the Sitgraves National Park near Snowflake, Arizona. One of the gang was Travis Walton. At the end of the day they were driving their truck back to their base when all of the witnesses saw a large gold UFO at treetop height, apparently solid and displaying windows and a dome on top.

Six of the crew stayed in the truck but Travis Walton ran towards the object while the rest shouted for him to come back. They witnessed a blue ray fired from the UFO which knocked Walton into the trees; they saw little else as they fled the area to report the incident to the local police.

It was five days before Travis Walton was located and during that time there was considerable pressure on the gang to explain what had happened to him. There were suggestions that they had murdered Walton which were particularly distressing to one of the gang, Walton's brother Duane. However, despite these pressures three of the gang refused to go into the woods at night, and as the sheriff who headed the search party said: 'One of the men was weeping. If they were lying, they were damn good actors.'

In order to clear their names of a potential murder charge the witnesses took **polygraph** tests at the Arizona State Office for Public Safety. One of the gang was apparently too upset to take the test with reliability but the other five passed. The examiner, Cy Gilson, commented, 'I gotta say they passed the test.'

Travis Walton turned up five days later.

According to him he had been abducted by the UFO and had encountered entities similar to those often reported in abductions, i.e. short, thin figures with large domed bald heads, huge black eyes and reduced facial features. More unusually, Walton also remembers a human-like or even human person aboard the flying saucer, and he recalled being taken for what seemed to be some sort of space flight, or at least was shown a convincing hologram projection of one.

Travis Walton also took a lie-detector test under Dr Gene Rosenbaum who stated, 'This young man is not lying . . . he really believes these things.'

Walton was apparently amazed to discover that he had been away five days and had five days' beard growth. He believed he had only been absent for a short period of time.

The case gave rise to much controversy. Some research

groups seem to have 'adopted' Walton and fully support his case while others claim it was a fake. Those who disbelieve Walton say that the gang was behind with its work and would lose valuable payments if they could not explain the delays. They point to the fact that the witnesses received a $5,000 'reward' from the *National Inquirer* newspaper for the most valuable UFO report of the year.

Those who support the case argue that such an extraordinary story would be an unlikely invention just to explain delays in tree-felling and point to the positive lie-detector tests.

It has been over twenty years since the incident and none of the witnesses has broken ranks and confessed to a hoax; given the nature of the fame of the case, anyone doing so would probably command considerable publicity and financial reward. This must be regarded as supportive of the claims.

WANDERKA, JOSEF

Probably the single most bizarre encounter case was reported from Austria in September 1955 by Josef Wanderka.

He was driving a moped along the road when, not paying proper attention, he accidentally drove straight up the ramp of a UFO and into the arms of tall aliens. He apologised for doing so, the aliens explained in German that they had arrived from Cassiopeia, and got him to explain to them how the moped engine worked. Josef apparently gave them an anti-Nazi lecture, they got bored and threw him off the ship. They did make the suggestion that he could create a movement for world equality.

WAR OF THE WORLDS

In 1938 Orson Welles broadcast the story of H. G. Wells' *War of the Worlds* as if it were a real event actually happening in the locality. There was some panic arising from this though detailed analysis has shown that most of the hysteria was only in the pages of the newspapers and not actually in the streets.

This broadcast, and particularly the reported reaction to it, has long been held to be the reason why exposing UFO-related material to the general public should be achieved gradually over a long period. In fact, many analysts now believe that even a major disclosure of such material would not cause the slightest panic. In reality the greatest problems, assuming that concealed material contained proof of extraterrestrial visitation, would be the damage to, or collapse of, certain institutions such as religion, finance, etc.

Reasonably enough, this consideration would be sufficient to make any major government tread with caution.

WARD, GEORGE

In the late 1950s George Ward was Secretary of State for Air and appears to have undertaken a policy of **debunking** UFO sightings on the basis that they were either explainable or unexplainable only because of lack of evidence. However, when challenged by author Desmond Leslie, Ward apparently commented: 'What am I to say? I know it wasn't a balloon. You know it wasn't a balloon. But until I get a saucer on the ground in Hyde Park and can charge the public sixpence a go to enter, it must be balloons, otherwise the government would fall and I would lose my job.'

That sounds more like a committed politician than a committed disbeliever.

WARMINSTER, WILTSHIRE

In 1965 Gordon Faulkner photographed a banded disc-shaped UFO over Warminster in Wiltshire, which was highly publicised in tabloid newspapers such as the *Daily Mirror*. Immediately there were rashes of photographs of similar objects making headlines in the newspapers; all came from Warminster which instantly became one of the most famous **UFOcals** in the world. For around a decade it was to remain the British centre of Ufology, largely due to the diligent efforts of a local devotee, Arthur Shuttlewood.

Warminster was, of course, a collection of UFO cases as are all UFOcal events but, of more significance, Warminster was a sociological event. There were **skywatches** taking place all around Warminster and particularly the two main hills in the area, Cradle Hill and Starr Hill. It saw the birth of a camaraderie amongst young people involved in the embryonic UFO subject and although very little was learned about UFOs a great deal was learned about people involved in the business, their motivations and their needs.

Warminster's cases included mostly lights and discs in the sky, and some cases of a contactee-like nature; abductions were not yet accepted in UFO literature but it is held by many to be highly likely that some abductions passed by because of the lack of investigation into particular cases.

By the same token Warminster was very much an example of 'me too' syndrome; when something of interest attracts the public's attention, other people begin reporting it also, on a 'me too' basis. This is not to say that they are jumping on a bandwagon or lying but there is a tendency to look into the sky and to see quite normal things through more suspicious eyes when media interest is channelled on the one subject.

Warminster was the scene of several hoaxes played on the Ufologists; the unscientific approach of many at the time led to most of these being accepted as real until they were later exposed.

Anybody witnessing events at Warminster was able to learn a good deal about what was right and what was wrong with the study of Ufology. Its more sensible methodology in these modern times is due largely to lessons learned in those early years.

WARNETON, BELGIUM

A businessman (name withheld) was driving home from a business course near Warneton in Belgium when his car lights and radio cut out. The driver brought the car to a safe halt and as he was about to get out saw by the side of the road what appeared to be a dome-topped object.

Two entities approached him, some 4½ feet tall, each having a pear-shaped face, greyish skin, small nose, slit mouth and large eyes – in other words very similar to the type of entity reported all around the world. As they approached the car one of them pointed a tube-like gun at the driver and he felt as if he was hit by an electric shock.

The entities apparently then ran back to the object which took off and it disappeared as if by magic.

It is possible that this is a rare case of an interrupted abduction as the disappearance of the entities corresponded with the arrival of another car whose driver came to the assistance of the principal witness. Most importantly, the second driver also saw the UFO.

However, American cases suggest that the abductors are quite capable of dealing with any interruptions by 'switching off' those they do not want involved; therefore memory recall and an analysis of missing time – perhaps unnoticed – could have told a different story.

WASHINGTON 'FLAP'

In July 1952 there was a concentration of UFO sightings over the United States capital, Washington DC. Among the many radar visual sightings were a significant number tracked by the nearby **Andrews Air Force Base**.

Some of the reports gave rise to particular concern as the UFOs flew over the White House, thereby entering forbidden air space. Although intense, the flap produced no significant UFO cases for investigation.

WEBB, EDDIE DOYLE

During the October 1973 wave of sightings in the United States Eddie Doyle Webb was blinded by several hours by a close encounter with a UFO. He had been driving a tractor trailer through the dawn when a bright aluminium object came up fast behind him. He awakened his wife who was asleep in the cab, but she did not see anything. Webb put his head out of the window and something like a ball of fire struck him in the face. He began screaming, 'I am burned, I can't see,' and Mrs Webb drove him to Barnes Hospital, St Louis, to attend an eye specialist.

Dr Harley Rutledge of Southwest Missouri State University Physics Department analysed glasses that Webb had been wearing and stated that, 'It appeared they were heated internally. The plastic apparently got hot and the mould came to the surface. The heat warped the plastic causing the lens to fall out.'

The nature of the experience remains a mystery, but there are many instances of burning and heat resulting from close encounters, whether the source is natural or artificial.

WEBSTER, BRIAN

In November 1983 Brian Webster was the head of the Ministry of Defence's Department **DS8** which investigates UFO reports. Questioned about the **Woodbridge** alleged close encounter and landing by a former head of DS8, Ralph **Noyes**, he replied, 'I can assure you . . . that there is no evidence of anything having intruded into British airspace and landing near RAF Woodbridge.'

WEGIERSKA GORKA, POLAND

In July 1954 an eleven-year-old girl was on holiday at Wegierska Gorka in Poland. She and her friends were playing in the woods, collecting mushrooms. Separated from her companions, she saw a glowing oval-shaped light near a cliff and walked towards it. As she approached it an entity nearby seemed to draw her into the object; she walked up some stairs and through the door.

There were a few more entities inside. They were basically of normal human shape though the witness noticed something like a hump on their backs, a feature that has occurred mostly in Polish or Iron Curtain reports.

The girl was instructed to lie down. She slept and has no further memory until seven hours after she had gone missing when she was found by her friends near the cliff where the object had been. Her mushroom basket was empty and all she had was a vague memory of flying.

None of this was remembered by the girl until 1986 when a conversation with some friends awoke memories in her.

It is interesting to consider at what time the 'influence' over her began; her separating herself from her friends may well have been a part of the abduction already underway. Jean-François **Boedec** has examined some cases of abduction and believes there is a 'build up' phase where the witness acts in a way that isolated himself from others, allowing the abduction to take place. This may be such an example.

WEISBERG, DR

In a memo probably made in 1949 by the director of the Borderland Sciences Research Foundation there is a description by a Canadian university physics professor, a Dr Weisberg, who apparently examined crashed saucers following retrieval. He gave the director a description of the disc as 'Like a turtle's back, with a cabin space some fifteen feet in diameter. The bodies of six occupants were seared and the interior of the disc had been badly damaged by intense heat.' Weisberg also apparently described the autopsy on the bodies and suggests that the UFO arrived at Edwards Air Force Base, where he examined it, after a clandestine transportation by road and rail.

WEITZEL, CRAIG R.

In 1980 **APRO** received a letter from a person purporting to be a United States Air Force airman at Kirtland Air Force Base but who remained anonymous, describing a close encounter near the air base in July of that year.

According to the letter Craig R. Weitzel and ten others, including the author of the letter, were at Kirtland Air Force Base when they observed a dull-coloured UFO land nearby.

Furthermore, an entity in a metallic suit was witnessed near the craft and Weitzel took several pictures of the object.

Of significance was the fact that although the event was not reported, Weitzel was accosted the following evening by an individual stating that he represented Sandia Laboratories on Kirtland Air Force Base who told Mr Weitzel that he had seen a secret craft that he should not have seen, its origin having been Los Alamos. Weitzel was warned not to discuss the sighting.

The author of the letter believes that the Sandia Laboratories have examined several crash retrieved saucers.

WELLS, GREGORY

On 14 March 1968 nine-year-old Gregory Wells was the subject of a UFO incident near Beallsville in Ohio.

Wells and his parents lived in a caravan parked near his grandmother's home. Near dusk he left his grandmother to return to the caravan and his grandmother suddenly heard him screaming. In the caravan his mother also heard the screams and the two women ran towards each other to find Gregory Wells on the ground, his jacket on fire.

The women doused the flames and the boy was hurried to hospital where he was treated for burns and shock.

Several witnesses had reported a cigar-shaped UFO at low altitude near the site at the time; when Gregory had recovered he explained that as he was on his way to the caravan he saw a huge lighted object hovering above the road and while he watched it a device emerged from the machine, pointed towards him and fired a beam of flame at him. The mother and grandmother had not seen the UFO. Their attention was focused entirely on Gregory, which is understandable.

There have been several cases of what appear to be heat attacks against people but most of these have been related to military or potential military installations. Any reason for shooting down a nine-year-old boy can only be wild speculation.

Many cases are suggestive of a natural phenomenon, perhaps a form of **ball lightning**, striking the witness, causing the burning, but this case would seem not to fall into that category as the boy indicates that a 'device' was pointed from the UFO towards him and fired the beam.

WERNER, FRITZ

Fritz Werner is the pseudonym given to an alleged employee of the Office of Special Studies at **Wright Patterson Air Force**

Base who, in 1953, was given the special assignment of examining a crashed flying saucer, which the Air Force explained was one of its own secret vehicles. Werner's job was to estimate the speed of the vehicle from the marks of the impact. Apparently he was then forced to take an oath not to reveal what he had been.

He describes the object as approximately thirty feet wide, and oval with an opened hatchway. Inside were swivel seats and several instruments. There was one remaining occupant of the craft some four feet tall and wearing a silvery metallic suit.

WERTZ, LAVERNE
When police officer Robert **Dickerson** reported seeing a UFO at Redmond Airport, he notified the flight specialist Laverne Wertz. Wertz and other FAA men watched the disc through binoculars for several minutes, giving clear corroboration of the report.

Wertz was later also ordered to make a check in flight for abnormal radioactivity and he and another pilot, using a Geiger counter, circled the area at various altitudes where the UFO had been seen. However, the results were given to the Air Force and never released.

WEXFORD, EIRE
Two teenage boys walking in the early evening in September 1924, in County Wexford, Eire, encountered an extraordinary UFO. It consisted of a solid beam of light several feet long, which was simply travelling through the air some feet off the ground. They watched it moving at approximately 10 miles per hour, climbing over a hedge and crossing a field. They had several minutes of observation before the object encountered a railway line and moved off along its length.

WHEELER, JIM
During a spate of sightings on the night of 2 November 1957 on Route 116 near Levelland in Texas, Jim Wheeler apparently almost drove into a huge bright object some 210 feet wide, shaped like an egg, sitting in the middle of the road. The main reason he didn't run into it was because as he approached it, his car engine and headlights cut out. Wheeler got out of the vehicle but the object drifted up into the sky and vanished. As the object receded, the engine and lights of Wheeler's car came back to life.

WHEN THE MAN IN THE MOON SEEKS A WIFE

In 1908 Percy Stowe made the science fiction film *When the Man in the Moon Seeks a Wife*. As far as our research can determine, this is the first film to depict a visit to the Earth by an alien.

WHITE MOUNTAINS, NH

(See **Hill**, Betty and Barney.)

WHITELEY, JAN

(See **Tujunga Canyon**.)

WHITMORE, W. E.

W. E. Whitmore was, at the time of the **Roswell** crash retrieval, the owner of radio station KGFL, which is local to the area. Whitmore interviewed 'Mac' **Brazel**, the farmer who had discovered the debris on his farm. Mr Whitmore's son, Walt Whitmore Jr, was later interviewed about the events of that time and remembered that his father had hidden Brazel in their family home in order to make sure the interview was exclusive. After the interview, when Brazel left, he assumed that the Air Force caught up with him.

Apparently attempts to broadcast the interview were prevented, particularly by a man who identified himself as the Secretary of the Federal Communications Commission in Washington DC. According to this individual, Whitmore's FCC broadcasting licence would be jeopardised if the story was transmitted. Just to reinforce the threat a New Mexico senator also contacted Whitmore advising him to comply with the order.

WILCOX, GARY

The day before the remarkable **Socorro** landing witnessed by officer Lonnie **Zamora**, at ten o'clock in the morning, farmer Gary Wilcox saw an object in a field which he first took to be a dumped refrigerator or possibly the wing tank or another part of a damaged aircraft. It was only as he got closer that he realised it was an egg-shaped object some 20 feet wide.

Two creatures appeared in front of him although he did not notice them step out of the object; they were approximately four feet tall and humanoid in appearance. They explained to him, in English, that he should not be concerned because they had talked to humans before and that they came from the planet Mars.

The two entities requested of him a bag of fertiliser but when Wilcox went to get it the craft took off, disappearing in just a few seconds (the craft and the speed of departure are both very similar to the details of the Socorro sighting). Nevertheless the witness left the bag of fertiliser at the place of the meeting and the next day it was gone.

WILCOX, MAJOR GEORGE B.
On 27 June 1947 amidst a flurry of activity in those weeks, Major George B. Wilcox of Warren, Arizona, reported watching eight or nine discs travelling at high speed, passing above the town at three-second intervals and heading east.

This report correlates with many others received around the area at the time, suggesting that something was very definitely on the move above the southern United States during that period.

WILCOX, SHERIFF GEORGE
It was to Sheriff George Wilcox that farmer 'Mac' **Brazel** first reported the apparent debris of a flying saucer on his farm, which was to lead to the **Roswell Incident** and cover-up of July 1947.

George Wilcox contacted the Roswell Army Air Base who instigated the examination.

WILKINS, DR PERCY
On 11 June 1954 one of the world's top astronomers, Percy Wilkins, an expert on Earth's moon, had a UFO sighting, one of a great many by astronomers over the years. During a plane journey on the east American coast, in the late morning, near Atlanta, Dr Wilkins saw two egg-shaped objects appear out of the clouds. He described them as like polished metal dinner plates reflecting the sunlight. They were later joined by a third object.

The astronomer believed that each of the objects was some 50 feet wide.

WILLIAMS, FRANK
During the many sightings at Levelland in Texas on Route 116 on the night of 2 November 1957 Frank Williams, speaking from a telephone booth near Whitharral in Texas, reported that he had come across a huge UFO which had 'car-stopped' his vehicle. Apparently the UFO was pulsating and Williams' car headlights were pulsating in counter rhythm. He had remained

in his car and finally the object rose and disappeared, leaving the car operating again. This account is very similar to that of Jim **Wheeler**, who had an encounter at more or less the same time in the same place.

WILLIAMS, WING-COMMANDER GORDON
Wing-Commander Gordon Williams was overall base commander of **Woodbridge RAF/USAF Air Base** during the alleged close encounter at the base in 1980.

In one very dubious report it is alleged that Wing-Commander Williams not only ventured into **Rendlesham Forest** to see the object but communicated with aliens while there.

WILSON, LIEUTENANT-GENERAL ROSCOE C.
In 1960 Lieutenant-General Roscoe Wilson, the Deputy Chief of Staff for the Air Force, announced Project Saint which was a defence operation, a forerunner of the modern day Strategic Defense Initiative or 'Star Wars' programme. General Wilson stated that the project would create a device in orbit which would rendezvous with unknown objects orbiting the Earth and destroy them if they proved hostile. It is highly likely he was referring to any orbiting Russian weapons rather than anything extraterrestrial, but several people have suggested that the more exotic possibility would not have been overlooked.

WINDOW AREAS
(See **UFOcal**.)

WISE BABY DREAMS
One of the more curious components of abduction stories in recent years, and particularly relating to the apparent hybridisation programme between aliens and humans where the human race is being used in some form of cross-breeding genetic analysis experiment, are the wise baby dreams.

These are generally reported by women abductees who see a baby which they feel is both alien and intelligent, which is of their own blood but also hybrid alien. They feel that these children are in some way bizarre or special.

There have been several cases where women have apparently been abducted during pregnancy and had the foetus removed, and even cases where the mother is abducted again at some later time and allowed to meet and bond with her baby on board a flying saucer where its alien nature is clear to see.

WITHDEAN, SUSSEX

On 4 February 1951 in the early hours of the morning a girl named only as Sheila was in her mother's garden when an object was seen there, grey-green and glowing, with a flattened dome. Three entities wearing buff-coloured clothing floated out of the object towards her, then returned to the object which took off and disappeared. They had the bald domed heads quite often described by UFO abductees.

There is no evidence of an investigation into any missing time or abduction here. Indeed, there is no knowledge of what took place other than as given above.

Twenty years later, Sheila, now living in Western Australia, encountered a UFO which forced her off the road near the Darling Hills.

WOLBERT, RICHARD

On 21 March 1973 there was a wave of reports around Saylors Lake in Pennsylvania. One of the reports came from the Assistant Chief of Police, Richard Wolbert, who apparently watched a teardrop-shaped object move across the sky, pass between the moon and the mountains and go down towards Shawnee just before 9.30 p.m. In all there were many dozens of reports from various people around this time in this place, suggesting some real event occurring in the air somewhere.

WOLF, LEONARD

Following a report on UFOs by **NICAP** (National Investigations Committee on Aerial Phenomena), a member of the Space Committee, representative Leonard Wolf, told the House of Representatives that he believed the report should be published to reduce the dangers of panic or concern amongst the American people. He stressed that he believed it was a careful evaluation of UFOs, in contrast to 'frauds and illusions'. Wolf went on to urge open hearings on the matter.

WOLSKI, JAN

On 19 May 1978 farmer Jan Wolski, driving a horse and cart near Emilcin in Poland, was suddenly stopped by entities with slanting eyes.

Investigators confirmed that Wolski has no knowledge of the UFO subject and indeed is basically an uneducated country-man; his descriptions were very simplistic. He described being taken up by a tube into a 'bus in the sky' which hovered above him. On board the entities undressed him and performed a medical examination before letting him go. Apparently there was no amnesiac block placed on him or arising in him from shock at the incident; all of his recall was in conscious memory.

Psychologists at the University of Lodz found that he was apparently sincere and truthful.

WOODBRIDGE RAF/USAF AIR BASE

In December 1980 it is alleged that a grounded UFO was seen in the **Rendlesham Forest** area outside the back gates of RAF/USAF Woodbridge in Suffolk, England.

There are various, and conflicting, reports about what occurred on the night. According to the official report made by the Deputy Base Commander, Lieutenant-Colonel Charles **Halt**, two security police witnessed lights outside the back gate and called for permission to investigate on the grounds that an aircraft might have crashed. Three patrolmen were sent and they reported seeing a glowing object in the forest, described as triangular in shape, about 9 feet wide and 6 feet high, and emanating a powerful white light. Other reports detail blue and red lights at various points on the object. It was either hovering or standing on short legs and as the patrol approached, it manoeuvred away slowly through the trees on to a nearby farm (causing some disturbance in the animals there) before disappearing into the sky very quickly. However, the object was briefly sighted again about an hour later.

Investigation the following day found three ground traces indicating possible landing leg depressions.

However, there are other stories of events that night including one that the overall commander of the base, Wing-Commander Gordon **Williams**, was present at the investigation and also communicated with aliens that had been seen apparently carrying out repairs to the craft.

It is alleged that many films and photographs were taken but that these were all confiscated by senior officers and have not been released.

Investigators examining these claims have obtained interviews with two of the patrol who investigated the UFO, airman John **Burroughs** and a second airman who remains anonymous and is given the pseudonym of James **Archer**. Basically their stories agree with the Deputy Commander's statement. Archer denies seeing aliens but saw shapes inside the object, to which he had approached within three feet, and commented, 'I don't know what they were but the shapes did not look human. Maybe they were like robots.'

One of the security police at Woodbridge, Sergeant Adrian **Bustinza**, came forward after the publication of a book, *Skycrash* by Jenny Randles, Brenda Butler and Dot Street (see References and Background Material), and told his detailed version of events in the forest that night. Again, for the most part, his account basically agrees with that of Lieutenant-Colonel Halt. He describes the object as being seen through a yellow mist like 'nothing I have ever seen before', and comments that it was a tremendous size compared to the clearing it was in and that he was surprised it was able to fit into the area. One major discrepancy arises in his description, however; he describes it as saucer-shaped rather than triangular-shaped, which would seem to be a very major disagreement considering both reports come from eye witnesses.

There is allegedly a tape recording made by Lieutenant-Colonel Halt and his men while in the forest investigating the event and part of this has been released by a former base commander at Woodbridge, Colonel Sam **Morgan**. On the tape various voices including Lieutenant-Colonel Halt's describe what they are supposed to be seeing as they pursue the object through the woods.

When challenged by a former Chief of the Defence Staff, Admiral-of-the-Fleet Lord **Hill-Norton**, the Secretary of State for Defence, Michael Heseltine, through Lord **Trefgarne**, released the statement that 'the events to which you refer were of no defence significance'.

As Lord Hill-Norton put it, there would seem to be some defence significance either in an unknown object's entering and possibly landing in British territory or, alternatively, a deputy base commander of an RAF/USAF base filing a ludicrous and make-believe report. Lieutenant-Colonel (now Colonel) Halt has confirmed subsequently that this memorandum is legitimate. He also went on to say, 'There are a lot of things that are not in my memo.'

WOODRUFF, R. S.
In many people's eyes the quality of the witness to a UFO event is as important as the event itself. On that basis one sighting of three red-lighted UFOs buzzing low over cars near Bethel in Vermont, USA, should rank highly. Witnesses in other cars watched a police car ahead being buzzed. The police car

contained a high State police official and the State pathologist, Dr R. S. Woodruff.

Calculation by the police indicated that the speed of the UFOs was some 2,000 miles per hour.

Despite the fact that the UFOs had come down precisely together in line of formation, slowed down and flown parallel to the ground, the Air Force explained that they were only meteors.

WRIGHT PATTERSON AIR FORCE BASE

Wright Patterson Air Force Base in America is a name that frequently occurs in the pages of this encyclopedia and in the annals of UFO research.

It is alleged that this base is the storehouse and examination facility for retrieved crash flying saucers and also for alien bodies.

Other stories have it that Wright Patterson contains a 'quick reaction force' designed to retrieve downed saucers, a sort of SAS or SWAT team to deal with aliens.

There is even an allegation that Senator Barry **Goldwater** attempted to gain entry to the base to examine UFO evidence but was refused by the then commanding officer, General Curtis LeMay.

WYKOFF, LIEUTENANT ROBERT C.

On 10 August 1950 Navy physicist Lieutenant Robert Wykoff, using Navy binoculars, watched a large disc-shaped UFO manoeuvring near Edwards Air Force Base, the scene of many such sightings.

X

X, DR, CASE OF

On 1 November 1968 a medical doctor in southern France (both the identity of the witness and the location are suppressed at the witness's request) had an extraordinary encounter which had even more extraordinary after-effects.

It was early in the morning, before four o'clock, when the doctor awoke to the cries of his young baby boy. The toddler was pointing towards the window; through the shutters the doctor could see what appeared to be flashes of brilliant light. He did not consider this out of the ordinary and decided to give the child a drink of water. Following this he opened a large window and observed two disc-shaped UFOs, white on top and red beneath, flying across his field of view. They were apparently heading towards the house as they appeared to be growing in size. The brilliant flashes that the doctor had previously observed were bursts of light being projected between the two discs.

While he watched, the two discs merged into each other, becoming one large disc which flipped over and fired a beam of light directly at the house and at the doctor himself. Instantly, with a loud bang, the disc disappeared, leaving a hazy presence in the air which gradually dissipated.

A few days earlier the doctor had injured his leg while chopping wood and still had a painful bruise at the time of the incident. Further back, during the Algerian War, he had suffered some severe wounds and partial paralysis. All of these pains and difficulties disappeared after the UFO encounter.

The story was not yet over, however. A few days later the doctor noticed a red triangular pigmentation around his naval though examination could not determine the cause. The same shape and marking appeared on the toddler's stomach a day or so later and for many years since there have been recurrences of these markings. The doctor had a dream in which the pattern was connected with the disc he had seen. The marks were recorded on film years after the event, suggesting a lengthy response to the initial incident.

Finally, there have been other changes to the family – of social outlook and attitudes towards mortality, and also a remarkable increase in paranormal activity taking place around them such as levitation, telepathy, etc.

XAVIER, TELEMACO

In September 1962 a wave of sightings struck Barcelos in Brazil. There were reports of multiple animal abductions; a number of chickens, pigs and cows all disappeared from the area.

On the night of 1 September 1962, from the town of Vila Conceicao, a man called Telemaco Xavier apparently disappeared in similar fashion. It seems that he was seen by three plantation workers walking alone down a road during the night. A glowing circular object swooped in over him, and three entities got out and grabbed Xavier, dragging him off.

He has never been seen since.

Y

YACANTO, ARGENTINA

On 3 July 1960, near Yacanto, Argentina, Air Force Captain Nyotti took a photograph of an object he could see hovering just off the side of the road he was driving on. The object was apparently conical, some 25 feet tall and 12 feet wide, and rotating slowly, making no sound.

Analysis by specialists of the Argentine Air Force apparently expressed no reservations about the photograph, thought to be important because of the competence and professional credibility of the witness.

YORITSUME, GENERAL

On 24 September 1235 the Japanese Warlord General Yoritsume was at military camp with his unit when a most extraordinary phenomenon was sighted. **LITS (Lights in the Sky)** were seen to be swinging and circling and looping, throughout the night and into the early morning.

Astronomers working for Yoritsume to investigate this phenomenon came up with perhaps the first explanation offered for UFOs. They said: 'The whole thing is completely natural, General; it is only the wind making the stars sway.'

YOUNG, JAN

When the March 1973 wave of saucer sightings in the United States got under way, one witness was Mrs Jan Young, who witnessed no fewer than twenty-five such discs in the area around Saylors Lake. These appeared to be red at first but as she got closer she could see that there was a blue light in the middle, blinking on and off, and four lights forming a circle around the edge.

Z

ZACATECAS OBSERVATORY
(See **Bonilla, José A. Y.**)

ZAMMIT, MRS
When Ed **Walters** first photographed his flying saucers in **Gulf Breeze** on 11 November 1987, there was some corroboration from a Charles I. **Somerby** and his wife and also a third corroboration from a Mrs Zammit, who apparently saw the blue beam that attacked Walters and reported it to the *Sentinel* newspaper nine days later. She had felt compelled to do so by the publicity surrounding the pictures but has since chosen to remain silent. The investigators on the Gulf Breeze case, particularly Gary A. Watson, have interviewed Mrs Zammit and are satisfied that her story is corroborative and truthful, and accept her need for no further undue publicity or attention.

ZAMORA, PATROLMAN SERGEANT LONNIE
On 24 April 1964 police officer Lonnie Zamora, at **Socorro** in New Mexico, was chasing a speeding car when he heard a sound and saw a blue-orange flame descending a hill near him.

Once on the brow of the hill Zamora saw, parked below him, a shining egg-shaped object and two people who were obviously startled at the appearance of his police cruiser. Zamora reported over the radio that he would be investigating and got out.

The 'people' apparently got back into the object which took off immediately, levelled off and flew away across country.

Inspection of the landing site showed clear landing marks in the sand, and burn marks in the vegetation. There were some 'footprints' thought to relate to the entities nearby.

Dr J. Allen **Hynek** investigated the case for Project **Blue Book** and stated, 'Of all the close encounters of the third kind, this is the one that most clearly suggests a "**nuts-and-bolts**" physical craft.'

During the investigation even the principal civilian investigator, Ray Stanford, saw a similar object in flight in the days after this report. His book *Socorro Saucer* (see References and Background Material) is a most detailed analysis of the whole investigation.

ZECHEL, W. T.
In 1978 a former research director of **Ground Saucer Watch** and former radio operator for the Army Security Agency, W. T. Zechel, founded **CAUS (Citizens Against UFO Secrecy)**, with the aim of preventing the United States government from covering up its knowledge of UFOs and particularly crash retrieved saucers.

ZEEHAS
When receiving the limited communications he did, Ed **Walters**, the principal witness of the **Gulf Breeze** sightings, was apparently referred to by the aliens at Zeehas. Precisely what the word is supposed to mean is not determined even by Walters though he speculates one rather unpleasant connotation, which is that he is in some way their pet and that is their name for him!

ZETA RETICULI 1 AND 2
During the Betty and Barney **Hill** encounter, Betty Hill remembered a 'star map' which had been shown by the captain of the flying saucer that had abducted her. The star map was reported to various people in the United States and eventually Marjorie **Fish** reconstructed a likely approximation of the stars involved in the map. On that basis it appears that the aliens who abducted Mrs Hill and her husband, and who are very similar to many other aliens reported particularly on the North American continent, come from planets around one of the stars Zeta Reticuli 1 or 2.

It has to be said that the reliability of an unlabelled map seen for a few seconds during a traumatic experience, and recalled years later by regression hypnosis, must be questioned. Indeed, it has been speculated that the construction shown to Mrs Hill could be more of an illustrative device for showing to captives than a navigational device for use aboard the ship since it apparently had no detail or scale.

Other astronomers have called into question the assumptions made in reconstructing the star map and believe that the best line of fit is not necessarily the only line of fit, even assuming that the home world of the aliens comes within optical range of the Earth. If not, then of course the map is a red herring for one reason or another.

The Zeta Reticuli system is approximately thirty light years from our sun.

ZHANG PO COUNTY, CHINA

An open-air film was being attended by some 3,000 people at Zhang Po County in China on 7 July 1977 when two orange glowing UFOs swept in towards the crowd. So close did they approach that the witnesses felt the heat and heard humming sounds and indeed it appears that the objects had almost landed before they ascended and disappeared.

Unfortunately there was some considerable panic caused by the low approach; two were killed and two hundred people injured.

Examination of the film that was being shown showed that there was no optical illusion or light effect caused by the transmission and therefore the objects were external to that event.

ZHOU QINGTONG

In October 1978 Air Force pilot Zhou Qingtong of China and many others witnessed a UFO over their airfield. It was apparently huge in size and in sight for several minutes, exhibiting bright lights. Zhou Qingtong commented that all the witnesses were fighter pilots and could say with some authority that the object was not an aeroplane.

ZIENA

Very few aliens actually have names but Sid **Padrick**'s contact from the stars offered Ziena as a name.

ZIGEL, DR FELIX YUREVICH

Dr Felix Yurevich Zigel is a Doctor of Science and Assistant Professor of Cosmology at Moscow Aviation Institute. He was formerly Head of Cosmonaut Training for the USSR. He announced in 1967 that UFOs were worthy of scientific study, also making an open television broadcast to the people of the Soviet Union requesting reports be submitted as this was 'a serious challenge to science'. (See also **Stolyarov, Major-General Porfiri**.)

Zigel also appeared to the international UFO community at large, recognising it was a problem that would require such co-operation for solution.

Generally speaking UFOs were not officially accepted in the USSR and for Zigel to operate as he did during a period of very strict censorship is a tribute to his efforts. Since *perestroika*, UFOs have become relatively acceptable.

ZOHN, DR C. J.

On 29 June 1947, just days after Kenneth **Arnold**'s sighting which publicised the UFO phenomenon, rocket expert C. J. Zohn, stationed at White Sands proving grounds in New Mexico, apparently watched a huge, silver, circular disc at a height of 10,000 feet above the installation.

ZOPPI, FRANCESCO

In October 1977 Major Francesco Zoppi of the Italian Air Corps and his co-pilot were on a training flight in their helicopter when they encountered a bright orange circle ahead of them, moving at a speed matching their own. There were other helicopters in the squadron who corroborated the sighting; the object vanished at 'a speed impossible for any aircraft of this world to equal'. It had not been detected on radar.

AFTERWORD

I could not resist the following entry as a close for this encyclopedia, if only to show that there can be great humour in Ufology. It comes from Stephen Pile's book *The Return of Heroic Failures* (I am indebted to the author and publisher, Martin Secker and Warburg, for their permission to reproduce the article in full). Even Mr Pile listed it among 'stories we failed to pin down' and so I make no claims whatsoever for its authenticity. It seems to me though that, if true, it is a case that neatly reconciles ground-based and air-based UFO sightings, crash retrieval stories and the UFO-related city blackouts that occur from time to time, to say nothing of bizarre entity sightings.

THE LEAST SUCCESSFUL SUNBATHER

In 1983 a Californian sunbather decided to acquire the perfect tan. Hearing that a better-quality ray was available above the urban smog, he attached forty-two helium balloons to his deckchair which was itself tethered to the earth by means of a long rope.

He was supposed to rise 6,000 feet and there bask in the ultraviolet possibilities. However, he did much better than this when his rope snapped and the deckchair rose, untrammelled, to a height of 15,000 feet, where a passing airline pilot reported him as a UFO sighting.

Prepared for all possibilities, he pulled out an air pistol and shot the balloons one by one. His deckchair demolished a power cable, blacking out the whole area, and he arrived back on earth much paler than when he left.

REFERENCES AND BACKGROUND MATERIAL

BOOKS
ALLINGHAM, Cedric, *Flying Saucer from Mars*, Muller, 1955
ANGELUCCI, Orfeo, *Secret of the Saucers*, Amherst Press, 1955
ARNOLD, Kenneth and PALMER, Ray, *The Coming of the Saucers*, private publication, 1952
BASTERFIELD, *Close Encounters of an Australian Kind*, Reed, 1981
BERLITZ, Charles and MOORE, William, *The Roswell Incident*, Granada Publishing, 1980
BETHERUM, Truman, *Aboard a Flying Saucer*, De Vorss, 1954
BLUM, Ralph and Judy, *Beyond Earth*, Corgi, 1974
BOWEN, Charles (ed.), *Encounter Cases from Flying Saucer Review*, Signet, 1977
The Humanoids, Futura, 1974
BUTLER, Brenda, STREET, Dot and RANDLES, Jenny, *Skycrash*, Neville Spearman, 1984
CASSIERER, Manfred, *Parapsychology and the UFO*, private publication, 1988
CHAPMAN, Robert, *UFO*, Granada, 1968
COLLYNS, Robin, *Ancient Astronauts: A Time Reversal?*, Sphere, 1978
von DANIKEN, Erich, *Chariots of the Gods?*, Souvenir Press, 1969
The Gold of the Gods, Souvenir Press, 1972
Return to the Stars, Souvenir Press, 1970
DRAKE, W. Raymond, *Gods and Spacemen in the Ancient East*, Sphere 1973
EMENEGGER, Robert, *UFOs Past, Present and Future*, Ballantine, 1974
EVANS, Hilary, *The Evidence for UFOs*, The Aquarian Press, 1983
Visions, Apparitions, Alien Visitors, The Aquarian Press, 1984

EVANS, Hilary with SPENCER, John (eds.), *UFOs 1947–1987*, Fortean Tomes, 1987. (Contributors: V. J. Ballester Olmos, Ken Behrendt, Michel Bougard, Bill Chalker, David Clarke, Hilary Evans, Robert Girard, Richard Haines, Kim Hansen, Cynthia Hind, Peter Hough, John Keel, Alex Keul, Anders Liljegren, Claude Mauge, James McCampbell, Kevin McClure, Bertram Meheust, Michel Monnerie, Mark Moravec, Grenville Oldroyd, Ken Philips, John Prytz, Jenny Randles, John Rimmer, Andy Roberts, Chris Rutkowski, Bronislaw Rzepecki, Martin Shough, Willy Smith, John Spencer, Dennis Stacy, Leonard Stringfield, Clas Svahn, Jacques Vallée, Maurizio Verga, Enrique Vicente, Nigel Watson, Rob Westrum.)

EVANS-WENTZ, W., *The Fairy Faith in the Celtic Countries*, Oxford University Press, 1911

FESTINGER, REICHER and SCHACKER, *When Prophecy Fails*, Harper & Row, 1964

FLAMMONDE, Paris, *UFO Exist!*, Ballantine, 1976

FOWLER, R., *The Andreasson Affair – Phase Two*, Prentice-Hall, 1982
The Watchers

FRY, Daniel W., *The White Sands Incident*, New Age, 1954

FULLER, John G., *The Interrupted Journey*, Souvenir Press, 1966

FURNEAUX, Robert, *The Tungus Event*, Panther, 1977

GOOD, Timothy, *Above Top Secret*, Sidgwick & Jackson, 1987

HARTLAND, Edwin S., *The Science of Fairy Tales*

HIND, Cynthia, *UFOs – African Encounters*, Gemini, 1982

HOBANA, Ion and WEVERBERGH, Julien, *UFOs from Behind the Iron Curtain*, Bantam, 1975

HOPKINS, Budd, *Intruders – The Incredible Visitations at Copley Wood*, Random House, 1987
Missing Time, Richard Merrick, 1981

HOLZER, Professor Hans, *The UFOnauts*, Panther, 1979

HYNEK, Dr J. Allen, *The Hynek UFO Report*, Sphere, 1978

JOHNSON, Frank, *The Janos People*, Spearman, 1980

JUNG, C. G., *Flying Saucers: A Modern Myth of Things Seen in the Skies*, Arc, 1959, 1987

KEEL, John, *The Cosmic Question*, Panther, 1978
Operation Trojan Horse, Putnam, 1970
Strange Creatures from Time and Space, Sphere, 1976
Visitors from Space, Panther, 1975 (first published as *The Mothman Prophecies*)

KEYHOE, Major Donald E., *Aliens from Space*, Panther, 1975
  Flying Saucers from Outer Space, Tandem, 1969
KINDER, Gary, *Light Years*
KLARER, Elizabeth, *Beyond the Light Barrier*, Howard Timmins, 1980
KLASS, Philip J., *UFO Abductions – A Dangerous Game*, Prometheus, 1988
  UFOs: The Public Deceived, Prometheus, 1983
LE POER TRENCH, Brinsley, *Mysterious Visitors*, Pan Books, 1975
  Operation Earth, Tandem 1974
  Temple of the Stars, Fontana, 1973
LESLIE, Desmond and ADAMSKI, George, *Flying Saucers Have Landed*, Futura, 1953, 1977
LORENZEN, Coral E., *Flying Saucers*, Signet Books, 1966 (first published as *The Great Flying Saucer Hoax*)
LORENZEN, Jim and Coral, *UFOs over the Americas*, Signet, 1968
MENGER, Howard, *From Outer Space to You*, Saucerian, 1959
MICHEL, Aimé, *The Truth about Flying Saucers*, Corgi, 1958
MOONEY, Richard, *Gods of Air and Darkness*, Panther, 1977
  Colony Earth, Granada, 1975
RANDLE, Captain Kevin, USAF (Retd), *The UFO Casebook*, Warner, 1989
RANDLES, Jenny, *Abduction*, Robert Hale, 1988
RIMMER, John, *The Evidence for Alien Abductions*, Aquarian Press, 1964
ROGO, D. Scott, *Alien Abductions*, Signet, 1980
RUPPELT, Captain Edward J., *The Report on Unidentified Flying Objects*, Doubleday, 1956
SAGAN, Carl, *Other Worlds*, Bantam, 1975
SAUNDERS, David and HARKINS, Roger, *UFOs? Yes!*, Signet, 1968
SCULLY, Frank, *Behind the Flying Saucers*, Henry Holt, 1950
SHUTTLEWOOD, Arthur, *The Flying Saucerers*, Sphere, 1976
SPENCER, John and EVANS, Hilary (eds.), *Phenomenon*, Macdonald, 1988. (Contributors: Lionel Beer, Kenneth W. Behrendt, Bill Chalker, David Clarke, J. Danby, Paul Devereux, Hilary Evans, Stephen Gamble, Kim Hansen, Cynthia Hind, Budd Hopkins, Peter Hough, John A. Keel, Bertil Kuhlemann, Pierre Lagrange, Anders Liljegren, James McCampbell, Kevin McLure, Mark Moravec, Gerlad Mosbleck, Paul Norman, John Prytz, Jenny Randles, John

Rimmer, Andy Roberts, Chris Rutkowski, Bronislaw Rzepecki, John Shaw, Martin Shough, Dr Willy Smith, John Spencer, Dennis Stacy, Clas Svahn, Dr Allen Tough, Mauritizio Verga, Nigel Watson, Michael Wootten.)

STANFORD, Ray, *Socorro Saucer*, Fontana, 1978

STEIGER, Brad (ed.), *Project Blue Book*, Ballantine, 1976
   The UFO Abductors, Berkley, 1988

STRIEBER, Whitley, *Communion*, Century Hutchinson, 1987
   Transformation, Century Hutchinson, 1988

STRINGFIELD, Leonard, *Situation Red*, Fawcett-Crest, 1977

TIME-LIFE editors, *Psychic Powers*, Time-Life, 1988

VALLÉE, Jacques, *Dimensions*, Souvenir Press, 1988
   The Invisible College, E. P. Dutton, 1975
   Passport to Magonia, Spearman, 1970

VALLÉE, Jacques and Janine, *Challenge to Science*, Neville Spearman, 1967

WALTERS, Ed and Frances, *The Gulf Breeze Sightings*, Bantam Press, 1990

MAGAZINES AND PERIODICALS

Anomaly, Alan Cleaver (ed.)

BUFORA Journal and Bulletin 1968–1988

Cuardernos de Ufologia, Julio Arcas and Jose Ruesga (eds.)

Fortean Times, Robert Rickard and Paul R. A. de G. Sieveking (eds.), 1987

Italian UFO Reporter, Gian Grassino, Eduardo Russo, Paolo Toselli and Maurizio Verga (eds.)

The Journal of Transient Aerial Phenomena, 1980–1988

MUFON UFO Journal, Dennis Stacy (ed.)

Mystery of the Circles, compiled by Paul Fuller and Jenny Randles, BUFORA Publications

OVNI Presence, Yves Bosson (ed.), 1988

A Sample Survey of the Incident of Geometrically Shaped Crop Damage, C. P. Fuller, commissioned by BUFORA and The Tornado and Storm Research Organisation, 1988

SOBEPS News, Michel Bougard (ed.)

UFOAFRI News, Cynthia Hind (ed.)

UFO Brigantia, Andy Roberts (ed.)

UFO-IFO, Ian Mrzygrod, Scufori-Probe Production

UFO Report: America's Captured Flying Saucers – Cover-up of the Century, Gray Barker, 1977

UFO Times, Michael Wootten, BUFORA Publications

The Encyclopedia of the World's Greatest Unsolved Mysteries

JOHN and ANNE SPENCER

Mysteries surround every aspect of our lives

Man has been intrigued by the unknown since the dawn of time. This book is a fascinating and authoritative catalogue of the most enduring and intriguing of the phenomena which, at the present time, defy explanation.

From Alien Abductions and Angels, to Werewolves and Zombies, this encyclopedia, compiled by two eminently qualified researchers of the paranormal, examines the latest evidence for over eighty fascinating unsolved mysteries, including:

- Automatic Writing
- Poltergeists
- Crop Circles
- Stigmata
- Near-Death Experiences
- UFOs
- Witchcraft

John and Anne Spencer have been active researchers of the paranormal for over twenty years. John Spencer is Chairman of the British UFO Research Association. He and his wife are at the forefront of experimental work into many unsolved mysteries.

NON-FICTION / PARANORMAL 0 7472 5013 8

A selection of non-fiction from Headline